JOSHUA, JUDGES & RUTH

the Smart Guide to the Bible™ series

BE SMART · BE INSPIRED ·

Rebecca Bertolini
Larry Richards, General Editor

THOMAS NELSON
Since 1798

NASHVILLE   DALLAS   MEXICO CITY   RIO DE JANEIRO   BEIJING

Joshua, Judges, & Ruth
The Smart Guide to the Bible™ series
© 2008 by GRQ, Inc.

Published in Nashville, Tennessee, by Thomas Nelson. Thomas Nelson is a trademark of Thomas Nelson, Inc.

Thomas Nelson, Inc. titles may be purchased in bulk for educational, business, fundraising, or sales promotional use. For information, please e-mail SpecialMarkets@ThomasNelson.com.

General Editor: Larry Richards
Managing Editor: Michael Christopher
Scripture Editor: Deborah Wiseman
Assistant Editor: Amy Clark
Design: Diane Whisner

ISBN 10: 1-4185-1005-X
ISBN 13: 978-1-4185-1005-3

Printed in the United States of America
08 09 10 11 RRD 9 8 7 6 5 4 3 2 1

Introduction

Welcome to *Joshua, Judges, & Ruth—The Smart Guide to the Bible*™. This book is designed to put at your fingertips all the information and assistance you will need to fully understand why God left this record and communication for us today. You are about to discover a fascinating commentary that is both enlightening and pertinent, simple and entertaining. I pray this book will change your outlook forever. You can't help but learn more about God's Word.

To Gain Your Confidence

God left the Bible—his message to mankind—for people of all ages, cultures, and educational backgrounds. Everything he wanted us to know about himself, his dealings with people, and the way he has moved throughout history is recorded in these pages. God yearns for us to deepen our comprehension of him and broaden our relationship with him. That is why *Joshua, Judges, & Ruth—The Smart Guide to the Bible*™ will not be a complicated dissertation full of ancient Hebrew language explanations, arguments about dates, or debates over genealogical data.

Thumb through the pages and see for yourself. This book is full of lively conversation about the biblical text, fascinating opinions from a variety of experts, and illuminating definitions of terms. God *wants* you to comprehend his ways. Therefore, the goal of this book is to lay open God's Word in a plain and straightforward style so that no matter who you are, you can enjoy furthering your acquaintance with God.

Why Has God Intervened in Human History?

At the beginning of time as we know it, God longed for a relationship beyond that of the heavenly beings whose duties bound them in admiration and devotion to him. So he created a universe and a human pair to place within it. Adam and Eve, with a free will to enjoy God and flourish in his presence, could also opt to forfeit that privilege. What joy it would have brought to the heart of God if mankind had chosen to embrace all that he offered of himself. Instead, the first man and woman decided, out of selfishness and pride, that they could do better without him and so consigned themselves to a life separated from the God who knew them best and loved them most.

Every human being who has ever walked the face of this planet has made a similar series of wrong choices, so this story is as much about us as it is about Adam and Eve. Because they wanted to go their own way their souls were subject to death, their bodies to decay, and their world to a state of constant decline.

But God did not want to leave them to wallow in their misery and suffering, so he worked out an alternate method to save them from themselves. Plan "B" began with the selection of a man named Abraham. God desired to raise up a nation, through this man and his wife, Sarah, that would live within the protection of the universal laws he had set up. These parameters would bring the most joy and fulfillment to the people he had designed. He longed to see all nations observe his hand of blessing on the race of Abraham and be drawn to God by their example. The last part of the plan would involve providing from among their descendants a savior—God born in human form—who could bring deliverance from the consequences of evil.

Where in Biblical History Do Joshua, Judges, and Ruth Fit?

From this humble beginning, each of the twelve sons of Jacob produced many generations of children until they numbered about two and a half million people.[1] At this time they were living in Egypt because of a seven-year famine in which the only available food was stored in vast repositories along the Nile River. After the drought became a thing of the past, Abraham's descendants stayed on, living side by side in peace with the Egyptians.

Some time elapsed before Pharaoh recognized the threat in this sheep-raising group of people living within Egypt's boundaries. Should they take up weapons to overthrow his system of government, he could not very well defend his interests.

At the same time, he could scarcely overlook the manpower they could supply in the building up of his great public works projects. So he enslaved the entire nation and worked out vicious schemes to keep them weak and groveling.

At this time, God raised up a man to rescue his chosen people. His name was Moses—brought up as royalty in Pharaoh's own court and tempered by forty years on the back side of the desert. With God's miraculous help, Moses led the entire nation of Israel away from bondage on a difficult journey through wilderness country to a land that God had promised would be their very own.

On the brink of entering this coveted homeland, Moses died. He was the only leader they had ever known. Enter Joshua—and all the extraordinary circumstances and events God would work out to bring his people success in their new place of residence.

Directly on Joshua's heels follows the rule of the judges, men and women who filled the leadership gap and temporarily liberated the fallen nation from the depths of humiliation and subservience. And in the midst of this chaos unfolds the story of Ruth, a woman of surprisingly noble character.

What Are Joshua, Judges, and Ruth All About?

The events in these books document an unparalleled time in the history of the nation of Israel. Joshua, at Moses's death, ably steps in as the captain of their fighting force and champions Israel's cause all over the Middle East in the land that we now know as Israel. He successfully trounces their dangerous and immoral neighbors, then helps Israel settle into the land and make it their home.

But as soon as the generation that experienced victory firsthand passed on, strict adherence to God's principles was neglected. Their descendants embarked on a wretched pattern of rancorous living, followed inevitably by God's disciplinary correction. They got their act together for a little while and then fell directly back into the sordid habits they couldn't seem to shake. Although God raised up provisional leaders from time to time (the judges), his real desire was that they look to him as their authority to know the blessings of obedience that their fathers experienced. Unfortunately, this group of people (not unlike ourselves) seldom caught the vision and most often did what seemed right to them.

This, in fact, gave rise to one of the most telling statements in the book of Judges, repeated word for word in two places: "In those days there was no king in Israel; everyone did what was right in his own eyes" (17:6; 21:25 NKJV).

The story of Ruth shines in radiant contrast to the other depressing events that came out of the time of the judges. In spite of many challenges, this foreign woman made a personal choice to follow the authority of the God of the Bible. The outcome was joy and blessing for herself and those she loved.

Why Study Joshua, Judges, and Ruth?

Every part of the Bible is useful for one of the following purposes:
- Instructing and teaching knowledge and wisdom
- Revealing harmful attitudes and conduct
- Demonstrating how to change damaging behavior
- Training in patterns of godly living

Therefore, our study of Joshua, Judges, and Ruth will give us a more complete picture of the God of the Bible and push us along the road to spiritual maturity. Often, we tend to concentrate more on certain portions of the Bible that are easier for us to understand. Perhaps we park on what makes us feel the most comfortable. Joshua, Judges, and Ruth were written about a period of time that many have chosen to overlook. But a second glance reveals a rich heritage of living stories and eternal truths, amazing events, and basic principles. These books of the Bible will also answer some challenging questions. Here are a few:

- Are we all doomed to make the same mistakes over and over?
- Why does God allow suffering?
- How can I pass on a living faith to those who come after me?
- Is killing ever appropriate?
- How can I conquer fear and anxiety?

Which Translation of the Bible Should You Use?

For our study I have chosen the New King James Version (NKJV) of the Bible as the most accurate and readable. There are several translations from the original Hebrew that are adequate, but upon examination you will find that the NKJV states the original author's words quite reliably and remains one of the easiest to read in our English vernacular.

How to Use *Joshua, Judges, & Ruth—The Smart Guide to the Bible*™

As you read this book, keep in mind that it is divided into three sections. The first section will deal with the book of Joshua, the sixth book of the sixty-six books within the covers of your Bible. The next division will cover the book of Judges, a book that follows the time period of Joshua's leadership and thus comes right after Joshua in the Bible. The last section of this book will discuss the book of Ruth, which comes after the book of Judges even though its events took place sometime during the rule of the judges.

The best way to begin is to sit down with this book and your Bible.

- Start the book at chapter 1.
- As you work through each chapter, read the accompanying Bible verses from your Bible.
- Use the sidebars loaded with icons and helpful information to give you a knowledge boost.
- Answer the Study Questions and review with the Chapter Wrap-Up.

- Then go on to the next chapter. It's that simple!
- This book contains a variety of special features to help you learn, as explained in the section coming up soon, called "Understanding the Bible Is Easy with These Tools."
- It will also be helpful to remember the following:
  - There will be several interchangeable terms. For example, *Scripture, Scriptures, Word, Word of God, God's Word,* and other variations are all ways of referring to the Bible. I will use each one at various times, but I will use "Bible" most of the time.
  - The word *Lord,* in the years before Christ, refers to *Yahweh* (or *Jehovah*), the God of Israel. After Jesus was born that same title was used for *him.* He was the God of the Bible in human flesh.
  - The offspring of Abraham are called: *Israelites, children of Israel, Hebrews,* and the *chosen people.* Any one of these may be used to refer to the nation that came from Abraham's family line. Actually, *Israel* was the name that God gave to Abraham's grandson Jacob, and since the entire family came through his part of the line, any variation that uses his name makes the most sense.

One Final Tip

Sometimes when we sit down to read what God has written to us, our minds are already so full of the day's anxieties and plans for the next event that we can scarcely concentrate on the words before us. If we allow a few moments of restful prayer, dedicating our time to God, our hearts can be quieted and we can hear his voice. Ask God, through his Spirit, to be your teacher. Allow him to use his own words and the aid of this book to guide you into new discoveries and timeless truths. You are about to embark on the greatest adventure of your life.

About the Author

Rebecca Bertolini has devoted her adult life to teaching the Scriptures. She lives for those "Aha!" moments when truth comes alive to a wondering group of children, or a passage takes on new meaning for a struggling adult. Her striving for scriptural accuracy is exceeded only by her passion for practical application. Best of all from the reader's point of view, her experience in education, both secular and sacred, helps her present biblical information in a provocative and transforming style.

About the General Editor

Dr. Larry Richards is a native of Michigan who now lives in Raleigh, North Carolina. He was converted to Christianity while in the Navy in the 1950s. Larry has taught and written Sunday school curriculum for every age group, from nursery through adult. He has published more than two hundred books that have been translated into twenty-six languages. His wife, Sue, is also an author. They both enjoy teaching Bible studies as well as fishing and playing golf.

Understanding the Bible Is Easy with These Tools

To understand God's Word you need easy-to-use study tools right where you need them—at your fingertips. The *Smart Guide to the Bible*™ series puts valuable resources adjacent to the text to save you both time and effort.

Every page features handy sidebars filled with icons and helpful information: cross references for additional insights, definitions of key words and concepts, brief commentaries from experts on the topic, points to ponder, evidence of God at work, the big picture of how passages fit into the context of the entire Bible, practical tips for applying biblical truths to every area of your life, and plenty of maps, charts, and illustrations. A wrap-up of each passage, combined with study questions, concludes each chapter.

These helpful tools show you what to watch for. Look them over to become familiar with them, and then turn to chapter 1 with complete confidence: You are about to increase your knowledge of God's Word!

Study Helps

The thought-bubble icon alerts you to commentary you might find particularly thought-provoking, challenging, or encouraging. You'll want to take a moment to reflect on it and consider the implications for your life.

Don't miss this point! The exclamation-point icon draws your attention to a key point in the text and emphasizes important biblical truths and facts.

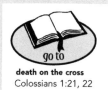

death on the cross
Colossians 1:21, 22

Many see Boaz as a type of Jesus Christ. To win back what we human beings lost through sin and spiritual death, Jesus had to become human (i.e., he had to become a true kinsman), and he had to be willing to pay the penalty for our sins. With his <u>death on the cross</u>, Jesus paid the penalty and won freedom and eternal life for us.

The additional Bible verses add scriptural support for the passage you just read and help you better understand the <u>underlined text</u>. (Think of it as an instant reference resource!)

How does what you just read apply to your life? The heart icon indicates that you're about to find out! These practical tips speak to your mind, heart, body, and soul, and offer clear guidelines for living a righteous and joy-filled life, establishing priorities, maintaining healthy relationships, persevering through challenges, and more.

This icon reveals how God is truly all-knowing and all-powerful. The hourglass icon points to a specific example of the prediction of an event or the fulfillment of a prediction. See how some of what God has said would come to pass already has!

What are some of the great things God has done? The traffic-sign icon shows you how God has used miracles, special acts, promises, and covenants throughout history to draw people to him.

Does the story or event you just read about appear elsewhere in the Gospels? The cross icon points you to those instances where the same story appears in other Gospel locations—further proof of the accuracy and truth of Jesus's life, death, and resurrection.

Since God created marriage, there's no better person to turn to for advice. The double-ring icon points out biblical insights and tips for strengthening your marriage.

The Bible is filled with wisdom about raising a godly family and enjoying your spiritual family in Christ. The family icon gives you ideas for building up your home and helping your family grow close and strong.

Isle of Patmos
a small island in the
Mediterranean Sea

something significant had occurred, he wrote down the substance of what he saw. This is the practice John followed when he recorded Revelation on the **Isle of Patmos.**

What does that word really mean, especially as it relates to this passage? Important, misunderstood, or infrequently used words are set in **bold type** in your text so you can immediately glance at the margin for definition. This valuable feature lets you better understand the meaning of the entire passage without having to stop to check other references.

the big picture

Joshua

Led by Joshua, the Israelites crossed the Jordan River and invaded Canaan (see Illustration #8). In a series of military campaigns the Israelites defeated several coalition armies raised by the inhabitants of Canaan. With organized resistance put down, Joshua divided the land among the twelve Israelite

How does what you read fit in with the greater biblical story? The highlighted big picture summarizes the passage under discussion.

what others say

David Breese

Nothing is clearer in the Word of God than the fact that God wants us to understand himself and his working in the lives of men.[5]

It can be helpful to know what others say on the topic, and the highlighted quotation introduces another voice in the discussion. This resource enables you to read other opinions and perspectives.

Maps, charts, and illustrations pictorially represent ancient artifacts and show where and how stories and events took place. They enable you to better understand important empires, learn your way around villages and temples, see where major battles occurred, and follow the journeys of God's people. You'll find these graphics let you do more than study God's Word—they let you *experience* it.

Chapters at a Glance

SECTION THREE: RUTH

Section One
JOSHUA

Introduction to the Book of Joshua

What Is the Book of Joshua About?

Led by Joshua, Israel conquers and possesses the land in the Middle East that is now called by their name. The first half of the book describes Israel's seven-year combat with the **pagan** nations already in residence. Like any good general, Joshua leads his army in a campaign to divide the country in warfare right down the middle before continuing to win the southern and northern halves. The later chapters of the book of Joshua find the leader parceling sections of the newly subdued lands among the different family groups that make up the nation of Israel. Before his death, Joshua charges the people to hold fast to God and his way of success.

Who Is Joshua?

Born as a slave in Egypt, Joshua would have been in the prime of his life when Moses held aloft his legendary staff and <u>split</u> the great Red Sea right down the middle for the ancestors of Abraham to cross unharmed. Joshua's heart must have sunk with the rest of his brethren to see their Egyptian oppressors in chariots bearing down upon their heels. But the roar of the returning waters and the frantic cries of the drowning enemy would inscribe an indelible message of God's enduring faithfulness on his heart. That event—and the miracles to follow—personally confirmed God's <u>promise</u> to Joshua that he would bring this fledgling nation to a land they could call home.

The barren wilderness crossing, with his fellow Jews, continued to be a schoolroom experience for this young leader-in-training.

- It was Joshua who <u>captained</u> Israel's defending forces in the desert against an **Amalekite** attack while Moses's aching arms were held to the sky with the help of **Aaron** and **Hur**. From this, Joshua would learn that victory comes from God, not an individual's own strength, courage, or ingenuity.

go to

split
Exodus 14:5–31

promise
Deuteronomy 6:10–12

captained
Exodus 17:8–16

pagan
lifestyle of defiance toward God

Amalekite
barbaric descendants of Esau

Aaron
first high priest of Israel

Hur
coworker with Moses and Aaron

go to

climbed
Exodus 24:12–14;
34:29

convince
Numbers 13, 14

commissioning
Numbers 27:18–21

died
Joshua 24:29

Mount Sinai
6,000–8,000 ft.
granite peak in the
Sinai Peninsula

• It was Joshua who <u>climbed</u> lofty **Mount Sinai** with Moses while God's presence enveloped the mountain peaks in the form of a cloud. He camped on the slopes of Sinai until Moses descended with the Ten Commandments and a face that shone with the light of God's glory. From this, Joshua would understand the importance in the life of a leader to schedule time in the presence of God.

• It was Joshua (with his friend Caleb) who tried to <u>convince</u> the people, standing on the border of the new land for the first time, to take possession of what God had already granted them. His countrymen were picking up stones to kill him, but he stood firm. From this, Joshua realized that the majority is not always right, and being right is not always comfortable.

God was preparing Joshua for the eventual death of Moses and his own transition into leadership. Forty years after their journey began, God made the observation at Joshua's <u>commissioning</u> that life's lessons had been learned well, for his own Spirit rested in a special way on Joshua.

When Did Joshua Live?

If Joshua was almost forty when Moses brought God's people out of Egypt, Joshua would have been around eighty when he took over the reins of leadership.[1] The year was probably around 1407 BC, right in the very middle of the Bronze Age.[2] Amenhotep III was ruling as the pharaoh at this time, but there was no threat from Egypt even though the Israelite nation had once been under their dominating thumb. Amenhotep had lost interest in the Middle East and maintained a weak foreign policy, so Joshua could make a move against his Asiatic holdings and not worry about reprisal.[3] Joshua was 110 when he <u>died</u> at the end of the book, so the events recorded took place over about thirty years.

Who Wrote Joshua?

Many sources affirm that Joshua is the most likely candidate to have written the book that is named after him.[4] Here is a short list of reasons why Joshua is the probable author and the book was not written by an unknown, years later:

- Intimate biographical <u>details</u> are included around the events. Joshua was the key eyewitness.[5]

- Several stories are written in the first person, as if the author were a <u>part</u> of the action.

- A few of the people and places were still (at the writing of the book) <u>unchanged</u> since the time the events took place.

- The unity and flow of language and theme nullify the argument for multiple authorship.[6]

- The **Talmud** states that Joshua was the author with several small <u>sections</u> added by **Eleazar** and **Phineas** after his death.[7]

What Is the Theme of Joshua?

One of the main themes repeated in Joshua is that of success through obedience. Victory always came when God's people followed his instructions. Another truth, often stated, relates to God's <u>faithfulness</u>. He could be trusted to bring about everything that he ever promised. Also on display are the qualities of good leadership. From the example of Joshua, a person can observe the characteristics of a godly authority figure worth emulating. The last issue to boldly appear throughout the book of Joshua has to do with the inheritance of God's people. The land would be theirs for the claiming. However, their possession had to be maintained to be retained.

go to

details
Joshua 1:1–9

part
Joshua 5:1, 6

unchanged
Joshua 4:9; 5:9; 6:25

sections
Joshua 1:9–15;
15:13–19; 18:27–28;
19:47; 24:29–33

fathfulness
Joshua 23:14

Talmud
historical explanation of Jewish laws and traditions

Eleazar
high priest and third son of Aaron

Phineas
high priest and son of Eleazar

Joshua 1-2
Preliminary Preparations

Chapter Highlights:
• God's Mandate
• The Almighty's Atlas
• Joshua's Instructions
• Spies' Escapades
• Rahab's Settlement

Let's Get Started

If we affirm, as many do, that the last verses of Deuteronomy were written by Joshua, we can see the ease with which he carries us, without interruption, from one era into another.[1] In Deuteronomy he reverentially eulogizes the character of the former leader—Moses. He declares him to be a prophet unlike any other the people have ever known, a man whom God chose to speak with face-to-face, a miracle worker who overwhelmed all Israel with his awesome deeds while confounding the hierarchy of the most powerful nation of that time—Egypt. Even at 120 years of age, Moses had the sight and the strength of a much younger man. Moses was one in a million!

But like every other mortal, the time had come for him to die. However, unlike other men, he was not buried by his family and friends, nor was he remembered by a monument erected over his remains. God himself buried Moses opposite the valley of Beth Peor in **Moab**. No one would ever know exactly where.

As was the custom, the Israelites mourned after their departed leader for thirty days. They then turned to Joshua for direction, for they saw that he was filled with a spirit of wisdom after Moses's hands of blessing had rested on him. It was time to begin the transfer of authority.

Moab
a country east of the Dead Sea

Jehovah
God's name for himself meaning "I am what I am"

God's Mandate

JOSHUA 1:1 *After the death of Moses the servant of the LORD, it came to pass that the LORD, spoke to Joshua the son of Nun, Moses' assistant, saying:* (NKJV)

Verse 1 of Joshua, in the original Hebrew language, is not so much like a new beginning as it is a continuation of a narrative already under way. In this verse Joshua describes the character of Moses, delineates his own former role, and directs attention to the source of his new calling—**Jehovah** himself.

book
Joshua 24:29

Nun
an Ephraimite
through the line of
Beriah

Moses's designation as "servant of the LORD" bespeaks a familiarity with God that Joshua at this point does not yet have. Although Moses is called the "servant of the LORD" thirteen times in Joshua, it is not until the end of the <u>book</u> that Joshua is spoken of using the same term. This indicates a deepening of his relationship with God over time and through experiences to come.

Joshua portrays himself for now as the "son of **Nun**" (which serves the same function as a last name), and calls himself the assistant of Moses. There was no one more qualified to make a smooth transition into leadership than Joshua himself. He had been watching, listening, and learning at the feet of Moses for years. But lest anyone should question his immediate rise into the highest human position of authority within this nation, Joshua makes it clear that God himself has done the appointing.

> **what others say**
>
> **Warren Wiersbe**
>
> Leaders don't last forever, even godly leaders like Moses. There comes a time in every ministry when God calls for a new beginning with a new generation and new leadership . . . A wise leader doesn't completely abandon the past but builds on it as he or she moves toward the future.[2]

The Almighty's Atlas

JOSHUA 1:2–5 *"Moses My servant is dead. Now therefore, arise, go over this Jordan, you and all this people, to the land which I am giving to them—the children of Israel. Every place that the sole of your foot will tread upon I have given you, as I said to Moses. From the wilderness and this Lebanon as far as the great river, the River Euphrates, all the land of the Hittites, and to the Great Sea toward the going down of the sun, shall be your territory. No man shall be able to stand before you all the days of your life; as I was with Moses, so I will be with you. I will not leave you nor forsake you. (NKJV)*

The descendants of Abraham were encamped along the eastern bank of the Jordan River. The name Jordan actually comes from a root word that means "to descend"—which it does, very rapidly, from its origin in the snowy peaks of Mount Hermon to the Dead Sea, some 1,290 feet below sea level.

Forty years previously, having received God's law at Sinai, the Israelites had been given the same <u>opportunity</u> to enter the land. At that time, they made the calamitous decision to doubt God's power to keep them safe from the cruel and warlike people who lived there. This foolish choice consigned them to wilderness wandering until the disbelieving generation died off and was replaced by a new one with a new chance. What their elders never understood was that the act of "entering *into* the land of blessing" was simply a counterpart of the earlier miracle in Egypt of being "delivered *out* of the land of bondage." God parted the Red Sea to let them out and he would now part the Jordan River to let them in. The God that had the strength and resources to do the one was not unable or insufficient to do the other.

The land was offered as an unconditional promise. However, the enjoyment of that gift was up to them. Israel had the legal title from God's perspective, but they still had to do the work of conquest and settlement.

In verse 4 the boundaries are established—as far south as the Negev, as far north as the Lebanon Mountains, as far east as the Euphrates River, and as far west as the Mediterranean Sea. And in case there should be any misunderstanding, God threw in the clincher. All the Hittite country was to be included—which involved any of the land above that was currently occupied by this prominent ethnic group.

The Lord's presence would abide with Joshua as it had with Moses, and he would never be forsaken by God. Literally the Lord was saying, "I will not drop you." Joshua's trust in God was based in absolute certainty. He would not be left in the lurch with a million people in an unfamiliar place.

opportunity
Numbers 13, 14

key point

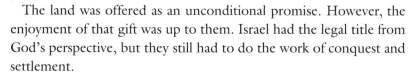

what others say

A. W. Tozer

We cannot think rightly of God until we begin to think of him as always being *there*, and *there first*. Joshua had this to learn. Now Moses is dead, and lest young Joshua be struck down with despair God spoke to reassure him . . . Nothing had changed and nothing had been lost. Nothing of God dies when a man of God dies.[3]

The Israelites had to conquer and claim the bounty and blessing of their inheritance before they could enjoy it. Even after they had taken up residence in the land granted by God, there had to be a continual effort to keep it in their own possession. So the "promised land" for the Christian is not a place in the hereafter called heaven, because that is a place that God alone is <u>preparing</u> for us to inhabit, and we will not have to struggle to keep it. Our inheritance is comprised of spiritual <u>blessings</u> of heavenly proportion meant for the here and now. However, to cash in on the benefit, these gifts must be actively <u>pursued</u> and laid hold of, or they will be lost.

Surefire Steps for Success

preparing
John 14:2–3

blessings
John 10:10;
Matthew 6:33;
1 Timothy 1:14

pursued
1 Timothy 1:18–19;
6:17–19

JOSHUA 1:6–9 *Be strong and of good courage, for to this people you shall divide as an inheritance the land which I swore to their fathers to give them. Only be strong and very courageous, that you may observe to do according to all the law which Moses My servant commanded you; do not turn from it to the right hand or to the left, that you may prosper wherever you go. This Book of the Law shall not depart from your mouth, but you shall meditate in it day and night, that you may observe to do according to all that is written in it. For then you will make your way prosperous, and then you will have good success. Have I not commanded you? Be strong and of good courage; do not be afraid, nor be dismayed, for the LORD your God is with you wherever you go." (NKJV)*

Do you think Joshua got the message that God wanted him to be strong and courageous after this encouragement was repeated three times in one short conversation? But God doesn't make Joshua drum up a sense of confidence on his own. Instead, he puts his own stamp of approval on all that Joshua is setting out to do, ensuring him of success.

He also reveals to Joshua that his accomplishments as a leader will not depend on natural talent or keen insight but will result from his own walk with God, and his degree of obedience. Any <u>deviation</u> from the principles that God has set down will put at risk the attainment of his goals. This all presupposes that Joshua is well-versed in the Scriptures and knows exactly what God wants. So he encourages Joshua to make a habit of thinking on God's Word, making it a part of every thought, word, and action. Literally, he should constantly "mutter it to himself."

And as a final vindication of Joshua's authority, God offers the assurance of his personal presence to be Joshua's constant companion.

Courage—when limited by our own resources and abilities—is foolhardy. But when braced by the assets and abilities of God it is wisdom.

Outstanding leadership is not achieved through a tight control over other people, but by God's tight control over us.

Christ is <u>with</u> us, his own children, all the time and in every place.

deviation
Deuteronomy
11:26–28

with
Matthew 28:19–20

what others say

Joni Eareckson Tada

You and I want all the maps, guides and compasses we can get our hands on as we plan our journey into marriage, a career, or a family . . . But when the sky grows dark and the path gets rough, our best resource is the Guide himself.[5]

request
Numbers 32

manna
food supplied by
God from heaven.

Joshua's Instructions

JOSHUA 1:10–11 *Then Joshua commanded the officers of the people, saying, "Pass through the camp and command the people, saying, 'Prepare provisions for yourselves, for within three days you will cross over this Jordan, to go in to possess the land which the LORD your God is giving you to possess.'"* (NKJV)

Joshua assumes the leadership role to which he's been appointed, and in turn passes on the commands he's received to the officers. Each soldier would be responsible for mustering his own supplies. The **manna** that had sustained them throughout the years of their wilderness wanderings was still available, but gradually their dependence on it would cease as more and more produce became available in the surrounding countryside.

The army does not head out immediately, but is given three days to get things in readiness. It is time to convert the promise of ownership into an actual possession of their own.

Like Birds of a Feather

JOSHUA 1:12–15 *And to the Reubenites, the Gadites, and half the tribe of Manasseh Joshua spoke, saying, "Remember the word which Moses the servant of the LORD commanded you, saying, 'The LORD your God is giving you rest and is giving you this land.' Your wives, your little ones, and your livestock shall remain in the land which Moses gave you on this side of the Jordan. But you shall pass before your brethren armed, all your mighty men of valor, and help them, until the LORD has given your brethren rest, as He gave you, and they also have taken possession of the land which the LORD your God is giving them. Then you shall return to the land of your possession and enjoy it, which Moses the LORD's servant gave you on this side of the Jordan toward the sunrise."* (NKJV)

The request had been made, during the days of Moses, by two and a half of the twelve Israelite family groups to settle on the east bank of the Jordan River. Part of the settlement agreement had been their commitment to continue the fight to the west of the Jordan on behalf of their brothers' lands. This was only fair, because the land they had chosen for themselves had been made secure by the effort of the whole body. Joshua holds them to their word by reminding them that the expectations remain.

Joshua commands the valiant men (those of particular strength and adeptness) to cross the Jordan, literally "in battle formation."

Moses
Exodus 33:14

The goal of the entire process of conquest and possession becomes the "rest" that those east of the Jordan have already obtained. "Rest" speaks of secure borders and inner peace. However, because of the inseparable ties between those who will settle on either side of the river, full rest cannot occur until *all* are able to experience it.

When God allows a period of rest and peace in our lives, we should consider what services we might render those who have not yet found victory and are still going through a time of strife.

Amen and Amen!

JOSHUA 1:16–18 *So they answered Joshua, saying, "All that you command us we will do, and wherever you send us we will go. Just as we heeded Moses in all things, so we will heed you. Only the LORD your God be with you, as He was with Moses. Whoever rebels against your command and does not heed your words, in all that you command him, shall be put to death. Only be strong and of good courage." (NKJV)*

Israel's response to Joshua is warm and affirming. "*All* that you command . . ." and "*wherever* you send . . ." are wholehearted and enthusiastic assurances of support. Their vow that they would obey just as they obeyed Moses is somewhat less encouraging as time and again they had rebelled against Moses and God's directives as administered by him. But the people's intent in this pledge is to affirm and support. Their prayers and supplications are fully behind Joshua as expressed in the utterance of their best wishes, "God be with you, as He was with <u>Moses</u>."

penalty
Proverbs 11:21

authorities
1 Timothy 2:1–2

call
Exodus 5:21

turn
Exodus 14:11

hungry
Exodus 16:2–3

thirsty
Exodus 17:2

bored
Exodus 32:1

mutiny
Numbers 14:2–4

endorsement
Numbers 12, 16

leadership
Hebrews 13:17

mirror
James 1:23–25

Their readiness to comply with God's will is so strong that they are prepared to put to death anyone who rebels. Disobedience is serious and the penalty against an offender must reflect that. Perhaps if such a law had been enforced in Moses's day, the insubordination and mutinous acts against him might have been prevented.

We need to pray for God's presence to motivate and empower the authorities God has placed over us.

Let's look more closely at the way the children of Israel responded to Moses's leadership. From the very first encounter, they call on God to judge Moses for making their burdens heavier. Fortunately, Moses overlooks their complaints and finally obtains permission for them to leave Egypt.

The next picture we have is of the entire nation standing on the brink of the Red Sea. God will work a mighty miracle and split the waters for them to cross, but they do not have the foresight to see what he intends and turn against Moses once again in abuse and anger. This scenario was repeated every time they faced a challenge—when they were hungry, when they were thirsty, and even when they were bored.

At last, Moses brings them to the threshhold of the Land of Promise. Even though he pleads with them to go in and receive God's blessing, they refuse. They mutiny against his leadership and decide to go back to Egypt without him.

In spite of God's continual endorsement of Moses's command, the children of Israel could not submit to his earthly leadership because they refused to submit, first, to the authority of God.

Keeping a heart that is soft and receptive to God, his Word, and the people he places in positions of spiritual leadership over us is vital to the health and vitality of our walk. The Bible says that when God speaks to us we are like individuals who look into a mirror. We see what needs to be changed, but what we do with that observation is up to us. We can walk away with a shrug, or we can go to work at improving and refining what needs correction.

go to

report
Numbers 13:31–14:3

alert
1 Corinthians 16:13

Jericho
ancient settlement
where the Jordan
River empties into the
Dead Sea

Joni Eareckson Tada

Hardened clay is brittle, easily damaged. If dropped, it can shatter into a thousand pieces. Dropped wax, however, only bends from the pressure of the fall. Impressionable and pliable, it can quickly be remolded. People are like that. People who are hardened in their resolve against God are brittle, their emotions easily damaged. But those who bend to the will of God find perfect expression in however God molds them.[7]

Spies' Escapades

JOSHUA 2:1–3 *Now Joshua the son of Nun sent out two men from Acacia Grove to spy secretly, saying, "Go, view the land, especially Jericho." So they went, and came to the house of a harlot named Rahab, and lodged there. And it was told the king of Jericho, saying, "Behold, men have come here tonight from the children of Israel to search out the country." So the king of Jericho sent to Rahab, saying, "Bring out the men who have come to you, who have entered your house, for they have come to search out all the country." (NKJV)*

Joshua's first act of leadership was one of espionage. His sending out of spies was not motivated by doubt but was a prudent military tactic. They were not determining if they could take the land but deciding the best method of attack. However, Joshua was determined to keep the spy mission a secret from the rank-and-file as he knew firsthand the demoralizing effect a negative <u>report</u> might have.

The focus of the reconnaissance mission was **Jericho**, the most likely location for their first military engagement. The spies would intuitively have found their way to the only type of residence in town where they could gather information and spend time without being suspect—the house of a prostitute. But they were spotted and followed to Rahab's, and she seemed to know who they were as well.

God wants us to be <u>alert</u> and prepared in our fight against our spiritual enemies.

go to

laws
Leviticus 19:11

change
James 1:17

judgment
James 3:1

converts
those who decide to
live for God

fear
awe inspired by
God's great works

admonition
instructions regard-
ing what pleases
God

Eugenia Price

To look first from the viewpoint of God gives us a starting place. We "know which way to turn" when trouble comes, when problems pile up suddenly . . . When legal complications or continuing failures or disappointments come, there is no wild rushing from place to place hunting a way out . . . We are not to be fools, but neither are we to panic or to begin to fight back hammer and tongs. There is no need to do either *if* we have begun to look at all of life, *before the trouble comes*, from the viewpoint of God.[8]

Lying for the Lord

JOSHUA 2:4–7 *Then the woman took the two men and hid them. So she said, "Yes, the men came to me, but I did not know where they were from. And it happened as the gate was being shut, when it was dark, that the men went out. Where the men went I do not know; pursue them quickly, for you may overtake them." (But she had brought them up to the roof and hidden them with the stalks of flax, which she had laid in order on the roof.) Then the men pursued them by the road to the Jordan, to the fords. And as soon as those who pursued them had gone out, they shut the gate.* (NKJV)

Rahab, a woman of the night, now performed one of the most astounding acts of faith mentioned in the Bible—she lied! Consider, however, that the laws of the Israelites had not been available to this woman, and oriental ethics commended the guarding of a guest as a high virtue of hospitality.[9] God does not change his standards as influenced by situational ethics, but he does accept a person where they are, the stricter judgment being withheld for those who ought to be more mature. Rahab jeopardized her own well-being to ensure the success of the Israelite spies' mission.

We must be sympathetic and patient with the character development of new **converts**, allowing time and space for them to grow.

Rahab hid two spies in her own home and helped them to escape at risk to her own life. This was an unparalleled act of faith for a woman who had never been raised in the "**fear** and **admonition** of the Lord." In addition, God must have moved the hearts of the king's messengers to be influenced by Rahab's suggestions—they

did not force an entry, search the premises, or even hesitate in their hot pursuit down the road.

go to

clients
Joshua 2:1

drying
Exodus 14:21–31

slaughter
Numbers 21:21–35

John Wesley	what others say

I am immortal until my work is done.[10]

Your Reputation Has Preceded You

JOSHUA 2:8–13 *Now before they lay down, she came up to them on the roof, and said to the men: "I know that the LORD has given you the land, that the terror of you has fallen on us, and that all the inhabitants of the land are fainthearted because of you. For we have heard how the LORD dried up the water of the Red Sea for you when you came out of Egypt, and what you did to the two kings of the Amorites who were on the other side of the Jordan, Sihon and Og, whom you utterly destroyed. And as soon as we heard these things, our hearts melted; neither did there remain any more courage in anyone because of you, for the LORD your God, He is God in heaven above and on earth beneath. Now therefore, I beg you, swear to me by the LORD, since I have shown you kindness, that you also will show kindness to my father's house, and give me a true token, and spare my father, my mother, my brothers, my sisters, and all that they have, and deliver our lives from death." (NKJV)*

The spies might have intended to bed down for the night, but their rest was interrupted by Rahab, who wanted to talk. Surely the difference between the demeanor of her regular clients and these Israelite visitors stood as a strong testimony of the type of God they served.

Rahab already knew a lot of Israel's history: the drying up of the Red Sea and the slaughter of Sihon and Og. Unknowingly, she now reveals an important piece of information that the spies will later pass on to Joshua.

But key to this passage is Rahab's statement about God's sovereignty. Unlike the Israelites, who were tempted to take for granted the God they served, Rahab was blown away by his extraordinary deeds. She waxes eloquent in her description of what he has done.

Red Sea
Exodus 14:19–29

fear
Exodus 15:15–16

Abraham
Genesis 15:16

nations
Isaiah 49:6;
Matthew 8:11

first
Hebrews 11:31

second
James 2:25

third
Matthew 1:5

life
Exodus 21:23

conversion
change of heart and
life

unrepentance
refusal to change a
reprobate lifestyle

righteousness
moral purity and
uprightness

Messiah
Christ, the long-
awaited deliverer

That, coupled with her plea to be saved, is a confession of faith reflecting a **conversion** within. Rahab is ready to risk all she has for a God she barely knows.

The crossing of the Red Sea happened a full forty years before Rahab mentioned it in this passage. The people of the land accepted the story as fact and allowed it to put fear in their hearts, but they did not change their behavior. Four generations earlier, God mentioned their **unrepentance** to Abraham, giving them four hundred–plus years to come to himself, but they would not. The last forty would have sealed their fate, as they knew of God but refused to develop a relationship with him. God has always desired that the Israelites would be the catalyst to bring all nations to himself.

Rahab is mentioned three times in the New Testament for her act of heroism. The first instance affirms that assisting the spies saved her physical life when Jericho was attacked. The second declares that her actions produced **righteousness** that would save her soul. And the third place she is mentioned is in the genealogy of Christ as the great-great-grandmother of King David and thus an ancestor of the **Messiah**!

Rahab's Settlement

JOSHUA 2:14–16 *So the men answered her, "Our lives for yours, if none of you tell this business of ours. And it shall be, when the LORD has given us the land, that we will deal kindly and truly with you." Then she let them down by a rope through the window, for her house was on the city wall; she dwelt on the wall. And she said to them, "Get to the mountain, lest the pursuers meet you. Hide there three days, until the pursuers have returned. Afterward you may go your way." (NKJV)*

There is a saying in Israelite law that in case of serious injury, a "life for a life" is required. Now this principle is being offered in reverse. If Rahab will keep silent about her rendezvous with the spies, they will grant her and her family an opportunity to live, as an even exchange for sparing their lives. In good faith she quietly helps them down from the wall, filling their ears with whispers of advice and caution.

For the most part, the towns in the land God was preparing for the Israelites were independent city-states, and their rulers were called kings. Jericho was a walled city of palm trees in an open valley, with flat-roofed houses upon which could be placed grain and stalks for drying. Archaeologists have uncovered houses located in the spaces between the inner and outer wall. Rahab's home would have been located in the western part of the wall, as it faced the only mountains in the region, one-half mile from the city.

The hills were perfect for hiding, with limestone cliffs some one thousand feet high and an abundance of caves. The city officials would have gone east on a road that came from Jerusalem and headed toward the Jordan. Except during flood stage, the river could be crossed at the place of the road by wading.[11]

covenant
binding two-sided agreement

I Solemnly Swear

JOSHUA 2:17–21 *So the men said to her: "We will be blameless of this oath of yours which you have made us swear, unless, when we come into the land, you bind this line of scarlet cord in the window through which you let us down, and unless you bring your father, your mother, your brothers, and all your father's household to your own home. So it shall be that whoever goes outside the doors of your house into the street, his blood shall be on his own head, and we will be guiltless. And whoever is with you in the house, his blood shall be on our head if a hand is laid on him. And if you tell this business of ours, then we will be free from your oath which you made us swear." Then she said, "According to your words, so be it." And she sent them away, and they departed. And she bound the scarlet cord in the window.* (NKJV)

The spies answer Rahab's plea for herself and her family by offering a **covenant** with three conditions: (1) the whole family must stay in Rahab's house, (2) a scarlet cord must be tied in the window, and (3) the covenant itself must be kept a secret.

previous
Numbers 13:31–33

faith
confidence and trust
based on conviction

justified
be released from the
guilt of sin

Zane C. Hodges

Although Rahab's faith began to operate the moment she "received the messengers," she could not really be **justified** by works until she had "sent them out another way." The reason for this is obvious when the story in Joshua 2 is carefully considered. Up until the last moment, she could still have betrayed the spies. Had she so desired, she could have sent their pursuers after them.[12]

Billy Graham

The **faith** that saves has one distinguishing quality . . . it is a faith that brings about a way of life. Some have quite successfully imitated this way of life for a time, but for those who trust Christ for salvation, that faith brings about in them a desire to live out that experience of faith.[13]

Local Gossip

JOSHUA 2:22–24 *They departed and went to the mountain, and stayed there three days until the pursuers returned. The pursuers sought them all along the way, but did not find them. So the two men returned, descended from the mountain, and crossed over; and they came to Joshua the son of Nun, and told him all that had befallen them. And they said to Joshua, "Truly the LORD has delivered all the land into our hands, for indeed all the inhabitants of the country are fainthearted because of us." (NKJV)*

After the deal has been struck, the spies follow Rahab's excellent advice and return in safety to disclose to Joshua two vital morsels of intelligence: (1) God would be faithful to deliver, and (2) the enemy was running scared.

apply it

How we view a situation is entirely a matter of perspective. The land was essentially in the same condition forty years previously, but the outlook of the previous set of spies was entirely different from that of the current men. The first report centered around the power and strength of the enemy and the size and fortifications of their cities. On this espionage mission, however, the spies have seen the land through the eyes of God. They return, full of excitement, expecting him to accomplish great things through them and for them.

Chapter Wrap-Up

- God makes it clear that the man of his choice to lead the nation of Israel after Moses will be Joshua. He promises victory, success and his own reassuring presence if Joshua will be courageous and follow carefully the law he has given. (Joshua 1:1–9)

- Joshua commands the troops to prepare for battle and reminds the tribes settling east of the Jordan that their work is not done. The people respond by affirming support. (Joshua 1:10–18)

- Joshua sends two spies to check out Jericho and the surrounding countryside. They meet Rahab, who puts her life on the line to save their own. She declares her belief in God and what he is about to do. (Joshua 2:1–13)

- The spies make a conditional covenant with the woman to save her life and the lives of her family. Rahab assists them in their escape, and they return with good news for Joshua. (Joshua 2:14–24)

Study Questions

1. What did God offer Joshua to bolster his self-confidence?

2. How can a person make God's Word an integral part of his or her own life?

3. Why did God choose a prostitute to help his people and to eventually become a part of the lineage of Christ?

4. How did Rahab demonstrate a living faith?

Joshua 3-4
Crossing the Jordan

Chapter Highlights:
- Educating the People
- Bathing from the Inside Out
- Crossing the River
- A Happy Ending
- Erecting the Memorials

Let's Get Started

The one event that the Israelites have been anticipating for as long as they've been alive is just about to happen. As children, they prayed for it at bedtime with their parents. As youth, they dreamed about it over the campfires at night. As adults, they discussed it with their neighbors in the doors of their tents. They were about to enter the land that was promised so long ago to **Abraham**, **Isaac**, and **Jacob**. But standing directly in the way of all their hopes and dreams was a rushing river that they could not ford.

go to

Abraham
Genesis 12:6–7

Isaac
Genesis 26:3

Jacob
Genesis 28:13

fifteen
Joshua 3:3, 6, 8, 11, 13, 14, 15, 17; 4:5, 7, 9, 10, 11, 16, 18

Educating the People

JOSHUA 3:1–4 *Then Joshua rose early in the morning; and they set out from Acacia Grove and came to the Jordan, he and all the children of Israel, and lodged there before they crossed over. So it was, after three days, that the officers went through the camp; and they commanded the people, saying, "When you see the ark of the covenant of the LORD your God, and the priests, the Levites, bearing it, then you shall set out from your place and go after it. Yet there shall be a space between you and it, about two thousand cubits by measure. Do not come near it, that you may know the way by which you must go, for you have not passed this way before." (NKJV)*

For three more days, the Israelites camp along the banks of the **Jordan**. No doubt their days are full of wonder and speculation at how God will be able to pull off a feat as great as transporting a whole nation of people and their gear from one side of the river to the other.

The emphasis in this story will be the **ark of the covenant**, as it is mentioned <u>fifteen</u> times in two chapters. The significance is that the ark (bearing the Word of God) embodies the very presence of God. So when it is carried before the people into the Jordan, it is as if God himself is leading the way. God would be going in front of them,

Abraham
patriarch of the Jewish people

Isaac
Abraham's son

Jacob
Isaac's son

Jordan
river defining the eastern entrance into the land

ark of the covenant
a box containing symbolic artifacts and God's own presence

go to

consequences
2 Samuel 6:6–7

triumph
Colossians 2:13–15;
1 Corinthians
15:20–23

ark
Exodus 25:10–22

manna
Exodus 16:31

rod
Numbers 17:8

dwelt
2 Samuel 6:2

believed
1 Samuel 4:1–11

commandments
laws given by God

manna
food provided by
God in wilderness

cherubim
angels with wings

directly into whatever danger lay ahead, and he was going first to be able to claim the land for his own people.

As always, God demands a holy reverence in his presence and requests that the people stay a thousand yards from either side of the ark of his covenant. There will be <u>consequences</u> if the ark is treated casually, yet it will be in full view of all who would cross.

Christ has gone ahead of us to <u>triumph</u> over the power of sin, the enemy of our souls and death itself.

what others say

Lloyd John Ogilvie

Our fears can be conquered only by One who made us, redeemed us, defeated the fear, which is the inner cause of our dread of life, and comes to us with power to make a difference in our hearts.[1]

The <u>ark</u> of the covenant was made sometime during the wilderness wanderings, of acacia wood, overlaid with gold. Two carrying poles ran through rings attached to the corners. It was around three feet, nine inches by two feet, three inches and a little more than two feet high. It contained the Ten **Commandments**, a jar of **manna**, and Aaron's budding <u>rod</u>. Across the top, called the mercy seat, two golden **cherubim** faced each other, and between them God himself <u>dwelt</u>. The ark itself was not magical, even though at times the people foolishly <u>believed</u> that its potency could bring supernatural power.

what others say

Bertha Spafford Vester

Long after the other tents were dark my husband and I sat on in the door of ours. The moon set behind the Judean hills, leaving us with the glow of the stars and the flicker of the camp lanterns suspended on poles to keep away jackals and hyenas. We spoke of the feelings of the Children of Israel when they came to the "swelling of Jordan" and by God's mighty hand were permitted to "cross on dry land" and entered upon new temptations to overcome.[2]

Bathing from the Inside Out

JOSHUA 3:5–6 *And Joshua said to the people, "Sanctify your-selves, for tomorrow the LORD will do wonders among you." Then Joshua spoke to the priests, saying, "Take up the ark of the covenant and cross over before the people." So they took up the ark of the covenant and went before the people.* (NKJV)

Consecration involved <u>washing</u>, clothing, bathing, and abstaining from sexual activity. More than an outward act alone, it demonstrated a cleansing of heart, renewal of soul, and a single focus on God alone. Consecration meant being set apart for a special service or activity.

Joshua speaks of the astonishing events God will perform the next day, building anticipation by not divulging the entire game plan all at once. He then starts the process by moving the priests with the ark to the front.

go to

washing
Exodus 19:14–15

devote
2 Timothy 2:20–21

consecration
to become sacred for God's use

sanctified
consecrated, set apart as holy

devote
to commit or desig-nate yourself to a particular purpose

---

what others say

George Sweeting

Fallow ground is dry, hard, unproductive soil. Prayer helps us to examine ourselves and see fallow ground in our lives that needs to be broken up . . . As long as we are unbroken, unre-sponsive, and unforgiving, we will be unproductive.[3]

Corrie ten Boom

One does not use the cat's saucer oneself. Why? Because it is set apart, not for you, but for the cat. If we are **sanctified**, we are set apart by the Lord for his service and for his honor.[4]

Before God can do amazing things in our lives, we must turn away from sin and **devote** ourselves to him.

Getting Their Toes Wet

JOSHUA 3:7–8 *And the LORD said to Joshua, "This day I will begin to exalt you in the sight of all Israel, that they may know that, as I was with Moses, so I will be with you. You shall com-mand the priests who bear the ark of the covenant, saying, 'When you have come to the edge of the water of the Jordan, you shall stand in the Jordan.'"* (NKJV)

apply it

To escape from Egypt took a measure of faith on the part of each Israelite citizen. If they were pursued, they would be taken back into a life of slavery. But to invade **Canaan** meant a commitment of their lives with no possibility of retreat. They were stepping into hostile territory with the river at their backs. God wants us to hazard our lives in reckless abandonment to him and in scrupulous obedience to his Word. A faith this profound and intense can <u>overcome</u> the world.

So God desires to show his great power in our lives, and we croak, "Now what shall I do . . . ?" The answer is really . . . "Take God seriously! Accept his enormous power in your life! Believe it, and be ready for miracles!"

what others say

Anne Ortland

A woodpecker was once pecking away on a great tree. Suddenly a huge bolt of lightning struck the tree and with enormous noise and force split it right down the middle, straight to its very roots. The poor little woodpecker found himself on the ground nearby, half-dead, his feathers torn and singed. And when he gathered himself together he croaked, "I didn't know I could do it!"[5]

Not Afraid of the Big Bad Wolf

JOSHUA 3:9–11 *So Joshua said to the children of Israel, "Come here, and hear the words of the LORD your God." And Joshua said, "By this you shall know that the living God is among you, and that He will without fail drive out from before you the Canaanites and the Hittites and the Hivites and the Perizzites and the Girgashites and the Amorites and the Jebusites: Behold, the ark of the covenant of the Lord of all the earth is crossing over before you into the Jordan. (NKJV)*

go to

overcome
1 John 5:4

Canaan
a pre-Israelite term
for the Promised
Land

God wants all Israel to know that just as he will miraculously convey them across a river, so he will drive their enemies out from before them as he had promised. He even makes a list of the most fearsome people groups, in case they should entertain any doubts that one of the following should prove too formidable.

The People of Canaan

Nationality	Locality
Canaanites	Seacoast and Jordan Valley
Hittites	Overall
Hivites	Near Shecem and Mount Hermon highlands
Perizzites	Central highlands
Girgashites	Small settlements east of Galilee
Armorites	Mountainous regions
Jebusites	Jerusalem and northern Palestine

Immediately after this recitation of potential enemies, Joshua draws the attention of the people back to the source of their hope and confidence. "Look at the ark," he says. "The Lord of all the earth will go before you." "All the earth" is an encompassing phrase that about covers any person, place, or thing that could bring them the slightest trepidation!

Each divine intervention in our lives should set the foundation of faith for the next.

Heaped-Up Waters

JOSHUA 3:12–13 *Now therefore, take for yourselves twelve men from the tribes of Israel, one man from every tribe. And it shall come to pass, as soon as the soles of the feet of the priests who bear the ark of the LORD, the Lord of all the earth, shall rest in the waters of the Jordan, that the waters of the Jordan shall be cut off, the waters that come down from upstream, and they shall stand as a heap.* (NKJV)

Twelve men, one from each tribe, are appointed for a service that will be delineated at a later point. And finally, after all their preparations are complete, Joshua gives the people a clue as to how the next exciting event is going to come about. In response to the action of the priests, stepping out boldly into the rushing torrent, God will stop the flow of the river and stack the waters in a heap.

There is a partnership in the service of God—I do my part and he does his.

Luci Swindoll

What are you resisting? Has God been nudging you into action and you've either said "no" repeatedly, or "well, maybe" so weakly that no one can hear it . . . The last thing you want to do just might be the best thing that ever happened to you. It might even be fun.[6]

Crossing the River

JOSHUA 3:14–17 *So it was, when the people set out from their camp to cross over the Jordan, with the priests bearing the ark of the covenant before the people, and as those who bore the ark came to the Jordan, and the feet of the priests who bore the ark dipped in the edge of the water (for the Jordan overflows all its banks during the whole time of harvest), that the waters which came down from upstream stood still, and rose in a heap very far away at Adam, the city that is beside Zaretan. So the waters that went down into the Sea of the Arabah, the Salt Sea, failed, and were cut off; and the people crossed over opposite Jericho. Then the priests who bore the ark of the covenant of the LORD stood firm on dry ground in the midst of the Jordan; and all Israel crossed over on dry ground, until all the people had crossed completely over the Jordan. (NKJV)*

Amy Carmichael

The Jordan, at the place where the nation of Israel would have crossed, would have been nearly a hundred feet wide and five to ten feet deep at flood stage. There are two times of overflow during the year—early summer and fall. Both were times of harvest. This event would have occurred during the greatest of the two—early summer, when spring rains and melting snow would have overwhelmed the banks.[7]

Joshua 4:1–16

The Lord finally tells Joshua why the twelve men have been selected. They are to erect two monuments, one at the spot where the priests are standing with the ark in the middle of the river, and the other to be announced shortly. Both would be made of river rocks, to memorialize the extraordinary events that took place on this spot.

Meanwhile, the soldiers from the two and a half tribes settled east of the river cross the empty riverbed first, and the rest of the people hurry after them. As the Israelites watch the entire miracle unfold before their very eyes, Joshua is validated in their minds as the leader chosen by God. When all is completed, God gives the word that Joshua is to command the priests to come up out of the Jordan.

Levitical
Deuteronomy 10:8

Levitical
descendants of Levi

The Bible narrative in this passage is a little confusing, with some repetition and backtracking, but coming across louder and stronger than the actual order of events is the habit pattern that is being established. God tells Joshua, Joshua tells the people, and the people do as they are told. This will serve them well in the years to come.

A Happy Ending

JOSHUA 4:17–18 *Joshua therefore commanded the priests, saying, "Come up from the Jordan." And it came to pass, when the priests who bore the ark of the covenant of the LORD had come from the midst of the Jordan, and the soles of the priests' feet touched the dry land, that the waters of the Jordan returned to their place and overflowed all its banks as before. (NKJV)*

This is the conclusion of the whole miraculous episode. The **Levitical** priests, still bearing the ark, walk up the banks while the tremendous energy from the pent-up force of the water rages once again down the channel, churning and foaming where their feet had stood only seconds before.

what others say

C. S. Lewis

If the ultimate Fact is not an abstraction but the living God, opaque by the very fullness of His blinding actuality, then he might . . . work miracles. But would He? Many people of sincere piety feel that He would not. Yet . . . I believe . . . there are rules behind the rules, and a unity . . . deeper than uniformity. A supreme workman will never break . . . the living and inward law of the work he is producing. But he will break without scruple any number of those superficial regularities and orthodoxies which little, unimaginative critics mistake for . . . laws.[8]

apply it

This account lays before us a plan to ford the impossibilities that stand in the way of God's design for our lives. We can follow the blueprint of Israel's success, for what they faced was not simply a geographical barrier but a <u>spiritual</u> one as well. Their preparations were not merely of weapons and provisions; they were to make ready their hearts and minds. When we view our struggles on this level, we will see God work as mighty a miracle for us as he worked for them. The first step is to <u>sanctify</u> and purify ourselves from any **encumbering** sin. Then we need to <u>follow</u> God's directing presence and let him be our guide. Finally, we need to <u>step</u> out in faith and trust that God will intercede and provide.

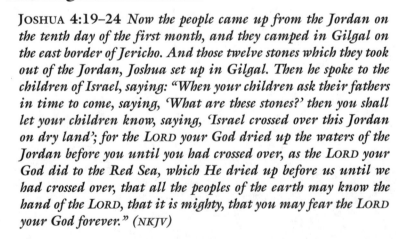

what others say

Ray Stedman

A helpful key in understanding God's teaching is to see that the visible, physical events recorded in scripture illustrate invisible spiritual situations and forces. The visible event is occurring *because of* the unseen spiritual situation . . . It is always a mistake to put great emphasis on a physical miracle [and] miss the point of what God is saying.[9]

Erecting the Memorials

go to

spiritual
Ephesians 6:12

sanctify
Joshua 3:5;
2 Timothy 2:21;
Hebrews 9:13–14

follow
Joshua 3:3–4;
John 10:4;
Isaiah 43:2

step
Joshua 3:15–16;
Philippians 3:12;
James 2:17

instructions
Exodus 12:1–3

encumbering
that which hampers, hinders, and impedes

JOSHUA 4:19–24 *Now the people came up from the Jordan on the tenth day of the first month, and they camped in Gilgal on the east border of Jericho. And those twelve stones which they took out of the Jordan, Joshua set up in Gilgal. Then he spoke to the children of Israel, saying: "When your children ask their fathers in time to come, saying, 'What are these stones?' then you shall let your children know, saying, 'Israel crossed over this Jordan on dry land'; for the LORD your God dried up the waters of the Jordan before you until you had crossed over, as the LORD your God did to the Red Sea, which He dried up before us until we had crossed over, that all the peoples of the earth may know the hand of the LORD, that it is mighty, that you may fear the LORD your God forever." (NKJV)*

Note that both Moses and Joshua gave important <u>instructions</u> on the tenth day of the first month. This date would fall during our March or April. Further, this was the day that the Passover lamb was selected. In other words, on the anniversary of their freedom from Egypt, the offspring of Abraham arrived in the land of promise.

Gilgal is an excellent place to set up camp as it has a natural water supply from the river, and with the Jordan on the one side and an open plain on the other, they would have no need to worry about a surprise attack. Here we find Joshua divulging the plan for the other twelve stones. They are to form a second memorial for the purpose of provoking questions from future generations so that they too can participate in the great deeds God has executed in this place.

Finally, God states why this miracle is significant. He has orchestrated the entire event to give incontestable proof of his strength, and to instill a reverence and an awe for who he is.

Gilgal
a town one and a half miles north of Jericho

what others say

Joni Eareckson Tada

As a youngster, I fostered the idea that God was on an ego trip, always telling people how wonderful He was . . . God wants us to get to know Him—not because He needs our worship but because we desperately need His strength. It has nothing to do with satisfying His ego but everything to do with finding life.[10]

Chapter Wrap-Up

- The people purify themselves and prepare to follow the ark of the covenant across the barrier of water that stands between them and the Promised Land. They are encouraged to remember that God is greater than their enemies. (Joshua 3:1–13)

- As soon as the priests' feet touch the Jordan River, the water piles up some miles upriver. The people cross in safety on dry ground. (Joshua 3:14–17)

- Twelve men are selected to set up two monuments, one in the river at the spot where the priests stood with the ark and another at Gilgal where they set up camp after the river crossing. (Joshua 4:1–18)

- The people are challenged to pass on the legacy of this event to future generations, and God states that the miracle's true significance is that it validates who he is. (Joshua 4:19–24)

Study Questions

1. What was involved in Israel's act of consecration?

2. What was Israel's three-step plan for victory?

3. Joshua listed Israel's potential enemies. What are the enemies of your soul, and how can you follow the example of the Israelites to act in faith against them?

4. What was the purpose of the two memorials?

Joshua 5-6
Conquest of Jericho

Chapter Highlights:
- Identification with God
- Cut It Out!
- Confrontation with God
- Stalking in Silence
- Conquest in Clamor

Let's Get Started

One piece of information can simultaneously strike two individuals, rejuvenating one with hope and courage and dispatching the other into the depths of despair. Such was the case with the news of what happened at the Jordan River. The Israelites rejoiced in the confirmation of their faith, strong in the conviction that God would make them triumphant. At the same time, the indigenous people of the land were filled with panic at the approach of the nation whose God could control the forces of nature.

In this chapter we find out what happened when God's people finally made it over the border into the land of promise.

key point

Identification with God

JOSHUA 5:1 *So it was, when all the kings of the Amorites who were on the west side of the Jordan, and all the kings of the Canaanites who were by the sea, heard that the LORD had dried up the waters of the Jordan from before the children of Israel until we had crossed over, that their heart melted; and there was no spirit in them any longer because of the children of Israel.* (NKJV)

The native people of Canaan were somewhere between complete demoralization and hysteria. When they originally heard the Israelites were stopped on the other side of the Jordan, they had to fight to maintain their composure. However, they were hoping the river barrier would grant them extra time to make preparations and mobilize for war. But the latest news sent them into complete pandemonium. The word went out that the entire company of Israelites miraculously crossed on dry ground through the middle of the impassable current and were now camped within walking distance of Jericho.

go to

disobedience
Exodus 32

urged
Deuteronomy 10:16

represent
Deuteronomy 30:6

inward
Jeremiah 9:25–26

not
Numbers 14:29

next
Numbers 14:31

blessing
Genesis 17:14

shame
Deuteronomy
30:2–3

Abraham
Genesis 17:10–13

apostasy
the renunciation of
God by word or
deed

Gentiles
non-Jews

Cut It Out!

the big picture

Joshua 5:2–9

God instructs Joshua to make knives out of flint and to circumcise all the males in the congregation of Israel. All the men of military age who came out of Egypt had died in the desert on the way because they never learned to obey God. So their sons, none of whom had been circumcised yet, were the ones Joshua would circumcise now. After this act is completed, they remain in the camp until fully healed.

The first generation of Israelites to leave Egypt were circumcised on the outside but full of <u>disobedience</u> and **apostasy** on the inside. Moses had constantly <u>urged</u> them to make circumcision more than just a physical act. He said that it should <u>represent</u> a heart that loves God, is yielded to him, and is ready to have anything superfluous cut away. Unfortunately, it is possible to have the outward sign without the <u>inward</u> change. And because the first generation did <u>not</u> keep covenant with God, he had no choice but to try again with the <u>next</u>.

Why had not the new generation been circumcised? We do not know, but we do know that there would be no <u>blessing</u> if there was no circumcision. With their willing subordination to God's commands at the Jordan, they are now ready in spirit and reality to do things God's way.

The timing is good, as the people of Canaan are paralyzed with shock and too afraid to attack. Joshua can now afford to let his soldiers be sidelined for a few days. Blessing will be obtained through weakness, and the <u>shame</u> of being a dominated people will finally be removed.

The act of cutting away the foreskin of an eight-day-old male in the nation of Israel began with a special covenant that God made with <u>Abraham</u> and was to continue through successive generations. This act set the people of Israel apart from the nations around them and became a symbol of their calling to a purer, higher life. Later, they even became known by the title "the circumcision," and this distinction became a real mark of racial and cultural pride. Other nationalities were referred to as "the uncircumcision" and were sometimes even viewed with contempt.

This subject became controversial in the early church (made up of a mixture of Jews and **Gentiles**). One side maintained that the rite should be enforced among Gentile believers, with the other side just as adamantly against it. In the end the outward act of circumcision was <u>dropped</u> as a prerequisite for Christian fellowship, and more important issues were addressed instead.

We can enter into the spirit of circumcision by putting aside our needless sin just as the physical act <u>puts</u> aside that which is unnecessary in the flesh.

apply it

what others say

Dale Evans Rogers

Oh, if I could only make some unbelieving folks understand! They seem to think I have "gone pious" because You have taken out of me all desire for some of my old, so-called "pleasures"—that I have "set myself up to be holy." Father, if I could only make them see that Dale Evans has died, and that a willing slave to Christ has been born in her place! When I asked You to make me over, that's exactly what happened.[1]

Although <u>**flint**</u> was in abundance in biblical lands, copper, bronze, and iron were preferred for tools and weapons at the time of Joshua. Even so, flint was probably part of the <u>tradition</u> of the original ritual.[2] It is also possible, via good "flint-knapping" techniques, to chip out a blade so sharp you can cut yourself just by picking it up. Far better to do this particular job with a knife of exquisite sharpness.

Confrontation with God

JOSHUA 5:10–12 *Now the children of Israel camped in Gilgal, and kept the Passover on the fourteenth day of the month at twilight on the plains of Jericho. And they ate of the produce of the land on the day after the Passover, unleavened bread and parched grain, on the very same day. Then the manna ceased on the day after they had eaten the produce of the land; and the children of Israel no longer had manna, but they ate the food of the land of Canaan that year. (NKJV)*

It was good that the children of **Israel** had already submitted to the act of circumcision since the original <u>instructions</u> for the Passover emphasized the importance of that rite. Now they are ready to celebrate. Scrupulously following <u>directions</u>, they begin on the fourteenth day of the month, <u>four</u> days after crossing the Jordan. This is the third recorded Passover meal. The <u>second</u> occurred on the first anniversary

go to

dropped
Acts 15:5–29

puts
Colossians 2:11–12

flint
Joshua 5:2–3

tradition
Exodus 4:25

instructions
Exodus 12:44, 48

directions
Exodus 12:6

four
Joshua 4:19

second
Numbers 9:4–5

flint
a hard grayish-black form of fine-grained quartz

Israel
name given to Jacob, Abraham's grandson

milk
Exodus 3:8

lesson
Deuteronomy 8:3

Jesus
John 6:48–51

forever
John 6:58

remembering
1 Corinthians
11:23–26

manna
a white honey-
tasting bread from
heaven

unleavened bread
a flat, unsalted
cracker-type bread

bitter herbs
probably wild let-
tuce, chicory, pep-
perwort, snakewort,
or dandelion

ingesting
absorption into the
body by swallowing

of the institution, but after that the holiday had probably not been observed at all.

Now that they were in the land that God described as "flowing with <u>milk</u> and honey" and had finally learned the <u>lesson</u> of humility that their dependence on the **manna** had encouraged, they were clearly at a turning point.

The Passover celebration commemorates the night God's angel of death "passed over" all of the homes in Egypt and killed the firstborn son of every family that did not sprinkle the blood of a lamb on the doorposts. The Egyptians suffered great loss, but the Israelites were spared because they followed God's instructions. The lamb was then roasted and eaten as they stood in traveling clothes, ready to leave the land of bondage at a moment's notice. They ate the lamb with **unleavened bread** (good for traveling) and **bitter herbs**, symbolic of the tyranny they had endured.

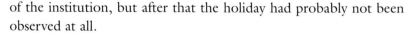

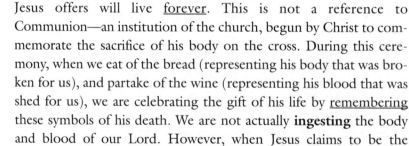

what others say

Alan Redpath

The manna was wilderness food; it suited a wilderness journey . . . God is always seeking to lead His children on to new
unexplored areas of the life of redemption . . . But how reluctant Christian people are to consider the possibility of going
on! . . . But there comes a moment in the training of a child of
God when the old ways have served God's purpose.[3]

Manna, a gift from heaven that sustained human life for a short period of time, is like <u>Jesus</u>. He is also a gift from heaven given to provide life. However, anyone who partakes of the nourishment that Jesus offers will live <u>forever</u>. This is not a reference to Communion—an institution of the church, begun by Christ to com-memorate the sacrifice of his body on the cross. During this cere-mony, when we eat of the bread (representing his body that was bro-ken for us), and partake of the wine (representing his blood that was shed for us), we are celebrating the gift of his life by <u>remembering</u> these symbols of his death. We are not actually **ingesting** the body and blood of our Lord. However, when Jesus claims to be the "Bread of Life," he is encouraging our spiritual appropriation of himself by faith for salvation.

Yes, *Sir!*

JOSHUA 5:13–15 *And it came to pass, when Joshua was by Jericho, that he lifted his eyes and looked, and behold, a Man stood opposite him with His sword drawn in His hand. And Joshua went to Him and said to Him, "Are You for us or for our adversaries?" So He said, "No, but as Commander of the army of the LORD I have now come." And Joshua fell on his face to the earth and worshiped, and said to Him, "What does my Lord say to His servant?" Then the Commander of the LORD's army said to Joshua, "Take your sandal off your foot, for the place where you stand is holy." And Joshua did so. (NKJV)*

Moses
Exodus 3:5

heavenly
Psalm 91:9–12;
2 Kings 6:15–17

spiritual
Deuteronomy
18:9–13;
Ephesians 6:12

theophany
appearance of God
in the form of an
angel or messenger

In the original Hebrew, "Joshua was near Jericho" meant that he was "in very close proximity" to Jericho. In other words, he was at the wall, probably under cover of darkness, looking for a weakness or trying to settle on a plan of attack. Intent on his mission, he is shocked to look up and see a man with a drawn sword. Joshua's quick inquiry could be expected: "Whose side are you on?" But the answer is entirely unanticipated. It does not fit neatly into either "friend" or "foe." And neither does the man who offers it.

This is not a representative sent from God, but a true **theophany**. Here are three reasons we can believe that this person that Joshua met is God himself: (1) Joshua recognized and worshipped him as God, (2) he commanded Joshua to take off his sandals as he did with <u>Moses</u>, and (3) the conversation in chapter 6 where the Lord is identified as the speaker is probably a continuation of this encounter in chapter 5. Verse 1 of chapter 6 is most likely parenthetical.

By not answering Joshua's original question, God is saying, "I am far more than an enemy or an ally—I am the commander!" That leaves Joshua in the position of field general, to carry out the commander's orders. And it makes Israel a mere division of God's army, alongside his <u>heavenly</u> hosts. In essence, the whole thing is really God's war and the conflict is no longer with just men and women, but against a <u>spiritual</u> wickedness that has a dominating grip on the land.

> ### what others say
>
> **John White**
> Earthly warfare is not the real warfare. It is but a faint, ugly reflection of the real thing. It is into the *real* war that the

go to

look
Exodus 33:20;
1 Timothy 6:16

image
John 1:18;
Colossians 1:15

Abraham's
Genesis 18:1–15

Jacob
Genesis 32:22–30

Gideon
Judges 6:11–22

Manoah
Judges 13:3–23

Moses
Exodus 33:18–23;
34:29–35

Saul
Acts 9:1–6, 15–19

transformed
2 Corinthians 3:18

preincarnate
before birth in
human flesh

beholds
sees

Christ's kingdom
the spiritual ruler-
ship of Christ among
the people of this
world

> Christian is to plunge. Wars on earth are but tremors felt from
> an earthquake light-years away. The Christian's war takes
> place at the epicenter of the earthquake. It is infinitely more
> deadly, while the issues that hang on it make earth's most
> momentous questions no more than village gossip.[4]

We know that **preincarnate** appearances of the Lord were not
God the Father, since no one can <u>look</u> upon his holiness and live.
The person Joshua saw would be the Christ, who alone reveals the
Father and is the <u>image</u> of the invisible God. No description is given
of what this person looked like—evidently, nothing about his physical appearance demanded attention. In this and other theophanies,
the one seen appears to be human until their words or actions proclaim otherwise.

<u>Abraham's</u> visit with the God-man brought the announcement
that he would be a father. <u>Jacob</u> had a wrestling match with the prebirth Christ. <u>Gideon</u> tried to feed the man he saw a goat-stew, and
<u>Manoah</u> was sure he was going to die after his confrontation. These
encounters were unexpected and full of drama. Not one of the individuals was ever the same again.

what others say

Jim Elliot

Moses and Joshua both came to the place where they had to
remove their shoes—to be a leader for God, one must take a
shoeless (uncovered) stand on holy ground.[5]

Charles Spurgeon

I desire . . . that you exercise your minds, your faith, your spiritual powers and vividly believe that Jesus is here; so believe
it, so that your inner eye **beholds** what you believe.[6]

Other people in the Bible had a personal encounter with the Lord.
It happened to <u>Moses</u> and <u>Saul</u>, and others. Meeting God changed
their lives and empowered them for work to come. Every great
Christian who has accomplished anything of merit for **Christ's
kingdom** has had a life-changing confrontation with the God of
the Bible before they ever became a useful servant. The more we
then seek his presence, the more we are <u>transformed</u> to look and act
like him.

preordained
decided in advance

earnest
a sign, or pledge, of
what is to come

A. W. Tozer

What ever else it embraces, true Christian experience must always include a genuine encounter with God. Without this, religion is but a shadow, a reflection of reality, a cheap copy of an original once enjoyed by someone else of whom we have heard.[7]

Stalking in Silence

JOSHUA 6:1–5 *Now Jericho was securely shut up because of the children of Israel; none went out, and none came in. And the LORD said to Joshua: "See! I have given Jericho into your hand, its king, and the mighty men of valor. You shall march around the city, all you men of war; you shall go all around the city once. This you shall do six days. And seven priests shall bear seven trumpets of rams' horns before the ark. But the seventh day you shall march around the city seven times, and the priests shall blow the trumpets. It shall come to pass, when they make a long blast with the ram's horn, and when you hear the sound of the trumpet, that all the people shall shout with a great shout; then the wall of the city will fall down flat. And the people shall go up every man straight before him."* (NKJV)

The citizens of Jericho did not think they could win in battle—their actions revealed their fear. Battening the gates, their strategy was purely defensive.

Now the Lord continues his conversation with Joshua. Adding to the encouragement that his presence alone would have provided, and to the reminder of who is in charge, God gives a list of instructions that must be meticulously followed for victory. He begins by saying that he has given—past tense—the city into their hands. The outcome of the battle has already been **preordained** and is an **earnest** of all the engagements to follow. What a relief to the mind of Joshua, who no longer must devise some sort of plan to undermine this "impregnable fortress."

But the scheme God unveils sounds absolutely ridiculous. How humiliating to march around the walls, within catcall distance, day after day for a whole week while nothing happens. However, there could be no better way to prove that God alone is the sole power behind the shellacking that will soon take place. No human military leader would ever have devised a plan like this!

There were seven priests, seven trumpets, and seven trips around the walls over seven days, signifying the completion of the first part of the large-scale conquest of the land of Canaan. The trumpets were made from rams' horns and would signal the arrival of God, Israel's commander-in-chief, along with the coming of Jericho's doom. At the long blast, everyone in the company would shout and the citadel would crumple.

The number seven in the Bible is significant—from the seven <u>days</u> of creation in Genesis and the seven last <u>sayings</u> of Christ in the **Gospels**, to the seven <u>churches</u> of Asia and the seven <u>seals</u>, <u>bowls</u>, and <u>trumpets</u> in **Revelation**. The number seven seems to represent a perfection or completion of the work of God.

The ram's horn was the most commonly mentioned musical instrument in the Old Testament. It can produce only a few pitches, and they sound more like elephant calls than melodious notes. It is often used to ceremonially announce a coming <u>victory</u> or the arrival of a <u>king</u>.[8]

key point

go to

days
Genesis 2:2–3

sayings
Matthew 27:46;
Luke 23:34, 43, 46;
John 19:26–28, 30

churches
Revelation 1:11

seals
Revelation 6:1

bowls
Revelation 16:1

trumpets
Revelation 8:6

victory
Judges 3:27–28

king
1 Kings 1:34

Gospels
the biblical biographies of Christ

Revelation
last book of the Bible

what others say

Charles R. Swindoll

God asks that we believe Him *regardless* of the risks—in spite of the danger—ignoring the odds. The ancient city of Jericho was defeated because Joshua and his troops defied the "normal procedure" of battle . . . never once fearing failure.[9]

Trial Run

the big picture

Joshua 6:6–11

Joshua passes on the directions as they were given him by God. He organizes the people in parade order with the ark in center focus, dominating the whole line. He adds the admonition to be silent until he commands otherwise, and Israel circles the city for the first time.

The repetition of God's instructions by Joshua highlights the importance of strict adherence to every detail. The ark is mentioned some <u>five</u> times in this short passage—a constant reminder of God's presence and leadership in this strange endeavor. There will be no military skill or prowess on the part of Joshua. His job is to simply carry out orders.

The less conspicuous we make ourselves, the more prominent God can become.

what others say

Martin H. Woudstra

In keeping with Hebrew narrative style these verses contain details not mentioned in the report of the Lord's words to Joshua. This narrative technique, skillfully using the same elements and adding new points as the narrative goes along, serves to build up to an effective climax, which will not occur until v.20 when the wall's collapse is actually reported.[10]

Conquest in Clamor

the big picture

Joshua 6:12–19

The Israelites get up early to march around Jericho and continue this regimen for six days. On the seventh day, they circle the city seven times. On the seventh time, after the trumpets blast, Joshua commands the people to shout and then reminds them that all the spoil is to be dedicated to God. Individual destruction (and national peril) will follow if anything is taken for personal gain. Rahab and her family are to be saved for the service she rendered in chapter 2.

five
Joshua 6:6, 7, 8, 9, 11

firstfruits
the first portion of any blessing from God

Rising early seems to show the eagerness of the people to obey. The walk around the city would be an easy twenty-five to thirty minutes, but the total from Gilgal and back is more like two hours.[11]

Joshua is serious about setting Jericho aside for God; it is not to be plundered for personal profit. He is aware of the principle of the **firstfruits**. This being the first capture in the land, the city essentially belongs to God.

To remind the Israelites from whose hand they received every blessing, the offering of the firstfruits was instituted during the time of Moses. It demanded that the first of any possession received from the hand of God was to be <u>dedicated</u> back to him—including animals, crops, and children. The firstborn children would have to be **redeemed**. Two additional purposes were achieved through the offering of the firstfruits. The people were <u>reminded</u> of the time when God saved their firstborn sons in Egypt. And some of the goods went to <u>supplement</u> the Levites, who would not own land but served God in the temple.

We should never offer to God whatever is left after we use what we need—he deserves the first and the best.

Total Collapse

JOSHUA 6:20–21 *So the people shouted when the priests blew the trumpets. And it happened when the people heard the sound of the trumpet, and the people shouted with a great shout, that the wall fell down flat. Then the people went up into the city, every man straight before him, and they took the city. And they utterly destroyed all that was in the city, both man and woman, young and old, ox and sheep and donkey, with the edge of the sword.* (NKJV)

After a slowly building climax that begins with the appearance of the commander in the last chapter, we now come to the culmination of the story. The walls literally fall "under themselves." It was not the reverberation from the voices of a vast company of people that brought this barrier down, but God's complete and effortless <u>mastery</u> over Israel's **unassailable** opponent. That and the simple <u>faith</u> of the children of God.

dedicated
Deuteronomy 26:1–10

reminded
Exodus 13:12–15

supplement
Deuteronomy 18:4–5

living sacrifice
Romans 12:1

mastery
Isaiah 45:2

faith
Hebrews 11:30

redeemed
bought back

living sacrifice
your desires die, God flourishes

unassailable
cannot be challenged

The walls of Jericho tumbled down upon themselves when God's people obeyed instructions and marched around the city for seven days. Many fortified cities at this time had walls up to twenty feet thick and over twenty-five feet high.[13] This was an act of God!

Jericho was less than one-half mile in circumference, at a total of seven acres. It was strategically located at the entrance to two passes through the hills—one heading toward Jerusalem and the other toward **Ai** and **Bethel**.[14]

The **Tel** es-Sultan, at the site of Jericho, was first excavated by John Garstang in 1930 and later by Kathleen Kenyon in 1952. They found walls of mud brick dating much earlier than Joshua's time. This city, ruled by the **Hyksos**, was destroyed by fire around 1560 BC and lay vacant for about 150 years. It was rebuilt about 1410 BC, reusing the same rampart but adding a new wall of mud bricks. This would have been the city of Joshua's time.[15]

True Blue

> JOSHUA 6:22–25 *But Joshua had said to the two men who had spied out the country, "Go into the harlot's house, and from there bring out the woman and all that she has, as you swore to her." And the young men who had been spies went in and brought out Rahab, her father, her mother, her brothers, and all that she had. So they brought out all her relatives and left them outside the camp of Israel. But they burned the city and all that was in it with fire. Only the silver and gold, and the vessels of bronze and iron, they put into the treasury of the house of the LORD. And Joshua spared Rahab the harlot, her father's household, and all that she had. So she dwells in Israel to this day, because she hid the messengers whom Joshua sent to spy out Jericho. (NKJV)*

days
Numbers 31:9, 13, 19

people of God
Hebrews 11:31; James 2:25

Ai
a Canaanite city east of Bethel

Bethel
a town about ten miles north of Jerusalem

Tel
artificial mound made of archaeological layers

Hyksos
intruding nation ruling from Egypt

Joshua sends the two spies to retrieve Rahab, most likely because they know where they're going. Rahab and her family are placed outside Israel's camp (probably for seven <u>days</u>) until they are ceremonially clean from any defilement. Any male relatives might have been circumcised. After her quarantine this former prostitute becomes one of the <u>people of God</u> and lives among them.

go to

occupied
Joshua 18:21;
Judges 3:13;
2 Chronicles 28:15

loss
1 Kings 16:34

Hiel
an Israelite entrepreneur during King Ahab's time

Bad News, Then Good

JOSHUA 6:26–27 *Then Joshua charged them at that time, saying, "Cursed be the man before the LORD who rises up and builds this city Jericho; he shall lay its foundation with his first-born, and with his youngest he shall set up its gates." So the LORD was with Joshua, and his fame spread throughout all the country. (NKJV)*

The bad news is that a curse now rests upon Jericho. The curse was not against re-inhabiting the city, as it has been occupied sporadically ever since and is a thriving town today. The curse was against the man who undertook the rebuilding of Jericho, perhaps as an act of presumption. It was dramatically fulfilled five hundred years later when **Hiel** of Bethel laid the foundation and rebuilt the walls at great personal loss.

The good news is that there is a blessing on the ones who have just conquered this place. Joshua's reputation (and consequently Israel's and the God it represents) is circulated all over the land.

The greater the final blessing, the more difficult the battle of faith to attain.

Chapter Wrap-Up

- The men of the Israelite camp undergo the knife in minor surgery to show submission to God by being circumcised. (Joshua 5:1–9)

- The whole camp celebrates the Passover and begins to live off the land instead of depending on a daily supply of manna. (Joshua 5:10–12)

- Joshua meets the Lord face-to-face and learns that God is in charge of the fighting forces. (Joshua 5:13–15)

- Instructions are given and followed as to the capture of the city of Jericho (Joshua 6:1–19)

- The city is devastated, Rahab is assisted, and rules are laid down for the disposing of the city's goods. (Joshua 6:20–27)

Study Questions

1. Why was circumcision important to God, and what is its personal application?

2. What did Joshua need to learn from his encounter with God?

3. Why should God's instructions be obeyed in every detail?

4. What is the principle of the firstfruits?

Chapter Highlights:
• **God Demands Attention**
• **Following Directions**
• **Getting It Right**
• **Covenant Renewal**
• **Cheers and Boos**

Let's Get Started

Chapter 6 of Joshua relates the glories of victory, but chapter 7 discloses the embarrassment of defeat. Six outlines the joyful results of obedience, while 7 recites the devastating consequences of sin. In the last chapter we heard about Joshua's fame, spreading across the land. The current chapter depicts the anger of God burning against the nation. And now we see that same Joshua, facedown before the Lord, pleading for the reputation of his people.

What brought such a reversal? What chilling change does the first word of the new chapter—an ominous "BUT"—signify?

fortress
Joshua 6:1–2

instructions
Joshua 6:18–19

God Demands Attention

JOSHUA 7:1 *But the children of Israel committed a trespass regarding the accursed things, for Achan the son of Carmi, the son of Zabdi, the son of Zerah, of the tribe of Judah, took of the accursed things; so the anger of the LORD burned against the children of Israel. (NKJV)*

Both this chapter and the last taught the fledgling nation of Israel what to do with obstacles in life. The first challenge came from without in the form of an impenetrable <u>fortress</u> that had to be overcome. The second challenge now comes from within, in the guise of a subtle enticement to a secret indiscretion. How they respond will determine the success they experience on a national level.

The <u>instructions</u> were clearly delineated, and the warning was very specific. But one man, Achan, gets sticky fingers and takes what is rightfully God's, misappropriating a sacred trust. Achan is the perpetrator, but all of Israel is to blame. In essence, even as he swipes a few articles from a vanquished city, Achan steals away the purity and holiness of an entire nation.

key point

go to

infectious evil
Isaiah 1:5–6

cherem
Deuteronomy 7:26

yeast
Galatians 5:9

member
1 Corinthians 5:9–11

body
1 Corinthians
12:12–13, 26

root
Hebrews 12:14–15

cherem
ban against confis-
cating goods

Paul
a prolific New
Testament writer

What makes this a national crime? What possible effect can it have on the lives of thousands of blameless Israelites, who were entirely unaware of what was going on? Achan's sin, minuscule as it seems, reveals an <u>infectious evil</u> that, if unchecked, can poison the entire body. If they can make an excuse in one area, they will in another. And just like a schoolteacher on the first day of school, who draws a hard line and makes example of any infringement, so God needs to enforce his standards from the very beginning.

In technical language, Jericho, the city they had just conquered, was under the **cherem**. More specifically, that meant whatever items were designated (in this instance, the loot and booty from the overpowered Jericho) were to be devoted to God alone. Often <u>cherem</u> indicated the articles in question were to be completely destroyed.[1] Other times, they were to be presented toward the service of the Lord. In this case, both were to take place. The plunder was to be divided, and some was to be eradicated and some was to be put into the treasury of the Lord.

what others say

John MacArthur

The smallest sin is so exceedingly vile that God, despite His infinite mercy, grace and forgiveness—will not and cannot overlook even one sin without exacting its full penalty.[2]

The principle of the small infecting the large is clear throughout Scripture, from the illustration of a little <u>yeast</u> spreading into every part of a lump of dough, to a sexually immoral church <u>member</u> ruining the reputation of an entire congregation. We see it in **Paul**'s allegory of the physical <u>body</u>, as compared to the church body. He says that even when one limb suffers, the entire body feels the pain. With respect to the body of Christ, we are hurt when even one member struggles or strays. A bitter or toxic <u>root</u> can grow into a plant wildly out of control, and it can bring trouble to everyone who touches its branches.

It is a fallacy to think that anything I do is acceptable as long as no one knows about it and it does not hurt anyone else.

go to

twelve thousand
Joshua 8:25

waited
James 1:4

plans
James 4:13–15

tabernacle
temporary place of
worship

> ## what others say
>
> ### R. Kent Hughes
>
> But the question is, how do the hidden sins—the sins others know nothing about—how do these hidden sins effect other believers? The answer is this: so-called hidden sins lead to a deterioration of character, reducing the ring of truth and reality of what we say and do.[3]

We Can Handle It

JOSHUA 7:2–3 Now Joshua sent men from Jericho to Ai, which is beside Beth Aven, on the east side of Bethel, and spoke to them, saying, "Go up and spy out the country." So the men went up and spied out Ai. And they returned to Joshua and said to him, "Do not let all the people go up, but let about two or three thousand men go up and attack Ai. Do not weary all the people there, for the people of Ai are few." (NKJV)

The spies' reconnaissance mission reveals that about twelve thousand men and women live in Ai. So they suggest that an Israelite detachment of two to three thousand soldiers will adequately squelch whatever military the citizens of Ai keep on retainer to guard their little settlement. However, it remains a little presumptuous of the spies to give advice. Their job is merely to stake out and report what they observe.

But even more presumptuous is Joshua's eagerness to follow their recommendations. We do not observe any counsel being sought of God, and Joshua does not take his plan to the **tabernacle** at Gilgal for approval. Surely, had he waited on the Lord, Joshua would have discerned immediately that there was a problem in the camp. Maybe he was still exulting in the success of his victory at Jericho. Perhaps he even had a sense of invincibility. At any rate, he acts on his own initiative.

We dare not make any plans without consulting the only one who can bring them about.

go to

hearts
Joshua 2:9, 11;

control
Daniel 2:21

garrison
military post where
troops are stationed

Petrified!

JOSHUA 7:4–5 *So about three thousand men went up there from the people, but they fled before the men of Ai. And the men of Ai struck down about thirty-six men, for they chased them from before the gate as far as Shebarim, and struck them down on the descent; therefore the hearts of the people melted and became like water.* (NKJV)

Ai is the quiet outpost of a larger settlement at Bethel. Little does Israel's army suspect, as they march up to the gates of the little town, that moments later they will be throwing down their weapons and fleeing for their lives. Thirty-six of them never make it farther than a nearby stone quarry before they are struck down. And now, the very words previously used to describe the terror of their countrymen at Israel's approach are used of Israel herself, for it says that "the hearts of the people melted and became like water." They are petrified.

Archaeology reveals that although Ai was not blessed with any natural barriers, it was well fortified with a stone rampart about eleven feet thick. The steep slope below the wall was faced with clay to prevent enemies from undermining the foundation. There were two tall towers guarding the entrance and others at intervals along the walls. Just inside the gates was a sturdy stone **garrison**.[5]

God is not only in control of who wins and loses, but in line with his ultimate purpose, he prescribes when and where the events will happen.

Spilling His Guts

> JOSHUA 7:6–9 *Then Joshua tore his clothes, and fell to the earth on his face before the ark of the LORD until evening, he and the elders of Israel; and they put dust on their heads. And Joshua said, "Alas, Lord GOD, why have You brought this people over the Jordan at all—to deliver us into the hand of the Amorites, to destroy us? Oh, that we had been content, and dwelt on the other side of the Jordan! O Lord, what shall I say when Israel turns its back before its enemies? For the Canaanites and all the inhabitants of the land will hear it, and surround us, and cut off our name from the earth. Then what will You do for Your great name?" (NKJV)*

bellyaching
Numbers 14:2–3

victory
Joshua 3:10

sadistic
gaining pleasure
from causing pain

Joshua looks for a way to vent his grief. Fortunately, his culture provides him with several methods. At the same time, he cries out to God in his distress and spreads out before the Lord all the hard questions he is dealing with.

His first reaction is to question God himself. He wants to know what **sadistic** nature could motivate a God who allows bad things to happen to good people. Then he personalizes his sorrow, questioning his own motives and the choices he has made that might have affected the outcome of this disaster. For a time he even feels speechless ("O Lord, what shall I say?"), but he quickly moves along to worry about his own welfare and what people will think of the nation he leads. Finally, almost as an afterthought, he ends with an expression of concern for the reputation of God himself. Perhaps he throws this in as the zinger that will motivate God to take some action to rectify the problem and intervene on his behalf.

Joshua has learned how to open his heart and spill out his emotions before the only one who can truly understand. However, some of his words come very close to blasphemy and echo the familiar <u>bellyaching</u> that the Israelites were already famous for. God graciously allows Joshua the space he needs to grieve.

Understand Joshua's frame of reference. He had believed with all his heart that God was on their side, and he was sure the children of Israel would never lose. As field general he had boldly declared to his troops that God was present with them and would bring them <u>victory</u>. Now his words stuck in his throat.

We can unleash whatever we are feeling and state whatever we are thinking directly to the Lord, even if it is not considered proper.

Joshua tears his clothes and tosses dust on his head. The ruined clothing indicates that his grief is irrevocable. The dust sprinkled on his head speaks of the insignificance of man, and his awareness that he is nothing. From dust he came, and to dust he will return.[6]

Here Comes the Judge

JOSHUA 7:10–12 *So the LORD said to Joshua: "Get up! Why do you lie thus on your face? Israel has sinned, and they have also transgressed My covenant which I commanded them. For they have even taken some of the accursed things, and have both stolen and deceived; and they have also put it among their own stuff. Therefore the children of Israel could not stand before their enemies, but turned their backs before their enemies, because they have become doomed to destruction. Neither will I be with you anymore, unless you destroy the accursed from among you.* (NKJV)

go to

favorite
Matthew 5:45

effective
Romans 5:3–5

infidel
someone with no belief in the true God

God's first pronouncement prods Joshua out of his melancholic funk. But not to worry—God is not ready to see his own reputation trampled under the foot of every **infidel** in the land. There is work to be done, and he needs to jolt Joshua, but good! He gets his attention by charging him not to grovel. Then God lists all the ways Achan's act of deception has slapped God in the face. Maybe Achan thought all he was doing was keeping back for himself a couple of things he wanted, but in doing so he:

1. broke faith with,

2. stole from,

3. lied to, and

4. schemed against

affront
Psalm 51:4

Presence
Isaiah 59:2

obey
Joshua 1:7–8

honest
Psalm 51:6

dwells
1 Corinthians 3:16

convict
John 16:7–8, 13

the God of the universe. In the face of this <u>affront</u>, God tells Joshua that Israel cannot prosper and his Holy <u>Presence</u> cannot go with them as before.

A covenant is a two-way street. God assured them of success and prosperity on the condition that they <u>obey</u> all the **law**, never veering from what it demanded. God could not overlook such a blatant disregard of the sacred pact he has made with his people. This is what God must communicate to his **emissary**, Joshua.

In acknowledgment of sin, it is important not to make a generic confession of "any sin I may or may not have committed." The **psalmist** says that God desires that we be <u>honest</u> with him (and with ourselves) deep down inside. This means I must come to a standstill and analyze what attitudes and actions within myself are in contrast to his perfect character. The **Holy Spirit**, who <u>dwells</u> in every believer, will bring us to see the truth and **convict** us of sin.

Under the Microscope

JOSHUA 7:13–15 *Get up, sanctify the people, and say, 'Sanctify yourselves for tomorrow, because thus says the LORD God of Israel: "There is an accursed thing in your midst, O Israel; you cannot stand before your enemies until you take away the accursed thing from among you." In the morning therefore you shall be brought according to your tribes. And it shall be that the tribe which the LORD takes shall come according to families; and the family which the LORD takes shall come by households; and the household which the LORD takes shall come man by man. Then it shall be that he who is taken with the accursed thing shall be burned with fire, he and all that he has, because he has transgressed the covenant of the LORD, and because he has done a disgraceful thing in Israel."' (NKJV)*

law
God's commandments in the Bible

emissary
special representative

psalmist
David, a Bible songwriter

Holy Spirit
one part of who God is

convict
to confirm guilt

go to

water
Exodus 30:20

heart
James 4:8

lots
Proverbs 16:33

consecration
to set apart as
sacred

defilement
that which pollutes

The first step that God outlines in the restoration process is that of **consecration**. This cleansing ritual involved washing with <u>water</u> on the outside and a cleansing of <u>heart</u> on the inside. God wants the stain of the sin in question to stand out ever so clearly.

The second step is to pinpoint the exact origin of the contamination. The **defilement** can then be drastically and irrefutably removed. It is not entirely clear from this passage how each responsible tribe, clan, family, and man is to be selected, but the hand of God will point to the guilty party.

what others say

V. Gilbert Beers

In times of great trouble, the ephod was often consulted to determine God's will. It was a beautiful sleeveless vest worn by the high priest. Attached to it was a breastpiece containing 12 precious stones, 1 for each tribe of Israel. Inside the breastpiece were the Urim and Thummim, which might have been two more precious stones that were probably used like <u>lots</u> to receive a yes or no answer to a question asked of God.[8]

Following Directions

JOSHUA 7:16–19 *So Joshua rose early in the morning and brought Israel by their tribes, and the tribe of Judah was taken. He brought the clan of Judah, and he took the family of the Zarhites; and he brought the family of the Zarhites man by man, and Zabdi was taken. Then he brought his household man by man, and Achan the son of Carmi, the son of Zabdi, the son of Zerah, of the tribe of Judah, was taken. Now Joshua said to Achan, "My son, I beg you, give glory to the LORD God of Israel, and make confession to Him, and tell me now what you have done; do not hide it from me."* (NKJV)

Joshua rises early in his impatience to take care of the problem and restore Israel to divine favor. There is no doubt as to the guilty party. The heavy finger of impeccable justice points squarely at Achan, now unmasked before the entire nation.

Joshua kindly calls Achan "My son . . ." (even though he should more correctly be labeled "rebel" or "thief"), and encourages him to tell all he has done. Joshua correctly surmises that Achan can give glory to God as righteous and just if Achan takes the blame and shame upon himself.

We should restrain our compulsion to further insult those suffering for wrongdoing and remain sensitive toward their pain.

apply it

Uncovering the Perfect Crime

JOSHUA 7:20–23 And Achan answered Joshua and said, "Indeed I have sinned against the LORD God of Israel, and this is what I have done: When I saw among the spoils a beautiful Babylonian garment, two hundred shekels of silver, and a wedge of gold weighing fifty shekels, I coveted them and took them. And there they are, hidden in the earth in the midst of my tent, with the silver under it."

So Joshua sent messengers, and they ran to the tent; and there it was, hidden in his tent, with the silver under it. And they took them from the midst of the tent, brought them to Joshua and to all the children of Israel, and laid them out before the LORD. (NKJV)

The basics of Achan's confession run along these lines: "I saw. I coveted. I took." Interestingly enough, Achan does not even need what he has stolen. He is not destitute. He does not desperately lack garments to clothe his wife or money to obtain medical help for his ailing children. He has plenty of <u>cattle</u>, donkeys, sheep, and able children. But he desires something *more*.

After Joshua hears Achan's admission, he quickly sends messengers to recover the plunder. They spread all of the booty before the Lord because he alone will be the final judge.

The garment in question was of Babylonian origin, and the main issue here was prestige and prominence. Anyone wearing such a robe would have driven his neighbors green with envy.[9]

something to ponder

The common shekel weighed about four-tenths of an ounce, thus making the silver here about 80 ounces and the gold around 20. Achan stole 200 shekels' worth of silver and 50 shekels' worth of gold, with a modern-day value of between $10,000 and $25,000.[10]

We Will Rock You

JOSHUA 7:24–26A Then Joshua, and all Israel with him, took Achan the son of Zerah, the silver, the garment, the wedge of

go to

cattle
Joshua 7:24

sow
Galatians 6:7

sacrifice
Leviticus 4:27–31

fall
1 Corinthians 10:12

sacrifice
shedding blood to
atone for sin

complicity
involvement in
wrongdoing

catharsis
purging of emotions

gold, his sons, his daughters, his oxen, his donkeys, his sheep, his tent, and all that he had, and they brought them to the Valley of Achor. And Joshua said, "Why have you troubled us? The LORD will trouble you this day." So all Israel stoned him with stones; and they burned them with fire after they had stoned them with stones. Then they raised over him a great heap of stones, still there to this day. (NKJV)

The Old Testament system of **sacrifice** makes ample provision for the atonement of a personal offense. However, any sin committed in continued rebellion cannot be simply dispensed with. Achan's silence during the process of determining the guilty party shows his hardness of heart. Basically, he only confesses when he has to.

Achan's family is no doubt involved in the caper he is trying to pull off. Practically speaking, Achan would have needed the help of his family to transport and conceal the offending objects under the floor of the tent. They indicate their **complicity** by maintaining a strict silence when revelation and confession are called for. The collaboration of his family includes them not only in the offense but also in the punishment.

Joshua's warning, "You brought us trouble, so God will bring you trouble," is not vindictive. The words merely rephrase the Scripture that says whatever you <u>sow</u>, you reap. Achan and his family violated God's covenant with the entire nation of Israel, so all of Israel participated in the **catharsis** by stoning the offenders and burning their bodies.

After removing the influence of the entire family through death, Israel erects a pile of stones over their remains. This memorial will serve not only to remind Israel of the defeat at Ai and the depth of one man's sin, but should encourage them to examine their own hearts lest they <u>fall</u> into a similar trap.

We can reflect over our defeats in two ways—to lament our stupidity or to validate what we have learned.

Ever After

JOSHUA 7:26B *So the LORD turned from the fierceness of His anger. Therefore the name of that place has been called the Valley of Achor to this day. (NKJV)*

Achan is put to death in a valley that means "the Valley of Trouble." The geographic place is called after the man Achan, for he was the "troubler" of Israel.

God's anger is assuaged as soon as the source is removed. His character demands a reaction of wrath when his holiness is under siege, but when the cause is removed, the perfect balance of his nature is visible to mankind once again.

Some have argued that the God of the Old Testament is a God of wrath, but the God of the New Testament is a God of love. On the contrary, we see both characteristics <u>spread</u> generously throughout the entire Bible. Actually, every demonstration of wrath is motivated by <u>love</u>. And we know that God has not changed, because the Bible declares that he is the <u>same</u> yesterday, today, and forever.

go to

spread
Isaiah 55:3;
Jeremiah 31:3–14;
Romans 1:18;
Hebrews 12:25–29

love
Hebrews 12:5–6

same
Hebrews 13:8

hope
Hosea 2:15

pastureland
Isaiah 65:10

joy
Psalm 30:5

something to ponder

what others say

Josh McDowell

We find judgment as well as love scattered very persuasively throughout the New Testament, and love and mercy as well as judgment throughout the Old Testament. God is consistent and unchanging, but different situations call for different emphases . . . The two testaments . . . reveal the same holy God who is rich in mercy, but who will not let sin go unpun-

The Valley of Achor in later passages comes to be called a "door of <u>hope</u>." God chooses to bless this region with restful <u>pastureland</u>, vineyards, and song. Doesn't that proclaim the richness of God's divine mercy? When the blight is removed, God restores productivity and blessing. He does the same in our own lives when he brings hope out of despair and <u>joy</u> from grief.

go to

anger
Joshua 7:26

foreordained
previously planned
by God

Getting It Right

JOSHUA 8:1–2 *Now the LORD said to Joshua: "Do not be afraid, nor be dismayed; take all the people of war with you, and arise, go up to Ai. See, I have given into your hand the king of Ai, his people, his city, and his land. And you shall do to Ai and its king as you did to Jericho and its king. Only its spoil and its cattle you shall take as booty for yourselves. Lay an ambush for the city behind it." (NKJV)*

As if to reinforce the conclusion of the last chapter where the Lord's fierce <u>anger</u> was finally satisfied, the words God now speaks are reassuring and energizing. Joshua's confidence is bolstered, and he is given the next step to follow.

God's strategy calls for the whole army, not just two or three thousand. One reason is that Bethel (the neighboring city of which Ai is just the suburb) is likely to get involved. Also, God wants to emphasize the unity of his people, as he did in Jericho.

As in Jericho, the victory is **foreordained**—only this time the Israelites are allowed to plunder possessions and livestock. If only Achan had been more patient and less greedy, he could have had all he wanted.

> **what others say**
>
> **Corrie ten Boom**
>
> I once visited a weaver's school, where the students were making beautiful patterns. I asked, "When you make a mistake, must you cut it out and start from the beginning?"
>
> A student said, "No. Our teacher is such a great artist that when we make a mistake, he uses it to improve the beauty of the pattern."[12]

Baiting the Trap

> **the big picture**
>
> **Joshua 8:3–13**
>
> Joshua chooses 30,000 of his best soldiers and sends them off at night to set an ambush behind the city of Ai. The next morning, he leads the rest of the company to camp in front of the city to the north. Another 5,000 take cover to the west. Joshua

Gilgal
Israelis' main head-
quarters about one
quarter mile from
Jericho

instructs the 30,000 to take over the city as soon as he and the main force start to run away from battle as they did before. As soon as the ambush has taken the city, they are to set it on fire. The smaller parties furtively take up their positions, and Joshua with the main body marches into the valley before Ai.

It is about fifteen miles from **Gilgal** to Ai and a climb of 3,200 feet.[13] The group of 30,000 is to enter the city by surprise from the rear, while the 5,000 are to cut off any reinforcements from Bethel and prevent the main ambush from being outflanked.

The fire will serve several purposes:

1. It will alert Joshua that the city is taken and that it's time to turn around and fight.

2. It will completely demoralize the enemy; when their homes and families are destroyed they will have nothing to fight for.

3. Israel's adversaries will panic when they realize that they are surrounded.

In verse 7, Joshua passes on the key to the entire conflict. "The LORD your God will deliver it into your hand" (NKJV). They had to be totally dependent on God.

All our anxious strategizing to ensure a successful life is futile without depending on God to bring it about.

apply it

Gotcha!

the big picture

Joshua 8:14-29

When the king of Ai sees Joshua and his army marching across the valley, he hurries out to meet them with his troops. Not realizing it's a setup, he pursues the Israelites toward the desert with his entire force. Not one man was left in Ai or Bethel.

At the right moment, God instructs Joshua to hold out his sword toward Ai. As he does, the ambushers rise up, capture the city, and set it on fire. As the men of Ai see the smoke, Joshua's men turn back. Now, for the first time the men of Ai realize they're trapped. Israel chases down every last one and then destroys

go to

Moses
Exodus 17:8–16

king
Joshua 12:16

law
Deuteronomy
21:22–23

the citizens still left in the city. Twelve thousand die. Joshua continues to hold his sword in the air until the battle is completely over.

Israel carries off the livestock and plunder, the city is left a permanent heap of ruins, and the king is hanged on a tree until evening. At sunset, Joshua instructs the people to take the king's body and throw it in the entrance to the city, raising a pile of rocks over his remains.

The king of Ai hurries out to a place overlooking the Jordan Valley, near where the Israelites had previously been routed. But his anticipation of an easy victory quickly vanished.

Joshua's signal weapon was probably like a scimitar (*kidon* in Hebrew)—a large blade that would mirror the gleaming sun.[14] If the reflected light could not be seen all the way back to the ambush, they likely had a relay system to carry the message that the sword was being held aloft. But the upraised weapon was more than just a signal to start the battle, for Joshua did not put it down until every last foe was conquered. The elevated sword was a symbol of their own inadequacy and a plea to God to work on their behalf, just as he had for <u>Moses</u> in a previous encounter.

Because every single man from Ai and Bethel had been led away from the city, the takeover was effortless. This account does not specifically record the defeat of Bethel, but later in the book of Joshua, Bethel's <u>king</u> is listed among those conquered.

The king of Ai was not cut down but was held responsible for the crimes of his people. He would be executed and displayed before the whole company as an example of what happens to those who mock God and his people. It was customary to impale a rebel's body on a sharp stick, but at sundown, according to the <u>law</u> of God, the body had to be removed. It was thrown into the very gate where the king had previously sat in state, proclaiming his unrighteous decrees and formulating his wicked deeds.

The city itself, whose very name meant "the ruin," fulfilled in history the judgment implied in its name and was never rebuilt.[15]

Joshua was a great general in the following ways:

1. He was wise and perceptive. Taking God's suggestion for an <u>ambush</u>, he saw what needed to be done and put the pieces together to make it happen.

2. He was cautious and <u>thorough</u>. He started the preparations the night before and provided for all eventualities.

3. He was helpful and <u>industrious</u>. He rose up early and did what he could to assist the people to get organized and moved into place.

4. He was courageous and <u>unflinching</u>. He was at the forefront of the main company of people and carried on with uplifted sword until the entire enemy was defeated.

go to

ambush
Joshua 8:2

thorough
Joshua 8:3

industrious
Joshua 8:10

unflinching
Joshua 8:26

what others say

Luis Palau

From man's perspective, the tools one needs to carve out a position of leadership in the world include a good-looking face, lots of charisma, regular press bulletins, and a media-wise public relations man. But don't try to use those tools to get ahead in the kingdom of God . . . What God looks for . . . is a servant's heart. And if you have a servant's heart, you can be greatly used of the Lord.[16]

<u>Covenant Renewal</u>

JOSHUA 8:30–32 *Now Joshua built an altar to the LORD God of Israel in Mount Ebal, as Moses the servant of the LORD had commanded the children of Israel, as it is written in the Book of the Law of Moses: "an altar of whole stones over which no man has wielded an iron tool." And they offered on it burnt offerings to the LORD, and sacrificed peace offerings. And there, in the presence of the children of Israel, he wrote on the stones a copy of the law of Moses, which he had written. (NKJV)*

go to

decreed
Deuteronomy
11:26–32

specifications
Exodus 20:25

burnt
Exodus 29:18

fellowship
Leviticus 7:15

plastered
Deuteronomy
27:2–3

praise
Psalms 9:1; 66:3;
96:3

know
Romans 2:13–15

curses
Deuteronomy 11:29

Christ
Galatians 3:13–14

absolute
Psalm 18:30;
Romans 7:12

altar
a flat-topped rock
where gifts are
offered to God

offerings
presentation back to
God of something
already his

atonement
reconciliation
between us and
God through Jesus's
death

absolute
a standard that
never changes

From a military standpoint, the next directive of Joshua's was foolish. Instead of capitalizing on his victories and reinforcing the momentum of this campaign, he takes time out for a pilgrimage. Actually, this step was already <u>decreed</u> for the children of Israel from the time of Moses.

So the entire nation wends its way to the Shechem Valley, a hollow two miles wide between the towering peaks of Ebal (3,085 feet) and Gerizim (2,890 feet).[17] Here they build an altar in line with God's <u>specifications</u>. Israel's uncut and unembellished stones stand in contrast to the Canaanite altars that already dot the land, carved with queer symbols and occultish phrases.[18]

Upon the **altar**, they sacrifice <u>burnt</u> **offerings**, which are entirely consumed by fire, and <u>fellowship</u> offerings in which portions of the animals are joyfully eaten by the presenters.

After the offerings are proffered, Joshua copies the law into <u>plastered</u> rock. This will be the first public display of the law, making its words more than an exclusive possession of Israel, but the responsibility of all nations to learn of them and abide by them. Anyone entering this land will now have access to a knowledge of God.

The roots of our worship present a contrast with most other religions—plain and natural instead of contrived and affected.

When God brings victory our first response should be one of grateful <u>praise</u>.

It is the mercy of God that we can <u>know</u> exactly what he wants and do not have to err in ignorance.

Ebal, the mountain from which the <u>curses</u> will be proclaimed, is the location where the altar was erected. So in the place where one would expect a curse, we find instead a sacrifice. Just so, <u>Christ</u> took away our curse when he was sacrificed for us. With his **atonement**, we receive blessings instead of curses.

---

what others say

Francis Schaeffer

Today most non-Christians exclude any real notion of the Law. They do this because they have no **absolute** anywhere in the universe and without any absolute, one cannot really have any morals as morals. For them, there is no circle inside which there is a right in contrast to that which is outside the circle and therefore wrong.[19]

Cheers and Boos

JOSHUA 8:33–35 *Then all Israel, with their elders and officers and judges, stood on either side of the ark before the priests, the Levites, who bore the ark of the covenant of the LORD, the stranger as well as he who was born among them. Half of them were in front of Mount Gerizim and half of them in front of Mount Ebal, as Moses the servant of the LORD had commanded before, that they should bless the people of Israel. And afterward he read all the words of the law, the blessings and the cursings, according to all that is written in the Book of the Law. There was not a word of all that Moses had commanded which Joshua did not read before all the assembly of Israel, with the women, the little ones, and the strangers who were living among them.* (NKJV)

Parts of this reading are meant to be **antiphonal**, with different parts of the congregation reciting various phrases and the whole company joining in with resounding "Amens!" Their location was perfect—it is said that a person can stand on top of Mount Ebal and talk to someone on Mount Gerizim without raising his voice.[20] Imagine, then, the entire nation gathered in this place—the **tribes** of Reuben, Gad, Asher, Zebulun, Dan, and Naphtali on the one side—with Simeon, Levi, Judah, Issachar, Joseph, and Benjamin on the other. The sound of their voices would ring from peak to peak!

Joshua did not omit or abridge one detail, and the message was heard by every age, rank, gender, and profession. The greatest to the least are <u>included</u> in the blessing and the curse of the law, with special mention of the aliens who live among them.

This would have been the first public rendering of God's commands since <u>Moses</u>'s death. It was actually appointed in the <u>law</u> to have this reading once every seven years. But here, at the outset, it was important to establish the rules from the very first inroads and activities in the land.

God had a special place in his heart for the <u>foreigners</u> who resided within the nation of Israel. He conscientiously instructed the Israelites in ways they could minister to their special <u>needs</u>. In the same way he also desires that we <u>show</u> people of all backgrounds, cultures, and nationalities what he is like through the caring things that we do—reaching out to everyone, even those outside our comfort zones.

go to

antiphonal
Deuteronomy 11:29; 27:14–26

tribes
Deuteronomy 27:12–13

included
1 Timothy 2:4

Moses
Exodus 24:7

law
Deuteronomy 31:10–13

foreigners
Exodus 22:21–23; Deuteronomy 10:17–19

needs
Leviticus 19:10; 23:22

show
Matthew 5:16

antiphonal
alternating responses between two groups

tribes
people groups within Israel related to each of the sons of Jacob

Chapter Wrap-up

apply it

- God alerts his people to sin in their midst by allowing them to experience failure in warfare. (Joshua 7:1–15)
- The Israelites uncover the problem and deal with the situation and the individuals involved as justice demands. (Joshua 7:16–26)
- Joshua carefully leads another military endeavor against the same city, this time with success. (Joshua 8:1–29)
- The whole nation offers sacrifices, hears the Word of the Lord read aloud, and responds to its message. (Joshua 8:30–35)

Study Questions

1. How can one person's sin have far-reaching effects?

2. How did God bring blessing out of fiasco?

3. What leadership qualities did Joshua possess?

4. What was the first thing the people did after they experienced victory?

Chapter Highlights:
• Gibeonite Trickery
• Deception Exposed
• Pass the Sunscreen
• Amorite Armored Assault
• Sortie of Southern Cities

Joshua 9–10
The Southern Invasion

Let's Get Started

The children of Israel (like most of us) had to learn the same lessons over and over. The Israelites were slow to understand that God must be <u>consulted</u> about *everything*. It was so easy to barrel into situations while depending on their own wisdom and strength. Only when they found themselves in trouble would they remember who was supposed to be leading them.

Think of the grief that could have been spared the entire congregation if Joshua had stopped to confirm his plans with the Lord before going to battle against Ai the first time. What victory could have been had if he'd waited on the Lord before doing anything at all?

go to

consulted
Psalm 25:9;
Isaiah 30:21

jurisdictional
authority over a
specifically defined
area

Gibeonite Trickery

JOSHUA 9:1–2 *And it came to pass when all the kings who were on this side of the Jordan, in the hills and in the lowland and in all the coasts of the Great Sea toward Lebanon—the Hittite, the Amorite, the Canaanite, the Perizzite, the Hivite, and the Jebusite—heard about it, that they gathered together to fight with Joshua and Israel with one accord. (NKJV)*

Most of the **jurisdictional** kings of this period are scurrying around making treaties with one another in an effort to stop the Israelites, headed their way. They are determined to fight it out and not give an inch of their lands to these people who threaten their way of life. Before this, Joshua has only faced individual cities; now his enemies are forming coalitions against him.

Many people will fight any change to the life they know, even a change for the better.

treaties
Exodus 34:11–12

terms
Deuteronomy
20:10–18

Egypt
Exodus 15:9–14

Amorite
Numbers 21:25–26

Hivites
Joshua 11:19

Word
Deuteronomy 7:1–6

Snow Job

JOSHUA 9:3–6 *But when the inhabitants of Gibeon heard what Joshua had done to Jericho and Ai, they worked craftily, and went and pretended to be ambassadors. And they took old sacks on their donkeys, old wineskins torn and mended, old and patched sandals on their feet, and old garments on themselves; and all the bread of their provision was dry and moldy. And they went to Joshua, to the camp at Gilgal, and said to him and to the men of Israel, "We have come from a far country; now therefore, make a covenant with us." (NKJV)*

In contrast to the rest of the nationals who are determined to fight God's people to the death, the Israelites are suddenly confronted with a group of people who are anxious to make peace. God did not want his people to share <u>treaties</u> with any of the local nations. However, he had made provision for distant countries to be spared if they were willing to exist under equitable <u>terms</u>. At face value, making an agreement with this obscure people group would be quite acceptable.

Oscar-Winning Performance

> ### the big picture
> #### Joshua 9:7–13
> The men of Israel question the foreign delegates about where they live because they know they should not make a treaty with a neighboring country. The men reply that they are Israel's "servants" from a distant land who have heard of God's reputation (citing <u>Egypt</u> and the <u>Amorite</u> kings east of the Jordan) and have come to make a pact of peace. They were sent by the elders of their country, they say, with fresh provisions and clean, serviceable clothing, but the trip was so long and difficult that their food is dry and their clothes are worn.

The leadership of Israel is initially suspicious: in the end they are completely hoodwinked. The envoys from Gibeon are careful to make no mention of Jericho or Ai, for if they had traveled from a remote area they could not yet have known of these victories.

In reality, however, Gibeon was very close to Ai and only about five miles northwest of Jerusalem.[1] Not only that, but the Gibeonites were <u>Hivites</u>, one of the nations that God had originally slated for destruction. To make a treaty with Gibeon was to go against the <u>Word</u> of the Lord.

The Cheater's Charter

JOSHUA 9:14–15 *Then the men of Israel took some of their provisions; but they did not ask counsel of the LORD. So Joshua made peace with them, and made a covenant with them to let them live; and the rulers of the congregation swore to them. (NKJV)*

direction
Numbers 27:21

alert
Proverbs 28:26

strategies
Ephesians 6:11

choice
Psalm 143:10

The men of Israel taste the food, relying on their own five senses to reveal the truth. God, who sees beyond every facade, could save them a lot of grief if they would come to him for <u>direction</u>. The particular treaty they agree to is one in which a weaker people (the Gibeonites) acquiesce to the control of a more powerful people (the Israelites) in return for protection.

There are three principles to learn from this story:

1. Never allow the glow of a previous victory to blind you. Stay <u>alert</u>.

2. The enemy of your soul is cunning and deceitful. Know his typical <u>strategies</u>.

3. No decision is too small for God. Present every <u>choice</u> to him.

Remember that your faith is in danger when you do not lay out all your options before the Lord and defer every decision to him.

what others say

J. Oswald Sanders

The story of the Gibeonites was so reasonable and consistent, their references to Jehovah so reverent, that Joshua accepted the evidence of sight without first seeking God's mind in prayer. His confidence was in his own good judgment and discernment rather than in God.[2]

Oswald Chambers

Never run before God's guidance. If there is the slightest doubt, then He is not guiding. Whenever there is doubt—don't.[3]

Deception Exposed

the big picture

Joshua 9:16–21

Three days later, Israel finds out the Gibeonites are neighbors, occupying four main cities: Gibeon, Chephirah, Beeroth, and Kirjath Jearim. But now Israel cannot attack them because they have sworn an oath before the Lord to let them live. The lay-people grumble, but the elders pacify them by appointing the people of Gibeon to the menial tasks of woodcutting and water carrying.

What a shock to find out the location of the Gibeonites' home! Beeroth, one of their cities, would actually have been in sight of the Israelite troops as they marched up to Ai.[4] They had been "hornswoggled"!

An oath, in the Bible, is intended to be a sacred and unbreakable pledge. It can never be revoked, even if obtained under false pretenses. When King **Saul**, later in history, disregarded the pledge that Israel made to the Gibeonites before the Lord, God judged the entire nation.

Woodcutters and Water Carriers

JOSHUA 9:22–27 *Then Joshua called for them, and he spoke to them, saying, "Why have you deceived us, saying, 'We are very far from you,' when you dwell near us? Now therefore, you are cursed, and none of you shall be freed from being slaves—woodcutters and water carriers for the house of my God." So they answered Joshua and said, "Because your servants were clearly told that the LORD your God commanded His servant Moses to give you all the land, and to destroy all the inhabitants of the land from before you; therefore we were very much afraid for our lives because of you, and have done this thing. And now, here we are, in your hands; do with us as it seems good and right to do to us." So he did to them, and delivered them out of the hand of the children of Israel, so that they did not kill them. And that day Joshua made them woodcutters and water carriers for the congregation and for the altar of the LORD, in the place which He would choose, even to this day.* (NKJV)

The answer seems obvious, but Joshua asks the Gibeonites why they would try to pull off a crazy stunt like this. They respond by explaining that, quite naturally, they were afraid for their lives. Now they are ready to do whatever is required of them. Looking into the future, the Gibeonites remain a significant presence within Israel and are woven into the plan of God for his people in the following ways:

go to

miracle
Joshua 10:10–14

tabernacle
2 Chronicles 1:3

ark
1 Samuel 7:1–2

exile
Ezra 8:20

observed
Joshua 2:10; 9:9–10

put
Joshua 2:12; 9:25

lied
Joshua 2:4–5; 9:9, 24

obtained
Joshua 2:14; 9:15

proved
Joshua 2:15–16; 9:25

separated
Joshua 6:25; 9:27

1. God performed a great <u>miracle</u> for their protection.

2. The <u>tabernacle</u> was pitched in the city of Gibeon for some time.

3. The <u>ark</u> of the covenant remained in Kirjath Jearim (another of their towns) for many years.

4. The Gibeonites who served at the temple were called "Nethinim" and were brought back by God from <u>exile</u> with the priests and Levites in later history.[5]

what others say

J. I. Packer

Our God is a God who not merely restores, but takes up our mistakes and follies into His plan for us and brings good out of them. This is part of the wonder of His gracious sovereignty.[6]

There are many similarities between Rahab and the Gibeonites:

1. Both <u>observed</u> and commented on God's intervention on behalf of his people.

2. Both <u>put</u> themselves at the mercy of the people of Israel.

3. Both <u>lied</u> to save lives.

4. Both <u>obtained</u> promises from Israel related to their safety.

5. Both <u>proved</u> their loyalty to the nation of Israel, Rahab by hiding the spies and Gibeon by taking positions of subservience without rebelling.

6. Both were from foreign origin and willingly <u>separated</u> from their former culture.

Amorite Armored Assault

JOSHUA 10:1–5 *Now it came to pass when Adoni-Zedek king of Jerusalem heard how Joshua had taken Ai and had utterly destroyed it—as he had done to Jericho and its king, so he had done to Ai and its king—and how the inhabitants of Gibeon had made peace with Israel and were among them, that they feared greatly, because Gibeon was a great city, like one of the royal cities, and because it was greater than Ai, and all its men were mighty. Therefore Adoni-Zedek king of Jerusalem sent to Hoham king of Hebron, Piram king of Jarmuth, Japhia king of Lachish, and Debir king of Eglon, saying, "Come up to me and help me, that we may attack Gibeon, for it has made peace with Joshua and with the children of Israel." Therefore the five kings of the Amorites, the king of Jerusalem, the king of Hebron, the king of Jarmuth, the king of Lachish, and the king of Eglon, gathered together and went up, they and all their armies, and camped before Gibeon and made war against it. (NKJV)*

Adoni-Zedek starts to put two and two together and realizes that his position, not very promising to begin with, is getting worse. First, the seemingly invincible fortress at Jericho was flattened. Then Ai was wiped out (and it was a fairly strong city, even though Israel had closed their eyes to this during their first attack).

Adoni-Zedek's assessment of Gibeon is that it is larger than Ai with an excellent force of fighting men. And now they've made peace with Israel! Outside of surrender, Adoni-Zedek's only recourse at this point is to merge with several other city-states and take the offensive.

Which End Is Up?

JOSHUA 10:6–10 *And the men of Gibeon sent to Joshua at the camp at Gilgal, saying, "Do not forsake your servants; come up to us quickly, save us and help us, for all the kings of the Amorites who dwell in the mountains have gathered together against us." So Joshua ascended from Gilgal, he and all the people of war with him, and all the mighty men of valor. And the LORD said to Joshua, "Do not fear them, for I have delivered them into your hand; not a man of them shall stand before you."*

Joshua therefore came upon them suddenly, having marched all night from Gilgal. So the LORD routed them before Israel, killed them with a great slaughter at Gibeon, chased them along the road that goes to Beth Horon, and struck them down as far as Azekah and Makkedah. (NKJV)

Since the agreement between Israel and Gibeon involves the subordination of one party for the protection of the other, it is now Israel's responsibility to answer Gibeon's need. They ascend from Gilgal, a distance of twenty miles, on a forced march of eight to ten hours, under cover of darkness.[7] Showing remarkable stamina, they were ready to fight a battle when they arrived. Of course, the Lord confused the enemy—so much so that they fled in opposite directions, to the northwest and the southwest. This shows the completeness of their whipping.[8]

what others say

Gigi Graham Tchividjian

"I want to be on the front lines," I complained to my friend . . . In reality, each one of us is on the front lines of service. In His providence He has placed us just where He wants us to be: in the roles of mothers, fathers, students, accountants, lawyers, pastors, secretaries, yes, even maids . . . for His glory.[9]

Hail to the Chief

JOSHUA 10:11 *And it happened, as they fled before Israel and were on the descent of Beth Horon, that the LORD cast down large hailstones from heaven on them as far as Azekah, and they died. There were more who died from the hailstones than the children of Israel killed with the sword. (NKJV)*

The last passage summarized the victory, while this section fills in some of the details. In addition to the pandemonium God places in the hearts of the enemy, he also bombards them with hailstones, killing more in this assault than all the weapons of the Israelites combined. Note that not one of God's people is hit.

go to

backward
2 Kings 20:9–11

ambassadors
2 Chronicles 32:31

Hezekiah
son of Ahaz ruling in Judah for twenty-nine years (716–687 BC)

Ahaz
twelfth ruler of Judah (732–716 BC)

Babylon
an ancient city-state located on the Euphrates River, north of the Persian Gulf

what others say

Charles Spurgeon

Let us expect to see the Lord glorified in our deliverance. Are we drawn out in fervent prayer? . . . Then the set time for His grace is near. God will lift Himself up at the right season. He will arise when it will be most for the display of His glory.[10]

Pass the Sunscreen

JOSHUA 10:12–15 *Then Joshua spoke to the LORD in the day when the LORD delivered up the Amorites before the children of Israel, and he said in the sight of Israel:*
"Sun, stand still over Gibeon;
And Moon, in the Valley of Aijalon."
So the sun stood still,
And the moon stopped,
Till the people had revenge
Upon their enemies.
Is this not written in the Book of Jasher? So the sun stood still in the midst of heaven, and did not hasten to go down for about a whole day. And there has been no day like that, before it or after it, that the LORD heeded the voice of a man; for the LORD fought for Israel. Then Joshua returned, and all Israel with him, to the camp at Gilgal. (NKJV)

In this same day, Joshua prays for the sun to "rest" or "cease" (*dom* in Hebrew).[11] And it was done just as Joshua requested so that the nation could avenge itself on its enemies. The words of a verse from the book of Jashur form two-part sections of well-balanced poetry and conclude with a three-part echo.[12] Jashur is not a part of the Bible and has not survived through history, but is simply interjected as a confirmation of the report found in these pages—and to make the story more vivid and dramatic.

A similar type of event in the days of **Hezekiah** is described by Isaiah, who called on the Lord and the shadow of the sun went backward ten steps down the stairway of **Ahaz**. The implication in Hezekiah's miracle was that it happened locally, for ambassadors from **Babylon** were sent to ask about what they had heard occurred in Israel as if it had not happened to them as well. So, using the illustration of Hezekiah, it is possible that God extended the direct or refracted light from the sun only in this particular place to serve

God's special purpose. This would also be consistent with the establishment of God's <u>laws</u> for day and night.[13]

Joshua's prayers caused light to remain in the sky until his soldiers were supplied with enough time to complete the job God had given them. God is not limited by any of the physical <u>laws</u> of the universe that keep us bound.

what others say

David Needham

For each of us there will be those times when in some mysterious way we will simply *know* that some specific thing is God's will. As we pray we may sense that we are living in His omnipotence—and we are! I doubt if Joshua gave much thought before he asked God to stop the sun. He just knew it was the right thing to do.[14]

Josh McDowell

Science and the Scriptures do not cancel each other out. They simply look at the world from different perspectives, but are not finally contradictory . . . The very origin of modern science rests upon the truth of the scripture. The fact that there is a God who created and designed an ordered universe prompted men like Newton to search for certain scientific laws to explain this order. So rather than science eroding the foundation of biblical authority, it must find its roots there.[15]

<u>D-Day</u>

> JOSHUA 10:16–19 *But these five kings had fled and hidden themselves in a cave at Makkedah. And it was told Joshua, saying, "The five kings have been found hidden in the cave at Makkedah." So Joshua said, "Roll large stones against the mouth of the cave, and set men by it to guard them. And do not stay there yourselves, but pursue your enemies, and attack their rear guard. Do not allow them to enter their cities, for the LORD your God has delivered them into your hand." (NKJV)*

The last chapter rehearsed the specifics of the battle in terms of the supernatural. This section of verses covers the same ground once again, bringing to light some of the details that carry the event to its conclusion. The Israelites need to slay as many men as possible in the open field, because once the adversary reaches a fortified city he is

laws
Genesis 8:22;
Jeremiah 33:20

laws
Job 38:4–7;
Matthew 8:23–27

go to

strategy
Joshua 8:6–7

confidence
Obadiah 3

committed
Joshua 10:6–7

relied
Joshua 10:8

offered some protection and is far more difficult to capture. That is why the <u>strategy</u> at Ai was designed to draw the enemy out where he would be more vulnerable.

Adoni-Zedek and his four counterparts become trapped in the very cave they hoped would keep them hidden. As always, when we put our <u>confidence</u> in anything other than God himself, we will be bitterly disappointed.

Subjugating in Style

JOSHUA 10:20–24 *Then it happened, while Joshua and the children of Israel made an end of slaying them with a very great slaughter, till they had finished, that those who escaped entered fortified cities. And all the people returned to the camp, to Joshua at Makkedah, in peace. No one moved his tongue against any of the children of Israel.*

Then Joshua said, "Open the mouth of the cave, and bring out those five kings to me from the cave." And they did so, and brought out those five kings to him from the cave: the king of Jerusalem, the king of Hebron, the king of Jarmuth, the king of Lachish, and the king of Eglon. So it was, when they brought out those kings to Joshua, that Joshua called for all the men of Israel, and said to the captains of the men of war who went with him, "Come near, put your feet on the necks of these kings." And they drew near and put their feet on their necks. (NKJV)

When Israel returns to camp after this campaign it is in safety; not one casualty on their side is mentioned. Not one resident utters a word of derision or mockery. The ceremony of putting the officers' feet upon the necks of the opponents is meant to bolster the morale of Israel's army, and to demoralize whatever foes are left to hear the report.

What are the key lessons from this military exercise for us to remember when we face battles in our own lives?

apply it

1. The Israelite army was <u>committed</u> to a principle. The defense of Gibeon was related to a promise previously made.

2. The army <u>relied</u> on God's help even though well-armed and competently trained.

3. The soldiers were ready to <u>participate</u> in the struggle. They did not just sit back and wait for God to act.

4. Joshua <u>prayed</u> in faith, believing God would work miracles.

5. Joshua <u>encouraged</u> the people not to be afraid but to be strong and courageous.

go to

participate
Joshua 10:9–10

prayed
Joshua 10:12

encouraged
Joshua 10:25

multiple
Joshua 1:6, 7, 9; 8:1;
10:8

> **what others say**
>
> **Joni Eareckson Tada**
>
> Why is it that so many Christians fail to conquer? Perhaps it's because we fail to mount up and soar with wings and choose instead to live on the same low level as our trials. Little wonder we blunder when the battlefield we choose is on an earthly plane. Christians are powerless there; that is, unless they shift to a higher battleground and choose weapons of warfare that are spiritual.[16]

Just Deserts

JOSHUA 10:25–27 *Then Joshua said to them, "Do not be afraid, nor be dismayed; be strong and of good courage, for thus the LORD will do to all your enemies against whom you fight." And afterward Joshua struck them and killed them, and hanged them on five trees; and they were hanging on the trees until evening. So it was at the time of the going down of the sun that Joshua commanded, and they took them down from the trees, cast them into the cave where they had been hidden, and laid large stones against the cave's mouth, which remain until this very day.* (NKJV)

Joshua seeks to share the message that has meant so much to him <u>multiple</u> times in the recent past. He wants to encourage the people in their endeavors, so he tells them to be strong and courageous. Then he disposes of the rulers of the opposition, to demonstrate, in part, the totality of God's deliverance. As God completely vanquished the leaders of this attack, so he will continue to dispel every fearsome foe.

go to

fought
Exodus 14:14; 23:27

refuge
Joshua 10:20

Negev
4,500 square miles of desert in southern Israel

Kadesh Barnea
land in northeastern Sinai and southern Israel

Gaza
an important seacoast town in southern Israel

Goshen
district in lower Canaan[18]

Gibeon
a city and people within the boundaries later allotted to Benjamin

seven
a number representing completion

annihilation
complete destruction

Max Lucado

God has proven himself as a faithful father. Now it falls to us to be trusting children. Let God . . . fill the void others have left. Rely upon him for your affirmation and encouragement. Look at Paul's words: "You are God's child and *God will give you the blessing promised*, because you are his child" (Gal. 4:7, emphasis added).[17]

Sortie of Southern Cities

Joshua 10:28–43

Joshua attacks Makkedah, leaves no survivors, and treats the king as he did Jericho's king. Israel attacks Libnah and Lachish and puts everyone to the sword. Horam and his army come from Gezer to assist Israel's adversaries but Joshua defeats him as well, leaving no survivors. Then they take up positions against Eglon and destroy all its inhabitants. After that, the army proceeds to Hebron, attacks it and the surrounding villages, leaving no survivors. From there, they turn around and attack Debir, leaving no one alive. In this way, they subdue the entire region—the hill country, the **Negev**, the western foothills and mountain slopes. They destroy everything that breathes just as they were commanded. The territory they overpower includes **Kadesh Barnea**, **Gaza**, **Goshen**, and **Gibeon**. All were conquered because God <u>fought</u> for Israel. Then the entire nation returns to Gilgal.

Exactly **seven** cities are listed in this particular narrative, suggesting that this is a summary and that these have been chosen to represent all the cities in this area. Only the bare details are given, and the accounts contain many repeated phrases.

Three of the seven are cities whose kings have already opposed Israel. So after having defeated them on the battlefield, the Israelites continue on to capture their towns. We know that some fled during the warfare to take <u>refuge</u> behind their walls, but no matter. The sweep of the campaign reaches everyone sooner or later, in swift and unequivocal **annihilation**.

These are wars of destruction and extermination, but not for the purpose of settlement, for there is a lot more to accomplish before the Israelites can even think of setting up housekeeping. But in a brief period they have secured complete control of the country. Individual tribes will finish the effort in the south when it is time for habitation. <u>Scattered</u> throughout the entire passage are reminders that the Lord is Israel's commander and that he has fought and delivered the land to their control.

go to

scattered
Joshua 10:8, 11–12, 14, 19, 25, 30, 32, 42

possible
1 John 4:4

what others say

Luci Swindoll

And consider this as a rule of thumb. God never calls without enabling us . . . If he calls you to do something, he makes it <u>possible</u> for you to do it. And let me go a step further: if you don't sense his strength and ability with you to do it, I would question the call.[19]

Chapter Wrap-Up

- A neighboring nation dupes Israel into making a treaty with their envoys by pretending to represent a country far away. (Joshua 9:1–15)

- After an agreement is signed, the Israelites realize how foolish they were not to consult with God, but now they are under oath to protect the Gibeonites. They make them to be their servants. (Joshua 9:16–27)

- Five nations band together to war against the nation Israel is bound to protect. In battle, God delivers them by sending confusion to the enemy, causing inclement weather, and changing the behavior of the sun. (Joshua 10:1–27)

- God continues to win battle after battle until the entire southern portion of the country is subdued. Israel returns to camp. (Joshua 10:28–43)

Study Questions

1. What mistake in judgment did the Israelites make, and what could they have done to prevent it?

2. How important is it for an individual or a group to keep their promises?

3. What miraculous event occurred in chapter 10 that the Bible says has never been duplicated?

4. What can be learned from the military endeavors of Israel about facing our own battles?

Joshua 11–12
Conquest of the North

Chapter Highlights:
- Fighting Their Foes
- Inventory of Invasions
- A Little R & R
- East of the Jordan
- West of the Jordan

Let's Get Started

Two precepts stand out above all the other truths in this chapter:

1. *Even when we are totally outnumbered and outclassed, there is hope when God is on our side.* The Israelites could never compete with the enormous army of troops that came together to make war against them. Militarily they were not even in the same league, except that God was on their side.

2. *The second principle builds on the first. Victory comes when we act on the promises of God, not on our own understanding or strength.* Joshua could have derived an entirely different picture of what was happening around him if he had not seen the situation through the eyes of God.

Fighting Their Foes

JOSHUA 11:1–5 *And it came to pass, when Jabin king of Hazor heard these things, that he sent to Jobab king of Madon, to the king of Shimron, to the king of Achshaph, and to the kings who were from the north, in the mountains, in the plain south of Chinneroth, in the lowland, and in the heights of Dor on the west, to the Canaanites in the east and in the west, the Amorite, the Hittite, the Perizzite, the Jebusite in the mountains, and the Hivite below Hermon in the land of Mizpah. So they went out, they and all their armies with them, as many people as the sand that is on the seashore in multitude, with very many horses and chariots. And when all these kings had met together, they came and camped together at the waters of Merom to fight against Israel. (NKJV)*

Jabin, king of Hazor, the largest and most strategic city in the northern realm, summons the kings of the mountains, the

Jordan Valley
a geological fault running north/south, 80 miles long

Hazor
the capital of several city-states in northern Israel and southern Lebanon

Jordan Valley south of the Sea of Galilee, the western foothills, and the dunes of Dor along the coast, to help him liquidate this presumptuous group of Israelite upstarts. Obviously, however, the reports of the Israelite victories in the south have caused some alarm. That Jabin enlists the help of the Jebusites shows that they are seeking help far and wide.

At the other end of the territory in the far north, they also ask the residents of the Mizpah Valley for help. The various kings then gather at Merom, located southwest of **Hazor**, which flows into the Sea of Galilee.[1] This was only a strategy meeting as they could not have carried on a battle at this location. Using chariots was impossible in the rugged terrain.

Meanwhile Joshua and his soldiers must have marched unopposed up the west side of the Jordan Valley, past towns left unattended while men and weapons were being gathered elsewhere in preparation for battle.[2]

To Infinity and Beyond

JOSHUA 11:6 *But the LORD said to Joshua, "Do not be afraid because of them, for tomorrow about this time I will deliver all of them slain before Israel. You shall hamstring their horses and burn their chariots with fire." (NKJV)*

Considering the uncountable forces arrayed against them, it is especially significant that God promises victory "tomorrow about this time." It will not be a long, drawn-out conflict, and they need not sweat the outcome. The enemy will be handed to them by God, already slain. As if to further bolster their confidence, he gives instructions for when they do overcome.

what others say

Charles Stanley

Have your fears become a controlling force in your life? Do you find yourself missing opportunities and experiences because of your fear of failure, rejection, or the future in general? God never intended for you to be controlled by fear. He is, however, willing to use your fears to move you to a place of greater dependence on him.[3]

The horses spoken of were not intended to carry mounted warriors into battle. At this time in history they were used only to pull the chariots.[4] God's instructions were explicit—he wanted them taken completely out of the picture. He did not want his people to <u>depend</u> on their own strength, or on any military power they might accumulate. And as a **prophet** later <u>warned</u>, horses and chariots would require them to maintain a professional army, and that was not God's intention.

Admonished Annihilation

JOSHUA 11:7–11 *So Joshua and all the people of war with him came against them suddenly by the waters of Merom, and they attacked them. And the LORD delivered them into the hand of Israel, who defeated them and chased them to Greater Sidon, to the Brook Misrephoth, and to the Valley of Mizpah eastward; they attacked them until they left none of them remaining. So Joshua did to them as the LORD had told him: he hamstrung their horses and burned their chariots with fire.*

Joshua turned back at that time and took Hazor, and struck its king with the sword; for Hazor was formerly the head of all those kingdoms. And they struck all the people who were in it with the edge of the sword, utterly destroying them. There was none left breathing. Then he burned Hazor with fire. (NKJV)

In essence, the alliance of northern kings was a boon for Joshua in that now he could defeat all the armies of the entire district with one major blow. Joshua's rapier-like thrust caught his opponents completely off-guard. Israel pursued their defeated foes as far as Greater Sidon (the mainland section of a Phoenician waterfront city on the Mediterranean), Misrephoth Maim (just south of Sidon on a promontory known as "the ladder of Tyre"), and the Valley of Mizpah (at the foot of Mount Herman).[5]

what others say

Arthur W. Pink

The total failure of Jabin's long-planned project demonstrated clearly that there is "no counsel against the Lord" which has the remotest possibility of succeeding. The best contrived policy against Him comes to foolishness.[6]

depend
Isaiah 31:1;
Psalm 20:7

warned
1 Samuel 8:11

prophet
someone who
speaks for God

Within twenty-four hours, Joshua's outnumbered and inferior force routs an army so vast it cannot be counted, and does it in a place where their superior weaponry cannot even be used.

The text states that everyone was put to the sword. The original Hebrew terminology reads more like: they were put "to the mouth (or the hilt) of the sword." The sword (*hereb*), the chief weapon of the Israelite soldier, had a blade of ten to twelve inches protruding from a hilt often fashioned like a lion's head with an open mouth.[7] It is spoken of as having two <u>edges</u> and when not in use was kept in a <u>sheath</u>. This could be fastened to a belt or removed when defense was not necessary.

Also used in warfare were <u>scimitars</u>, examples of which have been found in excavations and pictured on monuments. <u>Bows</u> and arrows were well-developed—arrows were made of wood with metal heads. Slings were loaded with stones, which were then whirled around the head and flung at their opponents. A <u>spear</u> or lance was probably the height of a grown man and could keep the enemy at bay when a warrior was involved in hand-to-hand combat. <u>Javelins</u>, for hurling, were counterbalanced with iron on the other end to match the weight of the metal head. Specimens of these types of weapons have been found in excavations.[8]

Forceful Fencing

edges
Hebrews 4:12

sheath
1 Samuel 17:51

scimitars
Joshua 8:18

bows
Joshua 24:12

spear
Numbers 25:7–8

javelins
1 Samuel 18:10–11

capital
Joshua 11:10

Jericho
Joshua 6:24

Ai
Joshua 8:28

left
Deuteronomy
6:10–11

JOSHUA 11:12–14 *So all the cities of those kings, and all their kings, Joshua took and struck with the edge of the sword. He utterly destroyed them, as Moses the servant of the LORD had commanded. But as for the cities that stood on their mounds, Israel burned none of them, except Hazor only, which Joshua burned. And all the spoil of these cities and the livestock, the children of Israel took as booty for themselves; but they struck every man with the edge of the sword until they had destroyed them, and they left none breathing. (NKJV)*

As the "<u>capital</u>" of an odd assortment of Canaanite kingdoms, Hazor was struck first, hardest, and its downfall was described in more detail than any of the other northern cities. Throughout the entire land, <u>Jericho</u>, <u>Ai</u>, and Hazor are the only cities put to the torch, the rest are <u>left</u> to be inhabited by the Israelites. The booty that remained, to be divided and shared by all, would have outfitted every household and padded their pockets. Since they already kept livestock, the animals they gained would have swollen their herds to enormous size.

Tel el-Qedah is the archaeological site of Hazor. In 1926–28, John Garstang found the ashes from Joshua's fire at this site with pottery dating around 1400 BC.[9] Further excavation by Dr. Yigael Yadin in 1955 revealed that, during Joshua's time, the city had a population of about 40,000 on 170 acres.[10] Also found in the Amarna Tablets (written to Pharaoh in 1380 BC by an Egyptian envoy in northern Palestine) are the words "Let my lord the king recall what Hazor and its king have already had to endure" (a reference most likely to the devastation by Joshua).[11]

Boss's Orders

JOSHUA 11:15 *As the LORD had commanded Moses his servant, so Moses commanded Joshua, and so Joshua did. He left nothing undone of all that the LORD had commanded Moses. (NKJV)*

Verse 15 describes how the authority system in Israel operates. This chain of command will work very effectively until a link is broken. The Scriptures are extravagant in their description of Joshua's obedience. Not only did he follow every instruction of the Lord's to the letter, but *nothing* was left undone.

what others say

Bill Gothard

God places every person under authority—the authority of parents, government, Godly church leaders, and employers. Every human authority, however, is under the authority of God and the Bible.[12]

Jerry Bridges

We must commit ourselves to obeying God in all of his commands. We cannot pick and choose according to our own values. A little bit of fudging on one's income tax return is sin just as much as outright theft; an unforgiving spirit toward someone else is just as much as murder.[13]

Inventory of Invasions

> JOSHUA 11:16–19 *Thus Joshua took all this land: the moun-*
> *tain country, all the South, all the land of Goshen, the lowland,*
> *and the Jordan plain—the mountains of Israel and its low-*
> *lands, from Mount Halak and the ascent to Seir, even as far as*
> *Baal Gad in the Valley of Lebanon below Mount Hermon. He*
> *captured all their kings, and struck them down and killed them.*
> *Joshua made war a long time with all those kings. There was not*
> *a city that made peace with the children of Israel, except the*
> *Hivites, the inhabitants of Gibeon. All the others they took in*
> *battle. (NKJV)*

This passage recaps what occurred in chapters 9 through 11. All
the geographic areas between the southern limits of Mount Halak
(southeast of the Dead Sea) and the northern border of Baal Gad (in
the Lebanon Valley northwest of Mount Hermon) are listed as captured. The conquest takes some time, during which the power of the
Canaanites to resist is shattered. Joshua could not have left controlling garrisons in every city, lacking sufficient men of war to do so,
but the land is now safe for individual tribes to occupy and continue
the program already begun.

Obstinate and Bullheaded

> JOSHUA 11:20 *For it was of the LORD to harden their hearts,*
> *that they should come against Israel in battle, that He might*
> *utterly destroy them, and that they might receive no mercy, but*
> *that He might destroy them, as the LORD had commanded Moses.*
> *(NKJV)*

God hardens the heart of every nation except the Gibeonites, *not*
to keep them from repenting but to keep them from surrendering
while still unrepentant. His justice demands a complete removal of
the various cancers represented by the countries in question.
Removing whoever refuses to repent is the only way to save the
land from recurring forms of evil.

Joe Aldrich

> The heart of man is pictured in scripture as the center of the rational-spiritual nature of man. It is the seat of love and hate, thought and conception, feelings and affection. The heart is that part of us which experiences joy, sorrow, anxiety and pain. It is the center of our moral life, the origin of all that is good and evil in thoughts, words and actions.[14]

God is not willing that any should <u>perish</u>. He promises that whoever <u>calls</u> upon his name will be saved and that as long as there is any hope of repentance, he will <u>wait</u> patiently. Knowing this, we must conclude that the people whose hearts were hardened by God had already decided they _would_ not believe, so God confirmed their choice by deciding they _could_ not believe. When a person <u>refuses</u> to believe the truth, God allows them to be deceived. The wonder of it all is that any of us have experienced God's mercy, all having <u>turned</u> aside from his perfect path to seek our own way.

Joni Eareckson Tada

> Maybe you've been dabbling in sin. Careless flirtations. Lazy thoughts. Fudgings of the truth. If you've been sweeping them under the carpet of your conscience, if you think, "God will always be there . . . He'll forgive me sooner or later . . . so I'll choose later," then wake up! . . . One day you may try to call on Him, and He won't be near.[15]

A Giant Problem

JOSHUA 11:21–22 _And at that time Joshua came and cut off the Anakim from the mountains: from Hebron, from Debir, from Anab, from all the mountains of Judah, and from all the mountains of Israel; Joshua utterly destroyed them with their cities. None of the Anakim were left in the land of the children of Israel; they remained only in Gaza, in Gath, and in Ashdod._ (NKJV)

go to

perish
2 Peter 3:9

calls
Romans 10:13

wait
Isaiah 48:9

would not
John 12:37–40

refuses
2 Thessalonians 2:10–12

turned
Romans 3:10–12

Anakites
Deuteronomy 9:2

rebelled
Numbers 13:28,
32–33

picture
Hebrews 4:7–11

reserved
Revelation 14:13

Anakites
a physically tall and
strong race

Now the Israelites encounter head-on what had previously been the object of their fears. The consternation that Israel felt over coming up against the **Anakites** was the reason they <u>rebelled</u> against entering the land of promise the first time. However, God's deliverance was not limited to the size or strength of the problem, and just as he provided victory in every other situation, he continued to do so with the Anakites. Gaza, Gath, and Ashdod are three of five Philistine cities located along the Mediterranean Sea. Basically, the coastal plain remains unconquered.

what others say

Corrie ten Boom

Somebody said to me: "When I worry I go to the mirror and say to myself, 'This tremendous thing which is worrying me is beyond a solution. It is especially too hard for Jesus Christ to handle.' After I have said that, I smile and I am ashamed."[16]

A Little R & R

JOSHUA 11:23 *So Joshua took the whole land, according to all that the LORD had said to Moses; and Joshua gave it as an inheritance to Israel according to their divisions by their tribes. Then the land rested from war. (NKJV)*

The apportioning of the land to the family groups in Israel begins immediately, but each of the tribes is expected to apply the lessons of war. The victory had been decisive, but they could enjoy it on a personal basis only as they continued to further their claims and acquisitions.

The text declares the land "rested." This is not the rest of the weary, where they collapse from the exhaustion of their labors. Nor is it the rest of the inactive, as if they know all that needs to be done but have put it off for another day. Rather, it is the satisfying rest of contentment that comes with the knowledge that they've successfully accomplished all that God has given them to do up to this point. This chapter marks the conclusion of the united warfare of the people of God in Canaan.

The rest that was granted the people of God at the completion of their warfare is but a <u>picture</u> of the rest that awaits us after our work on earth is done. It is <u>reserved</u> for those who have fought the good fight and remain faithful to Jesus. But even though the final rest is yet to be conferred, God offers a <u>sample</u> to us as believers here on earth. It is a <u>rest</u> found in the midst of service and it is something that the **unregenerate** can never experience.

go to

sample
Matthew 11:29

rest
Psalm 116:7

unregenerate
Isaiah 57:20

unregenerate
an individual not renewed by Christ

> ### what others say
> **Eugenia Price**
>
> Life was so good we felt almost afraid and ashamed to take it. We knew so well all about the suffering. And we knew we didn't have our joy because we *deserved* it. And out of this we realized also that when our cup is sweet we can do nothing but drink it deeply and thank Him for giving it to us.[17]

East of the Jordan

> ### the big picture
> **Joshua 12:1–6**
>
> The Israelites defeated two kings east of the Jordan River. They were Sihon, king of the Amorites, and Og, king of Bashan. Moses, the servant of God, with the help of the entire Israelite nation, conquered them. Then Moses gave this land to the tribes of Reuben, Gad, and half of Manasseh.

Included in this passage is an impressive description of the geographical details that demarcate the territory of Sihon and Og. This land becomes home to the two and one-half tribes that remain east of the Jordan.

Moses's title, "servant of the LORD," so perfectly communicates his chosen office that his name can scarcely be cited without it.

> ### what others say
> **D. L. Moody**
>
> Use me then my Savior, for whatever purpose and in whatever way, Thou mayest require. Here is my poor heart, an empty vessel; fill it with Thy grace. Here is my sinful and troubled soul; quicken and refresh it with Thy love. Take my heart for Thine abode; my mouth to spread the glory of Thy name; my love and all my powers, for the advancement of Thy believing people.[18]

go to

choose
2 Timothy 4:3–4

intolerable
Zephaniah 3:7–8

autonomous
self-governing

licentiousness
aggressive and
unchecked immoral
behavior

West of the Jordan

the big picture

Joshua 12:7–24

Joshua and the Israelites conquer thirty-one kings. Joshua gives their land as an inheritance to the remainder of the tribes of Israel.

The thirty-one kings mentioned in this passage were **autonomous** princes of individual city-states with local authority. Verses 9 through 16 recount the southern campaign, and 17 through 20 focus on the northern campaign. This list of kings is notable not only to point out how intimately God is involved in the details of our lives (proving that the individual is important in God's economy), but also to provide historical data that can be cross-referenced and validated via other literature. This inventory enumerates the significant military sites of the period and mentions kings found in other correspondence of the times.[19]

At the completion of these accounts depicting the slaughter and extermination of entire people groups, it seems appropriate to analyze the seeming barbarity and bloodthirstiness of the Israelite army. Liberal scholars and theologians claim these events to be in direct conflict with New Testament truth, and a transitional stage in Israel's evolutionary development.[20] Some even suggest that the Old Testament should be dropped from the canon.[21]

However, we cannot pick and <u>choose</u> what we like about God and throw out the rest without remaking God to fit our own human philosophy. There is a danger in projecting our system of morality onto God, because in doing so we create a god of our own intellects and emotions. Instead, we need to view the whole picture through the eyes of God himself. Why, then, would a loving God promote such carnage and destruction?

First, he was not arbitrarily wiping out one nation in favor of another. The Canaanites were abolished because their wickedness had reached a point that was <u>intolerable</u> and could not co-exist with God's holiness. Their religious observances had degenerated to embrace the most sordid **licentiousness** and brutality.[22] The Ras Shamra tablets, other relics, and pornographic statuary unearthed from this time period testify that the Canaanites' religions involved the prostitution of both sexes and demanded infant sacrifice.[23] Surely the cries of these innocent children reached the ears of God and <u>motivated</u> him to act in their behalf, bringing an end to this outrageous perversion. From the Bible itself, we continue to add to the list of <u>vulgarities</u> practiced by these people: incest, adultery, homosexuality, bigamy, and bestiality. We find they were also involved in the <u>occult</u> and Satan worship. When a nation's wickedness reaches an insufferable level, <u>judgment</u> must fall, or God would be guilty of injustice.

Second, if the Canaanites survived they would not be sinning in isolation. Their wicked ways would pollute the nation of Israel and drag them down into every imaginable evil. As if to prove this, Israel went on to practice every <u>impropriety</u> that was not completely wiped out.

Third, death is not the end of life. Blameless children who are killed find themselves in the <u>presence</u> of God. Therefore, death of the innocent is not the greatest evil that can befall a nation. On the other hand, allowing children to grow up in any pagan culture would be the greater evil.

Fourth, Israel was not given a blanket license to kill. They could not take a notion to simply murder anyone. The responsibility for this entire program of judgment fell squarely on the shoulders of God. Israel was simply the <u>tool</u> to carry out his purpose.

Fifth, God's severe treatment of sin included bringing pain and <u>suffering</u> upon his own Son in order to provide an alternate way of dealing with the problem. He has not removed himself from the issue, but remains actively involved in the process of **reconciling** those who respond to his gracious solution. Without his intervention, we would all be subject to <u>wrath</u>.

Finally, if any one of the nations involved had <u>turned</u> away from their evil practices, judgment would not have fallen. They had a <u>knowledge</u> of God and many <u>years</u> to respond before God at last hardened their hearts.

go to

motivated
Psalm 103:6

vulgarities
Leviticus 18

occult
2 Kings 21:2–6

judgment
Romans 2:5–6

impropriety
2 Kings 16:3; 23:7

presence
2 Corinthians 5:8;
2 Samuel 12:22–23

tool
Joshua 11:15

suffering
Isaiah 53:5–6

reconciling
John 3:17

wrath
Romans 1:18

turned
Jeremiah 18:7–8

knowledge
Joshua 2:10

years
Genesis 15:16

reconciling
to make two conflicting things compatible

what others say

Paul E. Little

Helmut Thielecke of Hamburg points out that a fabric viewed through a magnifying glass is clear in the middle and blurred at the edges. But we know the edges are clear because of what we see in the middle. Life, he says, is like a fabric. There are many edges which are blurred, many events and circumstances we do not understand. But they are to be interpreted by the clarity we see in the center—the cross of Christ.[24]

Chapter Wrap-Up

- The kings of the north form an alliance to fight against the invading Israelites. The coalition is doomed to fail in spite of their numbers and strength. (Joshua 11:1–15)

- This section summarizes the warfare that has already occurred in chapters 9 through 11. After the last victory, Joshua prepares to divide the land between the tribes and allow the country to be at rest. (Joshua 11:16–23)

- This section names the two kings and the territories conquered by Moses east of the Jordan River. (Joshua 12:1–6)

- This section lists the thirty-one kings and the territories conquered by Joshua west of the Jordan River. (Joshua 12:7–24)

Study Questions

1. What would be the danger if the Israelites learned to depend upon their own strength?

2. What was Joshua careful to do in chapter 11, verse 15?

3. What happened to the hearts of the people of the land when they refused to believe the truth?

4. List six reasons why extermination of the enemy was the only course of action for the Israelites.

Joshua 13-22
Division of the Land

Chapter Highlights:
- Caleb's Claim
- Taking Possession
- Cities of Refuge
- Establishing Accountability

Let's Get Started

Now that the main blitz of warfare is over, it's time for settling down and making this place a home. But it isn't first come, first served. The Israelites need to follow an orderly procedure of distribution, fair to every tribe, family, and individual. How do they determine where to divide each district, how large each parcel should be, and who gets first choice? As always, God has a plan. They just need to follow his directions for everything to come out all right.

continue
Exodus 23:29–30

Caleb's Claim

the big picture

Joshua 13:1-7

The Lord speaks to Joshua, reminding him of his age and the sections of land left to be subdued. Various regions are named, including the mountains from Lebanon to the Brook Misrephoth (Misrephoth Maim), from which God himself will drive out the Sidonians. All of this land will be included in the allocations for the nine and one-half tribes west of the Jordan River.

Joshua is probably ninety to a hundred years old at this point.[1] Thus God urges him to take the next step right away—dividing up the inheritance. The territories left to be conquered include (1) the land of the Philistines, (2) Israel's neighbors to the south, (3) the Phoenician coastline to the north, and (4) the northern mountains of Lebanon.

Five Philistine rulers are named, classified in the original language as "tyrants."[2] Despite the resounding victories already achieved, from one end of the land to the other, it isn't yet complete and God intends for the process to <u>continue</u> on an individual basis.

go to

praying
Matthew 26:41

failure
Joshua 13:13

inhabited
Joshua 16:10; 19:47

divided
Joshua 14:4

temptation
what we think is an
irresistible craving

flesh
the physical body
with its needs and
limitations

satiated
completely satisfied

Cynthia Heald

Certainly excellence in our lives is molded by discipline. Jesus' words are so true: "Keep watching and praying, that you may not come into **temptation**; the spirit is willing but the **flesh** is weak." So often my intentions are good, but . . . I don't exercise my will over my feelings or my lazy body![3]

Who Gets What?

the big picture

Joshua 13:8–14:5

The inheritance of Reuben, Gad, and half of Manasseh is delineated by describing its geographic boundaries and the primary towns they embrace. This was already laid out by Moses before the Jordan was crossed. Eleazar, Joshua, and representative leadership from each of the remaining tribes gather to determine further land arrangements by casting lots. The tribe of Levi is not included in this distribution.

Although this book primarily celebrates Israel's victories at the hand of the Lord, it also reveals that complete dominion is limited by Israel's failure to persevere in what they began. Some of the portions that were assigned to the individual tribes were never inhabited or enjoyed by them at all.

Of the twelve sons of Jacob, from whom the twelve tribes derive their names, Joseph's inheritance is divided between his two sons, Ephraim and Manasseh. But because Levi—as the clan of the priesthood—does not receive a grant of land, the country will still be divided into twelve portions. Levi is provided for in other ways, the most meaningful of which is that God himself will be their inheritance.

All of these instructions are followed "as the Lord commanded Moses," a refrain that is repeated over and over, as if to say—"obedience is paramount!" That land designations are determined by lot does not mean they are leaving these choices to fate. Rather, they are allowing God to determine who gets what.

what others say

Jim Elliot

Levi's inheritance is three times mentioned in this section . . . Nothing but Jehovah! What a poor tribe, we would say. How will they ever live? Ah, faith's eyes look up and are **satiated** with the unseen possessions in God's person. I would be so—nothing save God.[4]

Like the Levites, we can enjoy a special relationship with God when we make him our <u>inheritance</u>. This means to consider God a special <u>possession</u>, granted to us in place of material things that would demand our attention and energy. Nothing else will fill the places in our hearts that belong to him. He is our legacy waiting to be <u>claimed</u> and treasured.

A little sidelight from this passage is a brief mention of Balaam. Balaam was the pagan fortune-teller hired by Balak, king of Moab, to curse the Israelites. God caused a <u>donkey</u> to speak words of warning to Balaam, and after seeing the Angel of the Lord with a drawn sword, he was frightened into <u>blessing</u> Israel instead. Later, however, he <u>incited</u> Moabite women to seduce Israelite men, and through this brought devastation to God's people. Now we read that he is put to <u>death</u> with the sword.

Payment upon Promise

> JOSHUA 14:6–9 *Then the children of Judah came to Joshua in Gilgal. And Caleb the son of Jephunneh the Kenizzite said to him: "You know the word which the LORD said to Moses the man of God concerning you and me in Kadesh Barnea. I was forty years old when Moses the servant of the LORD sent me from Kadesh Barnea to spy out the land, and I brought back word to him as it was in my heart. Nevertheless my brethren who went up with me made the heart of the people melt, but I wholly followed the LORD my God. So Moses swore on that day, saying, 'Surely the land where your foot has trodden shall be your inheritance and your children's forever, because you have wholly followed the LORD my God.' (NKJV)*

The first person to ask for his inheritance is Caleb—the last is Joshua. So the entire distribution of the land at this time is framed by living examples of God's <u>faithfulness</u>.

Before the Exodus, Caleb's father (a foreigner descended from <u>Esau</u> through Kenaz) married a daughter of Hur from the family of Chelubai within the tribe of Judah.[5] She bore to Jephunneh a son whose name was derived from her family's name—Caleb.

Caleb was one of only two men in the previous generation to <u>believe</u> that God would do as he said and drive the nations out from before Israel. At that time, Moses <u>guaranteed</u> that Caleb would receive a special inheritance, and now it is time to pay up.

inheritance
Colossians 1:12–14

possession
Psalm 73:26

claimed
Philippians 3:12

donkey
Numbers 22:28–30

blessing
Numbers 23:11

incited
Numbers 31:16

death
Joshua 13:22

faithfulness
Numbers 14:24

Esau
Genesis 36:15

believe
Numbers 13, 14

guaranteed
Deuteronomy 1:36

apply it

God does not exclude anyone, on the basis of race or heritage, from becoming part of his family—or even serving in high places of leadership.

King of the Mountain

JOSHUA 14:10–15 *And now, behold, the LORD has kept me alive, as He said, these forty-five years, ever since the LORD spoke this word to Moses while Israel wandered in the wilderness; and now, here I am this day, eighty-five years old. As yet I am as strong this day as on the day that Moses sent me; just as my strength was then, so now is my strength for war, both for going out and for coming in. Now therefore, give me this mountain of which the LORD spoke in that day; for you heard in that day how the Anakim were there, and that the cities were great and fortified. It may be that the LORD will be with me, and I shall be able to drive them out as the LORD said."*

And Joshua blessed him, and gave Hebron to Caleb the son of Jephunneh as an inheritance. Hebron therefore became the inheritance of Caleb the son of Jephunneh the Kenizzite to this day, because he wholly followed the LORD God of Israel. And the name of Hebron formerly was Kirjath Arba (Arba was the greatest man among the Anakim). Then the land had rest from war. (NKJV)

Caleb stood firm in his convictions on that important day forty years before, and he continues to stand firm in what he believes God will do for him now. He asks for the territory of the Anakim—the race of giants who previously scared the socks off the trembling Israelites, standing at the border. So here he is, eighty-five years old, leader of the only family group to successfully <u>expel</u> the enemy from his land.[6] What is the key to his success? It is capsulized in one phrase, <u>repeated</u> several times for emphasis: "He wholly followed the LORD God of Israel."

Caleb leads his family to do what no other tribe could accomplish—drive the enemy—in this case a race of giant people—completely out of their land.

God delights in using people of any <u>age</u>, at any time of life.

go to

expel
Joshua 15:14

repeated
Numbers 14.24;
Joshua 14:9, 14

age
Psalm 92:12–14;
2 Corinthians 4:16

God deserves far more than our distracted and absentminded attentions. Further, there is a danger in allowing our love for God to grow <u>cold</u>. He declares that because of our lukewarm behavior, he desires to <u>spit</u> us out of his mouth. Double-mindedness and <u>neglect</u> only lead to disaster.

apply it

Taking Possession

the big picture

Joshua 15:1–17:14

The allotment for the tribe of Judah is described in great geographical detail, including Caleb's portion. In reward for the capture of Kirjath Sepher, Caleb grants his daughter's hand in marriage to Othniel. Caleb's daughter Achsah requests and receives the upper and lower springs to water her inheritance in the Negev. Then the townships are divided up to be distributed to each of the smaller clans of Judah. They cannot dislodge the Jebusites from Jerusalem and so live together with them.

Next, the allotments for Ephraim and Manasseh are described by drawing up their boundaries. They cannot dislodge the Canaanites from Gezer but put them under forced labor instead. Half of Manasseh's share consists of land east of the Jordan. There are several settlements that Manasseh cannot occupy because the Canaanites are determined to stay, but when Israel grows strong enough, they make the indigenous people work for them.

Divvying up the Lots

The precision with which the exact location of each **bequest** is laid out ought to encourage the tribes to value what they have received and take seriously their responsibility to free the inherited land from ungodly influences. When describing regional markers in terms of "going <u>up</u>" and "coming <u>down</u>," the Scriptures do not refer to north and south orientation but to geographic elevation.

This passage includes the <u>second</u> reference to Caleb and the inheritance he and Othniel fought to win. Caleb shares Kenaz, a common ancestor, with Othniel and in that sense is his brother, but when Othniel attacks and wins Kirjath Sepher, he becomes Caleb's son-in-law.[7] (Othniel later serves as a <u>judge</u> of Israel.) Caleb's daughter, rec-

go to

cold
Matthew 24:12

spit
Revelation 3:16

neglect
Daniel 9:13

up
Joshua 15:6

down
Joshua 15:10

second
Joshua 14:6–15;
15:13–17

judge
Judges 3:9–11

bequest
the act of passing on from one to the other

peace
Numbers 33:51–55

Moses
Numbers 27:1–11;
Joshua 17:3–4

Caleb
Joshua 14:12

continuance policy
allowing things to
go on as they always
had

apportionment
division and distribu-
tion

ognizing that land in the arid desert of the Negev is of no value without water, appeals for and receives springs to irrigate her portion.

The amount of space devoted to the description of each territory,
and the order in which they are presented, corresponds to the
importance of each tribe in Israel's history. Judah is treated most
thoroughly, followed by Ephraim, Manasseh and Benjamin. The rest
of the tribes are covered sparingly and with few details. Judah inher-
its more than one hundred cities with their surrounding villages.

But when it comes to Jerusalem, the nationals hang on and refuse
to leave because the people of Judah do not follow through on their
obligation to destroy every negative influence. It is not in God's will
for Judah to make peace. Nor is it God's intention for Ephraim and
Manasseh to put their **continuance policy** into motion—enslaving
those they were unwilling to kill or eject.

Also covered in the text, alongside the **apportionment** of the
land, is Joshua's effort to regulate and protect the individual rights
of the heirs. He carries out Moses's directions with regard to the
land of Zelophehad, who had no sons to whom he could pass on his
legacy. Each of Zelophehad's five daughters receives a portion, as do
the men of the other families.

I Think I Can, I Think I Can

the big picture

Joshua 17:15-18

Ephraim and Manasseh complain they do not have enough land
to situate all the people in their tribes. Joshua replies that they
could clear some of their forested land. They reply that even
then they would come up short, because the plains are populated with Canaanites who war with iron chariots. Joshua holds
his position and again encourages the tribes to drive the inhabitants out, even though the enemy has superior weaponry. He
confirms that Israel is stronger than her foes.

The tribes of Ephraim and Manasseh are presented with their quota of
land, disproportionately large and the most fertile of all in Canaan. They
have little reason to complain, but they are too lazy (or afraid) to remove
the residents of the plains because they possess iron chariots. What a contrast to Caleb, who couldn't wait to tackle even the most difficult challenge. Joshua knew they *could* and *should* handle it on their own.

In an effort to avoid the negative example of Ephraim and Manasseh, we need to fight the tendency to be frustrated by other people that we feel are holding us back from reaching our "full potential." It is so easy to wallow in "if onlys," to be absorbed with self-pity when we believe we deserve more than we have received. But sometimes we need to make better use of the <u>gifts</u> and resources we have instead of looking for greener grass.

apply it

> ### what others say
>
> **Charles R. Swindoll**
>
> Having some big struggles with envy? Eating your heart out because somebody's a step or two ahead of you . . . and gaining momentum? *Relax.* You are *you*—not them! And you are responsible to do the best you can with what you've got for as long as you're able.[8]

Each of the territories allotted to the clans of Manasseh in this section of the Bible are listed in the Samaritan Ostraca in 770 BC. This document records tax payments from various districts and was discovered in the palace of **Jeroboam II**. Many other names correspond as well.[9] The central ridge (where Joshua encouraged the descendants of Joseph to clear some of the trees) is devoid of any vegetation in our time. But excavations have unearthed acorns and **terebinth** seeds, deer antlers, and a boar's tooth. Another proof that this section was at one time heavily forested is that Saul's fortress in **Gibeah** was made of cypress wood and pine timber.[10]

Jeroboam II
son of Joash and a prosperous king of Israel (782–753 BC)

terebinth
a Mediterranean tree of the cashew family, yielding turpentine

Gibeah
capital city under the first king of Israel

U-Pick Portions

> ### the big picture
>
> **Joshua 18:1–10**
>
> The tabernacle is set up at Shiloh, and the whole assembly of Israel gathers to hear Joshua. He challenges the remaining seven tribes to take possession of what belongs to them. Under his direction, three men from each tribe are sent out to survey the balance of the land. After descriptions of the countryside and its townships are recorded and divided into seven parts, they return to Shiloh. The sections they have thus defined are then distributed by lot to the rest of the tribes.

go to

gifts
Matthew 25:14–30

go to

warned
Deuteronomy 32:15

blessings
Deuteronomy
33:27–29

shares
Joshua 19:9

smaller
1 Chronicles
4:24–27

together
Judges 1:3

forced
Judges 1:34

migrate
Judges 18:1–2,
9–13, 27–29

Leshem
Joshua 19:47

curse
Genesis 49:7

cruelty
Genesis 34:25–29

Jacob
Simeon's father

Until this point, the bulk of the Israelite congregation, as well as the Tent of Meeting, had remained in Gilgal. But now that the place where God's presence dwelt on earth has relocated, Joshua hopes to shake up the whole crowd. Some time has elapsed and the tribes appear to have grown complacent. It was too difficult to continue the warfare necessary to claim their own territory, and they were satisfied with the nomadic life, which was all they had ever known. For good reason, Moses had <u>warned</u> against the danger of becoming too comfortable with where they were. The <u>blessings</u> to be had would not come to those with their hands in their pockets.

> **what others say**
>
> **Dr. James C. Dobson**
> Great beginnings are not as important as the way one finishes . . . Most of life . . . is a marathon and not a sprint.[11]

Cities of Refuge

> **the big picture**
>
> **Joshua 18:11–19:48**
> The lands of Benjamin, Simeon, Zebulun, Issachar, Asher, Naphtali, and Dan are distributed by lot, with their towns and boundaries.

The remaining real estate is handed out to the tribes that are left. Simeon <u>shares</u> some of Judah's land, for Judah has more than it can handle and Simeon is a much <u>smaller</u> family group. Later, we find Simeon and Judah acting <u>together</u> to bring war against the Canaanites. The Danites are <u>forced</u> out of their territory and <u>migrate</u> to the north, settling in an area that was formerly known as <u>Leshem</u>.

Simeon received no territory of his own—only seventeen townships within the boundaries of Judah. This delegation fulfills **Jacob**'s earlier <u>curse</u> that Simeon's offspring would be dispersed throughout Israel. The punishment came out of an earlier <u>cruelty</u> that Simeon displayed (along with his brother) when he murdered and looted an entire city in a fit of rage.

All-Seeing Eye

guaranteed
Numbers 14:30

instances
Joshua 14:1; 17:4;
19:51; 21:1

plan
Jeremiah 29:11

communicate
James 1:5

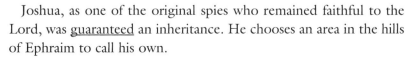

the big picture

Joshua 19:49–51

After all the districts are dispersed, the Israelites give Joshua an inheritance among them as God commanded. He asks for Timnath Serah, where he settles and builds a town. All of the distribution was done in the presence of the Lord at the entrance to the Tent of Meeting.

Joshua, as one of the original spies who remained faithful to the Lord, was <u>guaranteed</u> an inheritance. He chooses an area in the hills of Ephraim to call his own.

In the four <u>instances</u> where Eleazar and Joshua work together and are written up, Eleazar is always named first, out of respect for his crucial role of high priest.

The concluding verse in this passage is a solemn summary of the lot-casting ceremony performed under God's watchful eye. Nothing is done without his supervision.

what others say

J. I. Packer

Belief that divine guidance is real rests upon two foundation facts: first, the reality of God's <u>plan</u> for us; second, the ability of God to <u>communicate</u> with us. On both these facts the Bible has much to say.[12]

Our decisions in life are best served when we make them in the presence of the Lord and with his blessing.

"I Didn't Mean To . . ."

JOSHUA 20:1–6 *The LORD also spoke to Joshua, saying, "Speak to the children of Israel, saying: 'Appoint for yourselves cities of refuge, of which I spoke to you through Moses, that the slayer who kills a person accidentally or unintentionally may flee there; and they shall be your refuge from the avenger of blood. And when he flees to one of those cities, and stands at the entrance of the gate of the city, and declares his case in the hearing of the elders of that city, they shall take him into the city as one of them, and give him a place, that he may dwell among them. Then if*

go to

witnesses
Numbers 35:30

God
Deuteronomy 32:35;
Romans 12:19

provision
Acts 3:17–19

righteous
Romans 3:22

accusing
Psalm 31:19–21

Satan
Revelation 12:10

silenced
Romans 8:1

refuge
Psalm 91:1–2

against
Psalm 32:1–2

hides
Psalm 32:7

avenger
the person retaliating on behalf of another

statute of limitations
time in which legal proceedings must be started

the avenger of blood pursues him, they shall not deliver the slayer into his hand, because he struck his neighbor unintentionally, but did not hate him beforehand. And he shall dwell in that city until he stands before the congregation for judgment, and until the death of the one who is high priest in those days. Then the slayer may return and come to his own city and his own house, to the city from which he fled.'" (NKJV)

In the Hebrew economy, a person was considered blameless until proven guilty via the testimony of at least two witnesses. That the elders of the city are commanded not to "surrender" the accused assumes his innocence until proven otherwise. The provision of the cities of refuge makes the clear distinction between willful murder and manslaughter (literally in the original: "death through error and without knowing").[13] So if a person unintentionally took another's life, he could flee to the refuge of one of these cities and, after a preliminary hearing, be admitted as a resident. When his trial comes up before the assembly and he is acquitted of a willful crime, he may continue to make this city his home without fear of retribution from the **avenger** (literally: "close relative"), who might be feeling the need to protect his family's rights.[14] This provision basically limits the one who would vindicate a loved one's death by removing the personal right for vengeance and establishing it as a privilege to be exercised by God alone. The accused who was proven innocent would be free to leave the city of refuge without fear of revenge after the death of the current high priest. (The change of administration served as a **statute of limitations**.)

Just as the cities of refuge provided a place of safety for those who committed a wrongdoing (however unintentional), so God has made provision for us who also have violated his law but need his protection. We can be declared righteous by faith in him, and find refuge where accusing tongues cannot harm us. Even Satan, the greatest accuser of them all, is silenced, for God himself is our refuge. God no longer counts our sin against us but hides us from the trouble that threatens our souls.

Haven from Harm

JOSHUA 20:7–9 *So they appointed Kedesh in Galilee, in the mountains of Naphtali, Shechem in the mountains of Ephraim,* *and Kirjath Arba (which is Hebron) in the mountains of Judah. And on the other side of the Jordan, by Jericho eastward, they assigned Bezer in the wilderness on the plain, from the tribe of Reuben, Ramoth in Gilead, from the tribe of Gad, and Golan in Bashan, from the tribe of Manasseh. These were the cities appointed for all the children of Israel and for the stranger who dwelt among them, that whoever killed a person accidentally might flee there, and not die by the hand of the avenger of blood until he stood before the congregation. (NKJV)*

go to

Levites
Numbers 35:6

Moses
Deuteronomy
19:1–13

rebuke
Genesis 49:5–7

Levites
members of the
tribe of Levi who
cared for the house
of God

The cities were evenly distributed so that an individual would never be more than a day's journey from any place of sanctuary.[15] Golan, Ramoth Gilead, and Bezer were east of the Jordan. Kedesh, Shechem, and Kirjath Arba (Hebron) were to the west. All six cities were under the protectorship of the **Levites**, and their establishment was dictated since the time of <u>Moses</u>.

> **what others say**
>
> **S. I. McMillen, M.D.**
>
> Perhaps the Lord had the inspired writer record Psalm 46 for us in this atomic day: God is our refuge and strength, a very present help in trouble . . . Today the world outlook is darker than at any previous time in history. Yet to the believing Christian the gloom is only an indication of the imminent and glorious return of Jesus Christ.[16]

Leftover Levites

> **the big picture**
>
> **Joshua 21:1–42**
>
> The family heads of the Levites remind the leadership that God had previously determined that they should have towns and pasturelands within the borders of the other tribes. Each of the family units receives their allotments, including the six cities of refuge. All told, there were forty-eight towns with surrounding pastureland given to the Levites.

You'd never know from the way Levi began that he was destined to occupy a favored position in God's plan. Levi shared the <u>rebuke</u> of his father with Simeon for the cold-blooded murder of an entire town.

siding
Exodus 32:25–29

blessed
Deuteronomy
33:10–11

worship
Deuteronomy
10:8–9;
Numbers 1:50–51

gifts
Joshua 13:14

townships
Joshua 14:4

temple
Psalm 48

promise
Genesis 12:7

pledge
Exodus 3:17

commitment
Deuteronomy
11:24–25

reassurance
Joshua 1:5

foreknowledge
an awareness of
what is to come

Kohathite
Levites who are
priestly descendants
of Aaron

Babylonian exile
deportation to
Babylon in captivity,
605 BC, 597 BC,
and 586 BC

But unlike Simeon, whose tribe eventually faded into insignificance, the Levites later redeem themselves by <u>siding</u> with the Lord in spite of pressure from their peers to do otherwise. Consequently, they are <u>blessed</u> and given a special assignment in the service of the Lord. They do all the work involved in the <u>worship</u> of the Lord, from the transportation of the tabernacle, to the pronouncement of blessings upon the people. They are also to oversee the cities of refuge. So now, instead of a grant of land, they are

- to receive a portion of all the <u>gifts</u> brought to the Tent of Meeting
- to occupy <u>townships</u> within the territories of the other tribes, and
- to participate in a special way with God, who proclaimed himself to be their inheritance.

They were well provided for.

In God's prophetic **foreknowledge**, the **Kohathite** clan is strategically located near the future <u>temple</u> site (as yet undeclared), and also geographically preserved within the kingdom of Judah when the other tribes are scattered during the **Babylonian exile.**[17] In this way the worship of God would not be totally obliterated.

Word of Honor

JOSHUA 21:43–45 *So the LORD gave to Israel all the land of which He had sworn to give to their fathers, and they took possession of it and dwelt in it. The LORD gave them rest all around, according to all that He had sworn to their fathers. And not a man of all their enemies stood against them; the LORD delivered all their enemies into their hand. Not a word failed of any good thing which the LORD had spoken to the house of Israel. All came to pass.* (NKJV)

The last three verses are a glorious conclusion to the distribution and settlement of Canaan. God faithfully kept every oath, and not one word of all that he had sworn was left unfulfilled. From his first <u>promise</u> to Abraham and his continued <u>pledge</u> to the growing nation while they were still in bondage to Egypt, to his <u>commitment</u> at the time of the Israelite entrance into the land and his further <u>reassurance</u> to Joshua—*all* have been accomplished!

Arthur W. Pink

Herein is solid *comfort*. Human nature cannot be relied upon; but God can! However unstable I may be, however fickle my friends may prove, God changes not. If He varied as we do, if He willed one thing today and another tomorrow, if He were controlled by **caprice**, who could confide in Him? But all praise to His glorious name, He is ever the <u>same</u>. His purpose is fixed, His will is stable, His word is sure.[18]

Dr. John F. Walvoord

What is the greatest lesson I've learned? That God sustains us. In times of triumph, in times of sorrow, in times of achievement, in times of disappointment—our God is <u>faithful</u>.[19]

same
Hebrews 13:8

faithful
Lamentations 3:22–23

caprice
impulsive changes of mind

Establishing Accountability

JOSHUA 22:1–5 *Then Joshua called the Reubenites, the Gadites, and half the tribe of Manasseh, and said to them: "You have kept all that Moses the servant of the LORD commanded you, and have obeyed my voice in all that I commanded you. You have not left your brethren these many days, up to this day, but have kept the charge of the commandment of the LORD your God. And now the LORD your God has given rest to your brethren, as He promised them; now therefore, return and go to your tents and to the land of your possession, which Moses the servant of the LORD gave you on the other side of the Jordan. But take careful heed to do the commandment and the law which Moses the servant of the LORD commanded you, to love the LORD your God, to walk in all His ways, to keep His commandments, to hold fast to Him, and to serve Him with all your heart and with all your soul."* (NKJV)

The tribes east of the Jordan are dismissed with an excellent record of military service. As they leave, Joshua reminds them of the six most important fundamentals of their faith. They are to keep, to love, to walk, to obey, to hold, and to serve. Together these form the basis for a godly life; they speak of a wholehearted enthusiasm for the law as an expression of love and devotion to God. They describe a personal relationship rather than a formalized religion.

go to

abundant
John 10:10

hopeful
Jeremiah 29:11

guaranteed
Ephesians 1:3

Home Sweet Home

*JOSHUA **22:6–9** So Joshua blessed them and sent them away, and they went to their tents. Now to half the tribe of Manasseh Moses had given a possession in Bashan, but to the other half of it Joshua gave a possession among their brethren on this side of the Jordan, westward. And indeed, when Joshua sent them away to their tents, he blessed them, and spoke to them, saying, "Return with much riches to your tents, with very much livestock, with silver, with gold, with bronze, with iron, and with very much clothing. Divide the spoil of your enemies with your brethren." So the children of Reuben, the children of Gad, and half the tribe of Manasseh returned, and departed from the children of Israel at Shiloh, which is in the land of Canaan, to go to the country of Gilead, to the land of their possession, which they had obtained according to the word of the LORD by the hand of Moses. (NKJV)*

Joshua continues his address to the departing tribes by blessing them for their industry and fervor. His blessing includes bestowing material possessions, including livestock, precious metals, and clothing. Finally, the Reubenites, Gadites, and those from Manasseh who lived across the Jordan all took their leave.

apply it

A blessing in Scripture was more than just a wishful desire that another person would experience the best in life. Conferring a blessing was acting in God's behalf to secure the well-being of another. We know that God intends for our lives to be <u>abundant</u> and longs to assure us of a <u>hopeful</u> future. Thus the blessings that we offer family and friends today can be spoken encouragements, verbalizing what God has already <u>guaranteed</u> he will provide.

Misconstrued Messages

the big picture

Joshua 22:10–34

The three and a half tribes are dispatched to the other side of the river. When they come to Geliloth, they erect an imposing altar by the side of the river. Back in Shiloh, Israel prepares for war against them because of this atrocity, but first sends a delegation composed of Phineas the priest and one man from each of the other tribes.

They accuse their brothers east of the Jordan of breaking faith. They urge the tribes in question not to rebel against God, as the whole nation would suffer, but to join them on the other side to worship in unity.

Reuben, Gad, and half of Manasseh diffuse the concern by explaining that the altar was simply a replica to remind them of their common faith—not a place of worship where real offerings would be brought for sacrifice. The delegation is satisfied, and the members return to their homes in immense relief. The altar was named Witness, "for it is a witness between us that the LORD is God" (Joshua 22:34 NKJV).

The brothers east of the Jordan barely set foot on their own soil before they erect an altar. The larger group of their countrymen west of the Jordan are greatly alarmed. God has specifically declared that <u>sacrifices</u> should only be made at the Tent of Meeting, currently in Shiloh. To them this is an act of treachery, just as evil as the reproachful behavior of <u>Achan</u>. Remembering that occasion, they are well aware that the sin of one is the sin of <u>all</u>. If indeed the three and one-half tribes are violating the rules of worship, according to God's written <u>Word</u>, the remaining congregation is to cut them off and cut them down.

But they approach the situation at hand with care and tact. First, they form an investigating committee composed of spiritual leaders. Next, they arrange an opportunity to talk to those concerned face-to-face. In the interview they candidly express their uneasiness while keeping open the door of **restitution**.

The passionate reply of the east Jordanites conveys their agitation and concern.[20] They call on a combination of the names of the Lord: El, Elohim, and Jehovah, to deny the charge.[21] Their intent was simply to provide a visual reminder of the faith they held in common with their countrymen on the other side of the river.

The explanation is accepted, the leaders are satisfied, and the altar remains. Instead of a civil war destroying the nation, the misunderstanding has been corrected and peace has been maintained.

The method with which one group of Israelites dealt with a problem that arose between them and another group of Israelites is a good illustration to us. When we become aware of another believer who seems to be heading along a path that does not correspond with the teachings of God's Word, we dare not ignore their indiscretion,

go to

sacrifices
Leviticus 17:8–9

Achan
Joshua 7:1

all
Joshua 22:20

Word
Deuteronomy 13:12–15

restitution
making things right

apply it

go to

rebuke
Galatians 6:1;
Matthew 18:15

restoration
returning something
to its former condi-
tion

for it may reflect upon the name of Christ. Neither should we accost them in our outrage and buttonhole them to the wall. A gentle <u>rebuke</u> in private with the object of **restoration** is the place to start.

Chapter Wrap-Up

- Joshua's last assignment is the distribution of the newly conquered lands to each tribe. Caleb claims what was promised to him by Moses. (Joshua 13:1–14:15)

- The allotment starts with Judah, then Ephraim and Manasseh. But the rest need to be encouraged to survey the land so that it can be apportioned and settled. (Joshua 15:1–18:10)

- Benjamin, Simeon, Zebulun, Issachar, Asher, Naphtali, and Dan receive their portions, but Levi is given townships within the territories of the others. Six cities of refuge are established. (Joshua 18:11–21:45)

- The three and one-half tribes return home, only to be confronted by their brethren about an altar they fear will bring God's wrath. Their fears are allayed and the altar remains. (Joshua 22:1–34)

Study Questions

1. What did Caleb do that was worthy of acknowledgment? How did he accomplish what others could not?

2. What was the real issue when Ephraim and Manasseh complained about not having enough land?

3. How did God measure up when all the promises he'd made were considered?

4. Following the Israelite's example, what should a person do when they observe a brother or a sister involved in something questionable?

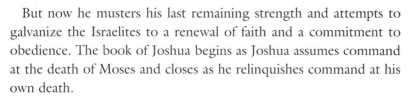

Joshua 23–24
Joshua's Farewell

Chapter Highlights:
- Final Sermon
- Thorns in Their Eyes
- A Word to the Wise
- Rekindled Pledge
- Laid to Rest

Let's Get Started

Old age sometimes brings more than gray hair or a slight stoop. There can be escalating pain, decreasing agility, and a gradual loss of the faculties that were once so sharp. Joshua's <u>age</u> first started telling on him some ten or twenty years previously, during the apportionment of the land of Israel to the twelve tribes.[1] During the intervening years, he watches as the children Israel, content to live side by side with their profane neighbors, slip into an increasing state of complacency and compromise.

age
Joshua 13:1

But now he musters his last remaining strength and attempts to galvanize the Israelites to a renewal of faith and a commitment to obedience. The book of Joshua begins as Joshua assumes command at the death of Moses and closes as he relinquishes command at his own death.

Final Sermon

JOSHUA 23:1–5 Now it came to pass, a long time after the LORD had given rest to Israel from all their enemies round about, that Joshua was old, advanced in age. And Joshua called for all Israel, for their elders, for their heads, for their judges, and for their officers, and said to them: "I am old, advanced in age. You have seen all that the LORD your God has done to all these nations because of you, for the LORD your God is He who has fought for you. See, I have divided to you by lot these nations that remain, to be an inheritance for your tribes, from the Jordan, with all the nations that I have cut off, as far as the Great Sea westward. And the LORD your God will expel them from before you and drive them out of your sight. So you shall possess their land, as the LORD your God promised you. (NKJV)

Joshua calls all Israel, but particularly the leadership, to hear a final message outlining the most significant topics within Israel that still need to be addressed. He reminds them that the Lord is the one

go to

offer
Joshua 1:4

claim
John 16:24

Isaac's
Genesis 27:1–29

Jacob's
Genesis 49:1–28

Moses's
Deuteronomy
31:14–22

received
Joshua 1:7, 9

passed
Joshua 10:25

who fought for them that they might obtain the inheritance currently in their possession.

But the Lord desires to continue the warfare on their behalf, so that the entire region he originally promised them would be under their control. Fact: God's original <u>offer</u> to Israel included approximately 300,000 square miles, but Israel never claimed more than 30,000.[2]

In the spiritual realm, we often do not take the trouble to <u>claim</u> and possess what is rightfully ours.

As a last opportunity for an individual to communicate with those he loves, deathbed speeches have characteristically been quite significant in the Bible. Sometimes they were filled with blessings—as <u>Isaac's</u> was to Jacob (who pretended to be Esau); sometimes they are prophetic—as <u>Jacob's</u> was to his twelve sons; and sometimes they are filled with warnings—as <u>Moses's</u> was to the nation of Israel. Whatever their contents, such messages were usually considered the most important information the dying party could give the ones left behind.

Straight as an Arrow

> JOSHUA **23:6–8** *Therefore be very courageous to keep and to do all that is written in the Book of the Law of Moses, lest you turn aside from it to the right hand or to the left, and lest you go among these nations, these who remain among you. You shall not make mention of the name of their gods, nor cause anyone to swear by them; you shall not serve them nor bow down to them, but you shall hold fast to the LORD your God, as you have done to this day. (NKJV)*

Joshua's message begins with the same encouragement he has <u>received</u> and <u>passed</u> on several times before. He is acutely aware that to consistently follow God's law will take just as much strength as conquering any foe in battle. He does not command. Rather he implores Israel in the areas he recognizes as their particular weak spots. Who better to know them than the one who led and lived among them all his life. He pleads with them . . .

1. Not to deviate from the instructions of God. In his Word they would find not only directives to follow and values to adopt, but God himself.

2. Not to mingle with godless people. He is not against interracial associations, but the mixing of religious practices and standards of morality would be inevitable as they merged.

3. Not to acknowledge alternate deities. Even to allow the names of other gods to pass over their lips is <u>forbidden</u>, because to mention them is to recognize them.

But not only should they shrink from any association with the pagan world around them, they need to expand their dependence on God. Holding fast to God means to "stick" or desperately "cling" to him as if there is no other option for survival.

Our spiritual mentors can help us to identify our weak spots, that we might conquer them before they conquer us.

go to

forbidden
Exodus 23:13

vineyard
John 15:1–6

cleaving
clinging closely

apply it

what others say

Tim LaHaye

Through the years I have watched thousands of Christians, some brilliant, others average, some with college backgrounds, others were scarcely educated, some had gone to Bible college and most did not. From each of those groups I have seen some remain continual babies while others grew strong in the Lord. The only thing they had in common was not their . . . education but whether they developed the habit of daily feeding their mind on the Word of God.[3]

Kay Arthur

Sometimes I find myself shuddering as I watch "Christian" television. I shudder because I know that thousands of untaught Christians are lapping up teachings which are simply not biblical. Yet they don't know better because they don't know God's Word! And they will *never* know it in its purity and authority and true transforming power until they study it for themselves.[4]

"Holding fast" or "**cleaving** to the Lord" in the Old Testament is the same principle as "abiding in Christ" in the New Testament. With this concept comes the whole picture of a <u>vineyard</u> in which

something to ponder

words
Joshua 1:5

failed
Joshua 7:4–5;
9:14–15

owed
Deuteronomy
6:10–12

omnipotence
all-encompassing
power

Christ is the vine and we are the branches. We cannot grow, flourish, or produce fruit unless we derive life-giving sustenance from the main vine. To detach is to wither and die.

Immense Muscle of Almighty

JOSHUA 23:9–11 *For the LORD has driven out from before you great and strong nations; but as for you, no one has been able to stand against you to this day. One man of you shall chase a thousand, for the LORD your God is He who fights for you, as He promised you. Therefore take careful heed to yourselves, that you love the LORD your God. (NKJV)*

That no one had been able to stand against the Israelite army was in direct fulfillment of God's <u>words</u> to Joshua at the beginning of his career. This display of power was so miraculous it had to be from God. If the Israelites were ever tempted to think it was their own prowess that had won the victory, all they needed to do was recall the times they had tried to do it on their own and abysmally <u>failed</u>. Thus it was for good reason Joshua concluded this recitation of God's **omnipotence** with a reminder to love God. They <u>owed</u> it all to him.

---

what others say

A. W. Tozer

What comes into our minds when we think about God is the most important thing about us. The history of mankind will probably show that no people has ever risen above its religion, and man's spiritual history will positively demonstrate that no religion has ever been greater than its idea of God . . . We tend by secret law of the soul to move toward our mental image of God.[5]

Thorns in Their Eyes

JOSHUA 23:12–13 *Or else, if indeed you do go back, and cling to the remnant of these nations—these that remain among you—and make marriages with them, and go in to them and they to you, know for certain that the LORD your God will no longer drive out these nations from before you. But they shall be snares and traps to you, and scourges on your sides and thorns in your eyes, until you perish from this good land which the LORD your God has given you. (NKJV)*

Just as Joshua had urged the Israelites to "cling" to God, now he begs them (using the same term in the original) *not* to "cling" to the Canaanites. He knows they cannot handle the pressures of **compromise** that mixed marriages introduce. Joshua's metaphors, comparing the infiltrating nations to thorns and snares, are not original with him. He is quoting the words of God through Moses.

go to

cling
Joshua 23:8

thorns
Numbers 33:55

snares
Exodus 23:33

curses
Leviticus 26:14–33

turn
Judges 2:10–13

compromise
exposure to danger and disgrace

credence
believability

what others say

Dewey Bertolini

A lot of people might feel differently about demanding their rights to live any way they please if they had to spend their time like I do—picking up the pieces. In my counseling ministry I have had to learn a very painful lesson . . . Sometimes the scars of rebellion last a lifetime. Sometimes the consequences of our disobedience may be eternal. The words, "And they lived happily ever after," do not always apply.[6]

A Word to the Wise

JOSHUA 23:14–16 *"Behold, this day I am going the way of all the earth. And you know in all your hearts and in all your souls that not one thing has failed of all the good things which the LORD your God spoke concerning you. All have come to pass for you; not one word of them has failed. Therefore it shall come to pass, that as all the good things have come upon you which the LORD your God promised you, so the LORD will bring upon you all harmful things, until He has destroyed you from this good land which the LORD your God has given you. When you have transgressed the covenant of the LORD your God, which He commanded you, and have gone and served other gods, and bowed down to them, then the anger of the LORD will burn against you, and you shall perish quickly from the good land which He has given you." (NKJV)*

The curses for violating the covenant are likewise drawn from previous writings, adding **credence** to Joshua's earnest warnings. In spite of his eloquence on the subject, the children of Israel would begin their turn from God in the very next generation, and his final predictions would come to pass eight hundred years later when the

go to

exile
2 Kings 24:10–25:21

defeat
Joshua 23:13

trapped
Joshua 23:13

disgrace
Joshua 23:15–16

obey
Joshua 23:6

separate
Joshua 23:7, 12

devote
Joshua 23:8, 11

carte blanche
permission to act
with total authority

apostasy
leaving the faith

nation was sent into <u>exile</u> under Babylonian rule.[7] Undergirding the harshness of impending destruction, however, is the unrelenting faithfulness of a God whose longing is to remain true to the promises of blessing and not to have to carry out the threats of discipline.

In this passage, Joshua outlines three results of **apostasy** and three safeguards against it. What happens when we turn our backs on what we know to be true?

1. We no longer experience victory; instead, we face <u>defeat</u>.

2. We become <u>trapped</u> by the very things we desire.

3. We make ourselves the objects of <u>disgrace</u> and destruction.

What can we do to escape these ends?

1. <u>Obey</u> God's Word.

2. <u>Separate</u> from the things that would bring us down.

3. <u>Devote</u> ourselves to God alone.

Rekindled Pledge

JOSHUA 24:1–4 *Then Joshua gathered all the tribes of Israel to Shechem and called for the elders of Israel, for their heads, for their judges, and for their officers; and they presented themselves before God. And Joshua said to all the people, "Thus says the LORD God of Israel: 'Your fathers, including Terah, the father of Abraham and the father of Nahor, dwelt on the other side of the River in old times; and they served other gods. Then I took your father Abraham from the other side of the River, led him throughout all the land of Canaan, and multiplied his descendants and gave him Isaac. To Isaac I gave Jacob and Esau. To Esau I gave the mountains of Seir to possess, but Jacob and his children went down to Egypt. (NKJV)*

At Shechem, a site of great spiritual significance, Joshua calls the leaders and the people together for the second installment of his final sermon. He begins the narrative from the beginning, when Abraham first heard the summons of God. Israel could trace its family roots back to the city of <u>Ur</u> beyond the river Euphrates. Now we find *why* it was important to remove Abraham from his point of origin. God wanted to detach him from the idolatrous worship of a plurality of fruitless gods and give him the privilege of depending entirely upon himself, the one true God.

Nahor is the second of **Terah**'s three sons to be mentioned here and the grandfather of Rebekah, who became Isaac's wife when Abraham sent his servant back to find a match for his son from among his own people. He traces the genealogy all the way to Jacob's sons, who were the founders of each of the family tribal units in Israel.

Abraham's descendants were granted the land of Canaan as a gift from God, but detoured in Egypt before obtaining the whole thing from the hand of God in battle.

Archaeological excavations at Shechem have uncovered **standing stones** and places of worship from almost every period of its existence.[9] It is a site with an ancient tradition of religious significance. Also recorded in the Bible are the following meaningful encounters:

1. God first presented the land to Abraham on this spot. (Genesis 12:6)

2. In this location, Jacob sets up an altar. (Genesis 33:18–20)

3. Joshua placed the law on plastered stones here. (Joshua 8:30–32)

4. It was in Shechem's vicinity that the Word of the Lord was read. (Joshua 8:33–35)

Ur
Genesis 11:31

Terah
father of Abraham

standing stones
a configuration of ceremonially placed stones

go to

blood
Exodus 7:19–21

scourge
Exodus 8:5–6

darkness
Exodus 10:21–23

sons
Exodus 12:29–30

plundered
Exodus 12:35–36

Nile
the only consistent
source of water in
Egypt

scourge
an agent of
punishment

pharaoh
highest ruler in
Egypt

Egypt's Embarrassing End

JOSHUA 24:5–7 *Also I sent Moses and Aaron, and I plagued Egypt, according to what I did among them. Afterward I brought you out. 'Then I brought your fathers out of Egypt, and you came to the sea; and the Egyptians pursued your fathers with chariots and horsemen to the Red Sea. So they cried out to the LORD; and He put darkness between you and the Egyptians, brought the sea upon them, and covered them. And your eyes saw what I did in Egypt. Then you dwelt in the wilderness a long time.* (NKJV)

Aaron and Moses were sent by God to bring the children of Israel out of Egypt. But they did not tiptoe quietly away. God brought about a miraculous deliverance, that even this generation could witness as they observed the hands-off policy of the country that had enslaved their parents before their demoralizing defeat.

By the time God was finished with the Egyptians, he had exposed a myriad of their false gods by causing a specific plague to fall relating to each one. For example: they worshipped the life-giving **Nile**, so God turned the water into <u>blood</u>; they worshipped frogs, so God caused the frogs to become a **scourge**; they worshipped the sun, so God brought such total <u>darkness</u> to the land that it could be felt. All in all, they experienced ten such plagues. The final one affected the highest god of them all—the **pharaoh** himself. All the firstborn <u>sons</u> were killed, including Pharaoh's heir. At last they pleaded with the Israelites to leave them alone.

But God was not through teaching Egypt a lesson. He saw to it that the people of this rich and opulent country showered their prosperity upon the Israelites as they took their leave. The Bible says that Israel completely <u>plundered</u> them.

Finally, God made sure that the mighty military force of their oppressing nation was <u>obliterated</u> in one **fell** swoop. After the children of Israel crossed the Red Sea in safety, God brought the waters crashing back upon Pharaoh's horses, charioteers, and armed troops. Not one person survived.

<u>Blessings from Curses</u>

JOSHUA 24:8–10 *And I brought you into the land of the Amorites, who dwelt on the other side of the Jordan, and they fought with you. But I gave them into your hand, that you might possess their land, and I destroyed them from before you. Then Balak the son of Zippor, king of Moab, arose to make war against Israel, and sent and called Balaam the son of Beor to curse you. But I would not listen to Balaam; therefore he continued to bless you. So I delivered you out of his hand. (NKJV)*

In this section of verses, through Joshua, God is reminding the Israelites about his care for them even when they were suffering the consequences of their own rebellion. By the time they confronted the Amorites and faced Balak, king of <u>Moab</u>, they had already been to the border of the Promised Land, refused to enter, and had been <u>cursed</u> by God to die in the desert.

In spite of this, God continued to show his loving-kindness to the nation he had chosen. He destroyed the <u>Amorites</u> and caused Baalam to repeatedly <u>bless</u> Israel rather than cursing them. God turned this dark time in Israel's history into a testimony of his love and compassion, in spite of their insubordination and alienation.

go to

obliterated
Exodus 14:8–28

Moab
Numbers 22:2–3

cursed
Numbers 14:32–35

Amorites
Numbers 21:25

bless
Numbers 24:10

looks beyond
Romans 5:8;
1 Timothy 1:15

fell
capable of killing

accrue
gather a substantial amount

what others say

Stanley E. Ellison

We naturally ask what God's purpose is in showing long-suffering to sinners. Negatively, it should be noted that its purpose is not to compromise with sin as allowing some kind of "indulgence." It is not some kind of emotional sympathy which wells up in God and makes his wrath capitulate in the face of human sorrow. God does not overlook sin, but rather <u>looks beyond</u> it. He looks beyond to the greater results and benefits which will **accrue** through his further work.[11]

go to

hornet
Exodus 23:27–28

everything
Psalm 44:1–3

people of God
Deuteronomy 7:6

Lord
John 15:5;
James 1:17

consistent
Revelation 2:5

Sting of the Hornet

JOSHUA 24:11–13 *Then you went over the Jordan and came to Jericho. And the men of Jericho fought against you—also the Amorites, the Perizzites, the Canaanites, the Hittites, the Girgashites, the Hivites, and the Jebusites. But I delivered them into your hand. I sent the hornet before you which drove them out from before you, also the two kings of the Amorites, but not with your sword or with your bow. I have given you a land for which you did not labor, and cities which you did not build, and you dwell in them; you eat of the vineyards and olive groves which you did not plant.' (NKJV)*

Now that Israel has crossed over the Jordan, God lists for them the people groups he delivered through warfare into their hands. The <u>hornet</u> that went before them is symbolic of the presence of God that put their terrified enemies to flight.

References to God occur seventeen times in verses 3 through 13, stating all the things God has done for them. Some examples: "I took," "I gave," "I sent," "I brought out," "I brought in," "I destroyed," and "I delivered." <u>Everything</u> that they had—any progress, any growth, or any advance—was because of the Lord. Reviewing where they had come from and relating it to where they are is Joshua's attempt to focus their attention upon a truth that he wished would impact every action of their lives—they had been brought out of idolatry for the sole purpose of becoming the <u>people of God</u>.

Any gifts, any power, and any deliverance I have are from the <u>Lord</u>.

apply it

Recalling what God has done in our lives can encourage us to a more <u>consistent</u> and focused walk.

Eeny, Meeny, Miney, Moe . . .

JOSHUA 24:14–15 *"Now therefore, fear the LORD, serve Him in sincerity and in truth, and put away the gods which your fathers served on the other side of the River and in Egypt. Serve the LORD! And if it seems evil to you to serve the LORD, choose for yourselves this day whom you will serve, whether the gods which your fathers served that were on the other side of the River, or the gods of the Amorites, in whose land you dwell. But as for me and my house, we will serve the LORD." (NKJV)*

Like any good preacher, Joshua doesn't simply restate God's Word. He brings his listeners to the point of commitment, that they might respond and receive the blessing. Regardless of the direction Israel would decide to take, however, Joshua and his family have already determined their own course.

The question he presents for their consideration is both **rhetorical** and open-ended, for there is only one rational answer. Would they choose to side with God, or would they opt for any of the innumerable idol-type gods in the land? After taking into account all that he had done, God deserves no less than complete and absolute commitment. But it was still up to them to decide.

go to

choose
Proverbs 1:28–30

response
Romans 5:8, 12:1;
1 John 4:19

rhetorical
a question with an obvious answer

> **what others say**
>
> **R. Kent Hughes**
>
> The Bible represents us as we are, made in the image of God. We are not robots. We are not helplessly subject to the cause and effect arrangements of life . . . Adam chose wrongly. Abraham chose rightly. And we, like the Israelites, can <u>choose</u> either way.[12]
>
> **Corrie ten Boom**
>
> God is voting for us all the time. The devil is voting against us all the time. The way we vote carries the election . . . Yes, Lord, I . . . choose to be yours.[13]

We need to choose what will control us—God or an imperfect substitute.

Our decisions should not be determined by what others around us are doing.

Loving and serving God is the only sensible <u>response</u> to his unswerving devotion and generosity toward us.

No Turning Back

> **the big picture**
>
> **Joshua 24:16–24**
>
> The people respond affirmatively to Joshua's challenge, vowing their intention to serve the Lord for all the good things he has

go to

gift
Romans 6:23

saying no
Matthew 16:24

desire
Romans 7:18–19,
24–25

Joshua 24:16-24

The people respond affirmatively to Joshua's challenge, vowing their intention to serve the Lord for all the good things he has done. But Joshua tells them he doesn't think they can serve a jealous and holy God. He warns them of the consequences of forsaking God midstream, but the Israelites claim they will not. Joshua asks them to serve as witnesses against themselves, and tells them to throw away the foreign gods they've already acquired.

Easily swayed, the Israelites are ready to submit in an instant to the Lord. But Joshua wants their response to be more than a superficial reaction to the emotion of the moment. It will mean an immediate change of lifestyle. They have already begun to collect an assortment of idols, and as long as they hang on to these, God cannot accept their flighty promises.

Joshua wonders if it is even possible for them to serve God at all. He asks them to witness against themselves—meaning, they must take responsibility for their own actions. And he gives them an opportunity to prove they mean what they say. They must get rid of their false gods.

J. B. Phillips

Man has rightly been defined as a "worshipping animal." If . . . he has no God he will unquestionably worship *some-thing*. Common modern substitutes are the following: the State, success, efficiency, money, "glamour," power, even security. Nobody, of course, calls them "God"; but they have the influence and command the devotion which should belong to the real God.[14]

Although responding to God's free <u>gift</u> of salvation seems an easy choice, we must remember that it demands <u>saying no</u> to our own desires every day. It is a blessed contradiction that even with a whole-hearted <u>desire</u> to please the Lord, we have not the strength nor determination to do so without his help.

As the Israelites were oblivious to the sin of idolatry in their lives, we too can carry on for some time without an awareness of the existence of sin in our own lives. Our idols—greed, wrong priorities, addictive behavior, jealousy, and selfishness—are composed of anything that gets in the way of our true worship of God.

Often the only way to wake up to the danger involved in practicing these things is to take them to their farthest logical conclusion. For the Israelites, it was not simply retaining a couple of little idols for good luck. It would come to mean the wholesale betrayal of a godly lifestyle for one of immorality. The act of nurturing a little <u>lust</u> is as bad as committing adultery, and the fostering of a little <u>hate</u> is comparable to murder.

Unchecked sin <u>declines</u> swiftly to an undesirable and ghastly end. We who have been <u>delivered</u> need to live above the **ignoble** deeds from which we were saved.

Reminiscent Relics

JOSHUA 24:25–27 *So Joshua made a covenant with the people that day, and made for them a statute and an ordinance in Shechem.*

Then Joshua wrote these words in the Book of the Law of God. And he took a large stone, and set it up there under the oak that was by the sanctuary of the LORD. And Joshua said to all the people, "Behold, this stone shall be a witness to us, for it has heard all the words of the LORD which He spoke to us. It shall therefore be a witness to you, lest you deny your God." (NKJV)

The covenant is sealed by the act of recording the contract in the Book of the Law. This expands the canon of Scripture beyond the first five books to include the now almost completed book of Joshua. Next, a large stone is erected to be an unspoken witness of the steadfast devotion and allegiance that were sworn in this place.

The history of Israel over the previous twenty-five years could be read upon the stones. There were twin <u>piles</u> in the Jordan River and near its banks at Gilgal to commemorate the notable crossing. Mounded over the bodies of Achan and his family was a rock <u>monument</u> to recall the influence of one small sin. A similar <u>stack</u> of stones was left over the deceased king of Ai, a reminder of the folly of opposing Almighty God. There were plastered <u>stones</u> with the commandments inscribed at Ebal and Gerizim, and now a large stone was placed under the oak at Shechem to celebrate their recent commitment.

go to

lust
Matthew 5:28

hate
Matthew 5:21–22

declines
James 1:15

delivered
2 Peter 2:20

piles
Joshua 4:8–9

monument
Joshua 7:26

stack
Joshua 8:29

stones
Joshua 8:32

ignoble
dishonorable

something to ponder

Laid to Rest

JOSHUA 24:28–31 *So Joshua let the people depart, each to his own inheritance.*

Now it came to pass after these things that Joshua the son of Nun, the servant of the LORD, died, being one hundred and ten years old. And they buried him within the border of his inheritance at Timnath Serah, which is in the mountains of Ephraim, on the north side of Mount Gaash. Israel served the LORD all the days of Joshua, and all the days of the elders who outlived Joshua, who had known all the works of the LORD which He had done for Israel. (NKJV)

The fact that each person was dismissed to his own inheritance is a "happy-ever-after" ending that carries the legacy theme from start to finish. Joshua has finally attained the full stature of Moses and is called (like his predecessor) the "servant of the LORD." This also provides another avenue to bring the book full circle.

Joshua's long and meaningful life has finally come to an end. One of the most significant accolades that could be awarded to an individual is conferred in the revelation that as long as Joshua's influence remained, the whole nation served the Lord. He was the model for their spiritual walk, and they emulated his example. He continues to shine throughout history as an exceptional leader and an exemplary mentor.

what others say

Stuart Briscoe

It's the "*ad infinitum*" idea of disciples making disciples which so intrigues me and which causes me to challenge you now. Take a good, hard look at your own learning-following-imitating discipleship. Then ask yourself who the people are around you whose lives are being so impacted by you that they too are about to begin, have just begun, or are faithfully following the discipleship road . . . Because . . . when the principle works, it is close to perpetual motion; but when some individual misses an assignment, the system is severely affected and the job the Master bequeathed to us does not get done.[15]

Pushing up Daisies

Eleazar
Joshua 14:1; 19:51

Joseph
Genesis 41:41–44

carried
Exodus 13:19

request
Genesis 50:25

faithfulness
Deuteronomy 7:9

delivering
Hebrews 6:9;
1 Peter 4:19

JOSHUA **24:32–33** *The bones of Joseph, which the children of Israel had brought up out of Egypt, they buried at* **Shechem**, *in the plot of ground which Jacob had bought from the sons of* **Hamor** *the father of* **Shechem** *for one hundred pieces of silver, and which had become an inheritance of the children of Joseph. And Eleazar the son of Aaron died. They buried him in a hill belonging to Phinehas his son, which was given to him in the mountains of Ephraim.* (NKJV)

Mention is made of two other prominent leaders who were buried: Eleazar, the high priest, and Joseph, the patriarch. Eleazar was the religious leader who figured most prominently in the land distribution. Joseph (one of the original twelve brothers who became next in command to a pharaoh) died while still in Egypt. His bones had been carried from Egypt in response to his personal request to be buried in the Land of Promise. Now that his wish is fulfilled, another theme is confirmed at the close of this era—the continued faithfulness of God.

Shechem
a central city, set between Mount Ebal and Gerizim

Hamor
the Hivite prince of Shechem during Jacob's time

Shechem
son of Hamor, seducer of Dinah, Jacob's daughter

repose
peacefully rest

exercised
repeatedly performing

what others say

George Mueller

Through reading of the word of God . . . the believer becomes more and more acquainted with the nature and character of God, and thus sees more and more . . . what a kind, loving, gracious, merciful, mighty, wise, and faithful Being He is, and, therefore . . . he will **repose** upon the *ability* of God to help him, because he has . . . seen instance upon instance in the Holy Scriptures in which His almighty power and infinite wisdom have been actually **exercised** in helping and delivering His people.[16]

Chapter Wrap-Up

- Joshua reminds Israel of past blessings and warns them of future consequences. (Joshua 23:1–16)
- Joshua reviews Israel's history from conception to the time of his death. (Joshua 24:1–13)
- Joshua encourages the people to make a commitment. (Joshua 24:14–27)
- Eleazar, Joseph, and Joshua are laid to rest. (Joshua 24:28–33)

Study Questions

1. What is a good New Testament picture of the principle of "holding fast" or "clinging" to God?

2. What are three results of apostasy as mentioned by Joshua, and what are the three safeguards against it?

3. Why did Joshua review all of Israel's history with them?

4. What action did the Israelites need to take in the affirmation of their covenant? Why?

Section Two
JUDGES

Introduction to the Book of Judges

What Is the Book of Judges About?

If the book of Joshua was all about achieving victory through obedience, then Judges is the account of failure through compromise. Judges follows the downward spiral of the nation of Israel through repeated cycles of apostasy and defeat. Few books of the Bible show **depravity** in all its perversity and corruption as does the book of Judges. God was forced to chasten Israel over and over by allowing their adversaries to harass, oppress, and even enslave them.

But as soon as Israel would repent and cry out for deliverance, God would send them a "judge" (*shopet* in the original) to bring them aid.[1] Different from the men and women of our day appointed to interpret law and administer justice in the courtroom, these judges were people raised up and empowered by God to meet specific crises in Israel's history. There were fourteen judges in all (twelve of whom are described in this book) bridging the gap between Joshua's leadership and that of Israel's kings.

Not one was a national leader who appealed to the whole country like Moses or Joshua, and most were limited in their capabilities, often possessing major defects or handicaps. Yet in spite of their personal weaknesses, God used these individuals to demonstrate his compassion and rescue his wayward people, time and again.

When Did the Judges Rule?

The most likely dates during which the judges would have offered periods of relief in the midst of the ongoing domination of other countries would have been 1380 BC through 1043 BC.[2] During this time, Tutankhamun, Rameses II, and Rameses III were reigning from Egypt; the **Phoenicians** were becoming a dominant trading power in the Mediterranean; silk fabrics were being created in China; a Hittite library was accruing tablets in eight different languages; and the city of **Troy** was at its sixth level as described in the *Iliad*.[3] This time period would have spanned approximately 325 years.[4] Viewed

depravity
state of moral corruption

shopet
magistrate

Phoenicians
citizens of a country on the coastal plain of Syria, known for shipbuilding and trade

Troy
port city in northwestern Asia Minor

Iliad
ancient Greek epic poem

go to

monarchy
Judges 17:6

Jebusites
Judges 1:21

Gezer
Judges 1:29

David
2 Samuel 5:6–9

Solomon
1 Kings 9:16–17

scribe
1 Samuel 10:25

Jebusites
pre-Davidic inhabitants of Jerusalem

Gezer
a city bordering the Philistine plain and controlling the highway from Egypt to Syria

David
second king of Israel

Solomon
third king and David's son

grace
undeserved display of mercy

repentant
turning away from sin

consecutively, the composite history of the judges would have taken more than 410 years, but as it was, they could rule concurrently in different parts of the land and their leadership at times would overlap.

Who Wrote Judges?

The author is unknown, but many suggest that it could have been Samuel, the very last of all the judges. The following are a few reasons why he is a likely candidate:

1. The author presupposes that there will eventually be a <u>monarchy</u>, so it would make sense that he would have been present during the transition from the rule of the judges to the rule of the kings. Samuel would qualify.

2. At the time of writing, the **Jebusites** were still in Jerusalem and **Gezer** was not an Israelite city. Later, **David** would capture Jerusalem once and for all, and Pharaoh would give Gezer to **Solomon** as a wedding present, so the book of Judges was probably written *after* the transition was made from the rule of judges to that of kings, but *before* David's victory over the Jebusites and Solmon's marriage to Pharaoh's daughter.

3. Samuel was raised in temple service and could do the work of a <u>scribe</u>, among other things. Writing would be natural for him.

4. The Talmud identifies Samuel as the author.[5]

What Is the Theme of Judges?

Judges is the portrait of a nation in decline. We watch as the Israelites abandon their mission to adopt the lifestyles of their contemporaries. When this happens, they forsake their faith and their whole system of government breaks down. They become the victims of the predatory nations around them. So the first theme would relate to the slippery slope of sin.

Meanwhile, God displays the magnificence of his **grace** in receiving and restoring the whole nation back to himself whenever his people turn to him. So the other major issue in the book of Judges concerns God's faithful mercy and lovingkindness to the **repentant** soul.

Judges 1:1–2:15
Leaderless Without Joshua

Chapter Highlights:
- **Triumphs They Have Known**
- **Capitulation and Failure**
- **Angelic Confrontation**
- **Disenfranchised Generation**

Let's Get Started

The book of Joshua begins with the words, "After the death of Moses . . . ," and the book of Judges follows suit. Only this time Joshua has died, and there is *no one* to take over the reins of command in his place.

This vacuum in leadership should prompt the Israelites to make God their supreme head and go directly to him for guidance and encouragement. This they do—at the start. But, as always, the way people end is far more significant than how they begin. At the launching of this chapter, some of the tribes ambitiously take up the conquest where the nation left off. But then they seem to hit a snag. What is holding them back?

cities
Joshua 19:9

Triumphs They Have Known

> **JUDGES 1:1–3** *Now after the death of Joshua it came to pass that the children of Israel asked the LORD, saying, "Who shall be first to go up for us against the Canaanites to fight against them?" And the LORD said, "Judah shall go up. Indeed I have delivered the land into his hand." So Judah said to Simeon his brother, "Come up with me to my allotted territory, that we may fight against the Canaanites; and I will likewise go with you to your allotted territory." And Simeon went with him.* (NKJV)

Because substantial pockets of resistance remain within the borders of the lands allocated to each tribe, there is work to be done before full occupation can take place. That Simeon and Judah would fight together is only logical; the <u>cities</u> offered to Simeon were located within the land already belonging to Judah. Again, God refers to the deliverance of the land as an accomplished fact. This assurance of success ought to serve as a motivating factor.

go to

Judah
Genesis 49:8–12

marching
Numbers 2:9

inheritance
Joshua 15

retaliation
Judges 20:18

Adoni-Bezek
a petty king whose name literally means "lord of Bezek"

Adoni-Bezek
cruelly cut off the thumbs and toes of seventy of his defeated contemporaries, and now when he is captured his enemies do the same thing to him

Bezek
a Canaanite town in Judah near Gezer

what others say

LeRoy Eims

The fellowship of believers is not only a matter of holding each other up, or becoming part of each other through care and concern and prayer. In addition to those things, each of us has a work to do, a job to perform, a task to accomplish. And until we give ourselves to that task, the whole body is out of kilter. Not one of us is unimportant. We all need to roll up our sleeves and pitch in with our whole heart.[1]

When Jacob blessed each of his twelve sons before his death, he indicated that Judah would be dominant and take a superior place. Years later, when it came time to begin the trek across the desert to the Promised Land, Judah set out first in the marching order. His was the first tribe to receive an inheritance, and later Judah would take the initiative in the retaliation against Benjamin for harboring wicked men. But now, Judah sets the example for the other tribes by being the first to take up arms and fight the Canaanites within the borders of their allotted land.

Thumbs and Toes

JUDGES 1:4–7 Then Judah went up, and the LORD delivered the Canaanites and the Perizzites into their hand; and they killed ten thousand men at Bezek. And they found **Adoni-Bezek** in Bezek, and fought against him; and they defeated the Canaanites and the Perizzites. Then **Adoni-Bezek** fled, and they pursued him and caught him and cut off his thumbs and big toes. And Adoni-Bezek said, "Seventy kings with their thumbs and big toes cut off used to gather scraps under my table; as I have done, so God has repaid me." Then they brought him to Jerusalem, and there he died. (NKJV)

Indeed, Judah and Simeon experience several victories. A case in point being their triumph over ten thousand men at **Bezek** and the capture of their monarch.

The action next taken was for the purpose of totally incapacitating a man for future service as a warrior. Removing his thumbs would completely hamper his effective use of a weapon, and taking off his big toes would keep him from ever again establishing a reliable stance in battle. God does not endorse this act of **retributive** justice, but the captive himself acknowledges that he deserves no better treatment.

Warm-Up Notes

JUDGES 1:8–10 *Now the children of Judah fought against Jerusalem and took it; they struck it with the edge of the sword and set the city on fire. And afterward the children of Judah went down to fight against the Canaanites who dwelt in the mountains, in the South, and in the lowland. Then Judah went against the Canaanites who dwelt in Hebron. (Now the name of Hebron was formerly Kirjath Arba.) And they killed Sheshai, Ahiman, and Talmai.* (NKJV)

Judah captures Jerusalem but does not maintain <u>control</u> for long. Later in Judges, Jerusalem is even regarded as a <u>foreign</u> city.

But in most of its initial efforts, Judah is successful. They subdue the central hills, the southern deserts, and the foothills leading toward the coast. This account of the early battles fought in the new land, serving as a prelude for the actual concert of events that will follow in the book, fluctuates back and forth between the present and some of the achievements already attained under Joshua. Like a repeating chorus, the victory over Hebron is sung once again.

A city twenty miles south of Jerusalem, at 3,040 feet in the Judean mountains, Hebron has a bit of biblical history.[2] Abraham, Isaac, and Jacob made Hebron their home at different times, and owned a plot of land here as a family burial place. Later, Hebron was presented to Caleb as a part of his inheritance. Caleb drove out the giant Anakim and occupied the town himself. It was assigned as a city of refuge, and David ruled there for seven and a half years as king.

Slay the Dragon for the Princess

JUDGES 1:11–15 *From there they went against the inhabitants of Debir. (The name of Debir was formerly Kirjath Sepher.) Then Caleb said, "Whoever attacks Kirjath Sepher and takes it, to him I will give my daughter Achsah as wife." And Othniel the son of Kenaz, Caleb's younger brother, took it; so he gave him his daughter Achsah as wife. Now it happened, when she came to*

go to

control
Judges 1:21

foreign
Judges 19:11–12

retributive
punishing or avenging for something done

capture
Joshua 15:15–17

marriage
Exodus 2:21

friendly
Numbers 10:29–32;
1 Samuel 30:26–29

ruins
Joshua 6:20

him, that she urged him to ask her father for a field. And she dismounted from her donkey, and Caleb said to her, "What do you wish?" So she said to him, "Give me a blessing; since you have given me land in the South, give me also springs of water." And Caleb gave her the upper springs and the lower springs. (NKJV)

Like a flashback, here is another account of the <u>capture</u> of Kirjath Sepher by Othniel to obtain the hand of Achsah (Caleb's daughter) in marriage. The springs requested by Achsah to be added to her dowry may be the ones about six miles southwest of Hebron on the way to Beersheba. This valley today is one of the best-watered areas in southern Israel.[3]

Debir (one of the towns occupied by Caleb's family) is believed to be located at Tel Beit Mirsim, thirteen miles southwest of Hebron. It was excavated in 1926 by Melvin G. Kyle and William F. Albright. From the remains, they determined that this city was controlled by Egypt until the fourteenth century BC. Above the bronze-age layer was found a burned-out layer (all that was left after Othniel's victory), and above that, remnants of Israelite life. Historical findings mesh perfectly with the biblical account.[4]

Close Encounters

JUDGES 1:16–18 *Now the children of the Kenite, Moses' father-in-law, went up from the City of Palms with the children of Judah into the Wilderness of Judah, which lies in the South near Arad; and they went and dwelt among the people. And Judah went with his brother Simeon, and they attacked the Canaanites who inhabited Zephath, and utterly destroyed it. So the name of the city was called Hormah. Also Judah took Gaza with its territory, Ashkelon with its territory, and Ekron with its territory. (NKJV)*

The Kenites were related to Israel by Moses's <u>marriage</u> to Zipporah. Although they preserved the identity of their clan, they remained <u>friendly</u> to Israel through the time of David. The City of Palms, which they leave to join the men of Judah in the Negev, is the site of the <u>ruins</u> of Jericho. All that would have been left at this time is an oasis of springs and palm trees.

The three Philistine cities that Judah takes—Gaza, Ashkelon, and Ekron—do not remain in Israelite hands for long. By Samson's day, all three are Philistine-<u>controlled</u> once again. However, it is to their credit that Judah made such brave inroads at this time. They were doing what God had called them to do.

controlled
Judges 14:19; 16:1; 1 Samuel 5:10

Well done
Matthew 25:14–30

promise
Joshua 17:18

demonstration
Joshua 11:4–9

Judah
Joshua 15:63

burning
Judges 1:8

> **what others say**
>
> **Joni Eareckson Tada**
>
> Picture yourself standing before God on the day that He rewards believers. You are longing to hear Him say, "<u>Well done</u> good and faithful servant," but as you glance to your left you notice Hudson Taylor, the famous missionary to China. To your right stands Corrie Ten Boom, the saint who put her life on the line to hide Jews from the Nazis. Somehow, you feel a little small and insignificant.
>
> There is no need to. God is only looking for you to be faithful to what He's called you to be and do.[5]

Efficiency and Deficiency

JUDGES 1:19–21 *So the LORD was with Judah. And they drove out the mountaineers, but they could not drive out the inhabitants of the lowland, because they had chariots of iron. And they gave Hebron to Caleb, as Moses had said. Then he expelled from there the three sons of Anak. But the children of Benjamin did not drive out the Jebusites who inhabited Jerusalem; so the Jebusites dwell with the children of Benjamin in Jerusalem to this day. (NKJV)*

As mentioned before, the five major cities of Philistine dominance emerged from the coastal plains, where iron chariots could be used effectively. Israel, on the other hand, occupied the Judean mountains where a chariot would be ineffective. But the most contested area remained the Shephelah—the foothills located between the two—where constant warfare needled and raged during the whole time of the judges and early kings.[6] Was it true that the presence of the enemies' superior weaponry kept Israel from possessing what God had said was theirs? No. They had both the <u>promise</u> of dominion and a <u>demonstration</u> of how it could be done.

The Benjamites did not dislodge the Jebusites living in Jerusalem any more than <u>Judah</u> had. Jerusalem sat astride the boundary between Benjamin and Judah. Because of its location, it did not strictly belong to either tribe. Even <u>burning</u> the town and

go to

place
Psalm 48:1–3

obey
James 1:25

Rahab
Joshua 2:14

informed
2 Corinthians 2:11;
11:3;
Ephesians 6:11

reconnaissance
exploration to
gather information

threatening its people with the sword made no lasting impact, and it would be many years before that holy <u>place</u> would be claimed for any time by the people of God. All in all, however, their successes up to this point outweigh their failures.

We need not weigh the pros and cons of what God tells us to do—simply <u>obey</u>.

I Spy an Entrance

JUDGES 1:22–26 *And the house of Joseph also went up against Bethel, and the LORD was with them. So the house of Joseph sent men to spy out Bethel. (The name of the city was formerly Luz.) And when the spies saw a man coming out of the city, they said to him, "Please show us the entrance to the city, and we will show you mercy." So he showed them the entrance to the city, and they struck the city with the edge of the sword; but they let the man and all his family go. And the man went to the land of the Hittites, built a city, and called its name Luz, which is its name to this day.* (NKJV)

The first fact we read in the tale of Bethel's capture by the tribes of Ephraim and Manasseh (the sons of Joseph) is that God's presence is with them, guaranteeing certain victory.

Their method of attack called for spying—quite literally "making a circuit with a view to **reconnaissance**."[7] In the process, they apprehend a resident who has come unsuspectingly out of the city, and inquire of him how to make an approach via the weakest and most vulnerable points of infiltration.

They offer mercy where they can, and like <u>Rahab</u> at Jericho, the informer and his family are offered escape from destruction. Unlike Rahab, however, who longed to unite unequivocally with the people of God, this unnamed citizen retires as soon as he can to his countrymen in another region. Perhaps he was more influenced by fear than by faith. The location of his new home is unknown, but we do know that he calls his new place of residence by the name of his old one, *Luz*.

We ought to make every effort to become <u>informed</u> and prepared to combat the enemy of our souls before we are involved in battle.

apply it

Jacob has a meaningful association with Bethel. This was where he had his dream of a stairway that reached up into heaven from which angels were ascending and descending to do their work. When he awoke he was overwhelmed with the feeling that this was the gateway to God's dwelling. An actual quote from Jacob, as he mused over the glory of what he had just witnessed, reads, "How <u>awesome</u> is this place!" After this encounter, he names the place Bethel, meaning "house of God," and the name stuck although, outside Israel, it was still referred to as Luz. Eventually, Bethel was as important in northern Israel as Jerusalem was to the south.[9]

something to ponder

Capitulation and Failure

What occurs in this section of verses has an overriding effect on the rest of the book. The failure of most of the tribes to rout out the enemy sets them up for disaster. Somehow they adopt a policy in which they attempt to use the Canaanites to increase their wealth and comfort. The mention of their strength (in occasionally subduing the native people by forcing them to labor) just makes this worse, for they had the power to carry out God's mandates but

go to

migrated
Judges 18

gift
1 Kings 9:16

associations
Psalm 1:1

chose instead a more cushy course of action. The tribe of Asher even moves right in without *any* effort to check the influence of their pagan neighbors. But their love of ease will become a source of agitation and unrest.

It is unusual to say that a larger number of people dwell among a smaller group. Therefore, when we read about Asher and Naphtali living among the inhabitants of the land, we must infer that the people of God are in the minority.

Dan was confined by the Amorites (whose boundaries are delineated here to show the strength and influence that they possessed), so this tribe <u>migrated</u> to Laish at the headwaters of the Jordan and renamed it Dan.

Some of the cities that remained impregnable to Israelite occupation during the time of the judges are designated in this passage; others are not. One that bears mention is Gezer, located eighteen miles northwest of Jerusalem, guarding a pass between the harbor at Joppa and the mountain city of Jerusalem. Entrenched behind walls fourteen feet thick, Gezer was able to resist Israelite dominance until the time of Solomon, when it was given to him as a wedding present.[10] Pharaoh of Egypt attacked and burned the city to the ground, then presented it as a <u>gift</u>.

> **what others say**
>
> **Charles R. Swindoll**
>
> Instead of the Hebrews keeping the upper hand, they opted for compromise with wrong . . . and they became victims instead of victors. Compromises like that never work . . . Even though we rationalize around our weak decisions and tell ourselves that wicked <u>associations</u> really won't harm us ("They'll get better, our good will rub off on their bad!"), we get soiled in the process.[11]

Angelic Confrontation

JUDGES 2:1–3 *Then the Angel of the LORD came up from Gilgal to Bochim, and said: "I led you up from Egypt and brought you to the land of which I swore to your fathers; and I said, 'I will never break My covenant with you. And you shall* *make no covenant with the inhabitants of this land; you shall tear down their altars.' But you have not obeyed My voice. Why have you done this? Therefore I also said, 'I will not drive them out before you; but they shall be thorns in your side, and their gods shall be a snare to you.'" (NKJV)*

Jericho
Joshua 5:13–15

response
Judges 2:4

serve
Joshua 24:31

Who was the Angel of the LORD? This would be none other than God himself—a prebirth appearance of Christ as previously experienced by Joshua before his military victory at Jericho. Only God could claim to have released their forefathers from Egypt, transferred the land as promised into their hands, and made a covenant to continue his miraculous support as long as they obeyed him. And only God would have a right to hold them accountable for their failures.

Why did this heavenly visitor come up from Gilgal? Perhaps he sought to revive the impressions Israel felt and the resolutions they made while they were encamped at that place. Gilgal was where they first submitted to the covenant of circumcision, launched the campaign to rid the land of sin's influence, and renewed their commitment with the reading and writing of the law and the burnt and fellowship offerings.

Where is Bochim? We do not know for sure, but we have the following clues. Bochim means "the weepers" and was so named *after* the people's response to the word of the Lord at this place.[12] Very possibly, God appeared to the people at or near **Shiloh**, as this location is the only likely place a substantial group of Israelites would have gathered on a holy day or day of worship. After the confrontation, it says the people offered sacrifices of repentance for their sins, and Shiloh is the site where that could be taken care of.

Shiloh
the hometown where people came to worship in the tabernacle

When did this event take place? Most likely the visitation occurred after Joshua's death. We know that, in spite of their tendencies to wander from the center of God's perfect will, Israel did serve the Lord throughout Joshua's lifetime and the lifetime of the elders who served with him.

go to

designed
Ephesians 2:10

obedience
1 Samuel 15:22

mourned
Luke 15:21; 18:13

something to ponder

what others say

Gerald L. Sittser

What instructions are to a new computer, the Ten Commandments are to people. They show us how to run properly. They are the divine instructions to the human machine, helping us to live well, productively, and happily. Sadly, the people of Israel spurned these commandments time and time again. They . . . paid dearly for their foolishness.[13]

We are invited to make the same choices as the people of Israel. We can toss aside the instruction book and guess how our lives ought to fit together, or we can trust our Creator, following his blueprint for the creation he <u>designed</u>, running as efficiently and creatively as he intended.

Crocodile Tears

JUDGES 2:4–5 *So it was, when the Angel of the LORD spoke these words to all the children of Israel, that the people lifted up their voices and wept. Then they called the name of that place Bochim; and they sacrificed there to the LORD. (NKJV)*

Israel wept aloud and offered sacrifices of appeasement to God, but it was only a superficial response. They were not in any way deterred from their idolatrous practices. God did not want their burnt offerings. He would much rather have received their whole-hearted <u>obedience</u>.

apply it

The grief that comes when we make a mistake should not merely be distress over being caught and corrected. A repentant heart is the only one that can truly profit from the discipline of God.

what others say

Kay Arthur

When was the last time you <u>mourned</u>—not because of what someone did to you or because of something that happened to you, but because what you did was wrong and it hurt God? . . . It's time for tears, Beloved. It's time to cry. It's time to pray, *"Oh God, break my heart with the things that break your heart."*[14]

Just as Bochim was named after those who wept over God's words of condemnation, so other locations have names that relate to significant events that occurred in those places as well. A few examples:

- <u>Zoar</u> means "small."
- <u>Bethel</u> means "house of God."
- <u>Mahanaim</u> means "two camps."
- <u>Gilgal</u> sounds like the Hebrew word for "roll."
- <u>Achor</u> means "trouble."

<u>Big Brother Is Watching</u>

Zoar
Genesis 19:22

Bethel
Genesis 28:19

Mahanaim
Genesis 32:2

Gilgal
Joshua 5:9

Achor
Joshua 7:26

verses
Joshua 24:29–31

degeneration
moral decline

JUDGES 2:6–9 *And when Joshua had dismissed the people, the children of Israel went each to his own inheritance to possess the land. So the people served the LORD all the days of Joshua, and all the days of the elders who outlived Joshua, who had seen all the great works of the LORD which He had done for Israel. Now Joshua the son of Nun, the servant of the LORD, died when he was one hundred and ten years old. And they buried him within the border of his inheritance at Timnath Heres, in the mountains of Ephraim, on the north side of Mount Gaash. (NKJV)*

Although the first verse of Judges stated that Judah's conquest began *after* Joshua's death, in this passage we find Joshua alive and well, dismissing the tribes to their respective inheritances like a ghost from the past. Many biblical writers follow a narrative style in which events are related to each other more by subject than chronology. So, after God's prediction that the Canaanites and their idols will become a snare, the author of Judges is now ready to unfold before our eyes the process of **degeneration** from beginning to end. He sets the stage by quoting several <u>verses</u> at the end of the book of Joshua, almost verbatim, bringing us up to speed with where it left off.

In spite of the emphasis in Scripture on the military exploits and the soldierly qualities of Joshua, there remains within him a deep devotion to God and an integrity of character. Many a man who becomes famous on the battlefield may find himself a nonentity in times of peace. Great warriors do not necessarily make great statesmen. But Joshua was a moral leader in civilian life as well as a capable general in war.

go to

righteous living
Joshua 24:31

honor
2 Timothy 2:20–21;
John 12:26

display
Isaiah 1:11–20

incorporating
Deuteronomy 6:5–9

transferred
2 Timothy 1:5; 3:16

many
John 14:6

squander
to wastefully expend

Baal
the most important
god of the
Canaanites

But far more important in God's eyes is Joshua's ability to do the work of a servant. There is no higher distinction than being useful to God and competent to please him.

Joshua did not claim his portion of the inheritance until everyone else was accommodated. Then he asked for a mountainous plot.

Egyptian writings of this period declare 110 years to be an ideal length of life.[15] True or not, the fact remains that conditions were ideal for the children of Israel while Joshua was alive. As long as he could track their every move, they stayed on the path of <u>righteous living</u> and God was free to perform great deeds to be witnessed by all.

There is no higher <u>honor</u> than to be called a servant of the Lord.

Disenfranchised Generation

JUDGES 2:10–13 *When all that generation had been gathered to their fathers, another generation arose after them who did not know the LORD nor the work which He had done for Israel. Then the children of Israel did evil in the sight of the LORD, and served the Baals; and they forsook the LORD God of their fathers, who had brought them out of the land of Egypt; and they followed other gods from among the gods of the people who were all around them, and they bowed down to them; and they provoked the LORD to anger. They forsook the LORD and served Baal and the Ashtoreths. (NKJV)*

How could an entire generation, raised by parents of principle and faith, grow up to **squander** their heritage and throw themselves into idolatry and licentiousness? Even while continuing to <u>display</u> many outwardly religious practices, their beliefs had no personal impact because they were not on a firsthand or an experiential level. God expected them to pass faith on through the generations by <u>incorporating</u> discussions of values into everyday situations. The missing factor was undoubtedly parental neglect, for we know that an active faith can be <u>transferred</u> by teaching and by living out God's Word.

Verse 11 refers to the deities of **Baal**. The verse speaks of Baal in the plural. In fact, there were many: Baal-peor, Baal-zephan, Baal-zebub, and Baal-berith, to name just a few. Any one or a combination of several were worshiped at this time. But our God is *not* one of several, and our faith is *not* just one road among <u>many</u> ways to get to heaven. The Bible makes it abundantly clear that God plus <u>any-thing</u> else is too much. When you worship <u>other</u> things you deny the source of them all.

Why did Israel ever fall into this type of behavior when it was so contrary to God's standards? Here are a few ideas with practical application:

- Perhaps Israel envied the gods of their neighbors as they looked out over their lush and fertile valleys and compared them with their own struggling farms on the rocky hillsides. We do the same when we view the prosperity of the godless and <u>wish</u> for the ease and opulence of their lifestyle.

- As the children of Israel settled into their distant neighborhoods, the trek to worship God at Shiloh must have seemed long and arduous, so some abandoned the discipline of worship. For us, being a faithful church member often takes time and energy that our workweek has already sapped away. Many times we are not <u>consistent</u> in our accountability.

- There was a sensuous and earthy appeal to the way other religions carried out their worship. The Israelites allowed themselves to be drawn into this depravity. We can also be attracted by the decadence and immorality of advertising and the media.

- Intermarriage led to the gradual infiltration of pagan ideas into the community. Also, it was politically correct to recognize the gods of Canaan when they made treaties with neighboring peoples, and these subtle compromises made them fudge everywhere else. Likewise, our friendship and business <u>ties</u> may lead us into things that we would not normally say or do.

What Goes Around Comes Around

JUDGES 2:14–15 *And the anger of the LORD was hot against Israel. So He delivered them into the hands of plunderers who despoiled them; and He sold them into the hands of their enemies all around, so that they could no longer stand before their enemies. Wherever they went out, the hand of the LORD was against them for calamity, as the LORD had said, and as the LORD had sworn to them. And they were greatly distressed. (NKJV)*

go to

anything
Matthew 6:24

other
Exodus 20:3

wish
Psalm 37:1–2

consistent
Hebrews 10:25

ties
2 Corinthians 6:14

warnings
Leviticus 26:15–17;
Deuteronomy 28:25

souls
John 8:44;
1 Peter 5:8

despoiler
robber of everything
valuable

The Israelites evidently do not believe God's <u>warnings</u> concerning their impending doom, as if his threats were meant only to frighten them. But his "selling them away" is the highest demonstration of divine displeasure, as if he no longer wishes to have any responsibility of ownership or identification.

Ironically, their new masters (i.e., the heathen gods of their oppressors) cannot prevent catastrophe or protect them from evil. They are no longer blessed when they go out to fight, but are left in a state of discomfort and anxiety.

Satan, as the great **despoiler**, longs to steal all we have that is good, including our bodies and <u>souls</u>.

Israel, in forsaking the Lord and embracing their pagan neighbors, gave up their only ally and became the victims of the very nations they tried to be like.

Chapter Wrap-Up

- The military exploits of the individual tribes are chronicled. (Judges 1:1–26)

- The lack of productivity and defeat of individual tribes are described. (Judges 1:27–36)

- God confronts the nation of Israel in a personal encounter. (Judges 2:1–5)

- Joshua's life and death are reviewed. (Judges 2:6–9)

- Israel falls away and becomes corrupt. (Judges 2:10–15)

Study Questions

1. What ingenuity did the house of Joseph display in getting into Bethel?

2. What was the essence of God's personal message when he confronted his people?

3. What caused the Israelites to lose their godly heritage in just one generation?

4. What are four possible reasons for Israel's decline during the time of the judges?

Let's Get Started

You would think that it would be easy to serve the Lord in times of prosperity and peace. But Israel found that abundance and ease made them <u>forget</u> the Lord and wander from his **principles**. Forsaking the God that had made, chosen, and accomplished great things for them was an act so presumptuous that heaven itself <u>shuddered</u> in horror. Not only did they turn their back on the Living Water, but they tried to dig their own dry wells. The futility of their attempts was absurd.

However, the only way for Israel to learn how unsatisfactory life would be without the Lord was to experience his absence firsthand. For this reason, God allowed the nations around them to act out their aggressions as they normally would. Then Israel learned what it was like to <u>serve</u> other people instead of God.

forget
Deuteronomy 28:47–48

shuddered
Jeremiah 2:12–13

serve
2 Chronicles 12:8

principles
fundamental rules of conduct

Apostasies Inventoried

> JUDGES 2:16–17 *Nevertheless, the LORD raised up judges who delivered them out of the hand of those who plundered them. Yet they would not listen to their judges, but they played the harlot with other gods, and bowed down to them. They turned quickly from the way in which their fathers walked, in obeying the commandments of the LORD; they did not do so. (NKJV)*

As we have mentioned, a judge in this time period is more like a vice-regent to represent the Lord than a justice in a courtroom. As a magistrate, the judge's duty is to handle religious and civic affairs (obviously long before the controversial issue regarding the "separation of church and state" was introduced in our own country), while leading military expeditions against Israel's foes. Judges are often thought of as "saviors" and "deliverers," because their leadership would usher in a time of peace and safety while Israel was temporarily released from the stranglehold of their oppressors.

But a transformation would seldom occur in the hearts of the people. Even during times of deliverance, they would not even listen to the judges—God's special emissaries. The Lord refers to their breach of contract in terms of a marriage agreement, calling their headlong pursuit after other things spiritual "adultery" and "prostitution."

apply it

Temporary, <u>outward</u> modifications are inconsequential without permanent, inward transformations.

> **what others say**
>
> **Fritz Ridenour**
>
> In the 1950's and 60's the United States fought "small wars" that it didn't really try to win. Containment was more of a goal than all out victory. A "peaceful settlement" was preferable to unconditional surrender. You can't fight that kind of war with sin. It will whip you every time. You have to decide which way you really want to go.[1]

Roller-Coaster Religion

JUDGES 2:18–19 *And when the LORD raised up judges for them, the LORD was with the judge and delivered them out of the hand of their enemies all the days of the judge; for the LORD was moved to pity by their groaning because of those who oppressed them and harassed them. And it came to pass, when the judge was dead, that they reverted and behaved more corruptly than their fathers, by following other gods, to serve them and bow down to them. They did not cease from their own doings nor from their stubborn way. (NKJV)*

go to

outward
Matthew 23:25–28

compendium
outline or survey

The majority of this chapter serves as a sort of **compendium** for the rest of the book, to be expanded and amplified in later chapters. It describes the downward spiral of corruption followed by oppression from Israel's enemies, and a period of deliverance from the hand of a judge. But every time Israel fell back into sin after the death of a leader, they found themselves in a deeper pit, wallowing in more corruption than ever before.

Humanity faces the same choices and struggles with the same temptations today as it did four thousand years ago.

go to

individuals
2 Chronicles 7:14

what others say

Dewey Bertolini

Contrary to much popular preaching today, we cannot *make* Jesus the Lord of our lives. He hasn't given us that option. He *is* the Lord of our lives. Nothing will ever change that. The options are reduced to but two: obedient submission resulting in God's blessing or defiant rebellion resulting in eventual destruction (Rom. 6:16).[2]

There is an amazing tendency among highly moral nations (given enough time) to degenerate and disintegrate from corruption within.

what others say

General Douglas MacArthur

In this day of gathering storms, as moral deterioration of political power spreads its growing infection, it is essential that every spiritual force be mobilized to defend and preserve the religious base upon which this nation is founded; for it has been that base which has been the motivating impulse to our moral and national growth. History fails to record a single precedent in which nations subject to moral decay have not passed into political and economic decline. There has either been a spiritual awakening to overcome the moral lapse, or a progressive deterioration leading to ultimate spiritual disaster.[3]

The only thing that can save our country from corporate decay and decline is <u>individuals</u> devoted to inner purity and personal adherence to the principles of God's Word.

In the Hands of an Angry God

JUDGES 2:20–23 *Then the anger of the LORD was hot against Israel; and He said, "Because this nation has transgressed My covenant which I commanded their fathers, and has not heeded My voice, I also will no longer drive out before them any of the nations which Joshua left when he died, so that through them I may test Israel, whether they will keep the ways of the LORD, to walk in them as their fathers kept them, or not." Therefore the LORD left those nations, without driving them out immediately; nor did He deliver them into the hand of Joshua. (NKJV)*

go to

treasuring up
Job 36:13

executed
completed

hitherto
before now

It is absurd to think that any nation can long escape the penalties of sin when its citizens are absorbed in it. God's wrath is aroused, as it always will be over the unnecessary pain and trouble that rebellion brings. He seeks a drastic method to get the Israelites' attention and bring them back to where they were when Joshua died.

Their delay in expelling the Canaanites was a result of Israel's lack of faith and industry. However, God can still bring about a useful result.

what others say

Jonathan Edwards

The wrath of God is like great waters that are dammed for the present; they increase more and more, and rise higher and higher till an outlet is given; and the longer a stream is stopped, the more rapid and mighty is its course when once it is let loose. 'Tis true that judgment against your evil works has not been **executed**; **hitherto** the floods of God's vengeance have been withheld; but your guilt in the meantime is constantly increasing, and you are everyday <u>treasuring up</u> more wrath.[4]

Foes Enumerated

JUDGES 3:1–2 *Now these are the nations which the LORD left, that He might test Israel by them, that is, all who had not known any of the wars in Canaan (this was only so that the generations of the children of Israel might be taught to know war, at least those who had not formerly known it),* (NKJV)

key point

Growth and knowledge have never come out of neglect or idleness, but from crisis and testing. The greatest lesson to be learned by the Israelites is one that has been forgotten with the passing of time. *God* will be the one to provide the victory, and only with *his* miraculous help can Israel destroy their enemies.

Why were the discipline of battle and an awareness of God's role as "miraculous deliverer" not fresh in their minds? Because they had not persevered in countering the foreign influence on their own soil, and now they have forgotten how. But even while reaping the fruit of their continued neglect, they could rediscover at any time what God intended for them to be and do.

> ### what others say
>
> **Marilyn Willet Heavilin**
>
> Trusting God takes an act of our will. It is <u>believing</u> something will happen before it happens. I can trust God to help me be kind to a person I do not like, but then I must approach that person with the intention and determination to be kind.[5]

Push 'Em Back, Way Back!

JUDGES 3:3–4 *namely, five lords of the Philistines, all the Canaanites, the Sidonians, and the Hivites who dwelt in Mount Lebanon, from Mount Baal Hermon to the entrance of Hamath. And they were left, that He might test Israel by them, to know whether they would obey the commandments of the LORD, which He had commanded their fathers by the hand of Moses. (NKJV)*

The five rulers of the Philistines would be the five kings of the coastal city-states: Gaza, Ashkelon, Ashdod, Ekron, and Gath. These cities were often referred to as the "Philistine **Pentapolis**."[6]

This is the first mention in Joshua or Judges of the Sidonians. They would be the Phoenicians just up the coast to the north. Mount Baal Hermon is near the source of the Jordan River, while Hamath is the point of access between mountain ranges to the town of Hamath.[7]

Mention is made once again of the remaining nations being used as a test. Two benefits have been listed—first, to teach Israel the type of warfare in which God is released by faith to achieve great things, and second, to prove their own faithfulness and commitment in the face of danger.

We should strive to please God in our endeavors so that we need not be <u>ashamed</u> by his evaluation of our work when we are tested. As with a precious metal, God will put us through the <u>fire</u> to purify away the dross, and only what has eternal implications will last. There is a <u>blessing</u> for those who persevere under trial and a reward in heaven to acknowledge those who stand firm throughout the tests of life.

apply it

Head Over Heels

go to

principle
1 Corinthians 15:33

Ham
Genesis 9:18–25

ancestors
Genesis 10:6, 15–19

JUDGES 3:5–6 *Thus the children of Israel dwelt among the Canaanites, the Hittites, the Amorites, the Perizzites, the Hivites, and the Jebusites. And they took their daughters to be their wives, and gave their daughters to their sons; and they served their gods. (NKJV)*

The Israelites are in a jam. As they rub elbows every day with their pagan neighbors, they also start joining with them in marriage. So here they are, coming together in the most sacred and intimate of human relationships without the most important thing in common—a mutual faith. Without that foundation they are doomed, for now the *enemy* is *family*!

The worst possible scenario unfolds as Israel's growing familiarity with the people of the land brings the adoption of their gods. It is a biblical <u>principle</u> that bad company corrupts good character, and in this instance their marriages with unbelievers caused them to give up the one thing that mattered the most—their God.

> **what others say**
>
> ### Karen Scalf Linamen
>
> I was in my early teens when my mother and I started praying for the man who would become my husband. I believe that those prayers reached across the miles and somehow, in some way, impacted the life of a high school kid named Larry who was living in Anderson, Indiana.
>
> But those prayers also had an impact close to home. They did something for me, as my folks and I walked the precarious line through my dating years. I believe my parents' prayers held up a standard—they reminded me that I belonged to God, that my future husband belonged to God, and that our life together was in God's hands.[8]

Originally the Canaanites were all descendants of <u>Ham</u>, one of Noah's three sons. Because Ham was disrespectful to his father, he received a curse that made him a servant of his brothers. Later, Ham's descendants moved into the area now known as Israel, and the nations in residence at the time of the judges were made up of the different family groups among his <u>ancestors</u>. They no longer maintain any ties with each other except a shared land and an occasional political treaty.

Othniel—The Spirit-Filled

JUDGES 3:7–8 *So the children of Israel did evil in the sight of the LORD. They forgot the LORD their God, and served the Baals and Asherahs. Therefore the anger of the LORD was hot against Israel, and He sold them into the hand of Cushan-Rishathaim king of Mesopotamia; and the children of Israel served Cushan-Rishathaim eight years.* (NKJV)

Like a distant memory, God was dismissed from the collective conscience of the Israelite nation in favor of the new and more appealing worship of the Baals and Asherahs. Asherah was the female consort of Baal. They are referred to in the plural as these gods took on various forms in different communities.

When lesser reproofs did not suffice, the Lord turned up the heat and subjected the Israelites to more <u>excruciating</u> forms of correction. The name Cushan-Rishathaim means "doubly-wicked" Cushan. He hails from Naharaim (or Mesopotamia). Mesopotamia was the fertile land around the upper and middle Euphrates, watered by the Tigris and Habar rivers.[9]

Dauntless Hero

JUDGES 3:9–11 *When the children of Israel cried out to the LORD, the LORD raised up a deliverer for the children of Israel, who delivered them: Othniel the son of Kenaz, Caleb's younger brother. The Spirit of the LORD came upon him, and he judged Israel. He went out to war, and the LORD delivered Cushan-Rishathaim king of Mesopotamia into his hand; and his hand prevailed over Cushan-Rishathaim. So the land had rest for forty years. Then Othniel the son of Kenaz died.* (NKJV)

Even though the sticky situation Israel now found herself in was her own fault, when the people cry out to the Lord he hears and answers. Othniel makes a good deliverer because he:

- Is experienced in warfare. He can handle weapons and do battle.
- Has shared in the conquest of Canaan. He is familiar with God's way of doing things.
- Is previously known for <u>heroism</u>. He is not timid or fearful.

excruciating
Leviticus 26:18–21

heroism
Joshua 15:16–17

go to

cry
Psalm 34:4

gave
John 14:26–16:7

rested
1 Samuel 10:10

rescued
1 Samuel 11:11

presumption
1 Samuel 13:13;
15:35

left
1 Samuel 16:14

indwelling
Romans 8:9

seal
Ephesians 4:30

indwelling
inhabiting, living
inside

endowed
provided with some-
thing desirable

seal
a closure that dis-
courages tampering

redemption
buying back to an
improved state

• Is from the tribe of Judah. He will get maximum support from this tribe in his campaigns.

After the Spirit of the Lord comes upon him, he overpowers the enemy king and performs the duties of a judge for forty years in peace.

When we <u>cry</u> out to the Lord in distress, he will hear and answer.

The spiritual empowering of an individual in the Old Testament is not the same act of **indwelling** that happens to a believer in the modern age, at salvation. Before Christ <u>gave</u> us his Holy Spirit, a person chosen by God for a particular task would be **endowed** with a special filling to enable him to perform the duty with strength and courage not his own. This did not necessarily produce any moral transformation in the individual. And the special enablement might leave at any time.

A good example is King Saul, upon whom the Spirit <u>rested</u> in the early years of his reign. With the strength he was given, he <u>rescued</u> a city and fought valiantly for his people. However, after several acts of <u>presumption</u> and disobedience on Solomon's part, the Spirit of God <u>left</u> him and he was tormented by an evil spirit.

In contrast, as followers of Christ, we have all the benefits of the Spirit's <u>indwelling</u> at the moment of regeneration. Some of the blessings are as follows:

• We are instructed in spiritual truth. (1 Corinthians 2:13; John 16:13)

• We are encouraged to be bold. (Acts 1:8)

• We are convicted of sin. (John 16:8)

• We are compelled to make good choices. (Acts 10:19–20; 13:2)

• We are taught what and when to speak. (Luke 12:12)

• We are set apart as holy. (1 Peter 1:2)

• We can produce fruit. (Galatians 5:22)

Best of all, the Spirit does not leave at will, but is a **<u>seal</u>**, identifying us with God until the day of **redemption**, when we will be joined with Christ, in our new bodies, forever, in heaven.

what others say

Billy Graham

Over 100 years ago, two young men were talking in Ireland. One said, "The world has yet to see what God will do with a man fully **consecrated** to Him." The other man meditated on that thought for weeks. It so gripped him that one day he exclaimed, "By the Holy Spirit in me I'll be that man." Historians now say that he touched two continents for Christ. His name was Dwight L. Moody.

This can happen again, as we open our lives to the recreating power of the Holy Spirit. No person can seek sincerely the cleansing and blessing of the Holy Spirit, and remain the same afterward.[10]

Ehud—The Left-Handed

JUDGES 3:12–14 *And the children of Israel again did evil in the sight of the LORD. So the LORD strengthened Eglon king of Moab against Israel, because they had done evil in the sight of the LORD. Then he gathered to himself the people of Ammon and Amalek, went and defeated Israel, and took possession of the City of Palms. So the children of Israel served Eglon king of Moab eighteen years. (NKJV)*

Israel repeats the same apostasy for which it had earlier been punished, and God allows Eglon, king of Moab, to exert power over them. The Moabites are located east of the Dead Sea. The Ammonites are northeast of Moab, and the Amalekites are **migrant nomads** from the south.

At this time, Moab conducts a successful campaign in the **Transjordan** area, defeating a portion of the eastern tribes and moving swiftly into the Jordan Valley. They make their capital in Jericho.[11]

It was longer (eighteen years) this time before Israel had the sense to cry out to God.

A careful correlation is drawn between the evil in which the Israelites indulge and the dispatching of wicked nations by God to oppress them.

go to

left-handed
Judges 20:16;
1 Chronicles 12:2

disarming
1 Samuel 13:19–22

ambidextrous
able to use right
and left hands with
equal skill

tribute
payment as a sign of
submission

Setting the Stage

JUDGES 3:15–17 *But when the children of Israel cried out to the LORD, the LORD raised up a deliverer for them: Ehud the son of Gera, the Benjamite, a left-handed man. By him the children of Israel sent tribute to Eglon king of Moab. Now Ehud made himself a dagger (it was double-edged and a cubit in length) and fastened it under his clothes on his right thigh. So he brought the tribute to Eglon king of Moab. (Now Eglon was a very fat man.) (NKJV)*

The deliverer that God provides comes from the tribe of Benjamin, which probably suffered the most at the hands of the Moabites. Benjamin was located front and center among the confiscated lands.

An interesting quirk that identifies itself with this tribe is the number of people who are either left-handed or **ambidextrous**. This characteristic, which in ancient times was considered a disability, was actually used advantageously by Ehud, who could keep his right hand free and easy while (under a fold of clothing, unsuspected by the adversary) grasping a sword in his left.

Undoubtedly, Moab maintained the same policies as most dominant nations, of disarming a subject people. For this reason, Ehud was forced to fashion a weapon of his own making. Ehud had access to Eglon by reason of the required yearly **tribute**.

There is a big difference between crying out in distress and crying out *to God* in distress.

The ancient historian Josephus shares a lot of biographical information about the Benjamite, Ehud. He says Ehud was a man of great courage and had a strong body fit for hard labor. Josephus suggests that Ehud had worked his way into the confidence of Eglon and was trusted by the king's attendants. They suspected nothing. When Ehud came at midday in summer, the guards who had not been dismissed for dinner were lethargic from heat. It was the perfect time to enact his plan.[12]

Aberrations to the Plot

JUDGES 3:18–19 *And when he had finished presenting the tribute, he sent away the people who had carried the tribute. But he*

himself turned back from the stone images that were at Gilgal, and said, "I have a secret message for you, O king." He said, "Keep silence!" And all who attended him went out from him. (NKJV)

fears
Psalm 27:1

services
Acts 4:18-20

With Ehud was a **posse** of men to help with the transportation of the tribute. Since it might have taken the form of agricultural produce, there would be a real need for **porters**.[13] Or perhaps, as is characteristic of oriental culture, this presentation demanded a display of ostentation. They would load on the shoulders of four or five in parade-style what could easily be carried by one.[14] At any rate, to avoid alarming anyone, Ehud sends them away.

posse
a group assembled for a purpose

porters
luggage or burden carriers

Whether Ehud himself lost courage and was on his way home when the sight of the idols at Gilgal infuriated him with holy wrath—or leaving and turning around at a certain point was all part of his plan—we do not know. At any rate, he returns with a confidential message for the king's ears only.

> what others say
>
> **William Secker**
>
> Another singular action of a sanctified Christian is to prefer the duty he owes to God to the danger he <u>fears</u> from man. Christians of all ages have prized their <u>services</u> above their safety . . . Were believers to shrink back at every contrary wind that blows, they would never make their voyage to heaven.[15]

Sharing Secrets

JUDGES 3:20–21 *So Ehud came to him (now he was sitting upstairs in his cool private chamber). Then Ehud said, "I have a message from God for you." So he arose from his seat. Then Ehud reached with his left hand, took the dagger from his right thigh, and thrust it into his belly. (NKJV)*

The king was left alone in his "summer parlor"—an upper room with latticed windows, well-ventilated for fresh air.[16] When Ehud says he has a message from *God* himself, Eglon pushes his corpulent body out of the chair in anticipation, probably quite an exertion.

At this moment Ehud presents the king with a very unusual visual aid to illustrate God's message concerning the conclusion of his life. God pronounces (and Ehud concurs) that it is time for Eglon to pass on the reins of leadership to someone else.

go to

justice
Romans 2:6

Josephus
Jewish historian and biographer from the first century

Seirah
an unidentified location

Relinquishing His Blade

JUDGES 3:22–26 *Even the hilt went in after the blade, and the fat closed over the blade, for he did not draw the dagger out of his belly; and his entrails came out. Then Ehud went out through the porch and shut the doors of the upper room behind him and locked them.*

When he had gone out, Eglon's servants came to look, and to their surprise, the doors of the upper room were locked. So they said, "He is probably attending to his needs in the cool chamber." So they waited till they were embarrassed, and still he had not opened the doors of the upper room. Therefore they took the key and opened them. And there was their master, fallen dead on the floor.

But Ehud had escaped while they delayed, and passed beyond the stone images and escaped to Seirah. (NKJV)

Now the urgency of a secret escape is upon Ehud, and he carefully covers his tracks and makes it as difficult to trace his actions as possible.

Some time elapses before the servants determine that even the private needs of an individual do not take this long. **Josephus** says it is even early evening before they unlock the door and discover the shocking truth.[18] Their leader has been assassinated!

In the meantime, Ehud has escaped all the way to **Seirah** in the hill country of Ephraim.

Horn's Holler

JUDGES 3:27–28 *And it happened, when he arrived, that he blew the trumpet in the mountains of Ephraim, and the children of Israel went down with him from the mountains; and he led them. Then he said to them, "Follow me, for the LORD has delivered your enemies the Moabites into your hand." So they went down after him, seized the fords of the Jordan leading to Moab, and did not allow anyone to cross over.* (NKJV)

Ehud issues a call to arms by "causing trumpets to be blown" (a more accurate translation) throughout the mountainous region of Ephraim.[19] The people respond by coming down from the hills where many have taken refuge.

With words of encouragement related to God's endorsement of the insurrection and blessing upon their endeavors, Ehud commands his afflicted countrymen to follow his direction. They take possession of the only route that the Moabite military in Israel would have to escape back to their homeland.[20]

Striking the Strong

> JUDGES 3:29–30 *And at that time they killed about ten thousand men of Moab, all stout men of valor; not a man escaped. So Moab was subdued that day under the hand of Israel. And the land had rest for eighty years.* (NKJV)

God (through Ehud) rallied his own exploited and browbeaten people to rise up and overthrow the tyranny of at least ten thousand armed and well-conditioned Moabites. The sturdy and robust Moabites probably made up armed service units stationed around Israel to put down uprisings while they were in power. The Scriptures state that every last one was cut down. In that act, Israel bought eighty years of freedom from the military presence of her enemies.

Shamgar—The Philistine-Goader

> JUDGES 3:31 *After him was Shamgar the son of Anath, who killed six hundred men of the Philistines with an ox goad; and he also delivered Israel.* (NKJV)

Shamgar is a foreign name. Anath is the name of the sister of Baal and the Canaanite goddess of war (among other things). Stating that Shamgar is the son of Anath could mean, then, that he was well-versed in warfare.[21] It could even mean that this heroic individual was not a native of Israel at all, but was sent by God from somewhere else to deliver them.

An ox goad is an instrument as much as eight feet long, normally tipped with metal on one end and chisel-shaped on the other for scraping out a plow-share.[22] Again, if weapons had been confiscated, at this time it would have been necessary to rely on implements like

lowly
1 Corinthians
1:26–29

excellency
Psalms 34:2; 44:8

suppression
forceful action to
restrain

these as weapons. But then, God has always preferred using the base and <u>lowly</u> to accomplish his purposes.

Shamgar's isolated exploit may have occurred under the leadership of another judge. Unlike what happened when other leaders delivered Israel, there is no new account of Israel's sins or the subsequent **suppression** by a dominant nation, or the length of time that the Israelites enjoyed a period of rest after his deliverance. Therefore, this may have been a one-time event that stands alone, or the six hundred Philistines may have been killed over the length of Shamgar's life.

When God chooses an unlikely method or instrument, the <u>excellency</u> of his wisdom and power can shine forth.

Chapter Wrap-Up

- An outline of Israel's continued cycles of corruption throughout the judges is given. (Judges 2:16–23)

- The reasons for warfare are discussed, and the people with whom the Israelites live and fight are listed. (Judges 3:1–6)

- Othniel is empowered by the Spirit to save Israel from a Mesopotamian ruler. (Judges 3:7–11)

- Ehud assassinates Eglon and drives the Moabites out of Israel. (Judges 3:12–30)

- Shamgar overpowers six hundred Philistines, with an ox goad as his only weapon. (Judges 3:31)

Study Questions

1. Describe a cycle in Israel's downward plunge.

2. What is one reason God allows evil to remain in our world?

3. What is the difference between the indwelling of the Holy Spirit in the Old Testament and today?

4. In the case of Ehud and Shamgar, how did God use the lowly and insignificant to work out his plan?

Judges 4–5
Deborah, a Lady Leader

Chapter Highlights:
- **Barak's Initiation**
- **A Deborah Tree**
- **Jael's Triumph**
- **Deborah's Song**
- **God's Victory**

Let's Get Started

God freely uses a woman to lead the nation of Israel at a time when finding a woman at the helm of any government was incredible. However, God has never performed any operation in the expected or traditional manner, so why should he start now? He delights in pushing over the walls and boundaries that individuals are so eager to erect, just to prove that he will not be put in a box.

With this introduction, meet Deborah, a musically proficient administrator who appears to face life without fear. The people adore her and her leadership, flocking to the hill country of Ephraim to receive her advice and encouragement. But what can she do about the cruelty of the Canaanites, who hold the helpless Israelites in a death grip? Apart from a miracle, Deborah has no option but to remain as vulnerable as the rest of her people.

Barak's Initiation

> JUDGES **4:1–3** *When Ehud was dead, the children of Israel again did evil in the sight of the LORD. So the LORD sold them into the hand of Jabin king of Canaan, who reigned in Hazor. The commander of his army was Sisera, who dwelt in Harosheth Hagoyim. And the children of Israel cried out to the LORD; for Jabin had nine hundred chariots of iron, and for twenty years he had harshly oppressed the children of Israel. (NKJV)*

After Ehud kicks the bucket, Israel once again plunges into a period of sin and **sedition**. The way the passage reads in the original language, they openly **defect** from the worship of the true God, even neglecting the regular temple services and duties.[1] This fresh outbreak of idolatrous living ushers in the next great period of judgment.

Until this point, Israel's oppressors had come from foreign soil, but now, the people they live with rise against them. Small rival kingdoms have sprung up around the land, loosely allied with one

sedition
rebellion against authority

defect
abandon allegiance to

go to

rebuilt
Joshua 11:11

eight
Judges 3:8

eighteen
Judges 3:14

rebuilt
Joshua 11:11

Jabin
Joshua 11:1

flounder
Matthew 9:36

leadership
Hosea 4:9

nominally
in name only

another, just as it was in Joshua's day. Jabin's monarchy is clearly the most powerful and holds the others under its influence.[2] Hazor, once the largest city in Canaan, has been <u>rebuilt</u>, and its nine hundred chariots are terrorizing Israel. These were especially formidable because the Israelites, unfamiliar with the process of forging iron, are incapable of producing anything like it.

The fact that Israel had once exerted control over them would encourage the Canaanites to inflict burdens and bondage upon Israel with glee. At the same time, Israel would have to choke on the realization that their current masters had formerly been in the palms of their hands, and if not for their own unbelief and idolatry would be there still.

Every time Israel falls into sin they wallow in their misery for a longer stretch before they think to call on God. First <u>eight</u> years, then <u>eighteen</u>, and now twenty have passed before they remember the source of their help and comfort.

Hazor, capital of the **nominally** associated Canaanite enterprises, has been <u>rebuilt</u> as a bustling city, nine miles north of the Sea of Galilee on the main route between Egypt and Mesopotamia. Its ruler, <u>Jabin</u>, shares his dynastic name with at least one descendant, probably in much the same way that the Philistine kings used the name Abimelech, or the kings of Damascus used Ben-Hadad.[3]

Harosheth Haggoyim, the residence of Jabin's commander, Sisera, has been identified with the modern Tel Amar, located where the Kishon River passes through a narrow gorge to enter the Plain of Acre. It is ten miles northwest of Megiddo in a region formally known as "Galilee of the Gentiles."[4]

People <u>flounder</u> when they have no one to follow.

No reverses are so trying as those which suddenly give the upper hand to people who have once been under our authority.

what others say

Howard Hendricks

Men make history and not the other way around. In periods where there is no <u>leadership</u>, society stands still. Progress occurs when courageous, skillful leaders seize the opportunity to change things for the better.[5]

A Deborah Tree

go to

honey
Psalm 19:9–10

Ramah
Joshua 18:25

Bethel
Joshua 18:13

Samuel
1 Samuel 7:16

JUDGES 4:4–5 *Now Deborah, a prophetess, the wife of Lapidoth, was judging Israel at that time. And she would sit under the palm tree of Deborah between Ramah and Bethel in the mountains of Ephraim. And the children of Israel came up to her for judgment. (NKJV)*

As we have said, finding a woman of that era, in a place of leadership, is truly amazing. Obviously she was exceptionally talented and capable.

Deborah is introduced as both a prophetess and a judge—one who can fearlessly declare the words of God, but can also arouse her people to fight at the appropriate time. Her name means "a bee," and like many names in the Bible, it carries a spiritual significance.[6] Like the tiny insect that spends its time feasting on that which is "sweeter than honey," so Deborah, as God's administrator, would have to spend time poring over God's law. And like the bee, ever industrious in the service of others, so Deborah occupies herself with the duties of prophetess and judge for the benefit of her people.

Ramah is in Benjamin, and Bethel is on the border between Benjamin and Ephraim, so both are located in southern Israel. This is the same area from which Samuel later successfully judged Israel.

Deborah is one of five women in the Old Testament to be called a prophetess. The other four are as follows (the last one being a false prophetess):

something to ponder

1. Miriam (Exodus 15:20)

2. Huldah (2 Kings 22:14)

3. Isaiah's wife (Isaiah 8:3)

4. Noadiah (Nehemiah 6:14)

Just as Deborah's name indicated what kind of a person she would be, so other figures in the Bible lived up to the labels put upon them by either their parents or the people who knew them best. Most significant are the individuals who started life with one name, but because of a positive change in character or purpose, God gave them an entirely different name. The following are some examples:

Antioch
Acts 11:26

look
1 Peter 3:15–16

refuge
Joshua 20:7

Tabor
dome-shaped sentinel in the Jezreel Valley

Esdraelon
Greek name for the Valley of Jezreel

What's in a Name?

Original	New	Meaning	Reference
Abram	Abraham	father of many	Genesis 17:5
Jacob	Israel	he struggles with God	Genesis 32:28
Gideon	Jerubbaal	let Baal contend	Judges 6:32
Solomon	Jedidiah	loved by the Lord	2 Samuel 12:25
Simon	Peter	rock	Matthew 16:17–18

We too have been given a new name. Like the believers in <u>Antioch</u>, we are known as Christians, or "Christ's ones." This is a title (with a built-in reputation) that we must honor and uphold. People will <u>look</u> to us to see how someone that belongs to the Lord reacts to pressure, success, temptation, and tragedy. Will we bring glory to God in what we say and do?

<u>Memo from God</u>

> JUDGES 4:6–7 *Then she sent and called for Barak the son of Abinoam from Kedesh in Naphtali, and said to him, "Has not the LORD God of Israel commanded, 'Go and deploy troops at Mount Tabor; take with you ten thousand men of the sons of Naphtali and of the sons of Zebulun; and against you I will deploy Sisera, the commander of Jabin's army, with his chariots and his multitude at the River Kishon; and I will deliver him into your hand'?"* (NKJV)

Deborah summons Barak from Kedesh (one of the cities of <u>refuge</u>) in Naphtali. (There are two other cities that bear the same name—one in Issachar and another in Judah.)⁷ She specifies two tribes in particular from which he is to draw fighting men—Naphtali and Zebulun. These two would be the most eager to furnish a force because (1) Barak would be well-known in his home region of Naphtali, and (2) both were geographically situated so as to receive the brunt of Jabin's harassment.

Barak is ordered to muster them at Mount **Tabor**, in the northeast part of the Plain of **Esdraelon**. If he would but lead the way, God promises through Deborah to lure the enemy into a trap, bringing ultimate destruction to Sisera and all his troops.

Tabor is a cone-shaped mountain that rises some thirteen hundred feet up from the valley below, and affords an unmistakable meeting place.[8] It is very fertile and entirely covered with a diversity of trees, as well as shrubs and plant life. Today, roads and paths on the south side permit a traveler to navigate all the way to the top, where he'll find a splendid view. On the northwest you can see the distant Mediterranean. To the south is the river Kishon, and farther on are the high mountains of Gilboa. Due east is the Sea of Galilee, one day away on foot. Mount Tabor is presently called Djebel Tour.[9]

God never asks us to do anything for him which he has not already underlinedplanned well in advance.

go to

planned
Psalm 33:10–11

trepidation
Exodus 4:10–17

question
Exodus 32:1–5, 21–24

true
Hebrews 11:32

God
Romans 4:21

Chicken-Livered

JUDGES 4:8–10 *And Barak said to her, "If you will go with me, then I will go; but if you will not go with me, I will not go!" So she said, "I will surely go with you; nevertheless there will be no glory for you in the journey you are taking, for the LORD will sell Sisera into the hand of a woman." Then Deborah arose and went with Barak to Kedesh. And Barak called Zebulun and Naphtali to Kedesh; he went up with ten thousand men under his command, and Deborah went up with him.* (NKJV)

Like Moses, who was filled with underlinedtrepidation at the thought of being a leader, Barak also struggled with feelings of inadequacy. Although Moses loved God, he let his fear run away with his emotions. And because he begged for someone else to accompany him, he ended up sharing his leadership with Aaron (even when Aaron's behavior at times was definitely under underlinedquestion).

Barak had a underlinedtrue but faltering faith as well, and so ended up sharing the honor of his victory with a woman (not Deborah, but someone else, yet to be introduced). Barak didn't want to be in this alone and pleaded for Deborah to accompany him, obviously placing more confidence in her than the underlinedGod that had created and empowered her.

Barak's hesitation forced two people to have to do the work that one able-bodied individual should have managed on his own. But in spite of this, Deborah and Barak begin the search for patriots in his own hometown.

If you are doing what God asks, then he will equip you for the task.

apply it

go to

presence
Psalm 139:7–11

existed
Joshua 19:33

Pamela Reeve

Faith is the handle by which I take God's promises and apply them to my particular problems.[10]

Don Baker

When I am finally able to accept my Father's perfect love for me, then my fears can relax. I know that He will not allow anything to enter my life without first giving it permission. And I know that He will not permit anything to enter my life without also providing His <u>presence</u>.[11]

Heber of Hobab

JUDGES 4:11 *Now Heber the Kenite, of the children of Hobab the father-in-law of Moses, had separated himself from the Kenites and pitched his tent near the terebinth tree at Zaanaim, which is beside Kedesh. (NKJV)*

In anticipation of the story to come, a parenthetical introduction of Heber is made. Heber, husband of the heroine you are about to meet (and distantly related to Israel through Moses), has separated from the main body of his clan and has settled near Kedesh (Barak's hometown).

An interesting reference is made to the "terebinth tree of Zaanaim," which has <u>existed</u> for some time and falls in the direct line of Sisera's escape route (as we shall see later).

Military Intelligence

JUDGES 4:12–13 *And they reported to Sisera that Barak the son of Abinoam had gone up to Mount Tabor. So Sisera gathered together all his chariots, nine hundred chariots of iron, and all the people who were with him, from Harosheth Hagoyim to the River Kishon. (NKJV)*

As soon as Sisera is informed of Barak's activities, he starts the move toward the river, drawn inexorably by the persuasive tug of God. But as he goes he gathers more and more of his troops, the centerpiece of which is his chariots of iron—swift and maneuverable weapons of destruction.

No man can <u>withstand</u> the irresistible draw of God's purposeful design.

withstand
Proverbs 21:1

marches
2 Samuel 5:24

Jael's Triumph

> JUDGES 4:14–16 *Then Deborah said to Barak, "Up! For this is the day in which the LORD has delivered Sisera into your hand. Has not the LORD gone out before you?" So Barak went down from Mount Tabor with ten thousand men following him. And the LORD routed Sisera and all his chariots and all his army with the edge of the sword before Barak; and Sisera alighted from his chariot and fled away on foot. But Barak pursued the chariots and the army as far as Harosheth Hagoyim, and all the army of Sisera fell by the edge of the sword; not a man was left.* (NKJV)

Standard principles of warfare would encourage Barak to establish himself on the high ground he already possessed, giving him an advantage over the approaching troops. But since God was going to do the fighting, this was unnecessary. With Deborah's assurance that God has gone ahead (a term used of a king who <u>marches</u> at the head of his army), Barak advances in his wake, straight for Sisera.[12]

By the time Barak and his soldiers arrive on the battlefield, all that is left is to pursue the enemy, now in flight. The Canaanites have abandoned the security of their infamous chariots and are running back in panic to wherever they came from. They were not as "invincible" as they thought, and every last one of them died on the point of a sword.

God's proper place is at the head of all our endeavors.

All the Better to Kill You with, My Dear

> JUDGES 4:17–18 *However, Sisera had fled away on foot to the tent of Jael, the wife of Heber the Kenite; for there was peace between Jabin king of Hazor and the house of Heber the Kenite. And Jael went out to meet Sisera, and said to him, "Turn aside, my lord, turn aside to me; do not fear." And when he had turned aside with her into the tent, she covered him with a blanket.* (NKJV)

intermarriage
Numbers 10:29

proselytes
religious converts

Sisera's pride and confidence had been in the strength of his chariot corps. He had undoubtedly mocked and despised God's people for their lack of sophistication. But in the end he was forced to abandon his treasured mode of transportation. His high-tech military machine had been derailed by a heavenly power he had not anticipated.

Leaving the rest of his army to flounder on their own, Sisera concentrates on saving his own neck. He heads north, probably with the hope of reaching Hazor—and safety. Finally, exhausted, he reaches the tent of Heber.

Jabin had not oppressed the nomadic Kenites; God was not judging *them*, so they had no reason to participate in Israel's uprising. Moreover, Heber probably felt it was good policy to preserve a strict neutrality, so Sisera had no reason to believe harm would come to him when he stopped to rest. What he did not know was that because of an <u>intermarriage</u> in years past, the Kenites were sympathetic to Israel's God. They were **proselytes** and worshipped God according to Mosaic Law, but without any claim to inheritance.[13]

Jael offers hospitality and gives Sisera a place to hole up until the heat's off. No one would search in a woman's tent for an outlaw. Rolled up in a blanket, placed inconspicuously in a corner, he would never be found.

Throbbing Headache

JUDGES 4:19–21 *Then he said to her, "Please give me a little water to drink, for I am thirsty." So she opened a jug of milk, gave him a drink, and covered him. And he said to her, "Stand at the door of the tent, and if any man comes and inquires of you, and says, 'Is there any man here?' you shall say, 'No.'" Then Jael, Heber's wife, took a tent peg and took a hammer in her hand, and went softly to him and drove the peg into his temple, and it went down into the ground; for he was fast asleep and weary. So he died. (NKJV)*

The details of the story are told in a slow, suspenseful manner. Sisera asks for water, but Jael deliberately gives him milk. Whether she had determined from the outset to murder the man, or the plan evolved in her mind as it played out in life, we do not know. But Sisera regards her refreshment as a seal of the normal covenant between host and guest that will ensure his protection. He trusts so implicitly and feels so weary that he soon falls asleep. But the cup of Sisera's iniquity is full, and his life is now forfeit to divine justice.

Jael is quite familiar with the use and function of the equipment for setting up the tent, as it is the Bedouin woman's responsibility to pitch camp wherever the family-at-large decides. The tent pin and mallet were probably made of wood.[14] In a moment, Sisera lies dead at her feet.

It was certainly not the traditional method of bringing a person down, but God doesn't operate out of convention, and he often uses people who are willing to step out of comfortable, established roles to take a risk.

key point

what others say

Patsy Clairmont

I can usually spot a rut-dweller from twenty paces (takes one to know one). They lack luster, imagination, energy, and interest. They tend to slurp, slump, and sleep a lot. They prefer to gripe rather than grow, and they enjoy whine with their candlelight.

Who really wants to be like that? I saw that hand! No, you don't. In your heart . . . you know ruts offer no future. At least not one with sparkle, celebration, and verve . . . His ways rescue us from our rut-dwelling ways.[15]

When we instruct those around us to cover for us, by saying, for example, that we are "not there" when we actually are but don't wish to be disturbed, we are doing them a disservice. We (1) cause them to participate in sin, (2) induce them to lose sensitivity of conscience, and (3) teach them to do more than lie *for* us—we teach them to lie *to* us. These offenses are a grievous injury to inflict on anyone, particularly people we care about.

Dead on Arrival

JUDGES 4:22–24 *And then, as Barak pursued Sisera, Jael came out to meet him, and said to him, "Come, I will show you the man whom you seek." And when he went into her tent, there lay Sisera, dead with the peg in his temple.*

further
Psalm 76:10

cruelest
Acts 2:23–24

tense
part of the verb that
expresses who, how
many, and when

So on that day God subdued Jabin king of Canaan in the pres-
ence of the children of Israel. And the hand of the children of
Israel grew stronger and stronger against Jabin king of
Canaan, until they had destroyed Jabin king of Canaan.
(NKJV)

Sisera died at the hands of a woman—a reality that brought
embarrassment and disgrace in that culture. Jael's act is methodically
described, but the victory is just as deliberately given to God.

The totality of the army's defeat breaks the vise grip of Jabin. So
thoroughly did Israel demoralize and destroy him and his people,
the term "King of Canaan" never again occurs after this event.

It is not necessary to justify the barbaric side of Jael's deed. Even
the harshest conduct in the Scriptures is able to <u>further</u> the cause of
God and his kingdom. Look at the cross itself. The <u>cruelest</u> act in
human history—the torture and death of a loving Creator at the
hands of hateful men—was the very thing that brought freedom and
victory for the believer.

Deborah's Song

JUDGES 5:1–3 *Then Deborah and Barak the son of Abinoam*
sang on that day, saying:
    "When leaders lead in Israel,
    When the people willingly offer themselves,
    Bless the LORD!
    Hear, O kings! Give ear, O princes!
    I, even I, will sing to the LORD;
    I will sing praise to the LORD God of Israel. (NKJV)

Chapter 4 gives the report of God's victory over the Canaanites in
prose. Chapter 5 goes over the same story, using poetry. This is actually a hymn whose ancient Hebrew style testifies that this account
was indeed written "on that day" or "about that time." Not only do
we recognize the author as an eyewitness because of the vivid details,
but we can most assuredly point to Deborah over Barak, as it was
written in the feminine singular **tense**.[16] This woman not only took
the position of authority in the field of battle, but she continues that
dominance in this expressive documentation of events.

The song begins and ends like many psalms—with a call to worship. God is praised when the leaders do what they are called to do

and the people follow suit with glad cooperation. Note that the act of sacrifice on the part of the people is done with an eager and enthusiastic spirit.

Since the office of kingship does not exist in Israel at this time, the cry to kings and rulers probably refers to foreign monarchs. So the audience of those who are meant to hear this song is not restricted to the Israelites alone. It is an appeal for all nations to hear and stand amazed at what God has done.

We should seek for ways to meaningfully react to God's great acts. We should not be able to <u>restrain</u> the emotion of our response.

go to

restrain
Luke 19:37–40

Nazirite vow
Numbers 6:1–21

sacrifice
John 15:13

giving
Matthew 16:25

what others say

Bill Bright

As a result of an extremely busy schedule which takes me from country to country and continent to continent, sometimes my body is weary, my mind fatigued, and my heart is cold—yet as I begin to praise God as an act of the will, reading Psalms of praise or entering into songs of worship, my heart begins to warm, and I sense the presence of God. Soon I am praising God out of a full and grateful heart of love for him.[17]

The original rendition is a little nebulous to a twenty-first-century audience, especially when the leaders in verse 2 are spoken of in the original translation as "the long-haired ones who let their hair hang loose."[18] A man who refrains from cutting his hair does not achieve a position of esteem in our day, but was evidently revered during the time of Deborah and Barak. This may refer to those who have taken the <u>Nazirite vow</u>—a special step of dedication in which a candidate displays his holy calling by not cutting his hair (among other things). Or perhaps the flowing hair was simply a symbol of age and the wisdom that it brings.

There is no sweeter offering that we can bring than the willing <u>sacrifice</u> of ourselves for God and others. As a matter of fact, <u>giving</u> is the only way to find true joy, not clinging to what we are afraid to lose.

apply it

Off the Richter Scale

go to

depiction
Numbers 10:12;
20:22

power
Exodus 19:16–18

power
Isaiah 63:1

fear
Psalm 31:19

JUDGES 5:4–5
LORD, when You went out from Seir,
When You marched from the field of Edom,
The earth trembled and the heavens poured,
The clouds also poured water;
The mountains gushed before the LORD,
This Sinai, before the LORD God of Israel. (NKJV)

A brief historical review follows the call to worship in which God's march (with Israel in tow) to Canaan is described. He starts at Mount Sinai and goes by way of Edom. This geographical <u>depiction</u> matches the actual movement of the people through the wilderness of Seir. There is an obvious contrast between the gods of Canaan, who supposedly offer fertility and ensure abundant crops, and the God of Israel. The latter comes out of the arid south, more specifically from the barren Sinai region, where he appeared to Moses, gave him the law, and entered into covenant with his people. He doesn't have anything to prove.

The reference back to this event implies that the same God who convulsed all of nature when he showed Israel his <u>power</u>—causing the mountains to "stream" or "flow down," in the original Hebrew—will be the same one that subdues their enemies in the present.

what others say

Earl D. Radmacher

God is infinite in power. We refer to this as his omnipotence, meaning that he has unlimited resources of power and is unlimited in his exercise of it . . . All of the human resources of power for both constructive and destructive purposes . . . even when combined, do not represent as much <u>power</u> as the omnipotence of God.[19]

A. W. Tozer

The fear of God is . . . astonished reverence. I believe that the reverential <u>fear</u> of God mixed with love and fascination and astonishment and admiration and devotion is the most enjoyable state and the most satisfying emotion the human soul can know.[20]

On the Wrong Side of the Bed

Shamgar
Judges 3:31

JUDGES 5:6–8
In the days of Shamgar, son of Anath,
In the days of Jael,
The highways were deserted,
And the travelers walked along the byways.
Village life ceased, it ceased in Israel,
Until I, Deborah, arose,
Arose a mother in Israel.
They chose new gods;
Then there was war in the gates;
Not a shield or spear was seen among forty thousand in Israel.
(NKJV)

These were not happy times, and they probably wished in the mornings that they would wake up and it would all be a dream. But a description of the bleak state of Israel in these pre-Deborah days provides a magnificent contrast to the deliverance when it comes.

Shamgar is mentioned as if his lifetime occurred during these days of struggle, confirming that his was not a separate time of revival and deliverance but a heroic deed spliced into the middle of Israel's bondage and suffering.

The highways were deserted, meaning commerce was impossible. The peasants deserted the villages for the protection of the walled cities, so agriculture was disrupted and crops were abandoned. The economy had come to an obvious standstill. Because Israel had chosen new gods, the besiegers had come to their very gates. This is where the government officials sat and conducted their business. Now they could not even administer their own affairs. Either the people were effectively disarmed or they did not dare to show any weapons in the presence of their enemies.

In the midst of this disaster, appears Deborah—called a "mother in Israel." This is a title of respect, honor, and distinction.

go to

weak
Hebrews 11:33–34

All Together Now

JUDGES 5:9–11
My heart is with the rulers of Israel
Who offered themselves willingly with the people.
Bless the LORD!
Speak, you who ride on white donkeys,
Who sit in judges' attire,
And who walk along the road.
Far from the noise of the archers, among the watering places,
There they shall recount the righteous acts of the LORD,
The righteous acts for His villagers in Israel;
Then the people of the LORD shall go down to the gates. (NKJV)

Deborah expresses gratitude for all the leaders who pulled together and proved faithful in time of crisis—those who responded to Barak's call and aroused the people with their positive example. But even while offering commendation for the human elements, she does not lose sight of God, the author of every blessing.

Then she calls for the attention of all classes of people. Deborah wants everyone to pay attention to the "archers" (a better rendition than "singers") who are telling about what took place in the battle. The picture is of a group of soldiers, newly returned from battle, refreshing themselves at the springs. The villagers are here to draw water and acquire the latest information and gossip, for this is the social gathering place where news is dispensed. They eagerly crowd around the warriors and listen intently as they relate their exploits and the marvelous intervention of God to bring them victory.

After learning of their deliverance, the townspeople quickly repossess the city gates from which they were previously expelled and once again administer justice in peace and safety.

Deborah is shown in the best light of all the judges in this book. In spite of the many demands on her time and energy, she had an innate sense of what was her responsibility and what belonged to someone else—or to the Lord. First, take a look at her multiple titles and abilities:

- prophetess (Judges 4:4)
- mother in Israel (Judges 5:7)
- **arbitrator** (Judges 4:5)
- leader (Judges 4:9–10)
- strategist in warfare (Judges 4:6, 14)
- lyricist and songwriter (Judges 5:1, 7)
- place-namer (Judges 4:5)

Like Deborah, we may wear many different hats and have many demands on our time. But we cannot do it all. Sometimes Deborah deliberately stepped back and let someone <u>else</u> do the work, or recognized that a certain task was out of her hands and could be accomplished only by <u>God</u> himself. Kingdom work is a <u>corporate</u> endeavor. The quickest way to reach maximum stress and burnout is to try to do the whole job by ourselves.

go to

else
Judges 4:14, 21; 5:2, 9

God
Judges 4:23

corporate
Galatians 6:2

arbitrator
judgment maker after hearing both sides

key point

<u>Wake Up and Smell the Coffee</u>

JUDGES 5:12–13
Awake, awake, Deborah!
Awake, awake, sing a song!
Arise, Barak, and lead your captives away,
O son of Abinoam!
Then the survivors came down, the people against the nobles;
The LORD came down for me against the mighty. (NKJV)

Any call to action must first start with ourselves. Deborah's song might be a war song, for Barak is next on the list and his charge is to chain up the captives, who appear to be ready and waiting. Indeed, after God was finished with the enemy, all that was left to do was chase and nab them.

The last call is more general in nature, to the people of God who were left after years of affliction. They are to rule the same mighty nation who had ruled them.

go to

asks
Psalm 42:5

appealed
Psalms 103:1; 104:1

revival
Psalm 85:6;
Habakkuk 3:2

revival
a renewal involving
the recovery of life

To appeal to herself, as Deborah did, calling on herself to wake up and break into song, is quite common in Hebrew poetry. The sons of Korah wrote a song that <u>asks</u>, "Why are you cast down, O my soul? And why are you disquieted within me?" In the same way, David often <u>appealed</u> to his inmost being to "bless the LORD."

what others say

Corrie ten Boom

The evangelist Gypsy Smith was asked one day, "What can I do so that a **revival** will take place in my church?" The answer was, "Go into your room and take a piece of chalk; draw a circle on the floor and kneel down in the middle of it. Then pray: 'Lord bring revival to my church, and begin in the middle of this circle.'"[22]

The Good Guys in the White Hats

JUDGES 5:14–15A
From Ephraim were those whose roots were in Amalek.
After you, Benjamin, with your peoples,
From Machir rulers came down,
And from Zebulun those who bear the recruiter's staff.
And the princes of Issachar were with Deborah;
As Issachar, so was Barak
Sent into the valley under his command; (NKJV)

Ten of the twelve tribes will be mentioned by name in this passage and the next. Five and a half responded favorably to Barak's summons: Ephraim, Benjamin, Machir (West Manasseh), Zebulun, Issachar, and Naphtali.[23] Those that volunteered first received the first mention. There is praise for these tribes, for their leadership, diligence, courage, and cooperation.

what others say

Leighton Ford

Studies of human behavior have shown that when we are faced with a responsibility we know we ought to accept, and we do nothing about it, it becomes harder for us to act than before.[24]

Lazy-U Ranch

anticipation
Psalm 40:8

JUDGES 5:15B–18
Among the divisions of Reuben
There were great resolves of heart.
Why did you sit among the sheepfolds,
To hear the pipings for the flocks?
The divisions of Reuben have great searchings of heart.
Gilead stayed beyond the Jordan,
And why did Dan remain on ships?
Asher continued at the seashore,
And stayed by his inlets.
Zebulun is a people who jeopardized their lives
*   to the point of death,*
Naphtali also, on the heights of the battlefield. (NKJV)

In this section there is a repeated phrase concerning Reuben's indecision. In the original language, one letter is different between the initial statement and its echo, best represented in English by making the meaning of the first—Reuben had many "resolvings" of heart, and the second—he had many "revolvings" of heart.[25] This tribe felt an original conviction, but when they did not act on what they knew to be right, their principles turned into empty deliberation.

Reuben, Gilead (Gad and Eastern Manasseh), Dan, and Asher were criticized for not joining their countrymen.[26] Judah and Simeon are not mentioned in either chapter.

Quiet campfires and tranquil flocks present quite a contrast to the war cries of clashing armies. Gilead did not even bother to lift a finger, and Dan (who had not yet migrated) was preoccupied with its own self-interest. Asher remains aloof, in stark contrast to the wholehearted efforts of Zebulun and Naphtali, who accomplish feats of daring even on the most dangerous parts of the battlefield.

> ### what others say
>
> **Lawrence J. Crabb Jr.**
>
> Something is terribly wrong when God's directions seem no more appealing than the harsh demands of an uncaring despot. Why do we sometimes respond to biblical instruction with a reluctant attitude of "doing one's duty" much as a recruit responds to the sergeant's command to get out of bed and do fifty push-ups? Why is there not a warm and confident <u>anticipation</u> as we follow the Lord, even when the path is steep and rocky?[27]

principalities
territories ruled by
local princes

Megiddo
a city on the plain of
Esdraelon

Kishon
a crooked stream
running from the
base of Mount
Carmel

atmospheric
related to climate

God's Victory

JUDGES 5:19–20
The kings came and fought,
Then the kings of Canaan fought
In Taanach, by the waters of Megiddo;
They took no spoils of silver.
They fought from the heavens;
The stars from their courses fought against Sisera. (NKJV)

The confederation of small Canaanite **principalities** originally led into war by Sisera is now left to fend for themselves at Taanach. Taanach is one of the cities on the plain of Esdraelon, and the waters of **Megiddo** speak of the **Kishon** and its tributaries.

Instead of swiftly subduing the Israelite rebellion and coming home loaded with the rich booty they had extracted from their hapless victims, the Canaanites did not obtain one coin or particle of silver.

As a matter of fact, it seems as if the stars themselves have arrayed against them and that the heavens have opened up in fury to bring them down. If we couple these few verses with the next section, we can see that this may refer to the vehemence of a sudden storm and the **atmospheric** conditions that seem adversely set against them.

Into the Jaws of Death

JUDGES 5:21–22
The torrent of Kishon swept them away,
That ancient torrent, the torrent of Kishon.
O my soul, march on in strength!
Then the horses' hooves pounded,
The galloping, galloping of his steeds. (NKJV)

During the summer months, the river Kishon dwindles to a mere stream, and under normal conditions, the Esdraelon Valley is an excellent place to deploy chariots and horsemen.[28] But conditions are not normal, and God causes the river to overflow its banks and all its tributaries to become saturated. To the Canaanites' surprise, the low-lying areas become enormously mucky and the wheels of their chariots mire in the mud. The horses panic and the sound of their stomping, in a frantic effort to escape, echoes through the valley. The Canaanites had been confident in the power of their chariots, but when their wheels became lodged in the mud they were trapped by the very equipment they relied on the most.

God once again overrules the forces of nature to bring the mighty energy of a storm in all its fury against the enemies of his people. The chariots in which they had placed their trust ensnared them, and thwarted any chance of escape.

Poles Apart

JUDGES 5:23–24
'Curse Meroz,' said the angel of the LORD,
'Curse its inhabitants bitterly,
Because they did not come to the help of the LORD,
To the help of the LORD against the mighty.'
Most blessed among women is Jael,
The wife of Heber the Kenite;
Blessed is she among women in tents. (NKJV)

The curse upon Meroz is in direct contrast to the blessing upon Jael that immediately follows. There is no further record of Meroz in history. Most likely, Meroz was a town located along the route of Sisera's flight, whose inhabitants made little effort to capture or kill him.

But Jael is praised above all other women of nomadic origin. When she had an opportunity to act on her convictions, she did not hesitate.

God asks each person to <u>do</u> what they can.

what others say

Corrie ten Boom

I am reminded of a story about the famous conductor, Sir Michael Costa. As he was conducting a rehearsal with hundreds of instruments and voices, the mighty chorus rang out with the thunder of the organ, the roll of drums and the blare of horns. In the midst of all this din, one man who played the piccolo, far up in a corner, said to himself, "It does not matter what I do," and ceased to play.

Suddenly, the great conductor stopped, flung up his hands, and quieted the performers. "Where is the piccolo?" he cried. His sharp ear had missed it, and the whole piece had been spoiled.[29]

do
1 Corinthians 15:58

go to

battle
Numbers 24:8

useful
2 Corinthians 12:9

Milk to Sleep By

JUDGES 5:25–27
He asked for water, she gave milk;
She brought out cream in a lordly bowl.
She stretched her hand to the tent peg,
Her right hand to the workmen's hammer;
She pounded Sisera, she pierced his head,
She split and struck through his temple.
At her feet he sank, he fell, he lay still;
At her feet he sank, he fell;
Where he sank, there he fell dead. (NKJV)

Most likely, the drink that Jael offers Sisera is a type of curdled milk still prepared today by Bedouin women. It is made by shaking fresh milk in a skin bottle, which ferments as it mixes with the stale milk still adhering to the skin from the previous use.[30]

It is proffered in a special dish of large size, fit for a lord. Sisera takes this as further proof of his acceptance and quickly falls into a deep sleep.

The story swiftly builds to a climax. Sisera's fall is described, not implying that he started from a vertical position but relating how he sinks from life into death. The action verbs are strong, similar to those used of swordsmen and archers in <u>battle</u>. Jael crushed, shattered, and pierced her victim. In the end, Sisera was just plain dead. In one simple act, doing what she thought she could, Jael liberated an entire nation.

what others say

Charles R. Swindoll

When I read that God is searching the planet for men and women (please stop and read 2 Chronicles 16:9a and Ezekiel 22:30), I do not find that he has a structured, well-defined frame into which they must fit. In fact, some of those God used most effectively were made up of the strangest mixture you could imagine . . .

I believe you anticipate my point. Let's be as open and flexible and tolerant as God is! Perhaps *you* don't fit the mold. Maybe you don't embrace the party-line system, so you're beginning to think "I'm not <u>useful</u> to God—I'll never be a leader in the ranks of Christianity." Take heart, discouraged believer.[31]

One for Me, One for You . . .

ruminations
chewing something
over again

JUDGES 5:28–30
The mother of Sisera looked through the window,
And cried out through the lattice,
'Why is his chariot so long in coming?
Why tarries the clatter of his chariots?'
Her wisest ladies answered her,
Yes, she answered herself,
'Are they not finding and dividing the spoil:
To every man a girl or two;
For Sisera, plunder of dyed garments,
Plunder of garments embroidered and dyed,
Two pieces of dyed embroidery for the neck of the looter?' (NKJV)

As Sisera lingers almost beyond the point of endurance for those who await his return, the thought occurs to his mother that the delay might mean that grief and shame have somehow become attached to this mission. But her maidens, knowing how to get her mind off such worries, direct her to a favorite subject. What souvenirs of war will Sisera bring home for her?

Insight is shown (perhaps because the author is a woman) into the female character, who (unlike the male, whose chief concern on the battlefield is to demonstrate his prowess and maintain his reputation) thinks mainly about the personal gain that success in combat will bring. Sisera's mother dreams of slaves, garments, and ornaments, for these are the traditional prizes of war. However, instead of showering family and friends with plunder, Sisera is in no position to provide them with anything. His mother's imagined glories are merely futile illusions.

These verses are not included to elicit sympathy for the other side. Rather, they demonstrate the impact of Jael's accomplishment. But for her the Israelites would be enslaved and destitute, while the Canaanites would be gleefully distributing the people and plunder they had appropriated.

You would think that the concept of the men taking women for the purpose of sport would be degrading to other women, but we find Sisera's mother and her maidens delighting in the thought. Their **ruminations** are a good indicator of the status of women at this time, and further emphasize the astonishing use of Deborah in God's economy. Deborah proves that women have merit and that God is not restricted by the closed-mindedness of the times.

all
Galatians 3:26–29

bigotry
intolerance toward
people who are
different

God can and will use people from <u>all</u> ages, genders, and walks of life, regardless of the **bigotry** of others.

There are three instances in the Old Testament where a woman is found looking out a window:

1. Sisera's mother (Judges 5:28)

2. Michal (2 Samuel 6:16)

3. Jezebel (2 Kings 9:30)

All three opposed God, and in the end all three had to suffer the consequences.

Ol' Sol

> JUDGES 5:31
> *Thus let all Your enemies perish, O LORD!*
> *But let those who love Him be like the sun*
> *When it comes out in full strength."*
> *So the land had rest for forty years. (NKJV)*

There is no concluding statement concerning the fate of Sisera's mother, although the implementation of this verse would bring about her downfall, along with all the other enemies of God.

The type of blessing here pronounced indicates the heart of the individual speaking rather than the need of God for the well-wishes of men and women. God *will* put his enemies in their places, and he *will* strengthen those who love him whether we desire it or not. But this poetic finale pleads quite eloquently for the wrong to fail and the right to prevail.

The last sentence resumes with prose to state how long the land of Israel will remain at rest.

Psalm 19:4–6 (NKJV) gives another fascinating word picture with the strength of the sun as its focus. The preceding verses have stated that the heavens declare God's glory and the skies proclaim the works of his hand. To demonstrate this, the sun comes forth every day like a "bridegroom coming out of his chamber" who "rejoices," or like a "strong man to run its race." The sun displays God's strength and vitality as it travels across the heavens.

Something to ponder

This is the kind of energy and vigor that Deborah desires for all of us who love the Lord.

Chapter Wrap-Up

- God calls Barak, through Deborah the judge, to deliver Israel from the Canaanites. With Deborah's assistance, he gathers an army and goes out to fight. (Judges 4:1–13)

- God wins the victory and in the end turns Sisera (the Canaanite commander) over to Jael (a Bedouin woman), who kills him with a tent peg. (Judges 4:14–24)

- Deborah and Barak sing about the circumstances that surround the battle, praising those who participated and questioning those who did not. (Judges 5:1–18)

- God is accorded credit for his miraculous intervention; Jael is blessed for her involvement; Sisera's mother is presented to show a contrast. (Judges 5:19–31)

Study Questions

1. Why did Barak want Deborah to go with him, and what were the consequences of his hesitation?

2. For what did Jael receive more praise than any other nomadic women?

3. When the call was issued to the tribes to assist in the uprising, who did Deborah call first? Why is this important?

4. What happened when Reuben did not act on his convictions? Why should we follow up on the promptings of our hearts?

Chapter Highlights:
• Gideon's Confrontation
• Deaf and Dumber
• Hero for a Day
• Gideon's Hesitation
• Gideon's Preparation

Let's Get Started

Fear is often the ball and chain that shackle us and prevent us from achieving our potential. The Midianites had browbeaten and demoralized the Israelites until they were broken in spirit and completely lacking in confidence. Among their number is a young man who can only be described as anxious and intimidated, until God starts working on him. Totally driven by fear, at first his only desire is survival.

But slowly and patiently, God opens for him a whole new vista of panoramic proportions. With little nudges, God encourages him to look beyond his own restricted world to see what he can do to free his people from their daily misery and suffering. God has chosen Gideon to liberate the nation of Israel, but first he must convince him that he is the man for the job.

key point

Gideon's Confrontation

JUDGES 6:1–5 *Then the children of Israel did evil in the sight of the LORD. So the LORD delivered them into the hand of Midian for seven years, and the hand of Midian prevailed against Israel. Because of the Midianites, the children of Israel made for themselves the dens, the caves, and the strongholds which are in the mountains. So it was, whenever Israel had sown, Midianites would come up; also Amalekites and the people of the East would come up against them. Then they would encamp against them and destroy the produce of the earth as far as Gaza, and leave no sustenance for Israel, neither sheep nor ox nor donkey. For they would come up with their livestock and their tents, coming in as numerous as locusts; both they and their camels were without number; and they would enter the land to destroy it.* (NKJV)

Israel's fourth period of oppression comes from the hands of the Midianites after the Israelites once again abuse God's generosity. The Midianites are tent-dwellers who live to the east and southeast of the Dead Sea.[1] In typical nomadic fashion, they set up temporary

go to

flee
Ruth 1:1

eat
Deuteronomy
6:10–12

Keturah
Genesis 25:1–6

Jethro
Exodus 3:1

guided
Numbers 10:29–33

advised
Exodus 18

curse
Numbers 22:4–7

seduce
Numbers 25:16–18

foray
Numbers 31:1–7

itinerant
traveling for work

voracious
consuming food in
great quantities

quarters on land that is not their own, using the surrounding pasture to accommodate the enormous appetites of their herds and helping themselves to whatever fruit and produce they can lay their hands on. Because of the sheer numbers of Midianites invading their land, the Israelites are helpless to defend what is rightfully their own.

The Midianites share a commonality with the Amalekites (who have infiltrated at the same time from the south) in that they are both **itinerant** drifters from the Syrian Desert region.[2] This is the first reference to an organized invasion in which camels are used, making raids from longer distances possible.

The ravaging is so comprehensive that all the Israelites can do is head for caves and mountain retreats for refuge. This may be the era in which Elimelech and Naomi flee from Bethlehem to Moab, be-cause food has become so scarce.[3]

God had planned that the Israelites should eat what they did not plant, but after their rejection of his plan, others eat what they have planted.

The Midianites were the descendants of Keturah, Abraham's sec-ond wife. Midian was one of her five sons, who himself bore five sons. When Abraham made provision for his heirs, he gave gifts to Midian and sent him and his brothers to the east to separate them from the son that God had promised to bless—Isaac.

On the one hand, Jethro (Moses's father-in-law, who was of Midianite ancestry) guided the Israelites during some of their wilderness wanderings, and advised Moses on a more practical form of government. On the other hand, we know also that the Midianites joined Moab in asking Baalam to curse Israel and tried to seduce them to accept immorality and idolatry, bringing a scourging plague upon the entire Israelite community.

Because of this, Moses led a foray against the Midianites, almost cutting down the entire race, some two hundred years before Gideon came on the scene. But now the Midianites have recovered and once again roam the fertile land of Israel to accommodate their **voracious** appetites. Retaliation could be an underlying motive for the severe devastation they leave in their wake.

Deaf and Dumber

go to

compression
Joshua 4:23;
Jeremiah 2:7;
Hebrews 3:7–8

consequences
Exodus 20:5

profit
Exodus 20:6

anoint
2 Kings 9:1–3

pronounce
1 Samuel 2:27–34

challenge
1 Kings 13

companies
1 Samuel 10:10;
2 Kings 2:3, 5, 7, 15

> **the big picture**
>
> **Judges 6:6–10**
>
> God sent a prophet, in response to Israel's cries of destitution, who reminded them how God had worked past miracles in their behalf. He said that Israel had ignored the Lord's request not to worship the gods of the land, and refused to listen when he spoke to them.

This impoverishing was a different kind of oppression than Israel had ever experienced before, but never had the punishment seemed so grievous. When they cry out to the Lord, he reminds them (through a prophet) of the merciful deliverance he characteristically enacts, but which they have forfeited through neglect and disobedience.

He speaks of bringing them out of Egypt's slavery and driving their enemies out of the land during conquest, as if they were personally present and years had not passed since their forefathers had experienced these wonders. This <u>compression</u> of many generations into one collective unit is quite common in Scripture. Even though these particular children of Israel only existed during the time of Israel's sojourn in Egypt in the sense that they were present in the makeup of their ancestors' genes, the legacy and heritage of the parents demands a strong accountability and responsibility in the children. They have had so much, but have only turned a deaf ear.

Each one of our actions and dealings must be evaluated in light of the knowledge that our heirs will reap the <u>consequences</u> of the poor decisions we make. Conversely, our offspring will also <u>profit</u> and greatly benefit from the positive associations and constructive projects we engage in. We do not exist merely for ourselves.

something to ponder

Unnamed prophets make frequent appearances in Scripture—the messages uttered being of far greater import than the bearers of the messages themselves. They <u>anoint</u> kings, <u>pronounce</u> judgments, and <u>challenge</u> nations.

Under Samuel, many unnamed prophets banded together and, in subsequent years, <u>companies</u> of them played an important role in the life of Israel.

Hero for a Day

> JUDGES 6:11–12 *Now the Angel of the LORD came and sat under the terebinth tree which was in Ophrah, which belonged to Joash the Abiezrite, while his son Gideon threshed wheat in the winepress, in order to hide it from the Midianites. And the Angel of the LORD appeared to him, and said to him, "The LORD is with you, you mighty man of valor!"* (NKJV)

The message to Israel came through a prophet; the message to Gideon came from God himself. We know that this appearance is of the Lord (and not just an angelic figure) because verse 14 refers to him as "the LORD" (Jehovah). And what dignified occupation is Gideon involved in when God comes to visit? He's hiding in a winepress, pounding wheat.

Without any introduction, God's first words are like a slap in the face. Gideon feels the mockery of such affirmation when he is so powerless to meet his own needs, much less those of the entire country.

Cisterns uncovered in archaeological research in Israel are generally underground cavities carved out of stone with two sections, one slightly below the other. In the upper area, a man would tread upon the grapes and after the liquid reached a certain height, the juice would enter a drain. The drain siphoned the flow to the lower vat. In this compartment the wine was stored.[4]

Gideon's Hesitation

> JUDGES 6:13 *Gideon said to Him, "O my lord, if the LORD is with us, why then has all this happened to us? And where are all His miracles which our fathers told us about, saying, 'Did not the LORD bring us up from Egypt?' But now the LORD has forsaken us and delivered us into the hands of the Midianites."* (NKJV)

Gideon doesn't beat around the bush. He blurts out the most difficult question in the universe, the question that is gnawing at his gut—why? Why has God allowed this to happen to him—especially if God is truly involved with what happens on earth and capable of interceding? Gideon is aware of the times when God has intervened in the past, so now he concludes that God no longer cares.

When the Lord speaks, he uses the singular tense, "The Lord is with *you* . . ." But when Gideon replies, he uses the plural, "if the Lord is with *us* . . ." He is careful not to monopolize the favor and desires to include all his suffering brothers and sisters.

If you look at the *size* of a trial, you may conclude that God is not willing or capable of intervention. The fact that we suffer does not mean God has irrevocably withdrawn his presence or support. In this particular instance, God was simply waiting for Gideon to act on his validation, whence deliverance would be found.

There is no struggle too <u>difficult</u> for God to handle or trial of life in which he cannot be <u>found</u>. He has both the strength and the desire to take care of us. There is nothing that can <u>separate</u> us from his love. He cannot forget us any more than a <u>mother</u> can forget a nursing infant. We are a part of him.

something to ponder

what others say

Vance Havner

If I could stand for five minutes at his <u>vantage point</u> and see the entire scheme of things as He sees it, how absurd would be my dreads, how ridiculous my fears and tears![5]

Who—Me?

JUDGES 6:14–16 *Then the LORD turned to him and said, "Go in this might of yours, and you shall save Israel from the hand of the Midianites. Have I not sent you?" So he said to Him, "O my Lord, how can I save Israel? Indeed my clan is the weakest in Manasseh, and I am the least in my father's house." And the LORD said to him, "Surely I will be with you, and you shall defeat the Midianites as one man." (NKJV)*

go to

difficult
Isaiah 43:2

found
Psalm 23:4

separate
Romans 8:38–39

mother
Isaiah 49:15–16

vantage point
Job 40:1–4

efficacious
having the power to produce a result

The Lord turns to Gideon and the look that he gives (in the original language) is **efficacious**—filled with the power to banish fear and inspire confidence.[6] God will need to give Gideon a boost because of the insecurities he feels over his origin and background. Gideon is the youngest son of Joash, of the clan of Abiezer, of the tribe of Manasseh. His home is in the obscure village of Ophrah, and as to spiritual heritage, his father is an idolater.

No matter. God's stamp of approval ought to be enough for anybody. God affirms that the Midianites will be dealt with in one clean sweep.

Poor origins and unstable backgrounds do not eliminate <u>anyone</u> from a place of service in God's design and program.

Many of the individuals God chose for the highest positions of leadership exhibited a spirit of reticent humility at their call. <u>Moses</u> keenly felt his insignificant position and propensity to stutter; <u>Saul</u> hid among the baggage at his coronation; <u>David</u> would not usurp the position of the outgoing ruler even after he'd been anointed king; <u>Isaiah</u> was insecure because he wasn't holy or pure enough; <u>Jeremiah</u> thought of himself as immature and unable to speak in public.

But it is only with those people who recognize their own insufficiencies that God can work. In our <u>weakness</u>, he can demonstrate his strength.

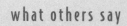

what others say

Sammy Tippet

True faith is simply our acceptance of His acceptance of us based on what Jesus did on the cross . . . We have a new power to accept ourselves as we are. That enables us to accept others in a revolutionary way. We can witness for Christ powerfully and boldly without fear of rejection. But most important, we have peace and contentment. That security gives us the ability to stand alone . . . for God. We have been <u>accepted</u> by Him and that's all that matters.[7]

anyone
1 Chronicles 29:12

Moses
Exodus 3:11; 4:10

Saul
1 Samuel 10:22–24

David
1 Samuel 24:4–7

Isaiah
Isaiah 6:5

Jeremiah
Jeremiah 1:6

weakness
2 Corinthians 13:4

accepted
Psalm 73:26

Talk About It over Dinner

JUDGES 6:17–19 *Then he said to Him, "If now I have found favor in Your sight, then show me a sign that it is You who talk with me. Do not depart from here, I pray, until I come to You and bring out my offering and set it before You." And He said, "I will wait until you come back."*

So Gideon went in and prepared a young goat, and unleavened bread from an ephah of flour. The meat he put in a basket, and he put the broth in a pot; and he brought them out to Him under the terebinth tree and presented them. (NKJV)

The most likely method of preparation in the oriental manner is to cut a portion of the meat into small pieces to be roasted on a skewer. This would be served in a small handbasket of leaves or rushes. The rest of the meat would be made into a stew to be served with unleavened bread.[8]

The whole process of serving a meal was for the purpose of discreetly determining "that it is really you." Gideon needed a way to decide if the guest was truly a supernatural visitor or just a well-intentioned prophet. How the offering was received would establish the value and import of the disturbing message that had been delivered. However scarce the provisions, Gideon looks for a confirmation that this whole episode is more than a stranger's whim and that the summons is backed by almighty God. So he gives the messenger the best that he has.

Now You See Me, Now You Don't!

JUDGES **6:20–22** *The Angel of God said to him, "Take the meat and the unleavened bread and lay them on this rock, and pour out the broth." And he did so.*

Then the Angel of the LORD *put out the end of the staff that was in His hand, and touched the meat and the unleavened bread; and fire rose out of the rock and consumed the meat and the unleavened bread. And the Angel of the* LORD *departed out of his sight. Now Gideon perceived that He was the Angel of the* LORD. *So Gideon said, "Alas, O Lord* GOD! *For I have seen the Angel of the* LORD *face to face." (NKJV)*

The Lord gives Gideon special orders for setting out the meal on an improvised altar. The fire that consumes the food is a mark of divine acceptance, just as it was in the days of Moses and <u>Aaron</u> at the dedication of the temple and later for the prophet <u>Elijah</u> on Mount Carmel.

Gideon recognizes at last that he has been speaking to God in the flesh, and fears <u>death</u> because he has heard that no one can look upon God and live. But, like <u>Abraham</u>, <u>Moses</u>, <u>Joshua</u>, and many others who see the figure of the **pre-incarnate** Christ in the Old Testament, Gideon's life is not in danger. The physical appearance of **Christ** can encompass all that God is in a <u>form</u> that is compatible with human existence.

go to

Aaron
Leviticus 9:24

Elijah
1 Kings 18:38

death
Exodus 33:20

Abraham
Genesis 18:1

Moses
Exodus 34:29

Joshua
Joshua 5:13–15

form
Philippians 2:5–8

pre-incarnate
before physical birth

Christ
Jesus, the Savior to come

key point

Why was God so gracious to accommodate Gideon's need for a sign? In later days, <u>Zechariah</u> the priest asks for a sign to affirm that the Lord has really spoken to him and is rebuked and punished. Even later, Jesus says that only a <u>wicked</u> and adulterous generation will ask for a sign.

God's response seems to be determined by where the person is coming from. Zechariah was a priest, ministering daily in the presence of the Lord, with all the wealth and knowledge of the Scriptures at his disposal. So, it's reasonable to assume that he'd done what he could on his own.

But on the contrary, the generation to whom Jesus refused a sign had refused to acknowledge the Lord even when he was standing right in front of them. They did not need to see miracles and wonders. They needed to see God himself.

But Gideon was raised during a time when no one was worshipping God and it would have been difficult to find out about God's ways. God had not been seen or heard from, directly, for years. So God is willing to start at ground zero and reach out to Gideon just where he is, even if that means he will need some extra assurances.

Not Your Time to Go

> JUDGES 6:23–24 Then the LORD said to him, "Peace be with you; do not fear, you shall not die." So Gideon built an altar there to the LORD, and called it The-LORD-Is-Peace. To this day it is still in Ophrah of the Abiezrites. (NKJV)

Whether God speaks to Gideon by audible voice or inner suggestion we do not know. But when he came it comforted and cheered, and when he left it created awe and wonder.

Zechariah
Luke 1:11–20

wicked
Matthew 16:4

turning points
Job 42:5–6

Although Gideon's call is to war, it is from the God who gives peace. Gideon builds an altar to commemorate the meeting and the message. And when the author of the book of Judges penned these words, it was still standing.

We all have <u>turning points</u> in our lives when God speaks to us in such a way that we can never remain the same.

Gideon's Preparation

JUDGES 6:25–27 *Now it came to pass the same night that the LORD said to him, "Take your father's young bull, the second bull of seven years old, and tear down the altar of Baal that your father has, and cut down the wooden image that is beside it; and build an altar to the LORD your God on top of this rock in the proper arrangement, and take the second bull and offer a burnt sacrifice with the wood of the image which you shall cut down." So Gideon took ten men from among his servants and did as the LORD had said to him. But because he feared his father's household and the men of the city too much to do it by day, he did it by night. (NKJV)*

Assignment number one involves putting his own house in order. Gideon's ability to follow through on this mission is essential, as it will (1) show his countrymen exactly where he stands, (2) prove to himself that he has the gumption to stand up against evil, and (3) serve as a test case. Will God defend Gideon against his own people? If so, then he can certainly do the same with his enemies.

Characteristically, Gideon is controlled by his misgivings, and this is no exception. He surrounds himself with ten of his servants and performs the task that God has asked, under cover of darkness. But the job gets done and Gideon is stretching himself to become more of the type of person God can use.

go to

complaining
Philippians 2:12–15

glory
Matthew 5:16

glories
Judges 6:13

sacrilege
desecration of something considered holy

apply it

> **what others say**
>
> ### Frank Minirth and Paul Meier
>
> Serving God can help alleviate your feelings of inferiority. As the writer of Ecclesiastes discusses throughout the last chapter of his book of wisdom, servanthood among God's people is the only thing that brings real meaning to life. Only as time passes . . . will the correlation between joy and ministry become clear. Then the divine mystery unfolds: happiness follows . . . helping others.[10]

Instead of <u>complaining</u> about the way things are, we should get out and do something! We give God <u>glory</u> when we are busy and industrious.

Humpty-Dumpty

> **the big picture**
>
> ### Judges 6:28–32
>
> After investigation, the townspeople discover that Gideon is the one who has torn apart their place of idol worship. They demand his life. Joash, Gideon's father, defends him by contending that if Baal is a real god, he can stand up for himself. He should not need mortals to defend him. The people listen to the reasoning of Joash and call Gideon "Jerubbaal."

The villagers are incensed by the **sacrilege** that Gideon has committed, and demand his life. The fact is, if God's law was still being kept, *they* would be the ones to be put to death for the worship of pagan gods. Israel has so twisted right and wrong that they are ready to kill the one they ought to applaud and support.

Perhaps the conscience of Joash has been prodding him for some time. Or maybe this act of bravery on the part of his son has brought a sudden conviction. Joash may have been the one to originally teach Gideon of Israel's former <u>glories</u>, although his ownership of idols shows he himself had not been faithful to the true God. But when the crisis came, Joash made the right choice.

His analysis brings the villagers to their senses. Why pray to some being to help you if it cannot even help itself? On the basis of his father's **oratory**, Gideon is not harmed and is given a new name, meaning: "let Baal plead." Now every time someone calls his name, it will be a reminder that Baal does *not* have any power and *cannot* even "put himself together again."

God is not God if he is <u>impotent</u>.

impotent
Isaiah 50:2

Ehud
Judges 3:27

oratory
gracious speech

impotent
without power

<u>Choosing Sides</u>

JUDGES 6:33–35 *Then all the Midianites and Amalekites, the people of the East, gathered together; and they crossed over and encamped in the Valley of Jezreel. But the Spirit of the LORD came upon Gideon; then he blew the trumpet, and the Abiezrites gathered behind him. And he sent messengers throughout all Manasseh, who also gathered behind him. He also sent messengers to Asher, Zebulun, and Naphtali; and they came up to meet them. (NKJV)*

After the nomadic people join forces and prepare for battle in the Jezreel Valley, the Spirit of the Lord envelops (literally: "clothes") Gideon so that he is enabled to accomplish the purposes of God.[11] He causes the trumpet to sound (like <u>Ehud</u>), calling the Israelites to arms.

The Abiezrites (Gideon's clan) rally first to his side. Then Manasseh follows with Asher, Zebulun, and Naphtali.

The Valley of Jezreel (synonymous with the Esdraelon Valley)[12] forms a triangle, eighteen by fifteen by twelve miles from end to end.[13] More specifically, this valley extends from Mount Carmel near the coast, all the way to the Jordan River, with one branch widening between Mount Tabor and the Hill of Moreh and another between the Hill of Moreh and Mount Gilboa.[14]

This is the heart of Canaan and has been the scene of many battles throughout history. The following individuals and groups have played a prominent role in this place: Barak, Gideon, Josiah, Holofernes, Vespasian, the Crusaders, Saracens, Turks, French, and General Allenby.[15]

go to

knows
Psalm 139:1–3

will
Isaiah 29:13

desires
Psalm 37:4

Dry as a Bone—Uh, Fleece

the big picture

Judges 6:36–40

Gideon pleads for two more signs. One night he asks that a fleece, placed on a threshing floor, be wet with dew by the next morning while the ground around it remains dry. The next night, he requests that the fleece remain dry while the ground around it becomes wet. God does just as Gideon asks.

God not only allows his words to be confirmed in an unusual way, but he does it with flair. The Scriptures say that in the morning, Gideon squeezed out a *bowlful* of water. The next night, the ground did not just show a slight amount of moisture. The Bible says it was *covered* with dew!

Obviously, the chances of a double sign like this occurring in nature, by pure coincidence, are most unlikely. But the God who <u>knows</u> the makeup of every individual in his creation knew that Gideon required an extra impetus to launch his career and graciously complied to his requests.

what others say

Gary Collins

Like many peak performers, most of the people who made a difference in the Bible were not well known. *Some Resisted* . . . Gideon was more cooperative, but twice he asked for a sign to be sure that he really was the man that God wanted to lead an army into battle.[16]

When it comes to finding out what God wants you to *do* in certain situations, your primary concern should be making sure you are the person he wants you to *be*. Once you are sure your life is in line with his <u>will</u>, you can make a decision knowing that you desire what he desires.

what others say

John MacArthur

The will of God is not, first of all, for you to go there or work here. The will of God concerns you as a person. If you are the right you, you can follow your <u>desires</u> and you will fulfill His will.[17]

what others say

Garry Friesen

The practice of "putting out a fleece" cannot be established by the scriptural passage on which it is based. For Gideon was not seeking a circumstantial sign, but a miraculous one; he did not use the fleece to obtain guidance, but to confirm guidance already given; and his motivation was not a desire to do God's will, but rather his reluctance to follow God's guidance because of his own doubts.[18]

Scaredy-Cats

JUDGES 7:1–3 *Then Jerubbaal (that is, Gideon) and all the people who were with him rose early and encamped beside the well of Harod, so that the camp of the Midianites was on the north side of them by the hill of Moreh in the valley. And the LORD said to Gideon, "The people who are with you are too many for Me to give the Midianites into their hands, lest Israel claim glory for itself against Me, saying, 'My own hand has saved me.' Now therefore, proclaim in the hearing of the people, saying, 'Whoever is fearful and afraid, let him turn and depart at once from Mount Gilead.'" And twenty-two thousand of the people returned, and ten thousand remained. (NKJV)*

The spring of Harod can be found today, fresh and sweet, at the foot of Mount Gilboa. Israel camped at this place with only 32,000 men, while Midian had at least 135,000.[19] That's an advantage for the enemy of four to one, but the Israelite army was still too large for God's purposes.

Actually, the <u>law</u> included a provision that allowed the faint-hearted to be sent home from military service, to maintain the morale of the remaining troops. But the current need might have induced many to participate in Gideon's campaign who really didn't want to.

When given the opportunity, two-thirds of the men return to their homes, leaving a paltry ten thousand. But Israel (as is true of us as well) needs God far more than he needs them.

We should never forget how little our own efforts impact our success and how vitally we require God's <u>support</u>.

go to

self
Isaiah 53:6;
1 Peter 2:25

sufficiency
ability to come up
with what is needed

endowments
the provision of gifts

Dog-lapping

the big picture

Judges 7:4–8

There are still too many men in God's reckoning. At the springs, the Lord instructs Gideon to separate those who use their hands to lap water like a dog from those who kneel down to drink. Gideon keeps the three hundred who lap, sends the rest of the men home, and retains the trumpets and provisions of all.

God has further sifting to do to separate the men he intends to use for this campaign from those he can use elsewhere. The defining line is positioned somewhere between the lappers and the non-lappers.

Two descriptions are given of the lappers: (1) "Everyone who laps from the water with his tongue, as a dog laps" (Judges 7:5 NKJV), or (2) they lap by "putting their hand to their mouth" (7:6 NKJV). Evidently they used their hands like a dog would use his tongue to rapidly scoop the water into their mouths. These are distinguished from the ones who kneel down to suck up long, successive draughts from the spring. The advantage for the lappers is twofold: (1) they could quench their thirst in less time, and (2) they could remain alert for battle.

The three hundred take over the provisions and equipment of the entire ten thousand. Thus they will have all the supplies they could possibly need.

However, the primary reason for the drastic reduction in the size of Israel's army is related to a lesson God desires to teach them about self-reliance. God does not want the soldiers to have any confidence in their own **sufficiency**. He wants their entire focus to be on *his* help and **endowments**.

key point

what others say

Patrick Morley

When we don't need to depend on Christ, we will not . . . Our natural tendency is to depend on <u>self</u>, not on Christ. Depending on Christ is an act of the will by faith, not the natural disposition of our heart.[20]

Like a Bad Dream

go to

committing
Isaiah 50:7

the big picture

Judges 7:9–15a

The Lord prompts Gideon to sneak down the valley to the camp of the Midianites with his servant. While there, Gideon overhears a man describing a dream he had to a friend. In his dream a loaf of barley bread comes tumbling into the Midianite camp, overturning and collapsing the tent. His friend replies that the dream means God has given the Midianites into Gideon's hand. Gideon responds by worshipping the Lord.

Perhaps the size of his tiny army has once again filled Gideon with misgivings. But now is the time to act boldly and with courage, so God offers one last sign without Gideon's even asking for it. The sign comes in the presence of Purah (Gideon's servant), who can then confirm that this authentication is not simply the delusion of a desperate man.

In this case, God uses a most unlikely source to encourage his chosen leader. Both the dream and its interpretation are put, by divine suggestion, into the mind and mouth of the enemy. But they are meant for the ears of Gideon.

The likelihood of a cake of barley overturning anything is very low, but so was that of three hundred untrained, inexperienced men defeating what seemed to Gideon an uncountable number. Only the poor, lower class would eat a cake made of barley flour (wheat was preferred), reminding Gideon of the status of Israel at this time—not only underrated but undesirable. But the insignificant and unappreciated will overcome even the mighty—like a bowling ball barreling through a set of pins. God is underwriting Gideon and the success of his endeavor, and Gideon rightly responds in worshipful gratitude.

what others say

Tim and Christine Burke

Several beneficial things did happen as a result of <u>committing</u> my career to the Lord. From that day on, I knew I had to concern myself only with my own effort and then trust the Lord with the results. If those results were good, it would be great, if they were bad, I would still believe he wasn't going to make his first mistake with me.[21]

apply it

The individual who receives the full <u>confirmation</u> of God (which a person certainly does at salvation) must respond in the same manner as Gideon. Upon hearing God's endorsement, Gideon knelt before God and worshipped in adoration and thanksgiving. In the same way, praise and <u>worship</u> ought to come from us as an automatic response to his acceptance and care.

Chapter Wrap-Up

go to

confirmation
John 5:24;
Romans 8:1;
Titus 3:5–7

worship
Psalm 27:4–5;
1 Chronicles 16:29;
Colossians 1:12

- God surprises Gideon with a personal challenge, and Gideon responds with hesitation. (Judges 6:1–24)
- Gideon takes a small step of obedience in tearing down his father's idols. (Judges 6:25–32)
- Gideon further tests his call and is filled with the Spirit of God. (Judges 6:33–40)
- God eliminates all the soldiers he does not need. (Judges 7:1–8)
- Gideon is provided with one last confirmation. (Judges 7:9–15)

Study Question

1. What is the first question that Gideon poses to the Lord? What is the answer?

2. What commonality did the following leaders experience: Moses, Gideon, Saul, David, Isaiah, and Jeremiah?

3. What was Gideon's first assignment, and what did its completion prove?

4. Is putting out a fleece a valid means of determining God's will today?

Judges 7:15b–8:35
Conditioning Gideon

Chapter Highlights:
- Gideon's Aggression
- The Race to Chase
- Gideon's Opposition
- Double Trouble
- Gideon's Remission

Let's Get Started

All told, Gideon has received a total of five confirmations to his call. Check out the following:

- His meal was consumed while the angel disappeared. (6:21)
- God protected him from the wrath of the townspeople. (6:30–32)
- The fleece was wet when the ground was dry. (6:37–38)
- The ground was wet when the fleece was dry. (6:39–40)
- The interpretation of the enemy's dream declared that Gideon would win. (7:13–14)

God's appeal to Gideon in the midst of his misery brings out the best in his character. In this chapter we will observe his success in rescuing Israel from the domination of Midian. Examining God's obvious call and Gideon's careful but certain response, we could easily believe that he would never again doubt God nor waver in his devotion to the Lord for the rest of his life.

However, after the initial squeeze is off, people tend to **regress** and relax in their passionate commitment for what is praiseworthy and honorable. Will Gideon be able to continue to eradicate evil in Israel and stimulate the people for good?

regress
return to a worse state

Gideon's Aggression

the big picture

Judges 7:15b–21

Emboldened by the words he has heard from the mouth of the enemy, Gideon returns to the Israelite camp and orders his men to get up, saying that God has given the Midianites into their hands.

As per Gideon's instructions, three companies of men place themselves around the perimeter of the Midianite tents with a trumpet in the right hand and a "pitcher" or jar in the left hand of each man. Each jar contains a torch. Soon after the change of

three
1 Samuel 11:11;
2 Samuel 18:2

psychologically
Ephesians 6:10–18;
1 Peter 1:13;
Romans 8:6

> guard in the Midianite camp, the Israelites follow Gideon's lead, blowing the trumpets, breaking the jars, holding the torches aloft, and shouting, "The sword of the LORD and of Gideon!" (Judges 7:20 NKJV). While the Israelites hold their position, the Midianites cry out and run.

The strategy that calls for the division of the ranks into three separate units to confront the enemy from multiple sides is an excellent ploy, adopted on many occasions by the Israelites.

The weapons are quite unusual, but serve their purpose in psychological warfare very well. The jars are made of earthenware; they can be easily broken, which generates an enormous clamor. The torches would be of pitch-smeared wood, so as not to be easily extinguished by wind or activity.[1] When the pots were shattered the torches would flare up and then provide just enough light for the Midianites to slaughter each other—but not enough for them to distinguish friend from foe. The trumpets would be ram's horns (*shofars*), typically used in warfare to signal and announce. The enemy's assumption would be that each trumpet represented an entire company of fighting men.

There are three watches throughout the night, of four hours each, the first beginning at 6:00 p.m.[2] Gideon chooses the time during which his rivals would have sunk into the deepest slumber, and in the ensuing fray, be thrown into the most bewilderment.

The cry that Gideon instructs his army to use includes the words he heard from the Midianite soldier, interpreting his buddy's dream. The man had said of the barley loaf that it could represent none other than "the sword of Gideon." So Gideon incorporates this notion into the slogan that the Israelites shout at the commencement of the battle: "The sword of the LORD and of Gideon!"

Most battles are psychologically won or lost in the mind long before they are ever actually fought.

The Race to Chase

the big picture

Judges 7:22–24

In the ensuing confusion, the Midianites turn on one another with their swords. Those who escape flee toward Beth Shittah.

go to

everyone
1 Corinthians
12:14–25

seed
Matthew 17:20

place
Isaiah 10:26

trophy
1 Samuel 17:57;
Matthew 14:8–11

The Israelites from Naphtali, Asher, and Manasseh are alerted and join in the chase, and soon after, Ephraim is also encouraged to stop the enemies' flight over the Jordan as far as Beth Barah.

The panic among the Midianites is unparalleled. Those who escape take the most natural line of flight to the east—down the valley, over the Jordan, and back to the regions from which they came.

The initial victory has been won by the three hundred handpicked specialists, but now even those who had previously been dismissed can help pursue the remaining enemy. Gideon's initial summons is to the tribes closest to the lines of flight. Then, when the pursuit continues, he asks Ephraim to seal off the escape routes farther away. Thus God enables three hundred Israelites—basically unarmed—to bring the forces of Midian into such confusion that they start a massacre among themselves.

There is an ideal place of service for <u>everyone</u> who is willing to help.

what others say

Andrew Murray

Dear Christian, I pray you, as you read God's wonderful promises and long to have them fulfilled, remember the grain of mustard <u>seed</u>. However small, if it be put into the ground and allowed to grow, it becomes a great tree. Take the hidden feeble seed of the little faith you have, with the word of promise on which you are resting; plant it in your heart.[3]

Two Heads Are Better Than One

JUDGES 7:25 *And they captured two princes of the Midianites, Oreb and Zeeb. They killed Oreb at the rock of Oreb, and Zeeb they killed at the winepress of Zeeb. They pursued Midian and brought the heads of Oreb and Zeeb to Gideon on the other side of the Jordan.* (NKJV)

Two Midianite leaders find shelter—one in the cavern of a rock, the other in the vat of a winepress. After they've been discovered and slain, the places where they have hidden take on *their* names, but the locations are never identified or mentioned in more than one other <u>place</u>.

In biblical times, the head of an enemy was considered quite a <u>trophy</u>.

Displaying the detached head of an enemy as a keepsake seems grisly to us today, but we have our own set of garish behaviors (<u>abortion</u>, **euthanasia**, <u>homosexuality</u>, and the flaunting of <u>pornographic</u> media, to name a few), all of which would have shocked the Israelites in Gideon's world. We have simply traded barbarities. Stepping back and viewing our world through the eyes of our Creator ought to grieve our hearts at the vulgarities we easily embrace as simply "part of our society."

Among ancient nations, princes and generals often took on the names of wild beasts. For example, here are the names of a few famous statesmen/warriors and their meanings:

- Gracchus   jackdaw
- Corvinus   crow
- Aquilinus   eagle
- Zeeb   raven
- Oreb   wolf [4]

Note especially the names of the last two, the Midianite leaders beheaded by the Israelites. Their names typify either what the individuals were like or how they wished to be perceived.

Gideon's Opposition

go to

abortion
Psalm 139:13–15

euthanasia
Psalm 139:16

homosexuality
Romans 1:26–27

pornographic
Matthew 5:28–30

euthanasia
to kill or allow someone to die who's old or sick

deferential
expressing polite respect

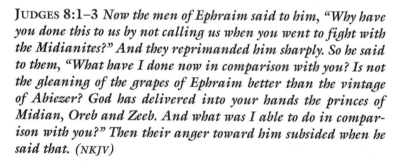

JUDGES 8:1–3 *Now the men of Ephraim said to him, "Why have you done this to us by not calling us when you went to fight with the Midianites?" And they reprimanded him sharply. So he said to them, "What have I done now in comparison with you? Is not the gleaning of the grapes of Ephraim better than the vintage of Abiezer? God has delivered into your hands the princes of Midian, Oreb and Zeeb. And what was I able to do in comparison with you?" Then their anger toward him subsided when he said that.* (NKJV)

There is a break in the action while Gideon settles a spat, but the pursuit resumes immediately after this interlude.

Ephraim enjoys a certain amount of prestige, partly because two prominent places of blessing—Bethel and Shiloh—are located within her borders. The Ephraimites have also come to expect the **deferential** treatment offered to the tribe from which Joshua descended.

In addition, there was a continuing <u>rivalry</u> between the families of Joseph's two sons, Ephraim always receiving the <u>foremost</u> blessing when placed side by side with Manasseh. With all these natural advantages, Ephraim highly resented being overlooked.

One other factor that could have been part of the equation might have been an underlying suspicion that Gideon was trying to deprive them of a share of the spoils. However, Ephraim had long been aware of the suffering of their countrymen and could have come forward at any time and volunteered to help, regardless of her ignorance of this particular campaign.

But Gideon chooses to respond with a sympathetic and self-effacing answer in spite of Ephraim's cutting criticism, and his reply diffuses their resentment. He conveys the impression that his own contribution is insignificant compared to the role they played in eliminating the notorious leaders of the adversary.

A <u>gentle</u> answer truly does turn away wrath, and the more we understand human nature, the more proficient we can become at using our speech to obtain <u>positive</u> results. There is an <u>appropriate</u> answer for every verbal challenge that is fired in our direction, and our **winsome** words can be very effective in silencing our critics. We can even bring <u>life</u> and <u>healing</u> by choosing carefully what we say.

go to

rivalry
Isaiah 9:21

foremost
Genesis 48:17–20;
Deuteronomy 33:17

gentle
Proverbs 15:1

positive
Proverbs 17:27

appropriate
Colossians 4:6

winsome
Titus 2:8

life
Proverbs 18:21

healing
Proverbs 16:24

bridge
Psalm 17:27;
Colossians 4:6

winsome
charmingly naive

what others say

Abraham Lincoln

If I were to try to read, much less answer, all the attacks made on me, this shop might as well be closed for any other business. I do the very best I know how—the very best I can and I mean to keep doing so until the end. If the end brings me out wrong, ten angels swearing I was right would make no difference.[5]

Gordon McMinn

Don't blow up bridges. You may find yourself tempted, at times, to focus on what someone else has "done" to you . . . Trouble is, bridges are difficult to build. Once destroyed it will be difficult, if not impossible, to build that span back again. And someday . . . some distant or not so distant day . . . you may want that <u>bridge</u> very much. So keep the roads open.[6]

go to

support
Ecclesiastes 10:12;
Titus 2:8

myself
Matthew 7:12

Scratch Our Back First

JUDGES 8:4–6 *When Gideon came to the Jordan, he and the three hundred men who were with him crossed over, exhausted but still in pursuit. Then he said to the men of Succoth, "Please give loaves of bread to the people who follow me, for they are exhausted, and I am pursuing Zebah and Zalmunna, kings of Midian." And the leaders of Succoth said, "Are the hands of Zebah and Zalmunna now in your hand, that we should give bread to your army?" (NKJV)*

Gideon's army had been equipped for a surprise attack, not the lengthy pursuit of a retreating foe, so they seek to obtain supplies from their brothers living on the other side of the Jordan. We know precisely where Gideon crossed the river, because Succoth is close to the east bank of the Jordan right where it emerges from the Sea of Galilee.[7] Gideon is now fifty miles from the scene of the battle, and his men are weary and famished.

The unpatriotic response of Succoth is another hint that the breakdown of tribal unity will eventually lead to a virtual separation between those living on one side of the river and those on the other. The eastern tribes might have thought that Gideon's victory was only a short-lived uprising that would soon be put down, and therefore they were afraid of the retaliation of the Midianites. Regardless, Gideon and his cause desperately needed food, and the leaders of Succoth turned a cold shoulder and taunted them over what remained to be done, instead of praising them for the great deeds they'd already performed.

We need to be careful that we do not discourage or demoralize by our thoughtless words those who come to us for support.

apply it

> **what others say**
>
> **Philip Yancy and Tim Stafford**
>
> I know how I love myself. It is the main preoccupation of my life—my first thought in the morning, my last at night. Jesus wants me to think about others. He wants me to praise their good traits just as wholeheartedly and enthusiastically as I congratulate myself for successes. He wants me to be as tolerant and kind and forgiving of them as I am of myself. In short, he wants me to act the way I would like people to act around me.[8]

Double Trouble

allows
Psalm 81:11–12;
Proverbs 1:23–31

leadership
Hebrews 13:17

JUDGES 8:7–9 So Gideon said, "For this cause, when the LORD has delivered Zebah and Zalmunna into my hand, then I will tear your flesh with the thorns of the wilderness and with briers!" Then he went up from there to Penuel and spoke to them in the same way. And the men of Penuel answered him as the men of Succoth had answered. So he also spoke to the men of Penuel, saying, "When I come back in peace, I will tear down this tower!" (NKJV)

Gideon is **piqued** that the people who could easily provide him with sustenance and relief are so callous and spiteful. He threatens them with trouble, but defers it until his return. He might have been afraid of losing time, or perhaps he harbors a secret wish that his warning will cause them to reflect and change their minds.

piqued
insulted and
resentful

A similar scenario occurs five miles down the road at Peniel, whose inhabitants respond with the same harsh insensitivity. Perhaps they even glance smugly at their tower, as if to imply that Gideon can threaten all he likes, but they will be safe. In their stubbornness and arrogance they have set themselves up for heartache.

> **what others say**
>
> **Greg Johnson**
>
> God is persistent, but he has a breaking point. No, he doesn't "give up" on anyone, but occasionally, the time arrives when God <u>allows</u> those who want to retain control of their lives to do so. Like the father in the story of the Prodigal Son (see Luke 15), God knows when arguments won't work, when the heart and mind are set on steering a different course, and when no amount of words can move the life's rudder of his child.[9]

If we align ourselves against the spiritual <u>leadership</u> that God has selected, we have chosen the wrong side.

Mopping Up

JUDGES 8:10–12 Now Zebah and Zalmunna were at Karkor, and their armies with them, about fifteen thousand, all who were left of all the army of the people of the East; for one hundred and twenty thousand men who drew the sword had fallen.

Then Gideon went up by the road of those who dwell in tents on the east of Nobah and Jogbehah; and he attacked the army while the camp felt secure. When Zebah and Zalmunna fled, he pursued them; and he took the two kings of Midian, Zebah and Zalmunna, and routed the whole army. (NKJV)

Zebah and Zalmunna are the greatest chiefs among the Midianites. As the leaders of the marauding nation who forcibly took lands and inflicted permanent injury and loss, they needed to be brought to justice.

By the time they reached Karkor (well to the east of the Dead Sea), they must have thought that they were home free.[10] However, the force that they began with is down to 15,000 men, having lost at least 120,000 in the initial encounter and subsequent chase. Zeb and Zal are undoubtedly licking their wounds but believing that at least they'd outrun the Israelites. They feel so secure that they forget to even set up a watch.

But they are not counting on the tenacity of Gideon, who is following a caravan route through Jogbehah some fifteen to twenty miles southeast of Peniel.[11] His sudden appearance, so far from the original scene of the battle, strikes terror into their hearts, and all they can do is scatter in alarm. Gideon at last captures the rulers of the vanquished Midianites.

Reaping Wild Oats

the big picture

Judges 8:13–17

Gideon returns from his last skirmish and catches a young man from Succoth who writes down the names of seventy-seven of the most prominent officials in Succoth. Gideon enters the town, presenting Zebah and Zalmunna, and carrying out his threat of vengeance on the town leaders. He also pulls down the tower at Penuel and kills the men of that town.

Gideon returns by a slightly different route so as to make his entrance into Succoth a surprise (Succoth is the town that not only refused to give assistance to her weary brothers but mocked Gideon in his quest). Gideon comes prepared to carry out the threat that he left them with and knows the exact individuals to hold responsible. The youth had probably scratched their names with a stick or pointed instrument on pottery or a piece of **shale**—a method commonly employed in the Old Testament.[12]

In effect, refusing to help these soldiers who were risking their lives to defend the freedom that was cherished by them all was an act of treason. Not only did they weaken them physically by refusing to supply their needs, but they weakened them emotionally as well. They derided and scorned Gideon's cause. As promised, Gideon repaid them for their malicious behavior. The method of punishment is not exactly understood, but somehow he tore their flesh on thorns and briers. And the tower that had seemed so invincible was demolished.

Princely Bearing

JUDGES 8:18–19 *And he said to Zebah and Zalmunna, "What kind of men were they whom you killed at Tabor?" So they answered, "As you are, so were they; each one resembled the son of a king." Then he said, "They were my brothers, the sons of my mother. As the LORD lives, if you had let them live, I would not kill you." (NKJV)*

Gideon is probably now back at his own hometown of **Ophrah**. Gideon puts a question to Zeb and Zal and soon gets his answer. As he surmises, they have killed his brothers.

This may have occurred during the years of the Midianite occupation, rather than during a battle. The Midianite leaders probably never thought they would be held accountable for the murder of some anonymous souls, when this guy, looking just like the men they killed, shows up. Their description gives us the only physical "picture" we have of Gideon.

In places where marriages with multiple wives are prevalent, to call someone the "son of my mother" is an even closer tie than to call them "my brother." As they were full-blooded siblings, Gideon feels the need to avenge their death. There is no executioner's office in Israelite government, so when blood-guiltiness needed to be punished it had to be done through the next of kin, unless the individual in question fled to a city of refuge and became subject to those laws.

shale
dark, fine-grained sedimentary rock

Ophrah
town in Manasseh, probably at the south edge of Esdraelon

POWs
prisoners of war

Zebah and Zalmunna, as foreign tyrants, would be accountable for the atrocities they had perpetrated on their subjects. Gideon can now settle his own private account while ridding the land of its tormenters at the same time.

Be a Man

JUDGES 8:20–21 *And he said to Jether his firstborn, "Rise, kill them!" But the youth would not draw his sword; for he was afraid, because he was still a youth. So Zebah and Zalmunna said, "Rise yourself, and kill us; for as a man is, so is his strength." So Gideon arose and killed Zebah and Zalmunna, and took the crescent ornaments that were on their camels' necks. (NKJV)*

In Gideon's time it would be considered a great honor for a youth to slay such important **POWs** as these Midianite leaders, and an equal disgrace to die at the hand of a child. But Zeb and Zal would much prefer to be dispatched via the clean blows of an experienced soldier rather than the tentative pokes and stabs of an amateur. Besides, they had their honor to uphold.

Since young people learn primarily through example, we undeniably provide instruction to them whenever we are in their presence by the way we conduct ourselves.

Strengthen your family

what others say

Susan Schaeffer Macaulay

There has never been a generation when children have so desperately needed their parents' time, thoughtful creativity, and friendship. The surrounding culture is deeply out of step with the Word of God.[13]

The specific word used for the camel's ornaments, in the original Hebrew, indicates that they were crescent-shaped figures. In corraboration of this, many moon-shaped ornaments have been excavated in sites all around Israel.[14]

Gideon's Remission

go to

king
1 Samuel 8:6–7

lifestyle
1 Samuel 8:11–18

initiate
Isaiah 41:10

retreat
Hebrews 12:1

hesitate
James 1:6

glory
Romans 7:18

monarchy
a state ruled by
someone (like a king
or queen)

JUDGES 8:22–23 *Then the men of Israel said to Gideon, "Rule over us, both you and your son, and your grandson also; for you have delivered us from the hand of Midian." But Gideon said to them, "I will not rule over you, nor shall my son rule over you; the LORD shall rule over you." (NKJV)*

As has happened many times in history, the citizens of the recently liberated country feel so much gratitude and admiration toward the military hero that they ask him to head their government as well. Gideon has outsmarted and outmaneuvered an army at least 450 times the size of his, and the Israelites desire to make him their king. This is the first mention of the people's desire to set up a hereditary **monarchy**.

They have forgotten the special way God has set up their government. Jehovah himself serves as their <u>king</u>, so they need not be subject to the exploitation and foolish whims of an earthly leader. Later, when they are forced to pay exorbitant taxes to fund their king's extravagant <u>lifestyle</u>, and their young men are required to fight in his personal army to expand the boundaries of his kingdom, they may change their minds.

Showing an excellent sense of judgment, Gideon turns down their proposal and points them to their rightful ruler.

The following are four principles to be derived from the life of Gideon, based on the word *nothing*:

apply it

- We should <u>initiate</u> *nothing* in our own strength.
- We should <u>retreat</u> from *nothing* to which we are called.
- We should <u>hesitate</u> in *nothing* with God's affirmation behind us.
- We should <u>glory</u> in *nothing* which God alone has accomplished.

Stop While You're Ahead

the big picture

Judges 8:24–27

Gideon hastens to put in a request. He asks that each soldier donate an earring from his share of the plunder (the defeated Ishmaelites wore earrings). They gladly comply and the total

go to

victory
1 Kings 18:16–40

melancholy
1 Kings 19:3–5

tribute
Matthew 16:15–19

rebuke
Matthew 16:21–23

Midian
the fourth of
Abraham's sons with
Keturah his concu-
bine

Ishmael
firstborn son of
Abraham by Hagar
(Sarah's Egyptian
maid)

ephod
sleeveless shoulder
vestment

prostituting
giving yourself away
in an unworthy
manner

weight comes to forty-three pounds, which does not include the wealth that the vanquished kings carried on their persons or around their camels' necks. Of this gold Gideon fashions an ephod, which he places in his hometown. Israel starts to worship it, and this object becomes a snare to Gideon and his whole family.

Having refused the kingdom, Gideon allows himself one small indulgence—that out of the battle bounty each man contribute one earring. They comply, eager to please. Considering the enormous wealth they had accrued, this donation was quite reasonable.

The Midianites were not strictly Ishmaelites, but as brothers, **Midian** and **Ishmael** had been banished to the eastern deserts at the same time. Their descendants had intermarried because they shared the same territory and lifestyle.

An **ephod** is generally part of a priest's attire—sometimes used to obtain guidance. Perhaps because of this function, Gideon's creation evolves into an object of worship.

When God first called Gideon and asked him to pull down the places of Baal and Asherah worship, he told him to erect a properly built altar to the true God. Perhaps this encouraged Gideon to think of himself as specially authorized to officiate in some aspects of religious observance. However, in the service of our God, human inventions should always be avoided.

Although the action of making an ephod may not have seemed to have enormous implications at first, by setting up this distraction Gideon brought ruin to his whole family. And soon the entire country was **"prostituting"** itself before what had begun as a personal immoderation.

apply it

We are most susceptible to depression, sin, and failure directly after a triumph in which we have been greatly used of God. Remember the prophet Elijah, who experienced revival at the hand of God on the top of Mount Carmel? After this tremendous <u>victory</u>, he went into a deep <u>melancholy</u> and begged to be allowed to die.

Peter was another who experienced his lowest points directly after his greatest achievements. In a conversation with the Lord, he recognized and declared Jesus to be the Son of God, receiving the highest <u>tribute</u> from Jesus's lips. But only a short time later he tempted Christ to avoid the inevitable suffering and death that must surely come and was given a stiff <u>rebuke</u>. Again, at Jesus's arrest in the garden, Peter experienced a moment of boldness and valiantly bounded to Jesus's <u>defense</u> with a sword. But several hours later, he found himself <u>denying</u> the Lord he loved three times.

The warning to us is clear. We need to be especially <u>watchful</u> and cautious at the very moment in which we'd like to relax and let down our guard.

defense
John 18:10

denying
John 18:15–18, 25–27

watchful
1 Corinthians 10:12

effect
Exodus 34:6–7

Ripe Old Age

> JUDGES 8:28–32 *Thus Midian was subdued before the children of Israel, so that they lifted their heads no more. And the country was quiet for forty years in the days of Gideon.*
>
> *Then Jerubbaal the son of Joash went and dwelt in his own house. Gideon had seventy sons who were his own offspring, for he had many wives. And his concubine who was in Shechem also bore him a son, whose name he called Abimelech. Now Gideon the son of Joash died at a good old age, and was buried in the tomb of Joash his father, in Ophrah of the Abiezrites.* (NKJV)

Having accomplished the primary mission for which he'd been sent, Gideon never quite recovers his former strength of spirit. He retires as an active, national figure a number of years before his death. He then becomes an extreme **polygamist**, and in choosing this way of life brings shame to his name.

The mention of the son of Gideon's **concubine** is important, for Abimelech's career will next be traced in Scripture. Perhaps the meaning of his name ("father-king") will prompt Abimelech to pursue an assertive course. The poor example of his father could certainly set him on a reckless and self-centered path. And there is always the residual <u>effect</u> of his grandfather's idolatry.

polygamist
a person who has more than one spouse at a time

concubine
a socially recognized mistress

I Don't Get No Respect

> JUDGES 8:33–35 *So it was, as soon as Gideon was dead, that the children of Israel again played the harlot with the Baals, and made Baal-Berith their god. Thus the children of Israel did not remember the LORD their God, who had delivered them from the hands of all their enemies on every side; nor did they show kindness to the house of Jerubbaal (Gideon) in accordance with the good he had done for Israel.* (NKJV)

The period immediately following Gideon's death finds the Israelite nation hurled all the way back into decline and decay. Here,

bona fide
authentic, genuine

a specific name of Baal is mentioned. It means "lord of the Covenant." How ironic that the true God had been the first to make a covenant with Israel. But they choose to break the **bona fide** covenant in favor of a cheap imitation with a stone idol.

What a tragic end to Gideon's excellent beginning! Already sorrow and shame stalk his family, foreshadowing what is to come.

Chapter Wrap-Up

- God, through Gideon, confuses the Midianite camp, slaughtering many and sending the rest on the run. (Judges 7:15b–25)
- Ephraim criticizes Gideon for not including them in the fight, and two Israelite towns refuse to aid Gideon's famished and exhausted troops. (Judges 8:1–9)
- Gideon pursues two Midianite chiefs, captures them, and returns to punish the towns that rebuffed him earlier. (Judges 8:10–17)
- Gideon avenges the murder of his brothers. (Judges 8:18–21)
- Gideon falls into sin, bringing sorrow to his family and trouble to all of Israel. (Judges 8:22–35)

Study Questions

1. How did Gideon respond to the criticism against his leadership?

2. Why were the inaction and derision of the people of Succor and Penuel so serious?

3. How had God designed the Israelite government to work? Why would demanding a king modify this perfect plan?

4. When and how did Gideon fall into sin?

Chapter Highlights:
- **Establishing His Position**
- **Buddies with Baddies**
- **Validating His Position**
- **Forfeiting His Position**
- **Others in His Position**

Let's Get Started

What kind of people live in Shechem, a bustling city in Ephraim? Most of the exploits in this chapter involve the citizens of Shechem, so a proper introduction should tell a little bit about who they are.

Remembering the Ephraimite's hasty <u>criticism</u> of Gideon for not including them in his initial call to arms, and looking at the Shechemites' impetuous response to Abimelech in the narrative we are about to read (first rashly vowing their support and later renouncing him as their leader), we might suggest that they are a volatile, high-strung people.

Enter Abimelech, the dishonorable son of Gideon's concubine who has high aspirations regarding his own Shechem-based leadership in Israel. He uses his knowledge of Ephraimite character and behavior to guarantee their cooperation. His goal is to get them distressed and agitated over the thought that Gideon's sons might try to rule over them, based on Gideon's former prestige. If the Ephraimites still cling to the imagined slight put upon them by this man, the thought of being dominated by his sons would be particularly distasteful. With all the arts of an aspiring **demagogue**, Abimelech offers to deliver them from this fate, thus elevating himself at the same time.

criticism
Judges 8:1–3

demagogue
a political leader who appeals to emotions

Establishing His Position

JUDGES 9:1–2 *Then Abimelech the son of Jerubbaal went to Shechem, to his mother's brothers, and spoke with them and with all the family of the house of his mother's father, saying, "Please speak in the hearing of all the men of Shechem: 'Which is better for you, that all seventy of the sons of Jerubbaal reign over you, or that one reign over you?' Remember that I am your own flesh and bone." (NKJV)*

slave
Judges 9:18

self-conceit
Psalm 36:2;
Galatians 6:3

toehold
the smallest inroad

noxious
poisonous

As the son of Gideon's concubine, Abimelech would traditionally be considered a part of his mother's family, not his father's. Customarily, a concubine would stay with her own clan, to be visited from time to time by her husband.[1] In the case of Abimelech's mother, who was a <u>slave</u> in Gideon's household, the emotional ties would still be as strong, although she is physically removed from her family.

Perhaps Abimelech's half brothers scorned him. We know that there was no love lost between them. Even so, Abimelech goes to Shechem to seek the help of his mother's family to support his claim to the throne. The office of judgeship is not a heredity one, and Abimelech has no claim on any position any more than his brothers, but he tries anyway.

Abimelech seeks to further the impression that all the sons of Gideon want to rule as kings, and that the ensuing dissension would be harmful for the nation. His basis for his own claim is not moral qualifications, experience in service, or prowess in defense of a national interest. As their kinsman, Abimelech simply assures them that he will be more likely to promote their own particular interests. They fall for the bait, and he secures their trust without having to earn it.

<u>Self-conceit</u> and ambitious envy are character flaws that we cannot allow even a **toehold** in our lives.

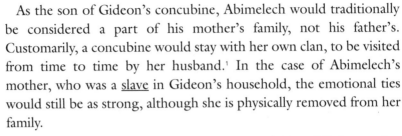

what others say

Lloyd John Ogilvie

One of the major causes of stress is combative competition—more accurately, envy. Rooted in a lack of self esteem, it grows in the soul-soil of comparisons and blossoms in **noxious** thorns of desire for what others have or achieve.[2]

Buddies with Baddies

JUDGES 9:3–4 *And his mother's brothers spoke all these words concerning him in the hearing of all the men of Shechem; and their heart was inclined to follow Abimelech, for they said, "He is our brother." So they gave him seventy shekels of silver from the temple of Baal-Berith, with which Abimelech hired worthless and reckless men; and they followed him.* (NKJV)

The people of Shechem concur with Abimelech's plans, even so far as dipping into their own pocketbooks to help him pull it off. The suggestion of preferred treatment brings visions to their minds of prosperity and prestige. Perhaps they even dream that Shechem will become the capital of the new kingdom.

In antiquity, temples were the centers of great wealth. People would bring gifts to present to the deities, and public funds would be kept there for safekeeping.[3] This is probably not the first time—nor would it be the last—that temple <u>treasuries</u> would be used to further political or military ends. Seventy pieces of silver is not a huge sum, but it does demonstrate that the citizens were backing Abimelech's cause.

Abimelech uses the funds to hire a gang of vagabonds—idlers and scoundrels—who are used to living off the resources of other people, and the most obvious individuals to implement his plan.

go to

treasuries
1 Kings 15:18–19

catalyst
something that
brings about change

Adler
Austrian psychiatrist,
associate of
Sigmund Freud

Kissinger
America's secretary
of state from 1973
to 1977

aphrodisiac
intensifying physical
desire

---

what others say

Bill Hybels

Power, simply defined, is the ability to control resources to secure one's destiny. Kings and slaves, wars and treaties, colonies and nations, coups and elections all share the common denominator of power. Through the centuries, from the time of the Fall, it has been the single greatest **catalyst** of history. **Adler** described it as the great human obsession. **Kissinger** referred to it as an **aphrodisiac**. The apostle Paul linked it, more times than not, to something he called sin.[4]

Executing Their Deaths

JUDGES 9:5–6 *Then he went to his father's house at Ophrah and killed his brothers, the seventy sons of Jerubbaal, on one stone. But Jotham the youngest son of Jerubbaal was left, because he hid himself. And all the men of Shechem gathered together, all of Beth Millo, and they went and made Abimelech king beside the terebinth tree at the pillar that was in Shechem.* (NKJV)

Abimelech puts into practice a ruthless custom still in vogue today—although carried out more discreetly. He puts to death any persons of rank who might contend with him for his position. In this case, it's his own flesh and blood. Like animals offered in sacrifice,

go to

tower
Judges 9:46

Jacob
Genesis 35:4

Joshua
Joshua 24:24–27

lengths
Ecclesiastes 6:7;
Philippians 3:19

self-centered
Romans 12:3

apply it

citadel
a fortress used as a
place of refuge

they were not slain in a fair fight but were butchered on stone. Only the youngest of Abimelech's brothers is able to escape, by hiding. He will appear later in the story.

Beth Millo literally means the "house of the fill." It is surmised that this refers to the huge earthen platform (dug out and repacked with dirt) upon which a towering structure of this era would be built.[5] Since we read later about the "**citadel**" or "<u>tower</u>" of Shechem, many believe this location is one and the same.

Abimelech will not be the first king in Israel, but he will be the first to be crowned.

Ironically, the coronation took place at a spot of great religious significance. Here, <u>Jacob</u> put away his foreign gods, and in this place <u>Joshua</u> erected a pillar to witness Israel's renewal of their covenant with God. So where idols were previously denounced, they are now worshipped. And the stone that once witnessed Israel's devotion to God alone currently witnesses their intent to serve another. This account should remind us that every step should lead us closer to God, and every obligation should further the companionship that once existed between us.

To what <u>lengths</u> would we go to ensure our own success?

what others say

Keith Miller

I believe we deceive ourselves about our own selfishness and egocentricity, because we are afraid a revelation of our true nature would alienate us from our chosen associates. Further, we cannot face the Biblical implication that the true nature of man is such that each of us is really engaged (however unconsciously) in the building up of the kingdom of Keith or Joe (or whatever *your* name is). We must find an appropriate audience because a kingdom with no subjects to respect the king is untenable . . . We are <u>self-centered</u> little children at heart bent on our own self-gratification.[6]

Crux of the Chronicle

the big picture

Judges 9:7–15

When Jotham is told of Abimelech's coronation, he climbs up Mount Gerizim and shouts for the residents of Shechem to hear: A kingdom of trees approaches an olive tree requesting that he be their king. But he refuses because he does not wish to give up his current position in the production of oil, in which even gods and men are honored. The trees move on, asking a fig tree to rule over them. He too abstains on the grounds that the manufacture of fruit (good and sweet) is more important.

They next approach a grape vine, but he recognizes his value in the production of wine, to cheer both gods and men. Finally, the trees invite a thornbush to be their leader. The thornbush agrees, inviting them to rest in his shade, but threatens that, if they do not accept him on his own terms, fire will come out of him, even consuming the cedars of Lebanon.

very
Judges 9:19

sacrifices
Numbers 15:10

treatise
a formal work on an extensive subject

libation
pouring out of liquid as a sacrifice

Jotham, Abimelech's only surviving son, climbs the eight-hundred-foot slope of Mount Gerizim to the south of Shechem.[7] A triangular rock juts out from the side of the mountain, forming a natural pulpit. From there, a person can be heard all the way across the valley in which Shechem is located.[8]

Jotham's **treatise** is delivered immediately after the murder of his family and the crowning of Abimelech, for during his speech he speaks of the Shechemites' actions that <u>very</u> day. The townspeople are gathered outside to celebrate the inauguration, so they would hear every word.

The story features four primary characters: the olive, the fig, the vine, and the thorn. It has two obvious morals:

1. Only disreputable individuals feel the need to lord over others. Those with worthwhile occupations are already busy making contributions to the society in which they live.

2. Those who seek honor without personal merit, and those who confer it unjustly, will become a source of misery for one another.

The wine does not cheer God in the sense that he enjoys imbibing now and then, but when wine is employed in <u>sacrifices</u> as a religious **libation**, he is pleased to graciously accept that which is sincerely presented.

The only options that remain for those who have chosen the thornbush are unpleasant. Either they can languish in the protection of its "shade," or it will scorch them with its destructive fire. That its blaze consumes even the cedars of Lebanon means that even the most influential people of the land will not escape the devastation it brings.

fire
Psalm 58:9

unguents
healing or soothing
ointments

poultice
a warm, moist,
external preparation
to ease pain

Olive trees flourish around Shechem. They are a native of Asia, later transplanted into Egypt, along the Barbary Coast, and into southern Europe. The wood of the olive is yellowish, veined, fragrant, and not easily injured.[9] The fruit of the olive must be prepared in brine or hot water to purge its bitterness. Its oil forms the base for perfumes and **unguents**, can be lighted in lamps, and is used in cooking like butter.[10]

The fig tree is the most common tree in Israel and has become a symbol of Israel's wealth and abundance. Its fruit is more of a food staple than a luxury, as it is in other parts of the world.[11] It can be eaten straight from the large clusters that hang from the tree, or dried in the sun and pressed into cakes.[12] A **poultice** for boils can be made from the pressed fruit. The trees themselves grow as large as thirty feet and provide welcome shade in the hot climate.[13]

The Bible mentions grapevines more than any other plant. The grape harvest usually begins in September, and if the crop is good the entire month will be filled with feasts of celebration. The women pick the grapes from the vines, and the men trample them with their bare feet to crush out the juice.[14]

The thornbush probably refers to a species of buckthorn that is a native of Syria and Israel. It is remarkable for the length and abundance of its spines, and the combustible nature of its wood.[15] It is used to make a quick <u>fire</u>, green or dry. These brambles can be seen throughout the valley, all around Shechem.

Fables are stories in which creatures take on human characteristics to convey a deeper message or moral. Prophets and teachers in Bible times often used this tactic to communicate spiritual truth, for several reasons: (1) fables arrest attention in a way that a statement of fact never could; (2) they convey wisdom or information more easily, by bringing home a point before prejudice can bar the entrance of truth; and (3) they can hold an audience spellbound until the end of the dialogue and full application has been revealed.

respond
Ephesians 4:19;
1 Timothy 4:2

what others say

Dr. George Bush

We have in this address of Jotham, the oldest, and one of the most beautiful parables on record . . . In the East especially, where the imagination and the whole mental temperament is more fervid and glowing than elsewhere, this veiled form of instruction has always been in high repute . . . Does a man of low caste wish to unite his son in marriage to the daughter of one who is high, the latter will say, "Have you heard that the pumpkin wants to be married to the plantain-tree?" Is a wife sterile, "The cocoa-nut tree in Viraver's garden does not bear any fruit." Has a woman had children by improper intercourse, it is said of her husband's garden, "Ah, the palmirah-trees are now giving cocoa-nuts." . . . A short fable, together with its "moral," is more easily remembered than a labored argument or the same truth expressed in abstract terms.[16]

I Hate to Speak and Run

the big picture

Judges 9:16–21

Jotham continues his narration, telling the people that if they have acted honorably and fairly in their treatment of Gideon and his family, then he wishes mutual joy upon both them and Abimelech. However, if the revolt against Gideon's family, the murder of his brothers, and the crowning of Abimelech were *not* in good faith, he calls for the fire from Abimelech to consume the citizens of Shechem and Beth Millo, and for it to be reciprocated. Then Jotham flees for his life to Beer and lives in that place.

Jotham lays out the evidence and asks the people to draw their own conclusions. After this they can never again claim ignorance, but it is doubtful that they have any guilt or conscience left to act upon. His conclusion is both a prediction and a curse. Given the character of the people involved, devastation is inevitable.

Jotham's departure is understandably abrupt. Circumstances had stirred his emotions to a fever pitch, but after he delivers his appeal he makes a quick exit. Since *Beer* means "well," there are many places Jotham could have gone to, but the most likely is Beer-Sheba or El-Bireh.[17]

We need to make sure we never get to the point in our lives where we can no longer <u>respond</u> to a call for repentance.

go to

Saul
1 Samuel 16:14

contrary
Judges 9:5;
1 Samuel 15:23

unworthy
Judges 9:56;
1 Samuel 15:35

clung
Judges 9:45;
1 Samuel 18:6–29

reprehensible
deserving censure

Validating His Position

JUDGES 9:22–24 *After Abimelech had reigned over Israel three years, God sent a spirit of ill will between Abimelech and the men of Shechem; and the men of Shechem dealt treacherously with Abimelech, that the crime done to the seventy sons of Jerubbaal might be settled and their blood be laid on Abimelech their brother, who killed them, and on the men of Shechem, who aided him in the killing of his brothers.* (NKJV)

The type of government that Abimelech practiced is entirely different from the mild and gentle authority of a judge. The more precise meaning in the original language implies he exercised "despotic coercion."[19] After a honeymoon lasting three years, whatever harmony he began with begins to disintegrate. The very people that Abimelech relied on to attain his present position make *him* the target of their lawless behavior. And God sends a spirit of animosity to rankle and fester between them.

An evil spirit afflicted <u>Saul</u>, the first true king of Israel, as well as Abimelech, the first counterfeit king of Israel. Both committed acts <u>contrary</u> to God's expressed law, both were <u>unworthy</u> candidates for the positions that they held, and both <u>clung</u> to their authority with ego-driven tenacity.

Mounting Mutiny

JUDGES 9:25–26 *And the men of Shechem set men in ambush against him on the tops of the mountains, and they robbed all who passed by them along that way; and it was told Abimelech.*

Now Gaal the son of Ebed came with his brothers and went over to Shechem; and the men of Shechem put their confidence in him. (NKJV)

never
Psalm 49:13–14

joy
Isaiah 16:9–10

The secret dissatisfaction finally takes on an outward form. The ambush in the mountain passes is most likely set up to discredit Abimelech. If travel along accustomed caravan routes is made unsafe, then ordinary citizens can no longer trade with the surrounding areas. Their economy will suffer, and people will blame Abimelech for not providing adequate protection.

Around this time, Gaal, a man well-known by the citizens of Shechem, who has recently returned with a crowd of relatives, pushes to the forefront. Under his leadership, discord will spread into open revolt.

Any position of authority, questionably attained, <u>never</u> stands secure.

A Lampshade on His Head

JUDGES 9:27–29 *So they went out into the fields, and gathered grapes from their vineyards and trod them, and made merry. And they went into the house of their god, and ate and drank, and cursed Abimelech. Then Gaal the son of Ebed said, "Who is Abimelech, and who is Shechem, that we should serve him? Is he not the son of Jerubbaal, and is not Zebul his officer? Serve the men of Hamor the father of Shechem; but why should we serve him? If only this people were under my authority! Then I would remove Abimelech." So he said to Abimelech, "Increase your army and come out!" (NKJV)*

Shechem is observing the festival at the harvest of the vintage. For the Israelites, this is traditionally a time of singing, dancing, and great <u>joy</u>. However, a pagan element has entered in, and here we find the Shechemites partying in the temple of Baal. The Canaanite brand of this celebration would include excessive drinking and immorality.[20]

Sometime in the middle of all the revelry and carousing, Gaal, either puffed up with too much wine or his own foolish arrogance, starts to rag on the absent Abimelech, loading his name with reviling and reproaches. Whereas Abimelech always stressed his

Arumah
Judges 9:41

aristocracy
noble families of
high social status

Arumah
town near Shechem

relationship to his Shechemite mother, Gaal stresses Abimelech's relationship to his Israelite father, as if it is a link of shame and disparagement.

Shechem, the city's founder, was the son of Hamor, ancient **aristocracy** in Canaan.[21] Because intermarriage between Israelites and Canaanites had become so prevalent, many of the citizens of Shechem could trace their lineage back to their Canaanite origins. So Gaal contends that the family of Hamor has a stronger claim to the people's allegiance than the usurper, Abimelech.

Gaal ends with a challenge to Abimelech and his whole army, claiming that, with the people behind him, he could get rid of the whole lot.

Ready and Waiting

the big picture

Judges 9:30–34

Zebul, the governor Abimelech has placed over Shechem, hears Gaal and secretly sends messengers to inform Abimelech. He suggests that Abimelech hide his men in the fields outside the city during the night, then when Gaal comes out to make good the threats of the night before he will be waiting.

Abimelech follows Zebul's advice, setting up four companies of men in concealed positions.

Zebul is the deputy that Abimelech has set up to rule in his absence. It is supposed that Abimelech lives in **Arumah**, and would consequentially need a representative to carry out his political wishes in Shechem. The original language in this passage emphasizes that the message Zebal sends is delivered craftily, or in fraud.[22] In other words, he pretends that the dispatch concerns an entirely different subject than it actually does. His life may be forfeit if he shows any sympathy toward the establishment, so he diplomatically conceals his true leanings.

Zebul's memo tells Abimelech to take quick action if he wants to save his kingdom. Abimelech follows his counsel and sets up troops to speedily squash the rebellion.

Put Up or Shut Up

disaster
Psalm 11:5–6;
Romans 2:7–9

> **the big picture**
>
> **Judges 9:35–41**
>
> Just as Gaal stands at the entrance to the city, Abimelech's soldiers rise from their places of hiding. Gaal turns to Zebul and tries to point out the people he thinks he sees descending from the mountains. Zebul tries to persuade him it is just shadows playing on the mountaintops. Again Gaal describes a group of people coming from the center of the land and another company from the "soothsayer's tree."
>
> This time Zebul reminds him of the boastful speech he gave the night before and suggests he back up his words with action. So Gaal leads out a citizen group from Shechem to fight against Abimelech. But the resistance group is completely routed and Abimelech chases them all the way back to the city gate, slaughtering many on the way.
>
> Abimelech retires to Arumah, and Zebul expels Gaal and his brothers from Shechem.

At first Zebul plays down Gaal's apprehension concerning the force that he imagines he can make out, possibly to give Gaal less time to prepare his troops. Zebul and Gaal engage in such familiar conversation it becomes obvious that Zebul has concealed his true sentiments until now. But when Gaal brings up the people he's *sure* he sees approaching for the second time, Zebul throws off all disguise and openly taunts him for his arrogant renunciation of Abimelech the night before.

"Aren't these the men you ridiculed? Go out and fight them!"

Gaal rallies whatever cronies and allies he can scrape together, but it is too late and his followers are not prepared to meet Abimelech's trained force. The revolt ends almost as soon as it begins, and Gaal is expelled from Shechem with all of his relatives. This is another example of the impulsive fickleness of the people of this locale, which so often invited <u>disaster</u>.

Forfeiting His Position

> **the big picture**
>
> **Judges 9:42–45**
>
> The next day, when the people went out of the city to their fields, Abimelech had three companies of soldiers awaiting

avenge
Judges 9:24

slow
Nahum 1:2–3

unpunished
Romans 1:32

miserable
Proverbs 24:24–25

stand
Psalm 103:6

slain
Deuteronomy
21:1–9

government
Proverbs 11:11;
14:34

justice
Proverbs 17:15

crown
1 Kings 12:1

venerates
respects

them. Two companies attacked those who were in the fields, while the third set an ambush behind them at the city gate. The entire day Abimelech pressed his advantage until all the people were captured or killed. Then he destroyed the city and scattered salt over it.

No doubt the Shechemites assume that once Abimelech has withdrawn his troops, the matter has been concluded and life can resume as it was before. They do not anticipate Abimelech's vindictiveness. The wrath of a thwarted demagogue is not easily assuaged.

Abimelech shows the Shechemites no mercy, but the campaign against them leaves him little to rule. The salt is meant to turn the once productive valley into a barren, uninhabitable wasteland.

God brought this disaster to <u>avenge</u> the crime against Gideon's seventy sons. The Lord is <u>slow</u> to anger, but when judgment is appropriate he inflicts it without hesitation. God cannot allow sin to go <u>unpunished</u>, for it is human nature to get away with as much as it can. Righteous people are <u>miserable</u> when sin is allowed to run rampant. God must maintain the equilibrium that only a strict <u>stand</u> against evil can bring.

what others say

John W. Lawrence

When someone is murdered in our area, we may say, "This is no concern to me. Let me just go on and live my life, and I will mind my own business." But this is not our option. In Deuteronomy 21 when an Israelite found someone <u>slain</u> lying in the field and it was not known who did it, the elders from the city closest to the field were required to go out into a valley and sacrifice a heifer . . . Little do we understand that even today when a murder is committed and the murderer is not brought to justice, wrath is treasured up against the city. This is the reason for the sacrifice and for the plea for mercy in Israel. When innocent blood is shed, wrath is reserved for a day of destruction.[23]

Our job in all this is to support the facilitation of law and order, and to build a system of <u>government</u> (wherever possible) that **venerates** what honors God and condemns what breaks his heart. If a person needs to be brought to <u>justice</u>, we must see that it prevails.

Shechem is later rebuilt, but not for two hundred years. After Solomon's death, all of Israel gathers at Shechem to <u>crown</u>

Rehoboam king. Later, Jeroboam makes Shechem his capital and <u>fortifies</u> the walls. Shechem seems to continue with questionable <u>importance</u> until it later becomes known as the leading city of the Samaritans.[24]

go to

fortifies
1 Kings 12:25

importance
Hosea 6:9;
Jeremiah 41:5

woman
2 Samuel 11:21

Imbedded in His Mind

the big picture

Judges 9:46–55

Many of the citizens of Shechem, when they heard what had transpired in their city, assembled in the temple of Berith. Abimelech instructed his men to bring branches and put them in a pile, then lit the whole thing on fire. About a thousand men and women died.

Next, Abimelech went to Thebez, besieged the city, and captured it. The citizens had a tower inside the city, and all the people locked themselves in. As Abimelech approached the entrance to set this place on fire as well, a woman dropped an upper millstone off the roof onto his head and cracked his skull. Abimelech ordered his armor-bearer to run him through with a sword, so that it wouldn't be said that a woman had killed him. His servant complied, and when the soldiers of Israel saw that he was dead they went home.

The walled city of Shechem had the extra bonus of an outlying tower for added defense. It was adjacent to the temple, so when the people were told of the destruction of their town they put themselves under the protection of their idol. But this precaution was *not* in their own best interest, for when Abimelech torched the structure all the remaining citizens went up in a blaze of glory.

Thebez may be the modern city of Tubas—thirteen miles north of Shechem.[25] The people here probably participated in the festival of the grape harvest leading to Gaal's revolt, and were thus held equally responsible in the mind of Abimelech.

The army of Abimelech comprised the men of Israel. The rebellion of the Shechemites had such Canaanite overtones that Gaal's uprising would have been viewed as anti-Israelite. So in these skirmishes, Israel would undoubtedly back Abimelech's cause.

For all of Abimelech's efforts to avoid the disgrace of dying at the hands of a woman, three thousand years later we still ascribe his death to the <u>woman</u> with the millstone. A later biblical reference in the book of Samuel also names her as the cause of death.

go to

disintegration
2 Samuel 20:22;
1 Kings 22:34–36

danger
1 Corinthians 10:12

every
Romans 7:15–18;
Matthew 26:41

prolific
highly productive

insidiously
subtly harmful

During this time in history, polishing off a leader, instead of incensing his followers, often brought an awkward <u>disintegration</u> of his cause. After Abimelech's demise, the soldiers simply pack up and go home.

The stone that stopped Abimelech in his tracks would have been eight to ten inches long and several inches thick.[26] Mills for grinding grain were typically made of two large stones. One moved back and forth or rotated on the lower one, crushing any grain between them.[27] Many such stones are still being found from antiquity in archaeological digs all over the land of Israel.

Abimelech had his seventy brothers killed on a single stone, and now a single stone kills him. An additional irony is that Jotham had predicted that fire would come from Abimelech to destroy the Shechemites. In actuality, it *was* fire that wiped them out.

Paying the Piper

JUDGES 9:56–57 *Thus God repaid the wickedness of Abimelech, which he had done to his father by killing his seventy brothers. And all the evil of the men of Shechem God returned on their own heads, and on them came the curse of Jotham the son of Jerubbaal.* (NKJV)

Sin produces **prolific** offspring. Thus Gideon is punished for his improper elevation of the ephod in the barbaric death of his sons. The Shechemites are punished for their treachery to Gideon's sons by the assault of Abimelech. Abimelech is punished for his part in the deaths of his brothers and the extermination of the Shechemites. Thus evil repays evil and sin fathers sin.

We are in <u>danger</u> when we find ourselves shaking our heads at the vice we see in others without taking a hard look at ourselves.

something to ponder

what others say

Aleksandr Solzhenitsyn

[It would be different if there were] evil people somewhere **insidiously** committing evil deeds, and it were necessary only to separate them from the rest of us and destroy them. But the line dividing good and evil cuts through the heart of <u>every</u> human being.[28]

go to

concentrate
1 Thessalonians
5:5–6

recognition
1 Peter 4:11

Others in His Position

JUDGES 10:1–2 *After Abimelech there arose to save Israel Tola the son of Puah, the son of Dodo, a man of Issachar; and he dwelt in Shamir in the mountains of Ephraim. He judged Israel twenty-three years; and he died and was buried in Shamir.* (NKJV)

Tola is the sixth judge, and the second of the minor judges (Shamgar being the first). Verse 1 says that Tola rose to "save" Israel, implying a military victory. With the exception of Shamgar, none of the adversaries during the reign of a minor judge are named.

Shamir is probably in the vicinity of Jezreel in Ephraim. Although Tola hails from Issachar, he has chosen to judge from Ephraim, probably because it is more centrally located.

We are not given any other information about this man. We simply know that he did what God called him to do and met a need that no one else could meet.

Thirty's My Favorite Number

JUDGES 10:3–5 *After him arose Jair, a Gileadite; and he judged Israel twenty-two years. Now he had thirty sons who rode on thirty donkeys; they also had thirty towns, which are called "Havoth Jair" to this day, which are in the land of Gilead. And*

go to

captured
Numbers 32:41

twenty-three
1 Chronicles 2:22

Jair died and was buried in Camon. (NKJV)

The judge in these verses is named after an ancestor who <u>captured</u> <u>twenty-three</u> towns in Gilead and called them Havoth Jair, meaning the "settlements of Jair." By now the number of captured villages includes seven more.

Each of the thirty towns is controlled by one of his sons riding on one of his donkeys. Their mode of transportation was an indication of status or rank, as being chauffeured in a presidential limousine might be a mark of privilege in our day.

Jair's control of the tribes east of the Jordan may have overlapped with Tola's leadership among the western tribes. Again, there is not an abundance of information on this man, but it is interesting to note the facts that God (through the author of Judges) chooses to include.

Chapter Wrap-Up

- Abimelech goes to barbaric lengths to establish himself as a king in Israel. (Judges 9:1–21)
- Abimelech fights to maintain his throne in the face of disloyalty and subversion. (Judges 9:22–41)
- Abimelech seeks to destroy all who have been critical of his leadership and in the process is himself destroyed. (Judges 9:42–57)
- God raises up two men to lead as judges after Abimelech's death—Tola and Jair. (Judges 10:1–5)

Study Questions

1. How far did Abimelech go to ensure his own success?

2. What mistakes in judgment did Gaal make when he was putting Abimelech down and building himself up?

3. How did each individual in this chapter reap the consequences of his or her actions?

4. List the facts you know about Tola and Jair.

Judges 10:6–12:15
Jephthah, Plus Three

Chapter Highlights:
- Rejection and Remorse
- Leadership and Letters
- Victory and Vows
- Criticism and Chastisement
- Influential and Important

Let's Get Started

An illegitimate, disinherited son of a prostitute is chosen by God to bring restoration to Israel. Struggling with feelings of inferiority from the rejection of his brothers and the abuse of the community, this unlikely hero extends to Israel's enemies a surprisingly sophisticated offer of diplomacy. When they do not respond favorably he advances to meet them.

However, in this unpredictable roller-coaster plot, our hero seeks to gain certain victory by making a foolish vow to God. He tells God that if he will give him success in this one venture, he will offer as a sacrifice whatever comes out of the door of his house when he returns home. When the time comes, who or what will pay this price?

Rejection and Remorse

the big picture

Judges 10:6–10

Israel again forsakes the Lord and serves not only the Baals and Ashtoreths, but the gods of Aram, Sidon, Moab, Ammon, and Philistia. The true God becomes angry and sells them into the hands of the Ammonites and Philistines. For eighteen years the Ammonites oppress them, even crossing over the Jordan, until Israel cries out to God, admitting her sin.

Israel has become a universal idolater, accepting all gods. But to do this the nation has had to renounce the *true* God. The following are some of the deities they would have revered:

- Aram's Hadad and Rimmon
- Sidon's Phoenician Baal
- Moab's Chemosh
- Ammon's Molech
- the Philistines' Dagon and Baal-zeboul[1]

sinful
1 John 1:8;
Romans 3:10–11

cannot
Matthew 6:24

gospel
good news recorded
about Christ

Given the Philistine encroachment on the west and the Ammonite intrusion on the east, Israel was getting the big squeeze. Jephthah will deal with Ammon in these few chapters, and Samson will take care of the Philistines in the chapters to follow. The oppression that these two countries bring is spoken of in the original language as the crushing and breaking to pieces that happens when two millstones grind whatever is between them.[2]

Israel seems to be incapable of doing the right thing, wallowing in sin and degradation with scarcely a whimper of protest until the pressure of God's chastisement becomes too excruciating. But as long as there is breath there is hope, and Israel in her suffering at last remembers the God she once knew. She cries out to him in repentance, acknowledging her specific offenses of omission (forsaking the Lord) and commission (serving other gods).

Distractions to our worship of the true God are as numerous today as they were for Israel in the time of the judges.

You <u>cannot</u> serve God and anything else, you end up *only* serving everything else.

You've Made Your Bed

the big picture

Judges 10:11–16

The Lord lists for Israel many of the nations that he has saved them from: the Egyptians, the Amorites, the Ammonites, the Philistines, the Sidonians, the Amalekites, and the Midianites. Now, however, God threatens to save them no longer. He tells them to ask for help from the other gods they have chosen over him.

But when the Israelites put away the foreign gods and begin to serve the Lord, pleading with him to save them from their enemies (and then he can do what he likes with them), he can no longer bear to keep them in misery.

God's List of Defeated Nations

Nation	Israelite Leader	Reference
Egyptians	Moses	Exodus 12:31–36; 14:5–30
Amorites	Moses	Numbers 21:21–35
Ammonites	Ehud	Judges 3:13–15
Philistines	Shamgar	Judges 3:31
Sidonians	(Perhaps allied with Canaanites; suffered defeat under Barak)	
		Judges 4:23–24
Amalekites	Ehud	Judges 3:13–15
Midianites	Gideon	Judges 7:22–8:21

God's warning that he would no longer save the Israelites is conditional, based on who they have determined to serve at the moment. If they elevate something else to the position that God rightfully deserves, then they should depend on their object of worship to act in place of God. But if they put God in the position of prominence where he belongs, then he is free to work in their behalf.

Israel would be far more comfortable if they could learn to live within God's laws, but that they must discover on their own. Yet when they finally turn back to God he will no longer stand aloof. His heart will be touched and he will be moved to action.

We are far happier when we learn to live within God's stated limits.

apply it

prodigal
Luke 15:11–24

surrender
Romans 6:13

well-being
Psalm 145:17–20

turning
Isaiah 55:7

mercy
Jonah 1:1–2; 3:10

Mizpah
Joshua 11:3

renunciation
denial or rejection of
something

what others say

Larry Burkett

A kindergarten in one town sat right on a corner by a busy highway. Although the school had a nice yard in which the children could play, at recess they would huddle right up against the building. The cars whipping by frightened them.

One day, workmen erected a steel fence around the school yard. From that point on, the children used the entire playground. The fence did not limit their freedom; it actually expanded it.[5]

Like the <u>prodigal</u> son who finally realizes that even his father's servants are in a better position than he is, Israel throws herself on God's mercy, saying, "Do with us whatever you think best, but please rescue us now."

Until we are ready for whatever God has for us, no matter how difficult, we have not yet learned the full lesson of submission. Submission's demand of complete <u>surrender</u> is tempered by the knowledge of God's true desire for our <u>well-being</u>. We can be assured that whatever he has in mind, it is better than any other options.

True confession must bring more from us than temporary grief. It must bring a **renunciation** and <u>turning</u> from the offense.

God always reserves the right to show <u>mercy</u> to the truly repentant.

Leadership and Letters

JUDGES 10:17–18 *Then the people of Ammon gathered together and encamped in Gilead. And the children of Israel assembled together and encamped in Mizpah. And the people, the leaders of Gilead, said to one another, "Who is the man who will begin the fight against the people of Ammon? He shall be head over all the inhabitants of Gilead."* (NKJV)

Here we find the two armies, Israel and Ammon, facing each other. However, Israel is not quite ready for battle. They are missing something. They have no captain! Here they are, on the verge of battle, desperately trying to fill the most vital position in the entire army. Since no one appears qualified, they open up the post for volunteers and throw in a little status and prestige as incentive.

There are several towns called Mizpah. Israel probably assembled for battle at the <u>Mizpah</u> in Manasseh.

Robin Hood and His Merry Band

go to

tradition
Genesis 21:10

JUDGES 11:1–3 *Now Jephthah the Gileadite was a mighty man of valor, but he was the son of a harlot; and Gilead begot Jephthah. Gilead's wife bore sons; and when his wife's sons grew up, they drove Jephthah out, and said to him, "You shall have no inheritance in our father's house, for you are the son of another woman." Then Jephthah fled from his brothers and dwelt in the land of Tob; and worthless men banded together with Jephthah and went out raiding with him.* (NKJV)

Jephthah was renowned for his strength and prowess. Living on the frontier (Tob was probably northeast of Gilead),[6] he undoubtedly made frequent rendezvous into the land of the Ammonites to retaliate and plunder. Reports of his success would have made the Israelites admire his pluck and skill.

His courage would have been fueled with bitterness over his "unfair" exclusion from family and society, and a personal drive to prove his worth. According to Israelite <u>tradition</u>, even the lawful children of a second wife or concubine would not inherit a father's estate, much less any children produced from an illicit affair. But that in no way excused Jephthah's half brothers for driving him away, nor the officers of the city for going along with them.

The men that gathered around Jephthah were "vain" men—considered wild and reckless by the more respectable members of Jewish society.[7] But even though these men were unruly, they respected Jephthah, for they chose to follow his leadership.

Following the Leader, Wherever He May Go

the big picture

Judges 11:4–11

When the Ammonites declare war against the Israelites, the elders of Gilead approach Jephthah about becoming their commander. Jephthah reminds them that they once drove him away. The elders admit that they are now in trouble and offer to elevate him to a continuing position of leadership if he will fight the Ammonites. Jephthah restates their promise and the elders reiterate their intention. This commitment was confirmed by the people in the presence of the Lord, at Mizpah.

go to

authority
James 3:1;
Hebrews 13:17

compensated
counterbalanced

After a brief biographical description outlining Jephthah's background, we return to the battlefield where Israel and Ammon are arrayed against each other. In the absence of a commanding officer, the elders of Gilead remember the stories of Jephthah's exploits and consider him a potential captain.

Jephthah's first response is quite natural, "You didn't lend a hand when I needed help, so why should I go out of my way for you now!" The elders acknowledge their former guilt, but prove their present sincerity by the offer of permanent command should he come to their aid now.

Jephthah does not appear to be motivated by ambition; he bases his faith in the success of this venture on the intervention of God. The conference with the elders of Gilead was a private one in which they sought him out in the land of Tob. But the confirmation of the people occurs in a public ceremony performed before the Lord at Mizpah.

People who have the <u>authority</u> to see that justice is carried out work a great evil if they neglect to use that power.

what others say

Charles R. Swindoll

Nurtured in an overcrowded cage of half-brothers, he was the constant target of verbal putdowns and violent profanity. Putting it mildly, Jephthah wasn't wanted. He **compensated** by becoming the meanest kid on the block.

Suddenly a change occurred . . . The Jews needed a leader with guts to stand against the fiery foes from Ammon. Guess who the Israelites thought of? . . . What a deal! Asking Jephthah if he could fight was like asking Al Hirt if he could blow some jazz or A. J. Foyt if he could drive you around the block. That was Jephthah's day in court.[8]

If Jephthah had not been ill-treated (despised by his family and expelled by his countrymen), he would never have had the opportunity to develop his military skills or distinguish himself in a way to catch the attention of the local leadership. Jephthah needed the prodding of negative circumstances to prepare him for the position God intended him to fill.

Likewise, the detrimental incidents and events in our lives may include the very experience and impetus we need to fill a position or meet a need that we otherwise could never handle. <u>Nothing</u> happens by accident. Not one event is a divine mistake or calamity. God has the master plan, and he is arranging all our "disasters" into successful achievements.

nothing
Genesis 50:20

Ammon Was Here

JUDGES 11:12–13 *Now Jephthah sent messengers to the king of the people of Ammon, saying, "What do you have against me, that you have come to fight against me in my land?" And the king of the people of Ammon answered the messengers of Jephthah, "Because Israel took away my land when they came up out of Egypt, from the Arnon as far as the Jabbok, and to the Jordan. Now therefore, restore those lands peaceably." (NKJV)*

Though it has already been confirmed that Jephthah was a man of courage, he first sends messengers to negotiate a settlement if at all possible. The reason given by the Ammonites for the attack is purely bogus, as will be attested in a moment, but the initial claim is that Israel took over their land when they came up from Egypt. The territory in dispute is bordered by the Arnon River on the south, the Jabbok on the north, and the Jordan on the west.

To Whom It May Concern

the big picture

Judges 11:14–27

Jephthah's reply lays out the following defense: As Israel progressed from Egypt to the Promised Land, she requested permission to pass through Edom and Moab. But the kings of both countries refused to grant access, so Israel skirted around them so as not to trespass. Next, the Israelites came up against Sihon, king of the Amorites, and asked if they could pass through his land to reach their destination. He responded by challenging them to war. God gave Israel the victory, and the land in question passed into their possession.

Jephthah's defense continues: If God gave Israel that land, what claim does Ammon have? If Ammon's god, Chemosh, gave them territory, would they turn around and give it away? Furthermore, Balak, a great king in Moab's recent history, never contested Israel's claim, and neither did anyone else for three hundred years. Finally, Jephthah throws the whole issue open to God and asks him to make a judgment.

Lot
Genesis 19:36–38

Lot
Abraham's nephew

Jephthah's argument is well-conceived and laid out with precision in a letter. A foundational point that he did not state, but was well understood by both parties, was that even before Israel came onto the scene the Ammonites had lost their claim to the disputed land when the Amorites were victorious over them. Then, when the Amorites provoked an attack against the Israelites and lost, the land again exchanged hands, this time falling into the possession of God's people.

Jephthah is careful to point out how vigilantly the Israelites guarded against causing any offense to Moab. Both Jephthah and the king of Ammon act as if Moab and Ammon are one and the same. Indeed, both peoples are descended from **Lot** and remain closely allied.[9] Strictly speaking, "Molech" was the god of Ammon and "Chemosh" was the god of Moab, but the two countries' intimate association with each other links their worship as well. Here Jephthah argues out of Ammon's own admitted principles; a nation is expected to occupy whatever their god gives them.

Balak, a famous Moabite king, set a precedent when he did not dispute Israel's title. Being the ruler from whom the Amorites had originally taken the land, he would have had a stronger legal claim than the current king of Ammon.[10] But Balak never met Israel in battle or disputed their occupancy. Now, Jephthah challenges: Do you arrogantly presume yourself superior to the legendary Balak?

The contention that Israel has occupied the land for three hundred years is indisputable. The implication being, if this land was really the Ammonites', why didn't Ammon do anything about it before now? The final appeal is to God himself, that he will judge righteously and with integrity.

The Moabite Stone, although not authored until the time of the Israelite kings, attributes the victories of Moab to the "favor" of Chemosh and the victories of Israel to the "anger" of Chemosh.[11]

This bluish basalt stone was found in 1868, twenty miles east of the Dead Sea. It stands four feet high, two feet wide, and carries an inscription of Mesha, a king of Moab. While the French and the Germans were negotiating for this piece of antiquity, the Arabs broke it into pieces to make charms, but later the pieces were secured and reassembled, saving the inscription. This stone now rests in the Louvre.[12]

Victory and Vows

desired
1 Samuel 15:22

everything
2 Peter 1:3

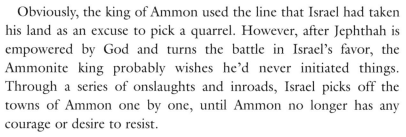

Judges 11:28–33

the big picture

The king of Ammon did not pay any attention to the message that Jephthah sent. Then the Spirit of the Lord came upon Jephthah. Jephthah advances against the Ammonites and as he does so, he vows that if the Lord will give him the victory, he will sacrifice as a burnt offering whatever comes out of his house to meet him when he returns in triumph from the battle.

God gives Jephthah the victory against the Ammonites, devastating twenty of their towns and completely subduing them.

Obviously, the king of Ammon used the line that Israel had taken his land as an excuse to pick a quarrel. However, after Jephthah is empowered by God and turns the battle in Israel's favor, the Ammonite king probably wishes he'd never initiated things. Through a series of onslaughts and inroads, Israel picks off the towns of Ammon one by one, until Ammon no longer has any courage or desire to resist.

We know that God chose Jephthah as his man to accomplish his purposes because God's Spirit came upon him with special power. God gave him victory after glorious victory. But Jephthah foolishly obligated himself with a further act of commitment that would turn his joy into despair. He probably intended his vow to demonstrate an extra measure of devotion, but it was not needed or even <u>desired</u>, and shows instead a lack of faith in God's enabling power.

what others say

Lewis Sperry Chafer

He [the Spirit of God] often came upon people as revealed in the events . . . in the Old Testament. He came upon them to accomplish certain objects and left them, when the work was done, as freely as he had come. So far as the record goes, no person in that whole period had any choice, or expected to have any choice, in the sovereign movements of the Spirit.[13]

God has given us <u>everything</u> we need to do his work; we need not strive to achieve an extra measure of his power.

go to

hates
Proverbs 6:16–19

sacrifice
Deuteronomy 12:31;
Leviticus 18:21,
24–25

Jacob
Genesis 28:20–22

Israel
Numbers 21:2

Hannah
1 Samuel 1:11

sailors
Jonah 1:16

Preposterous Promise

JUDGES 11:34–35 *When Jephthah came to his house at Mizpah, there was his daughter, coming out to meet him with timbrels and dancing; and she was his only child. Besides her he had neither son nor daughter. And it came to pass, when he saw her, that he tore his clothes, and said, "Alas, my daughter! You have brought me very low! You are among those who trouble me! For I have given my word to the LORD, and I cannot go back on it."* (NKJV)

It is obvious that seeing his only daughter be the first to greet him upon his return had never occurred to Jephthah. The supreme exhilaration of the moment changed in an instant to sorrow. The Ammonites could not bring him down, but his own irresponsibility could. For women to meet a returning conqueror with songs and dances, accompanied by musical instruments, was not the least bit unusual.

It's also possible that Jephthah, having been born in a loose, degenerate period of Israel's history, and having spent much of his life in a foreign land among outlaws, might have sunk into a state of semi-paganism. Influenced by the heathen worship all around him, he might have felt that God required a payment for his success. But God does not play the barter game.

Jephthah's promise, neither desired nor required, put him in the awkward position of doing one of the following: either lying to God or killing his daughter. God <u>hates</u> a lying tongue, but neither does he in any way condone human <u>sacrifice</u>. It is detestable to him. The sacrificial killing of sons and daughters was one of the main reasons he drove the former possessors out of the land when Israel came.

Vows were encouraged in the Scriptures to give ordinary people the opportunity to demonstrate the love they felt in their hearts, by presenting special gifts or services above and beyond what was required. Many were good and appropriate:

- <u>Jacob</u> resolved to give back to God a tenth of his possessions.
- <u>Israel</u> purposed to completely destroy an enemy nation.
- <u>Hannah</u> offered to give her son back to the Lord.
- <u>Sailors</u> in Jonah's boat recognized God's power and made suitable vows.

But once a vow was verbalized, God required that it be <u>kept</u>. Even if the fulfillment of the obligation brought <u>pain</u>, God expected an individual's promise to be carried out.

However, when the observance of a vow breaks the law of God, keeping the oath becomes a greater evil than breaking it. The Bible relates an example of a vow rashly given in the account of Saul's clash with the Philistines. Saul made an <u>oath</u> that whatever soldier ate before he had avenged himself on his enemies would be cursed. Of course, the army became faint from the heavy exertion of battle because they had not received any sustenance. By the time their obligation was fulfilled, they were so famished they were ready to eat raw meat. Saul's thoughtless vow caused the entire army to sin, for God had made it clear that eating meat with blood was <u>forbidden</u>.

Jonathan, his son, was not present when Saul pronounced his oath. So when Jonathan came across a honeycomb in the forest during the combat, he most naturally helped himself. Saul was prepared to put his son to <u>death</u> for breaking the vow, but the soldiers would not allow him to take Jonathan's life, for they recognized that a greater wrong would be committed than the breaking of an oath.

Keeping his vow caused an entire army to do evil and almost made him guilty of the murder of his own son. Better the foolish pledge had never escaped his lips—but once the promise was made, multiple wrongs could not make it right.

kept
Deuteronomy 23:21–23

pain
Psalm 15:1, 4

oath
1 Samuel 14:24–33

forbidden
Deuteronomy 12:23–25

death
1 Samuel 14:43–45

<u>Delete That File</u>

the big picture

Judges 11:36–40

Jephthah's daughter appears quite ready to allow her father to fulfill his vow, but requests that she and her friends be permitted to camp in the hills for two months to mourn, for she will forever remain a virgin. He grants her petition, and after two months she returns, and Jephthah does to her as he vowed.

Thus began the special tribute by Israelite young women each year in commemoration of Jephthah's daughter.

If Jephthah could start the book of his life all over again, surely this is one chapter he would choose to leave out. But nobody is given the opportunity to rewrite what has already been recorded, and now he must go on. First let's look at some ambiguities:

faith
Hebrews 11:32–33

rewards
Psalm 127:3

- *Question:* If Jephthah were under the influence of the Holy Spirit, how could he have made such a foolish vow?

- *Question:* Doesn't Jephthah's victory over the Ammonites validate God's approval of his promise?

- *Question:* How could a man, commended for his <u>faith</u>, do something so contrary to God's nature and divine command?

- *Question:* Why did God intend for Jephthah's daughter (God was certainly in control of who went through Jephthah's door) to be the one to greet him, knowing the nature of Jephthah's promise?

In the first place, as is typical of every example of Spirit-filling in the Old Testament, Jephthah's endowment was bestowed to enable him to perform a specific work. This did not sanction his behavior outside what God called him to do. Neither did it add any virtue to his character, or prevent him from committing sin.

Second, we cannot read in any event of Scripture the proof that God is pleased with an action that is entirely of man's own invention and enterprise.

Finally, God allowed what naturally would have occurred to occur. Perhaps he wished to forever confirm to those who would read this story that the God of heaven did not need a man's impetuous promise to carry out what was already in his will. Perhaps God also wished to remind Jephthah that it was not his own cleverness that won the victory, for Jephthah was *not* wise when it came to *this* foolish choice. On the contrary, it was God's decree that brought the Ammonites to their knees.

At any rate, good lessons could still come out of this experience, but God did *not* desire Jephthah to follow through on his promise. Ignorance and pride would be the only barriers preventing Jephthah from recognizing his stupidity and repenting before God from his given course.

The lament of Jephthah's daughter is primarily over her lost opportunity. In that era, childlessness was considered a misfortune, for bearing heirs was the only way to preserve the family name and was said to continue a woman's influence long after she was gone. Children were considered <u>rewards</u> from the Lord.

In the end, we do not actually know for sure that Jephthah offered his daughter as a sacrifice. Logistically, this would have been difficult, for to carry out a sacrifice of this kind under the **auspices** of the priests in the temple would have **desecrated** that holy place, and Jephthah did not have the authority to perform any sacrificial ceremonies by himself.

The Scriptures simply say that Jephthah "carried out his vow with her which he had vowed" (Judges 11:39 NKJV). At face value it appears that Jephthah took the life of his daughter, but some believe that this rendering gives a certain amount of leeway, allowing him to do to her what was equivalent to the original vow. For example, he could have offered her in consecrated service to God.[14] Or maybe she could have been **redeemed** like a firstborn son who was to be given to the Lord.

go to

redeemed
Exodus 34:19–20

whence
James 4:1

auspices
help or support of

desecrated
religiously offensive

redeemed
to liberate with payment

whence
from what place

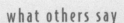
what others say

Vance Havner

Trouble sets in when we begin to take some of our weight off God and lean upon ourselves or others. From . . . the day you start that sort of thing, you may count on wars within and without. ". . . **whence** come wars and fightings among you?" One reason is, we fear that God's promise is not enough, we must supplement that with resources of flesh.[15]

Criticism and Chastisement

JUDGES 12:1–3 *Then the men of Ephraim gathered together, crossed over toward Zaphon, and said to Jephthah, "Why did you cross over to fight against the people of Ammon, and did not call us to go with you? We will burn your house down on you with fire!" And Jephthah said to them, "My people and I were in a great struggle with the people of Ammon; and when I called you, you did not deliver me out of their hands. So when I saw that you would not deliver me, I took my life in my hands and crossed over against the people of Ammon; and the LORD delivered them into my hand. Why then have you come up to me this day to fight against me?" (NKJV)*

This is the second time the Ephraimites accost a leader over an imagined neglect. Their intimidation is both physical and personal. Jephthah responds that he had requested help from them from the beginning, but they had refused to come to his aid. So he risked his life in a desperate undertaking without them, and they respond with hostility instead of gratitude.

Those who are most often at fault try to shield themselves by blaming the innocent.

blaming
Matthew 7:3–5

dialects
regional variety in a
language

A Matter of Pronunciation

JUDGES 12:4–7 *Now Jephthah gathered together all the men of Gilead and fought against Ephraim. And the men of Gilead defeated Ephraim, because they said, "You Gileadites are fugitives of Ephraim among the Ephraimites and among the Manassites." The Gileadites seized the fords of the Jordan before the Ephraimites arrived. And when any Ephraimite who escaped said, "Let me cross over," the men of Gilead would say to him, "Are you an Ephraimite?" If he said, "No," then they would say to him, "Then say, 'Shibboleth'!" And he would say, "Sibboleth," for he could not pronounce it right. Then they would take him and kill him at the fords of the Jordan. There fell at that time forty-two thousand Ephraimites. And Jephthah judged Israel six years. Then Jephthah the Gileadite died and was buried among the cities of Gilead. (NKJV)*

Jephthah's remonstrations are in vain, for Ephraim is intent on a quarrel. The final insult that incites Gilead to action appears to say that the tribes east of the Jordan are made up of the debris or refuse of Ephraim and Manasseh. Gilead's army had already been dismissed, but now they issue another call to arms to put down Ephraim's threat of violence.

At the fords of the Jordan, the individuals who attempt to cross are asked to say "Shibboleth" (an ear of corn), for the first consonant was mispronounced in the Ephraimite dialect.[16] (The existence of **dialects** during the time of the judges was another indication of national disunity.)

Ephraim is finally put in their place after forty-two thousand of their citizens are cut down. Finally, Israel can settle down to six years of relative quiet, after which Jephthah passes on and leaves a void for someone else to fill.

Influential and Important

JUDGES 12:8–10 *After him, Ibzan of Bethlehem judged Israel. He had thirty sons. And he gave away thirty daughters in marriage, and brought in thirty daughters from elsewhere for his sons. He judged Israel seven years. Then Ibzan died and was buried at Bethlehem. (NKJV)*

The only particulars we are given on Ibzan's life are (1) his place of birth, (2) his place of burial, and (3) the size of his family. Evidently he followed the practice of marrying his offspring into influential families outside his own district, to strengthen his political ties.

go to

gap
Ezekial 22:30

tenure
length of time a position is occupied

Just the Facts, Ma'am

JUDGES 12:11–15 *After him, Elon the Zebulunite judged Israel. He judged Israel ten years. And Elon the Zebulunite died and was buried at Aijalon in the country of Zebulun. After him, Abdon the son of Hillel the Pirathonite judged Israel. He had forty sons and thirty grandsons, who rode on seventy young donkeys. He judged Israel eight years. Then Abdon the son of Hillel the Pirathonite died and was buried in Pirathon in the land of Ephraim, in the mountains of the Amalekites. (NKJV)*

Again, only a few facts are documented about each of these leaders. Most of Elon's name is found in the last syllable of the town in which he was buried, so perhaps this place was named in his honor.

Abdon was a resident of Pirathon in Ephraim (probably Fer'ata, six miles southwest of Shechem).[17] He was most known for his sons and grandsons and the donkeys they rode. His **tenure** may have been concurrent with the Amalekite occupation (clarifying why an Ephraimite town was located in Amalekite hill country).

what others say

Floyd Schwanz

God works through people. He always has, and He always will. Not notebooks and tapes, not well-machined organizations, not just a few professionally trained persons—God works through ordinary people who are committed to love the people around them God's way.[18]

God uses ordinary people to step into the gap and further his kingdom on earth.

something to ponder

Chapter Wrap-Up

- Israel suffers under the invading Ammonites and turns from her sin. (Judges 10:6–16)
- Israel calls Jephthah to be their leader, and he tries to make peace without war. (Judges 10:17–11:27)
- Jephthah defeats Ammon and deals with the consequences of a foolish vow. (Judges 11:28–40)
- Jephthah deals with criticism at home and punishes the offenders. (Judges 12:1–7)
- Three more minor judges led Israel, in varying degrees. (Judges 12:8–15)

Study Questions

1. To what point did the Israelites have to come before they were ready to submit to God?

2. How did Jephthah's ill-treatment prepare him for leadership?

3. What is the purpose of a vow, and what obligation is inherent in one?

4. Were the last three judges recognized for stupendous feats of prowess and skill?

Judges 13-14
Samson's Strength

Chapter Highlights:
- Samson's Calling
- Phantom of the Field
- Samson's Birth
- Samson's Courting
- Samson's Riddle

Let's Get Started

No one is quite certain where the Philistines came from—possibly the Aegean Islands or the island of Crete. But when they descended on the coast of Israel they were called the "Sea People" because they emerged from the waters of the Mediterranean.[1] They had been in Israel at least since <u>Abraham's</u> time, first settling in the southwest corner. But since about 1200 BC their numbers had increased, and so had their influence.[2]

go to

Abraham's
Genesis 21:32–34

Shamgar
Judges 3:31

Judah
Judges 15:11

They were warlike and powerful, skilled in the art of crafting iron weaponry. This gave them an immense advantage over the Israelites, who always felt overwhelmed by anyone who fought in chariots. Each of the Philistine's five coastal cities was ruled by a lord who handled the smaller decisions; the larger ones were voted on by the general populace.[3] This system of government also placed them in a superior position to Israel, who by this time was a conglomeration of weak and bickering tribes.

<u>Shamgar</u> checked the influence of the Philistines only temporarily, and now they are again exerting a lot of clout. For forty agonizing years (the longest recorded oppression in the book of Judges) they increase the heat, <u>Judah</u> receiving the brunt of the pressure.

Samson's Calling

JUDGES 13:1 *Again the children of Israel did evil in the sight of the LORD, and the LORD delivered them into the hand of the Philistines for forty years. (NKJV)*

The story of Samson is preceded by one full generation of oppression. The historian actually picks up the account from chapter 10, verses 6 and 7, where God, grievously saddened by the evil that he sees, deliberately sells Israel into the hands of the Ammonites and Philistines. When Israel repented, God allowed Jephthah to deal a death blow to the Ammonites, and now God will groom Samson to

go to

Joshua
Joshua 5:13–15

Gideon
Judges 6:11–24

Christ
John 1:3

Sarah
Genesis 11:30

John
John 1:20

Manoah
Judges 13:16–22

Sarah
Genesis 17:1–8;
18:9–15

scourge
something used as a
punishing agent

barren
not able to bear
children

confess
to declare a belief

save Israel from the Philistines' **scourge**. But before Samson appears on the scene, life is grim and depressing at best.

what others say

Oswald Chambers

In certain moods we wish God would make us do the right thing, but He will not; and in other moods we wish He would leave us alone altogether, but He will not.[4]

The Patter of Tiny Feet

JUDGES 13:2–3 *Now there was a certain man from Zorah, of the family of the Danites, whose name was Manoah; and his wife was barren and had no children. And the Angel of the LORD appeared to the woman and said to her, "Indeed now, you are barren and have borne no children, but you shall conceive and bear a son. (NKJV)*

Just as he appeared to <u>Joshua</u> and <u>Gideon</u>, the Lord himself visits Manoah's wife with an announcement that will change her life forever. No longer will she be despised in the culture of the day as a woman unable to bear children, but the ultimate honor of every Israelite wife will fall upon her. She will mother a child.

Telling Manoah's wife that she is both sterile and childless seems to us to state and restate the obvious. This pattern of speech is commonly used in ancient Israelite culture. For example, the Scriptures affirm that <u>Christ</u> made all things, then reaffirm that without him nothing was made that was made. In another place (very similar to the passage we are looking at), it states that <u>Sarah</u> was **barren**, and (as if it were not already declared) she had no children. And yet again, <u>John</u> the Baptist did not fail to **confess**, but it says that he confessed freely.

Annunciations are associated with the births of important people. They are pronouncements of the soon arrival of someone special who has a singular role to fulfill. Besides the appearance of the "Angel of the LORD" to <u>Manoah</u> and his wife, there are three other prominent examples in the Bible:

1. Abraham and <u>Sarah</u> were told they would have a son who would father an entire nation.

2. Zechariah received the announcement that he and his barren wife would become the parents of John the Baptist, the one to prepare Israel for the coming of the Messiah.

3. Mary entertained a heavenly visitor, who came to foretell the birth of Jesus, the Savior of the world.

The astonished reactions of each party, so visited, vary greatly. One thought he was going to die, another laughed out loud, a third verbally **parried** the messenger and was left speechless, and the last felt so blessed she wrote a song to commemorate the event. But all of them realized that these were no ordinary encounters, and they would never be the same.

Zechariah
Luke 1:8–20

Mary
Luke 1:26–38, 46–55

all
Leviticus 11:1–47

parried
used cleverly evasive words

abstinence
restraint from indulging in something

Never Lower His Ears

the big picture

Judges 13:4-7

The angel continues his instructions to the woman. She may not drink wine or any fermented drink, nor may she eat anything unclean, because the son that will be born to her is to be set apart to God from birth as a Nazirite. He will begin the deliverance of Israel from the Philistines.

The woman tells her husband about the strange encounter. She describes her visitor as a man of God who looked as awesome as an angel. She didn't know his name or where he'd come from, but repeated the conversation as best she could.

The fact that God asks the *mother* to subject herself to Nazirite law as long as she is carrying this child confirms that a fetus can already be considered a human being in the eyes of God. Although as yet unborn, the role that Samson will play demands a certain discipline even in the womb. Because the child will be nourished by what the mother eats, his separation and consecration must begin even before birth.

Even on a natural level, **abstinence** from alcoholic beverages would promote health and strength in the child. As to unclean foods, certain meats were forbidden for all Israelites, not just Nazirites, but perhaps this distinction was no longer being observed at this time and the angel felt an extra caution was required.

go to

David
2 Samuel 5:25

human
Jeremiah 1:5

plant
1 Corinthians 3:5–9

lay
1 Corinthians
3:10–11

Nazirite
Numbers 6:2–21

yoke
something oppressive and restrictive

persona
image or identity

futility
action with no effect

The Israelites still had some time to wait for God's deliverance, for Samson wasn't even born yet. After that he had to grow to maturity before he could rescue his nation. Even then, his efforts would only initiate the liberation. Other judges and rulers would continue the work of throwing off the Philistines' heavy **yoke**, until almost total deliverance is finally achieved at the time of David.[5]

The woman calls her visitor a man but seems to have her suspicions that he's much more than human. His **persona** exactly fits her impression of what an angel must be like.

> **what others say**
>
> **Charles Caldwell Ryrie**
>
> God's concern and creative power are extended to prenatal life. This teaching would make it impossible to consider the embryo or fetus "just a piece of tissue" or "an insensible blob of tissue." The very least one must say is that at the moment of conception there exists a potential human being (or better, a human being with potential) which is sacred and valuable to God as evidenced by God's personal involvement.[6]

Just as Samson's role will only *begin* the work of liberation, leaving it to others to further the process until the Philistines no longer pose any threat to the nation of Israel, so it is with the work of the kingdom going on all around us. One person may plant in the heart of another a seed of faith. But it may be another individual's job to water the plant so it may continue to grow. Both have an equally important role in the process and must realize the **futility** of striving alone. So too, one person may lay the foundation for spiritual growth in another's life, but it may be the duty of someone else entirely to build on that foundation.

In the final analysis, it will be God who grants the victory over the Philistines, God who ensures that the proper growth and development take place, and God himself who is the only foundation worth building upon. Helping others attain spiritual maturity is a corporate endeavor that happens only under the blessing of God.

When an individual would decide to take the Nazirite vow, he signified by his behavior a deep commitment to God and his service. He would not cut his hair or shave his beard; he could not drink wine or other alcoholic beverages; and he had to stay away from anything dead or in any state of decay. Even if one of these regulations was broken by accident, he was required to shave his head and face, bury the hair, and start the vow all over again.

pray
Genesis 17:18;
1 Chronicles 29:19

what others say

V. Gilbert Beers

The Nazirite vow could be taken for as little as 30 days, or for an entire lifetime. Parents could take the vow for their children before they were born, and the children were bound by it. Samson was a lifetime Nazirite because his mother and father had made this promise to God (Jud. 13:5,7).[7]

Phantom of the Field

JUDGES 13:8–10 *Then Manoah prayed to the LORD and said, "O my Lord, please let the Man of God whom You sent come to us again and teach us what we shall do for the child who will be born." And God listened to the voice of Manoah, and the Angel of God came to the woman again as she was sitting in the field; but Manoah her husband was not with her. Then the woman ran in haste and told her husband, and said to him, "Look, the Man who came to me the other day has just now appeared to me!" (NKJV)*

Could Manoah have been skeptical that such an important message would come through a woman? Did he find it hard to believe that his wife really got all the details straight? Giving him the benefit of the doubt, he may have simply desired more instruction and guidance at the prospect of such a critical event. At any rate, his prayer is a wonderful model for any expectant parents: "Lord, teach us what we shall do for the child who will be born."

It is ironic that when the angel makes his second appearance in response to Manoah's plea, it is once again to the *woman* and Manoah is nowhere around. Perhaps this is a touch of gentle humor on the part of the Lord, to remind us that God will not be influenced by man's biases or predispositions. The woman, however, hurries away to get her husband, desiring that he share in her experience (and probably hoping to prove that she had not been delusional).

One of the most important things a parent can do for his or her child is to pray.

apply it

go to

convey
Philippians 2:12–14

pragmatic
concerned with
practical results

integral
an essential element
of a whole

what others say

Karen Scalf Linamen

I believe there are three reasons a parent must learn to pray—
effectively, regularly, and with power—for their children . . .
The first reason is simply and profoundly this: the world in
which we are raising our children is fraught with temptations
and treachery . . . We pray because our children are in danger; we also pray because we were created to pray. To deny
our need for prayer leads to stifled growth, pain, suffering,
and even spiritual death . . . The third dynamic that can send
us to our knees is perhaps the most **pragmatic** of all. We pray
because prayer works.[8]

Follow the Formula

the big picture

Judges 13:11–14

Manoah follows his wife to see the angel. On receiving the affirmation that he is the same visitor who had delivered the first
message, Manoah asks for guidelines for raising the child. The
angel reiterates the same instructions he'd given to the woman.

Instructions given firsthand are more easily understood than those
delivered through another source. For this reason, it was important
to Manoah that, whoever this man was and whatever message he had
to relay, it would be heard and experienced by himself personally. He
asks, "What is the rule (or *mishpot* in Hebrew, meaning "prescrip-
tion") to follow regarding the training and education of the boy?"[9]

The angel answers by repeating the directions concerning the conduct of the mother, seeming to indicate that if they made the
Nazirite restrictions a part of their household now, then the child
soon to be born would easily fall into the same patterns.

Whatever you desire to build into the life of a child—character
traits, special disciplines, internal values—must first be incorporated
into your own life as the parent or teacher. You cannot speak out of
a vacuum; you cannot share from inexperience; and you cannot pass
on a passion that does not burn first in your own soul. Take the
virtue that you wish to impart, deeply implant it as an **integral** part
of yourself, let it work itself out in your everyday experience, and
then consider how you might <u>convey</u> it to another. Chances are, by
that time, you'll already have done so.

Strengthen your family

Joni Eareckson Tada

When I fail to study the real thing, my paintings show it. They lack life if I've only worked from photographs or other people's ideas. And what is true for the artist is true for the Christian . . . If a painting is to shine with life, it must represent the real thing. If a Christian is to shine with the <u>light</u> of Jesus, it will mean taking time to get close to the real thing, or in this case, the real Person.[10]

light
Matthew 5:16;
2 Corinthians 3:18

previous
Exodus 23:20–21

enigmatic
difficult to enterpret

ineffable
incapable of being
expressed in words

divinity
that which makes up
God

Samson's Birth

JUDGES 13:15–18 *Then Manoah said to the Angel of the LORD, "Please let us detain You, and we will prepare a young goat for You." And the Angel of the LORD said to Manoah, "Though you detain Me, I will not eat your food. But if you offer a burnt offering, you must offer it to the LORD." (For Manoah did not know He was the Angel of the LORD.) Then Manoah said to the Angel of the LORD, "What is Your name, that when Your words come to pass we may honor You?" And the Angel of the LORD said to him, "Why do you ask My name, seeing it is wonderful?"*

Manoah offers to prepare a meal for his guest, but what he suggests is not appropriate for the person he is entertaining. Actually, a burnt offering would be more suitable, as the visitor is the Lord himself, not just a mere man. The Lord's reply is not a rebuke; rather, it's an honest statement declaring the true nature of things.

Still bumbling around, Manoah next asks the Lord's name, wanting to know how he should address his guest. Again the Lord's answer seems **enigmatic**, but God is not playing mind games with Manoah. His holy name is **ineffable** and marvelous beyond human comprehension, for it encompasses all that he is.

In a <u>previous</u> passage, God sent an angel ahead of the Israelites to prepare the way for them as they entered the Promised Land. That angel possessed the same rights as God (an authority to be obeyed and the ability to forgive sins). But the real key to his identity is revealed in God's affirmation that "my Name is in him," meaning "my nature is in him." He held within his person true **divinity**.

A name is a label of identification, and Manoah's visitor (bearing a name too wonderful to be represented by the language of mortals) is clearly none other than God himself.

name
Isaiah 57:15

Gideon's
Judges 6:22

confidence
Colossians 2:2–3;
Hebrews 10:22–25

face
Exodus 33:18–20

embodiment
tangible expression
of an idea

pre-incarnate
before birth

The Light Dawns

the big picture

Judges 13:19–23

Then Manoah took a goat and sacrificed it with his grain offering on a rock. As the flames blazed up from the altar, Manoah
and his wife saw an amazing thing. The angel ascended toward
heaven in the flame and disappeared. Finally Manoah realizes
who appeared to them and falls with his face to the ground, crying, "We shall surely die, because we have seen God!" (13:22
NKJV). But his wife reasons that God would not have accepted
their offering, shown them signs, or given them the message he
did if he simply intended to kill them in the end.

Manoah is starting to get the picture when he takes the grain he has set
aside as an offering to God (along with the goat), and selects a rock from
which to make a sacrifice. But seeing the Lord ascend in the flame is such
an astonishing sight that at last he is convinced beyond the shadow of
any doubt. His visitor is *the* angel of the Lord.[12] His reaction to this discovery is the same as <u>Gideon's</u>. He is sure he is going to die.

His wife remains composed, recognizing that dead couples do not
parent babies. God will not go back on his promise now.

My <u>confidence</u> and assurance in life are based on the depth of my
trust and expectation in God.

Manoah's fear for his life is not entirely without reservation. When
God allowed Moses to view his "goodness" on parade, he acknowledged that if anyone should look directly at his <u>face</u>, they would die.
At that time, he was speaking of his form as it appears in heaven
without earthly modifications for our benefit. However, the **pre-
incarnate** figure of Christ, which he assumes to make many Old
Testament appearances, is fully compatible with human limitations.

Like Manoah, the individuals the Lord visits are often amazed that they can see God in the flesh and still live to tell about it. An example would be <u>Jacob</u>, who wrestled all night with "a Man." In the morning, he names the place Peniel (meaning "face of God"), saying, "For I have seen God face to face, and my life is preserved" (Genesis 32:30 NKJV).

go to

Jacob
Genesis 32:26–30

revelations
Psalm 19:1–6;
John 1:1–14;
Hebrews 1:1–2;
Romans 1:20

revelations
information newly
disclosed

omnipresent
everywhere

> ### what others say
>
> #### J. Dwight Pentecost
>
> In many different times and in many varied ways, God has revealed Himself to us. And every revelation has shown Him to be a God of infinite glory. These **revelations** were designed, not only to dispel our ignorance of Him, so that we might know Him, but also to bring those who know Him to worship, obedience and love for Him.[13]

Stirred with God's Spoon

JUDGES 13:24–25 *So the woman bore a son and called his name Samson; and the child grew, and the LORD blessed him. And the Spirit of the LORD began to move upon him at Mahaneh Dan between Zorah and Eshtaol. (NKJV)*

The name Samson comes from a root meaning the "sun."[14] Perhaps his mother was recalling in this designation the shining face of the angel who had announced his birth.

From time to time, Samson was led to display remarkable feats of valor and strength under the influence of the Spirit of God. This movement of the Spirit comes from another root word meaning "anvil."[15] So, like the repeated and violent strokes of a workman on an anvil, the influence of the Spirit in Samson's life is abrupt, impelling, striking, and forceful.

> ### what others say
>
> #### John F. Walvoord
>
> Although the Holy Spirit clearly indwelt some saints in the Old Testament, this does not seem to have been universally realized and, in fact, was only bestowed sovereignly by God to accomplish His purpose in certain individuals. The Spirit, being **omnipresent**, was *with* all those who put their trust in God even if not *in* them, and undoubtedly contributed to their spiritual life and experience.[16]

Samson's Courting

alliances
Deuteronomy 7:3–4

seems
Proverbs 12:15;
14:12

establishment
the institutions in a
society

JUDGES 14:1–4 *Now Samson went down to Timnah, and saw a woman in Timnah of the daughters of the Philistines. So he went up and told his father and mother, saying, "I have seen a woman in Timnah of the daughters of the Philistines; now therefore, get her for me as a wife." Then his father and mother said to him, "Is there no woman among the daughters of your brethren, or among all my people, that you must go and get a wife from the uncircumcised Philistines?" And Samson said to his father, "Get her for me, for she pleases me well." But his father and mother did not know that it was of the LORD—that He was seeking an occasion to move against the Philistines. For at that time the Philistines had dominion over Israel. (NKJV)*

Timnah was a frontier town of Dan, lying on the border of Philistine country about twenty miles west of Jerusalem.[17] The Philistines have probably taken over the town, put it under tribute, and settled down to live side by side with the Israelite residents.

Samson sees the wife he desires and urges his parents to start the ball rolling. Customarily, the parents were responsible for making marriage arrangements, and Samson was willing to let his parents take their rightful role as long as he got to pick the bride.[18]

God has warned the Israelites concerning the danger of making marriage <u>alliances</u> with the pagan people around them, for he knows the downward tug of an unspiritual partner is usually too hard to overcome. So the parents try to encourage Samson in another direction, but Samson has made up his mind. He literally says, "She is right in my eyes," revealing an incredibly self-absorbed attitude.[19] God, however, has plans to use this stubborn obsession to defy the Philistine **establishment**.

Samson's comment that the Philistine girl is "right in his eyes" typifies the general attitude of most Israelite citizens during this ungodly period in Israel's history. Instead of trying to please God and discern his will, they follow whatever suits their fancy. They do whatever they feel like at the moment.

I must never decide on the worthiness of anything based on how it feels or <u>seems</u>.

Leapin' Lizards . . . Uh, Lions!

JUDGES 14:5–7 So Samson went down to Timnah with his father and mother, and came to the vineyards of Timnah. Now to his surprise, a young lion came roaring against him. And the Spirit of the LORD came mightily upon him, and he tore the lion apart as one would have torn apart a young goat, though he had nothing in his hand. But he did not tell his father or his mother what he had done. Then he went down and talked with the woman; and she pleased Samson well. (NKJV)

Manoah and his wife agree to approach the potential wife's parents, no doubt with grave misgivings.

Perhaps Samson, in his eagerness, has gone on ahead, for he is alone when suddenly assaulted by a lion. The lion is "young," not in the sense that it is an incompetent whelp but, on the contrary, has recently come into its full strength and size and is more fierce than one that has mellowed with age.

Samson, in his own strength, may naturally have been stronger than other men, but the prowess described in this passage flowed from the Spirit of the Lord, which came upon him with enabling power. It is not obvious why Samson did not share this event with anyone, but it might have been a surprising display of modesty and humility on his part.

> **what others say**
>
> **Charles Spurgeon**
> We have plenty of people nowadays who could not kill a mouse without publishing it in the Gospel Gazette. Samson killed a lion and said nothing about it: the Holy Spirit finds modesty so rare that He takes care to record it.[20]

The Secret of the Savory Skeleton

JUDGES 14:8–9 After some time, when he returned to get her, he turned aside to see the carcass of the lion. And behold, a swarm of bees and honey were in the carcass of the lion. He took some of it in his hands and went along, eating. When he came to his father and mother, he gave some to them, and they also ate. But he did not tell them that he had taken the honey out of the carcass of the lion. (NKJV)

betrothal
becoming engaged

wrested
seized with force

nuptial
relating to marriage

antithesis
opposite

Traditionally, there existed a ten- to twelve-month interval between a **betrothal** and the wedding. During this time, the bride would prepare herself for marriage and the time when the bridegroom would take her away from her own family to join with his. There was no intimacy in courtship; communication and attention were limited during this time.[21]

By the time Samson returns along the road where he met the lion at an earlier date, the carcass is a naked skeleton (otherwise, the bees, according to their habits, would never have selected this spot to make a home). However, Samson may entertain some doubt as to the acceptability of even touching the *bones* (Nazirites are forbidden to touch a dead body), and perhaps that is why he does not even tell his parents of this incident.

He does not just help himself (*laka'h* in the original) to the honey, but has an encounter with the bees and subdues them. The word used is *radah*, giving the impression that he "**wrested**" the honey from them.[22]

Samson's Riddle

the big picture

Judges 14:10–14

Samson and his family follow the customary procedure in Middle Eastern weddings, Samson hosting a feast for the thirty companions he has been given. Samson proposes to his guests a little wager based on their ability to solve a riddle. Thirty linen garments and sets of clothes are on the line. They agree to the terms and he gives them the riddle: "Out of the eater came something to eat, and out of the strong came something sweet" (14:14 NKJV).

Conventionally, there were seven days of **nuptial** festivity, the men celebrating in one house and the women in another. The marriage would not be consummated until the seventh day.[23] Since they were removed by distance from any of Samson's friends, companions were provided. Perhaps they were Philistine young men especially picked to keep an eye on this Israelite, who undoubtedly bore himself with strength and vigor.

The riddle forms two perfect parallels, the first part being the **antithesis** of the second. Something to eat comes from something that eats, and something sweet comes from something strong (also meaning bitter or acrid).[24] The particular challenge in this riddle is not figuring out the individual parts but understanding how they relate to the whole. A lion would be the most ravenous predator and honey the sweetest food, but unless anyone in the wedding party had witnessed what Samson had seen, the answer would remain **ambiguous**.

Riddles were a common form of entertainment among Mediterranean nations. One party would propose a difficult or obscure question, and the other would seek the solution. To crack the brainteaser would bring honor and reward; to forfeit would bring shame and loss. One of the ways the **Queen of Sheba** sought to test the wisdom of Solomon was to pose a riddle to him. Later in history the Greeks, who were particularly fond of this type of amusement, called their verbal puzzlers "banquet riddles" or "cup questions."[25]

Solomon
Kings 10:1

ambiguous
having more than one possible meaning

Queen of Sheba
woman who traveled 1,200 miles to visit Solomon

> **what others say**
>
> ### Bob Phillips
>
> Q: How many feet are there in a pasture that is filled with 200 cows, 40 sheep, 7 dogs, 11 donkeys, and a farmer?
>
> A: Two. All the rest are hooves and paws . . .
>
> Q: How many seconds are there in a year?
>
> A: Only 12. The second of January, the second of February, the second of March . . . [26]

Kiss and Tell

JUDGES 14:15–17 *But it came to pass on the seventh day that they said to Samson's wife, "Entice your husband, that he may explain the riddle to us, or else we will burn you and your father's house with fire. Have you invited us in order to take what is ours? Is that not so?" Then Samson's wife wept on him, and said, "You only hate me! You do not love me! You have posed a riddle to the sons of my people, but you have not explained it to me." And he said to her, "Look, I have not explained it to my father or my mother; so should I explain it to you?" Now she had wept on him the seven days while their feast lasted. And it happened on the seventh day that he told her, because she pressed him so much. Then she explained the riddle to the sons of her people. (NKJV)*

secret
Proverbs 11:13

Recognizing the trouble this riddle will cause, the bride spends the entire seven days of the wedding celebration in tears. Particularly when her own people (struggling for three days and only coming up with dead ends) start to threaten her life, she uses every amount of persuasion she can muster to convince Samson to give her the solution. He finally reveals the answer, but it does not remain classified for long. Samson was not faithful to guard his own secret, so he should not have been surprised when his panic-stricken wife proved just as unreliable.

Plowing with His Heifer

JUDGES 14:18 *So the men of the city said to him on the seventh day before the sun went down:*
"What is sweeter than honey?
And what is stronger than a lion?"
And he said to them:
"If you had not plowed with my heifer,
You would not have solved my riddle!" (NKJV)

On the seventh day, Samson's companions suddenly pop up with a solution for the riddle and Samson is burning mad. He intimates with an apt expression that they never could have obtained the answer without the assistance of his bride.

Entirely New Wardrobe

JUDGES 14:19–20 *Then the Spirit of the LORD came upon him mightily, and he went down to Ashkelon and killed thirty of their men, took their apparel, and gave the changes of clothing to those who had explained the riddle. So his anger was aroused, and he went back up to his father's house. And Samson's wife was given to his companion, who had been his best man.* (NKJV)

Ashkelon was twenty-three miles away on the Mediterranean coast, so Samson's wrath must have burned hard and strong to provide the stimulus he needed to accomplish this task.[27] After marching in a rage all the way there, he kills thirty persons of consequence in order to obtain their "splendid and costly" clothing.[28] How he could have possessed himself of their garments without touching their dead bodies is a mystery (remember, the Nazirites were not to touch anything deceased), but he returns to the wedding feast and discharges his obligation.

Still in an angry funk, he proceeds back to his own father's house, not with the view of permanent desertion but to signify his displeasure at his wife's conduct. Meanwhile, the girl's parents are quite willing to terminate their association with this barbaric young man, and seize this opportunity to make the separation irrevocable. The bride was left in disgrace with the nuptials incompleted, so the parents offer her in marriage to the eager "best man."

Samson was in a unique position to humiliate the enemy. Had he organized a national uprising, a huge army of Philistines would have crushed Israel's meager forces, bringing immeasurable devastation and suffering to God's people. Instead, Samson was an individual with a personal chip on his shoulder and as such could disengage himself from the body of the Israelites and prevail over the Philistines one incident at a time.

Chapter Wrap-Up

- Samson was set apart as special before he was even born to start Israel's deliverance from the Philistines. (Judges 13:1–14)
- God makes himself known to Samson's parents, Samson is born, and begins to feel God's prompting. (Judges 13:15–25)
- Samson chooses a Philistine girl for his wife. (Judges 14:1–9)
- Samson is tricked out of an answer to a riddle and in revenge kills thirty men. (Judges 14:10–20)

Study Questions

1. Why was it important for Samson's mother to begin following some of the Nazirite distinctions before her son was even born?

2. Why did God keep his name a secret?

3. What was wrong with Samson's choice of a wife?

4. What enabled Samson to tear apart a lion with his own hands and kill thirty of the enemy at one time?

Judges 15-16
Samson Subdued

Chapter Highlights:
- Samson's Vengeance
- Bound and Gagged
- Samson's Response
- Samson's Capture
- Samson's Requital

Let's Get Started

Samson's life makes a fascinating psychological study. His behavior was erratic, to say the least. He brought about more miracles for God than any other judge, but at the same time committed more acts of disobedience and rebellion than any other. He was given a tribute in Hebrews, chapter 11, for deeds of <u>faith</u>, and yet for every positive characteristic, he had a morally weak **counterpart**.

He was ambitious to kill the Philistines, not out of a passion to preserve the reputation of God and his people but from a personal **vendetta** and desire for revenge. In spite of the Bible's teaching on the dangers of uncontrolled <u>anger</u>, Samson was driven to wreak havoc on his enemies out of passion and rage. His lustful self-indulgence put him into shameful situations, yet God brought severe devastation to the Philistines out of these very encounters. You might say that God used Samson in spite of who he was.

faith
Hebrews 11:32

anger
Ecclesiastes 7:9;
Matthew 5:22

counterpart
an opposing characteristic

vendetta
prolonged feud

Samson's Vengeance

> JUDGES 15:1–2 *After a while, in the time of wheat harvest, it happened that Samson visited his wife with a young goat. And he said, "Let me go in to my wife, into her room." But her father would not permit him to go in. Her father said, "I really thought that you thoroughly hated her; therefore I gave her to your companion. Is not her younger sister better than she? Please, take her instead."* (NKJV)

Samson eventually returns to his wife like a husband ready to kiss and make up (albeit with a goat instead of the proverbial bouquet of flowers behind his back). The wheat harvest would have made this around early June.[1] Time has cooled his resentment and he's ready to reconcile. However, the woman Samson thought belonged to him now belongs to someone else.

Samson is affronted. Acts of repudiation within the marriage at this time would only be displayed by a husband for a wife and not

resinous

containing a sub-
stance found in sap

the other way around, and Samson was never even apprised of the family's intentions. The girl's father tries to distract him with the physical endowments of a younger sister, but if Samson considered himself already married, this offer would be regarded as an invitation to commit incest.

Hightailing Through the Fields

JUDGES 15:3–5 And Samson said to them, "This time I shall be blameless regarding the Philistines if I harm them!" Then Samson went and caught three hundred foxes; and he took torches, turned the foxes tail to tail, and put a torch between each pair of tails. When he had set the torches on fire, he let the foxes go into the standing grain of the Philistines, and burned up both the shocks and the standing grain, as well as the vineyards and olive groves. (NKJV)

Samson is probably talking to himself in this passage. He determines to carry out his revenge on *all* the Philistines, as he no doubt believes the slight was not a personal one but came about because he was an Israeli. That shuffled the deck of blame to include every card-carrying Philistine.

The gathering of the foxes was not necessarily done in one day, and the devastation of the fields did not all have to originate from one place. This may have been an extended campaign in which he released the animals from different locations at different times.

The torches would probably have been made of **resinous** wood, which would continue to burn for some time. If Samson would have lit the brands tied to *individual* foxes, instinct would have made them run in fright directly back to their burrows, but by tying their tails together, they would be facing different directions and swerve from side to side as they constantly thwarted one another.

The Hebrew word for fox is the same word for jackal, and that is probably the animal designated here, for they are very numerous in the Middle East. They inhabit the brush country, deserts, and grasslands. Jackals are about three feet long and weigh about twenty-four pounds. They have erect ears, long legs for their size, and a slinking gait. They live in holes, travel in large packs, and prey upon helpless animals.[2]

Madder Than a Wet Hen

JUDGES 15:6–8 *Then the Philistines said, "Who has done this?" And they answered, "Samson, the son-in-law of the Timnite, because he has taken his wife and given her to his companion." So the Philistines came up and burned her and her father with fire. Samson said to them, "Since you would do a thing like this, I will surely take revenge on you, and after that I will cease." So he attacked them hip and thigh with a great slaughter; then he went down and dwelt in the cleft of the rock of Etam.* (NKJV)

loses
Proverbs 14:17

fissure
a long, narrow crack

quasi-historical
a fictional character
based on fact

The Philistines sustain no sense of loyalty for one another. When they reckon their trouble stems from the local girl that Samson chose, they burn her and her family to a crisp. But if they hope this action will appease Samson and halt any further hostility, they are sadly mistaken. Now he has an additional reason for resentment, and he is burning mad. He attacks furiously, with an intense and violent hatred, leaving many dead.

Having concluded his present rampage, he settles down in a cleft or **fissure** in the rocky hills near Etam, probably a natural fortress for defense. Etam is about two miles southwest of Bethlehem.[3]

In the original language, verse 8 uses an idiom to describe Samson's vicious attack on the Philistines. It literally reads that he attacked them "hip and thigh."[4] This would have been a common expression at the time, referring to the brutal force that he would have used against them. This same phrase is found on Babylonian cylinder seals, where Gilgamesh (a **quasi-historical** figure) is shown using this method in wrestling.[5]

In an effort to be in control, an angry person actually <u>loses</u> control.

what others say

Greg Johnson

The point is that anger opens the door. It allows the enemy to come inside the walls and destroy you . . . The answer is to give up . . . your belief that you always need to be in control. The truth is, you'll never be in total control—that's God's job. When you face a situation where you're tempted to vent your anger, remember that it's your job to control yourself and it's God's job to control the circumstances. It truly is the only way to keep Satan from destroying you from within.[6]

The fact that God uses Samson's wrath to restore partial freedom to his floundering people does not put a stamp of approval on his behavior. That would be equivalent to declaring that when God allowed an evil nation to triumph over Israel for the purpose of judgment, he actually endorsed that country or its wicked practices. To carry out his ultimate design, God will use many resources of questionable origin, because the whole world is at his disposal and <u>everything</u> is his to use as he pleases.

Family Feud

JUDGES 15:9–11 *Now the Philistines went up, encamped in Judah, and deployed themselves against Lehi. And the men of Judah said, "Why have you come up against us?" So they answered, "We have come up to arrest Samson, to do to him as he has done to us." Then three thousand men of Judah went down to the cleft of the rock of Etam, and said to Samson, "Do you not know that the Philistines rule over us? What is this you have done to us?" And he said to them, "As they did to me, so I have done to them."* (NKJV)

Israel exists at this time with a "survival only" mentality. So when the Philistines gang up on the tribe of Judah and demand Samson to be handcuffed and turned over to them, Judah anxiously attempts to comply. Now Samson is faced with two antagonists. The enemy—the Philistines, and his own family—the Israelites. The fact that they send three thousand men to capture a solitary individual is a tribute to Samson's strength.

It is interesting that both parties—the Philistines and then Samson himself—assert that the motive behind their shared animosity is **retaliation** for the unpardonable deeds of the other.

Bound and Gagged

everything
Psalm 24:1–2

retaliation
harming in response
to harm

JUDGES 15:12–13 *But they said to him, "We have come down to arrest you, that we may deliver you into the hand of the Philistines." Then Samson said to them, "Swear to me that you will not kill me yourselves." So they spoke to him, saying, "No, but we will tie you securely and deliver you into their hand; but we will surely not kill you." And they bound him with two new ropes and brought him up from the rock.* (NKJV)

Samson shows some strength of character in that he did not become angry at the cowardice of Judah or upset over their ungratefulness for the risks he undertook in fighting their common enemy. His main concern seems to be that they would not carry out any vindictiveness against himself. He is not actually afraid of what they might do to him, for he could break his bonds and fight them as easily as any other foe. His primary apprehension is related to what he might have to do to them in defense, were they to set themselves up against him. Samson had no scruples about slaughtering any number of Philistines, but he certainly did not wish to spill Israelite blood.

In this portion of the story, we have an excellent illustration of what Jesus would later do to bring us liberty from sin, which is *our* primary foe. Jesus, like Samson, voluntarily allowed himself to be bound by the very ones he had come to save, in order to bring about our deliverance.

Of course, that is where the parallel ends, but the freedom we experience now comes directly from the **subjugation** he had to suffer then.

Jesus
Acts 2:22–23

freedom
Romans 8:32

subjugation
being under control of another

Samson's Response

> JUDGES 15:14–15 *When he came to Lehi, the Philistines came shouting against him. Then the Spirit of the LORD came mightily upon him; and the ropes that were on his arms became like flax that is burned with fire, and his bonds broke loose from his hands. He found a fresh jawbone of a donkey, reached out his hand and took it, and killed a thousand men with it.* (NKJV)

Lehi was an Israelite town, undoubtedly occupied by Philistines by this time. As the Philistines view the figure of their archenemy approaching, tightly bound by new ropes, a spontaneous cheer breaks forth from their lips. But a moment later they watch as the bands *melt* (the literal Hebrew description), flowing off like a liquid substance from the body of Samson.[7]

Samson grabs the bone of an animal recently killed, as this bone would not be as easy to break as one dried, and with it kills a thousand men.

ditty
a short, popular
song

A Donkey's Bone for Donkeys

JUDGES 15:16–17 *Then Samson said:*
"With the jawbone of a donkey,
Heaps upon heaps,
With the jawbone of a donkey
I have slain a thousand men!"
And so it was, when he had finished speaking, that he threw the
jawbone from his hand, and called that place Ramath Lehi.
(NKJV)

Since the conquest by Samson was performed without an Israelite audience, if there is to be a song of victory, it must be sung and performed by Samson alone. The authentic rendition of this **ditty** involves a different play on words in Hebrew than the ones recorded in English for us, although the *effect* we derive from our translation would be much the same as in the original. The *actual* significance is not transferable from one language to another. The word for donkey and heap are the same in Hebrew, and so Samson pictures the Philistines falling into heaps from the jawbone of a donkey like a bunch of donkeys.[8]

Here we are given the full name of Lehi—Ramath Lehi (meaning "jawbone hill," after Samson's exploits). It is common to shorten the name of a place for convenience, as Salem is used for Jerusalem and Sheba for Beersheba.

It is disappointing to note that Samson does not give any particular glory to God for the defeat of his enemy in this poem. The attention seems riveted on his own personal accomplishments.

what others say

Samuel Brengle

If I appear great in their eyes, the Lord is most graciously helping me to keep little in my own eyes. He does use me. But I am so concerned that he uses me and that it is not of me that the work is done. The axe cannot boast of the trees it has cut down. It could do nothing but for the woodsman. He made it, he sharpened it, and he used it. The moment he throws it aside, it becomes only old iron. O that I may never lose sight of this.[9]

Water on Demand

needed
Philippians 4:19

JUDGES 15:18–19 *Then he became very thirsty; so he cried out to the LORD and said, "You have given this great deliverance by the hand of Your servant; and now shall I die of thirst and fall into the hand of the uncircumcised?" So God split the hollow place that is in Lehi, and water came out, and he drank; and his spirit returned, and he revived. Therefore he called its name En Hakkore, which is in Lehi to this day. (NKJV)*

Finally Samson gives an offhanded acknowledgment that God had something to do with his victory, but it is given in the form of a rebuke. In his weakened condition he feels as if he would be easy prey for the avenging Philistines. Like others who have but recently come from being greatly used by God, Samson has a temporary emotional crash in which he is overwhelmed with discouragement.

But God hollows out a deep, round basin (*maktesh*, in Hebrew), from which water bubbles up to refresh Samson and quench his thirst.[10] This place became known as *En Hakkore*, or "Spring of the Caller," to commemorate God's answer to Samson's call.

> **what others say**
>
> **Corrie ten Boom**
>
> Elijah had an attack of spiritual depression after his heroic effort on Mount Carmel (*see* 1 Kings 18, 19). He felt sorry for himself. What he really needed was sleep and food. God gave him both.[11]

God understands our times of depression and anxiety; even more, he knows exactly what is <u>needed</u> to bring us out of each funk.

Under New Management

JUDGES 15:20 *And he judged Israel twenty years in the days of the Philistines. (NKJV)*

This verse is a sort of conclusion to this portion of Samson's story. Other anecdotes from his life will be related in the next chapter, but they reveal more of Samson's inherent flaws and quickly degenerate to a final demise.

apply it

Samson's influence would have radiated out of southwestern Israel. These were the "days of the Philistines," when their oppres-

David
2 Samuel 3:18

sion in Israel was the greatest. Samson kept them in check, but their final decline did not come until <u>David</u> was given the throne some years later.

Samson's Capture

> JUDGES 16:1–3 *Now Samson went to Gaza and saw a harlot there, and went in to her. When the Gazites were told, "Samson has come here!" they surrounded the place and lay in wait for him all night at the gate of the city. They were quiet all night, saying, "In the morning, when it is daylight, we will kill him." And Samson lay low till midnight; then he arose at midnight, took hold of the doors of the gate of the city and the two gateposts, pulled them up, bar and all, put them on his shoulders, and carried them to the top of the hill that faces Hebron. (NKJV)*

Gaza was the capital and most significant of all the cities under Philistine domination. It is sixty miles southwest of Jerusalem and only two or three miles from the Mediterranean coast.[12] Samson seems to have no fear of entering his enemies' strongholds, perhaps indicating that he has begun to take his strength for granted.

But the real question is: Why is he there? Does he have too much unoccupied time and just pops in for a lark? The saying, "Idle time is the devil's playground," is certainly operative here, for no sooner does he enter the town, than he is taken in by a prostitute.

The news travels fast among the excited citizens of the city, and the final scheme they decide to adopt in order to capture the great Samson involves waiting in subterfuge until he emerges the next morning. But Samson has no plans to be caught unawares, so he makes his exit in the middle of the night, brazenly taking the very gates of the city, together with bars and posts, and depositing them on a hill outside the city. Unfortunately, the success of his fast-break serves to confirm to his perverted way of thinking that it doesn't matter what immoral activity he involves himself in, God will still be with him and protect him from harm.

what others say

Martin Luther

The human heart is like a millstone in a mill; when you put wheat under it, it turns and grinds and bruises the wheat to

> flour; if you put no wheat, it still grinds on, but then 'tis itself it grinds and wears away. So the human heart, unless it be occupied with some employment, leaves space for the devil, who wriggles himself in, and brings with him a whole host of evil thoughts, temptations, and **tribulations**, which grind out the heart.[13]

apply it

Idleness is more than a lack of industry; it is a sin that indulges many **indiscretions**.

Delighted with Delilah

JUDGES 16:4–5 *Afterward it happened that he loved a woman in the Valley of Sorek, whose name was Delilah. And the lords of the Philistines came up to her and said to her, "Entice him, and find out where his great strength lies, and by what means we may overpower him, that we may bind him to afflict him; and every one of us will give you eleven hundred pieces of silver."* (NKJV)

This is no less than an illicit and shameful affair. The woman is *not* called Samson's wife, and he makes *no* attempt to bring her home. He has come to believe that because of his continued success against the enemy, his excesses are acceptable. Now the enemy, with very little research, has been able to pinpoint Samson's source of weakness. The only thing the Philistines have left to figure out is his source of strength.

Delilah is the **mercenary** sort, who is quite willing to compromise this relationship for the sake of a little pocket money. In reality, the amount of silver the national leaders offer her totals more than 140 pounds![14] They are probably thinking that his extraordinary strength is derived from an **amulet** of some sort, or a spell that he chants when needing an extra burst of power. If they could just use Delilah to pinch the charm and hand it over to them, or find a curse to counter the effects of his deep magic.

Much of Samson's life was spent in the Valley of Sorek, now known as the Wadi es-Surar, starting fifteen miles northwest of Jerusalem and running all the way to the coast.[15]

The fact that an activity has become routine or commonplace does not make it normal or acceptable.

go to

idleness
Proverbs 18:9;
21:25;
2 Thessalonians 3:11

acceptable
2 Peter 2:18–22;
Isaiah 5:20;
Malachi 2:17

tribulations
afflictions

indiscretions
actions lacking judgment

mercenary
someone who works for personal profit only

amulet
an object providing protection

go to

commonplace
Hebrews 3:13

more
Ecclesiastes 6:7

tenuous
easily broken

Tim LaHaye

You can't fill your mind with filth and expect to feel clean. But this is the reason many Christians "don't see anything wrong" with certain sins. They have been indulging in sinful mental attitudes so long that sinful actions seem normal. I have had people try to justify adultery because they "didn't feel it was wrong." In actuality, they had felt it was wrong before it became <u>commonplace</u> in their thinking pattern.[16]

Can't Tie a Good Man Down

the big picture

Judges 16:6–12

Delilah starts asking Samson to divulge the secret of his strength. At first he says that he will become as weak as any other man if tied up with seven fresh bowstrings. With the enemy hidden in the room, she binds him as he suggested, but when she calls out that the Philistines are upon him, he easily breaks out of the strings that confine him. Again she asks for his secret. This time he declares that if fettered with new ropes, he will lose his strength. But after he's been tied, she once again calls out and he snaps the ropes as if they were threads.

If we read between the lines, it is not hard to believe that Delilah used all the arts of womanly persuasion. She may have started by admiring Samson's firm muscles, and then progressed to flattery and compliments for his most recent exploits. Eventually she pretends to wonder what makes him so strong.

However, Samson retains his self-possession at first. Perhaps tying him up (first with bowstrings of fresh animal gut, then with new ropes) is done in sport, as if to gratify her own curiosity. Samson no doubt thinks she feigns an attack by the Philistines merely to play a practical joke. He has no idea of the gravity of this game, or that his enemy is concealed within the very same room (or possibly an inner chamber).[17] The Philistines are watching for any indication that Samson's might has decreased before revealing themselves.

Craving personal gratification or acknowledgment puts us in the **tenuous** position of requiring <u>more</u> and more.

Hair Weaving

> JUDGES 16:13–14 *Delilah said to Samson, "Until now you have mocked me and told me lies. Tell me what you may be bound with." And he said to her, "If you weave the seven locks of my head into the web of the loom"—So she wove it tightly with the batten of the loom, and said to him, "The Philistines are upon you, Samson!" But he awoke from his sleep, and pulled out the batten and the web from the loom. (NKJV)*

Finally, Samson inches closer to the truth. One proof of a Nazirite's commitment to the Lord *is* related to hair. However, God's stipulation had nothing to do with a loom.

This time, Delilah waits until Samson is asleep before attempting to pull off her scheme of betrayal. But when awakened by her cries, Samson is as strong as ever. He drags the entire apparatus with him when he rises, even pulling up the post that secures it to the ground while the loom stays fastened to his head.

Baring His Soul

> JUDGES 16:15–17 *Then she said to him, "How can you say, 'I love you,' when your heart is not with me? You have mocked me these three times, and have not told me where your great strength lies." And it came to pass, when she pestered him daily with her words and pressed him, so that his soul was vexed to death, that he told her all his heart, and said to her, "No razor has ever come upon my head, for I have been a Nazirite to God from my mother's womb. If I am shaven, then my strength will leave me, and I shall become weak, and be like any other man."* (NKJV)

Over a period of time Delilah wears Samson down, insisting that if there is any affection at all between them, there will be no reluctance to share any private information. Of course, she never reveals her own hidden secrets about the bribe, the men in her closet, and the true motives behind her disarming words.

In all actuality, although Samson had taken a vow related to the cutting of his hair, there was no inherent strength in the tresses that fell from his head. He could just have easily said, "If I were made to drink an alcoholic beverage or touch a dead body, my power would leave."

From God's perspective, however, when Samson treated his vow so casually, offering it in exchange for the love of the woman he wanted, Samson forfeited what the vow represented. A Nazirite willingly accepted his restrictions because they set him apart as one who had a special relationship with God. Without God, Samson no longer had any gifts or abilities above those of an ordinary man.

apply it

Samson made no attempt to separate himself from a dangerous situation. We have an obligation to always be on guard, watching carefully to <u>avoid</u> error and steering <u>clear</u> of those who would drag us into sin. When we observe a setup that demands compromise, the Bible tells us to <u>run</u> in the other direction lest the temptation prove too strong. The best insurance is to <u>prepare</u> for the eventuality of attack, for it will surely <u>come</u>.

Free Shave and Haircut

go to

avoid
2 Peter 3:17

clear
Proverbs 4:14;
Luke 21:34

run
1 Timothy 6:10–11

prepare
Ephesians 6:13

come
1 Peter 5:8

dexterous
skillful in hand
movement

ministrations
treatment

JUDGES 16:18–20 *When Delilah saw that he had told her all his heart, she sent and called for the lords of the Philistines, saying, "Come up once more, for he has told me all his heart." So the lords of the Philistines came up to her and brought the money in their hand. Then she lulled him to sleep on her knees, and called for a man and had him shave off the seven locks of his head. Then she began to torment him, and his strength left him. And she said, "The Philistines are upon you, Samson!" So he awoke from his sleep, and said, "I will go out as before, at other times, and shake myself free!" But he did not know that the LORD had departed from him. (NKJV)*

Perhaps the earnestness with which Samson has spoken, or the look on his face, reveals to Delilah that this time Samson has revealed the truth. She calls back the authorities and they come with money in their hands.

It is a common custom in the Middle East for a woman to sit cross-legged on a mat, and a man to lay his head in her lap while she croons, sings, and caresses him to sleep. It seems that either Samson was a very sound sleeper, or the barber was particularly **dexterous**. However, if Delilah had been stroking his flowing locks as he fell asleep, he might have sensed nothing unusual in the continuing **ministrations** needed to remove his hair while he slumbered.

Samson awakes at Delilah's cry and has no idea that God has left him. Now he must face his enemies in his own strength, alone.

Blinded by Devotion

JUDGES 16:21–22 *Then the Philistines took him and put out his eyes, and brought him down to Gaza. They bound him with bronze fetters, and he became a grinder in the prison. However, the hair of his head began to grow again after it had been shaven. (NKJV)*

The Israelites consider the loss of eyesight to be an appalling <u>curse</u>. The eyes of Samson, which on many occasions had gazed with desire at various women, are now required of him, and he will never gaze at anything lustfully again. He is bound not as a common criminal with ropes or thongs but with metal **retainers**, and he is set to drudge at a degrading task that was usually assigned to animals.

As his hair begins to grow, so does his repentance, and as his repentance grows, so does his strength.

what others say

John Milton

Ask for this great deliverer now, and find him eyeless at Gaza, at the mill with slaves.[18]

Samson's Requital

JUDGES 16:23–25A *Now the lords of the Philistines gathered together to offer a great sacrifice to Dagon their god, and to rejoice. And they said:*
"Our god has delivered into our hands
Samson our enemy!"
When the people saw him, they praised their god; for they said: "Our god has delivered into our hands our enemy,
The destroyer of our land,
And the one who multiplied our dead."
So it happened, when their hearts were merry, that they said, "Call for Samson, that he may perform for us." So they called for Samson from the prison, and he performed for them. (NKJV)

The belated festival to celebrate Samson's capture is held at last in the temple of **Dagon**. We know some time has elapsed because Samson's hair is already growing back. Perhaps the Philistines waited to ensure that their captive was truly secure in his bonds (Samson

go to

curse
Proverbs 30:17;
1 Samuel 11:2

retainers
holding devices

Dagon
the father of Baal and god of vegetation

favorable
James 1:17

tribute
1 Peter 2:9

pantheon
all the deities of a
religion

had a history of breaking out of any kind of shackle), or maybe it just took some preparation time to pull off an event of this magnitude. At any rate, after honoring their god for his deliverance, the Philistine revelers decide to make themselves merry at Samson's expense and he becomes a laughingstock for the whole crowd.

Dagon, meaning "grain" in the Canaanite language, was originally one of the gods of the Canaanite **pantheon**, probably related to agriculture and produce. The Philistines adopted this god after they settled in the land and built temples to him throughout Israel. Archaeologists are aware of at least three temples, located at Gaza, Ashdod, and a well-excavated one at Beth-shan.

The ruins plainly show long halls, lined with pillars, providing support for the roof areas. Events of interest could be carried out in the central courtyard while hundreds of people could watch from the roof. The temples at Gaza and Ashdod were quite large, capable of holding thousands of people.[19]

Even heathens give glory to their worthless idols when they are victorious or prosper. How much more should we give our praise to the one and only true God, who is responsible for every <u>favorable</u> event and positive circumstance that graces our lives. God deserves our adoration and <u>tribute</u> for all the wonderful things he has done.

Last Gasp

JUDGES 16:25B–28 *And they stationed him between the pillars. Then Samson said to the lad who held him by the hand, "Let me feel the pillars which support the temple, so that I can lean on them." Now the temple was full of men and women. All the lords of the Philistines were there—about three thousand men and women on the roof watching while Samson performed.*

Then Samson called to the LORD, saying, "O Lord GOD, remember me, I pray! Strengthen me, I pray, just this once, O God, that I may with one blow take vengeance on the Philistines for my two eyes!" (NKJV)

Samson breathes out an anguished petition from the depths of his broken heart. His humiliation seems to have made him aware for the first time of God's role in his overall mission. No longer can Samson personally take revenge for every individual slight; he must now depend on God to give him the strength and opportunity if he is to bring about the destruction of his enemies. Once he recognizes his own helplessness, God can use him once again to destroy their common foe. This last act will vindicate both Samson's name and God's glory.

God hears and <u>responds</u> mercifully to us, especially when we call out to him in grief and anguish.

responds
Jeremiah 33:3

colonnade
rows of columns
supporting a roof

Buried in His Own Debris

JUDGES 16:29–31 *And Samson took hold of the two middle pillars which supported the temple, and he braced himself against them, one on his right and the other on his left. Then Samson said, "Let me die with the Philistines!" And he pushed with all his might, and the temple fell on the lords and all the people who were in it. So the dead that he killed at his death were more than he had killed in his life. And his brothers and all his father's household came down and took him, and brought him up and buried him between Zorah and Eshtaol in the tomb of his father Manoah. He had judged Israel twenty years. (NKJV)*

Samson's prayer to die is not a justification of suicide, for he no doubt saw his own end as the only way of bringing about the destruction of his enemies. His attitude toward dying should be seen in the light of a soldier's attitude as he rushes forward into certain death, knowing that in his final attack he will bring down many of his adversaries.

Samson applies heavy pressure on two of the pillars in the **colonnade**, which weakens the entire structure. The building crumbles to the ground in a heap of rubble. Raucous singing turns to agonized groaning, and shouts of triumph to shrieks of pain.

Samson obtained for Israel two full decades of peace, for all the rulers and lords of the Philistines would have been killed in the carnage. Samson's relatives were free to remove his body and give him an honorable burial.

God gave Samson the strength to kill more of his enemies in this last act (done with a humble heart) than he had in his entire life, when he swaggered around with a proud and boastful spirit.

Chapter Wrap-Up

- Samson takes his revenge on the Philistines for what he considers a racial slight, and for burning the woman he considers his wife. His own people turn him over to the enemy. (Judges 15:1–13)

- Samson breaks from his bonds and kills one thousand Philistines with the jawbone of a donkey. (Judges 15:14–20)

- Samson breaks out of a walled city when visiting a prostitute, then compromises his Nazirite commitment and loses his strength after becoming entangled in an illicit affair. (Judges 16:1–22)

- The Philistines make sport of the fallen hero, but he kills all their leaders and brings about his own death in one last stand. (Judges 16:23–31)

Study Questions

1. What did Samson do that was a perfect illustration of Christ?

2. What appears to be one of Samson's mistakes when he entered the town of Gaza?

3. What led to Samson's final downfall? Why could he not see what was happening to him?

4. How did Samson's last request show that he had changed?

Judges 17–18
Micah's Mistake

Chapter Highlights:
- Idolatry of Micah
- Irresistible Offer
- Exploits of Spies
- Confrontation of Warriors
- Settlement of Dan

Let's Get Started

The rest of the events in the book of Judges, after the life of Samson, do not follow in chronological order. You might say they are tagged on to the end of the book like random **appendices**.

Actually, the very first chapter of Judges prepares us for the events found here. It describes the <u>Amorites</u>' tight grip on the plains in the districts allotted to Dan, such that the members of that tribe do not dare to even descend from the hills. As a result, the Danites are confined to the mountain regions, which do not provide enough land for each family to have their own portion. In addition, the soil is full of boulders and difficult to farm. So the Danites feel like they've been cheated of their inheritance.

In these final chapters we find out how the tribe of Dan locates a place of its own, and why its worship varies from the manner in which the Lord originally designated. The whole story begins with an unprincipled and superstitious man named Micah, who stoops low enough to steal from his own mother.

go to

Amorites
Judges 1:34

yearly
Judges 17:10

appendices
separate material at the end of a book

shekels
main unit of currency in Israel

Idolatry of Micah

JUDGES 17:1–2 *Now there was a man from the mountains of Ephraim, whose name was Micah. And he said to his mother, "The eleven hundred shekels of silver that were taken from you, and on which you put a curse, even saying it in my ears—here is the silver with me; I took it." And his mother said, "May you be blessed by the LORD, my son!"* (NKJV)

After picking his own mother's pocket, Micah becomes alarmed when he hears her utter a curse against the thief who has helped himself to her cash. Micah later offered (and a Levite willingly accepted) ten **shekels** as a <u>yearly</u> wage, so it is no wonder that the mother wished ill upon the one who'd taken such a substantial amount as 1,100 shekels.

curse
Genesis 49:5–7

religiosity
Psalm 40:6–8

scribes
copiers of manuscripts of Scripture

profane
disrespectful to God

blaspheme
to treat God irreverantly

Being superstitious in nature, Micah offers to return the money. A well-founded <u>curse</u> could bring disaster and sorrow, even within one's own family. Better to remain poor than to suffer bad luck.

The name Micah is probably a shortened form of Mikayehu, meaning "who is like Jehovah?" Jewish scholars claim that because Micah became an idolater, the **scribes** who copied the ancient Scriptures regarded it as a **profane** gesture to have God's name connected with such practices. Accordingly, they took it into their own hands to shorten the name so that it would not **blaspheme** Jehovah.[1]

An Idol for God

JUDGES 17:3–4 *So when he had returned the eleven hundred shekels of silver to his mother, his mother said, "I had wholly dedicated the silver from my hand to the LORD for my son, to make a carved image and a molded image; now therefore, I will return it to you." Thus he returned the silver to his mother. Then his mother took two hundred shekels of silver and gave them to the silversmith, and he made it into a carved image and a molded image; and they were in the house of Micah. (NKJV)*

Micah's mother genuinely seems to desire to please the Lord by making this image of a false god. Perhaps she hopes to avert the curse on her son by using the restored money for a religious object to be located at Micah's house. These strange notions strikingly illustrate the confusion of the times. The religion of the Israelites has become a mixture of pagan idolatry intermingled with elements of true worship.

The image and the idol are most likely one and the same (as the original manuscripts permit this rendering as well).[2] There was not enough silver to mold a solid idol of any size, so it undoubtedly would have been a wood carving overlaid with metal. The remaining nine hundred shekels were probably used to procure the other articles of worship mentioned a little later.

Micah and his mother are like the blind and deluded people of every age, who never deal with the real issue of sin, but seek various human inventions to adapt God's plan in a *human* effort to please him. However, God is not looking for sacrificial acts or extra <u>religiosity</u>; he desires simple obedience to the set of precepts, set down from the beginning, that he knows will work best for us.

When we err he does not look for **oblations** and additional acts of **penance**, but a contrite heart and a repentant spirit.

If It Feels Good, Do It

JUDGES 17:5–6 *The man Micah had a shrine, and made an ephod and household idols; and he consecrated one of his sons, who became his priest. In those days there was no king in Israel; everyone did what was right in his own eyes.* (NKJV)

Micah tries to remember everything when outfitting his little **sanctuary**. To go along with the idol his mother had made he apparently adds other gods. He appoints one of his sons to perform the priestly duties required of a custodian of such images, and procures clothes suitable to the sacred office for him to wear.

The statement about the lack of leadership provides a possible motivation for the crazy deeds of this man and his whole generation. It suggests that Micah made such gross blunders because there was no one to take notice when he deviated from God's law. There was no one to judge whether an action was good or bad—no one to correct error, convince others of the truth, or punish wrongdoers. No one to hold up a higher standard.

go to

penance
Psalm 51:16–17

individualism
Isaiah 53:6

oblations
offerings given as a religious rite

penance
self-punishment to show sorrow for sin

sanctuary
holy place

inalienable
can't be transferred away

autonomous
a free and independent agent

---

what others say

Gerald Mann

The spirit of independence begins with all of the noble assumptions of the spirit of individualism. It says that every person has the **inalienable** right to think and choose for himself and that no power on earth can violate this right. But then it goes one fatal step beyond this position, and says, "Therefore, I'm free to behave as I like; I'm not responsible for the well-being of others; I'm absolutely **autonomous** and independent of the God who created me, of the world into which I was born, and of the human community in which I live."[3]

Irresistible Offer

JUDGES 17:7–10 *Now there was a young man from Bethlehem in Judah, of the family of Judah; he was a Levite, and was staying there. The man departed from the city of Bethlehem in Judah to stay wherever he could find a place. Then he came to the*

father
Judges 17:11

deserving
2 Kings 6:21;
Isaiah 22:21

Aaron
Numbers 18:1–7

Gershom
Judges 18:30

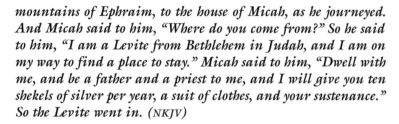

mountains of Ephraim, to the house of Micah, as he journeyed. And Micah said to him, "Where do you come from?" So he said to him, "I am a Levite from Bethlehem in Judah, and I am on my way to find a place to stay." Micah said to him, "Dwell with me, and be a father and a priest to me, and I will give you ten shekels of silver per year, a suit of clothes, and your sustenance." So the Levite went in. (NKJV)

Another indication of the negligence of the times is found in the mention of the young Levite's hometown. Levitical cities were scattered among the lands of the various tribes, but Bethlehem, in Judah, was not one of them. Evidently, the Levites had dispersed haphazardly all over the country without residing in the places God specified for their use.

Either this young man was struggling to find a livelihood or he was a wandering soul—perhaps both. As a Levite, he should have been involved with the work of the temple, but apparently he was not. The wages offered by Micah are suitable but not extravagant, job security and a position of prestige being the greater incentives.

Part of the Levite's job was to serve as Micah's father. In actuality, Micah was old enough to be a <u>father</u> to this young man instead. He meant, of course, that the Levite would serve as his "spiritual" father. This would be the first time a ministering leader would be called by this title. But it is found at other times in the Bible as well, generally used to address more <u>deserving</u> individuals, such as Elisha and Eliakim.

Father to a Father

JUDGES 17:11–13 *Then the Levite was content to dwell with the man; and the young man became like one of his sons to him. So Micah consecrated the Levite, and the young man became his priest, and lived in the house of Micah. Then Micah said, "Now I know that the LORD will be good to me, since I have a Levite as priest!" (NKJV)*

Micah did not have the authority to install a priest, and the Levite did not have the right to accept the position. The only Levites who were supposed to serve as priests were the descendants of <u>Aaron</u>. In the next chapter, we find out that the young man's name is Jonathan and that he is the son of <u>Gershom</u>, not at all in the priestly line.

Micah's feeling of comfort and security is not based in reality. He is ignorantly trusting in a "magic **talisman**" (the priest), believing that his presence will bring him good fortune.

God and his promises are the only <u>securities</u> upon which to base our confidence.

> **what others say**
>
> **Dr. S. Bruce Narramore**
>
> The sovereignty of God also means that when we seek to understand our lives, we must begin with God. Any other focus is doomed to failure. There are only two <u>perspectives</u> on all of life. One begins with God; the other begins with man. If we begin with God, we end up with a certain world view. If we begin with man, we end up with another.[4]

Exploits of Spies

JUDGES 18:1–2 *In those days there was no king in Israel. And in those days the tribe of the Danites was seeking an inheritance for itself to dwell in; for until that day their inheritance among the tribes of Israel had not fallen to them. So the children of Dan sent five men of their family from their territory, men of valor from Zorah and Eshtaol, to spy out the land and search it. They said to them, "Go, search the land." So they went to the mountains of Ephraim, to the house of Micah, and lodged there.* (NKJV)

Because of Dan's timidity they never seemed to claim the inheritance that was rightfully theirs. If they had forged ahead with the confidence of the Lord, God would have honored their faith and given them possession of the land. But instead they retreated. By now the tribe of Dan had been squeezed into the hills and had no room to spare.

So they send out spies (representing each of the five smaller clans within the tribe) to find a new home. As they pass through Ephraim they end up spending the night at Micah's house.

securities
Hebrews 6:18–19

perspectives
Matthew 7:13–14

talisman
an object with
magical powers

sanction
official permission

Richard Lee

When the great conqueror Napoleon and his armies crossed the Alps, his troops came into battle with the enemy. Napoleon's troops found themselves trapped in a valley, and many began to die in battle.

The great leader's heart went out to his men, so he turned to his bugler boy and said, "Son, sound the retreat." The boy did nothing. Again Napoleon said, "Son, blow the retreat or our men will die."

Then the bugler looked at his great general and said, "I'm sorry, sir, but I have forgotten the sound of retreat." Napoleon snapped back, "Then blow whatever you know how to blow!"

The boy placed the bugle to his lips and blew—charge, charge, charge! The troops of Napoleon thought, "Help is coming," and they fought with all their might. The enemy thought, "We must flee because reinforcements are on the way." Thus the battle was won and eventually the war, because one little bugler boy had forgotten the sound of retreat.[5]

Round Peg in a Square Hole

Judges 18:3-6

The spies recognize the voice of the young Levite, and turn aside to ask him what he is doing in this place. After he explains that Micah has hired him to be a priest, the men want him to ask God if their journey will be successful. The priest wishes them peace and assures them of God's approval.

The spies either knew of the Levite from a previous encounter or recognize from his dialect that he belongs to a different tribe. After learning that he is installed as a priest (a fact that seems to bring no surprise, again indicating that anything has become acceptable during this time), the men from Dan assume that, as clergy, he can perform the role of a fortune-teller.

The Bible does not record that the priest Jonathan even asks God before offering a confirmation and sending the men on their way. He gives his **sanction** in the form of such an ambiguous expression that whether the mission triumphed or failed, they could not blame him for giving them false encouragement—although they probably did not think it through at the time. Literally, he says, "Your way is before the Lord," meaning only that the Lord is aware of their course.[6] It is an extremely innocuous reply.

go to

safety
1 Thessalonians 5:3

attack
1 John 2:15–17

sanguine
cheerfully (even naively) optimistic

Easy Pickings

JUDGES 18:7 *So the five men departed and went to Laish. They saw the people who were there, how they dwelt safely, in the manner of the Sidonians, quiet and secure. There were no rulers in the land who might put them to shame for anything. They were far from the Sidonians, and they had no ties with anyone.* (NKJV)

Laish was populated by citizens from the city of Sidon, in Phoenicia, on the coast. This colony had not retained close ties with its mother country, and because its location was sheltered and remote, the people of Laish saw no need to maintain a high level of security. To all appearances, this **sanguine** and passive settlement was ripe for the picking.

In the spiritual life, we need to maintain a constant awareness of the forces that would seek to rob us of our peace, never settling into false illusions of <u>safety</u>.

what others say

Dr. Curtis C. Mitchell

But, not only does a good general want to know what the enemy is going to throw at him, he also wants to know where he is vulnerable . . . Where am I vulnerable to <u>attack</u> from the enemy: the world, the flesh, and the devil?[7]

Puzzling Over Plans

JUDGES 18:8–10 *Then the spies came back to their brethren at Zorah and Eshtaol, and their brethren said to them, "What is your report?" So they said, "Arise, let us go up against them. For we have seen the land, and indeed it is very good. Would you do nothing? Do not hesitate to go, and enter to possess the land. When you go, you will come to a secure people and a large land. For God has given it into your hands, a place where there is no lack of anything that is on the earth." (NKJV)*

The report of the spies could not have been more positive. But the people of the tribe appear to get cold feet at the last minute and wonder whether they are really ready to pick up stakes and move so far away from all they have previously known.

The five men encourage the whole group, telling them that the land is spacious, uncongested, productive, and could be easily taken.

We, too, need to induce one another to actively pursue heavenly gain. We need to encourage our fellow believers to follow whatever course God has called them to. Every time we get together as believers, our ultimate <u>goal</u> ought to be the mutual **edification** of one another.

Where in the World

JUDGES 18:11–13 *And six hundred men of the family of the Danites went from there, from Zorah and Eshtaol, armed with weapons of war. Then they went up and encamped in Kirjath Jearim in Judah. (Therefore they call that place Mahaneh Dan to this day. There it is, west of Kirjath Jearim.) And they passed from there to the mountains of Ephraim, and came to the house of Micah. (NKJV)*

Six hundred fighting men was a force considerably smaller than the <u>62,700</u> soldiers that the Danites were originally able to field before they entered the land. Either the six hundred were all the depleted force they had left after measurable defeat and discouragement, or the party that originally set out for the north is made up of only the more adventurous families of the tribe. We do know that some of the Danites remained in the area of **Zorah and Eshtaol**, for <u>Samson</u> and his parents made that region their home.

Kirjath Jearim means the "city of forests," and is about eight miles from where the journey began.[8] Mahaneh Dan simply means "camp of Dan," for this is where they made their first stop.[9] They happen to pass through Ephraim on the way to their new place of residence.

goal
Romans 14:19; 15:2

62,700
Numbers 1:38–39

Samson
Judges 13:2

edification
uplifting instruction

Zorah and Eshtaol
towns in the foothills of Dan's original allotment

Confrontation of Warriors

the big picture

Judges 18:14-17

The original five spies inform the rest of the company about Micah's little sanctuary and his priest. They turn aside to speak to him. The priest and the six hundred armed men stand at the gate, while the five spies go inside expressly to steal whatever sacred objects they can find.

The five spies indicate to the larger party that the priest and his religious accessories would be a valuable acquisition for their new settlement. They think this special paraphernalia will assure them of safety and prosperity. So, while the main party visits with the priest at the gate, a few of his new acquaintances sneak in to burglarize the shrine. Jonathan remains oblivious.

God alone can provide <u>happiness</u> and <u>security</u>.

go to

happiness
Proverbs 16:20

security
Hebrews 13:6

building
Matthew 7:24–27

> **what others say**
>
> **Arnold Prater**
>
> All about us men are feverishly <u>building</u> their lives on man-made things. They are hell-bent on getting things which do not abide—building houses on rebellious self-will, greed and satiety. They hope to find security in money. They fancy happiness is just ahead when they finally get enough.[10]

Take Me, I'm Yours

JUDGES 18:18–20 *When these went into Micah's house and took the carved image, the ephod, the household idols, and the molded image, the priest said to them, "What are you doing?" And they said to him, "Be quiet, put your hand over your mouth, and come with us; be a father and a priest to us. Is it better for you to be a priest to the household of one man, or that you be a priest to a tribe and a family in Israel?" So the priest's heart was glad; and he took the ephod, the household idols, and the carved image, and took his place among the people.* (NKJV)

When the priest finally figures out what is going on, he is surprised. But it doesn't take him long to recognize a break when he sees one. He forsakes Micah without even a backward glance, for a position of greater prestige and power. As a theoretical "representative of the Lord," he should have risen above his own selfish ambition and spoken out against the obvious theft that was going on. But he was not a pious man, and he was not living a righteous life.

Elisabeth Elliot

The Christian's distinctive mark is love. It was what set the Lord Jesus apart from all others. It was, in the end, what got him crucified. If we follow him in the marketplace, many of the self-promotion methods others use will be out of the question to us.[11]

Stop, Thief!

Judges 18:21–26

The Danites put their most precious possessions in front of them and continue on their journey. Meanwhile, Micah gathers together some of his sympathetic neighbors and takes off after them. The Danites ask him what's wrong, and Micah replies that they have taken his gods and his priest. The Danites answer that they will not be responsible if a hot-tempered man among them should attack and Micah should lose his life. So Micah goes home, recognizing that he's been beat.

The valuables are placed in front of the company of fighting men in case Micah should try to attack and retrieve his own property. He does, and at first the Danites feign innocence. But when they suggest that if he persists something bad might happen to him, Micah suddenly comprehends that he's bitten off more than he can chew. If these warriors and their families did not hesitate to rob him, they might just as easily murder him. And complaining of unscrupulous treatment to unscrupulous men invites more of the same.

Micah thus becomes a victim of his own depravity. He has placed so much store in his "sacred" objects that, when they are taken away, he has a serious problem. However, Micah stole a great sum of money from his own mother without any compunction. Now the tables have been turned.

Dr. Henry Cloud and Dr. John Townsend

God's world is set up with laws and principles. Spiritual realities are as real as gravity, and if you do not know them, you will discover their effects. Just because we have not been taught these principles of life and relationships does not mean they will not rule.[12]

Settlement of Dan

JUDGES 18:27–28 *So they took the things Micah had made, and the priest who had belonged to him, and went to Laish, to a people quiet and secure; and they struck them with the edge of the sword and burned the city with fire. There was no deliverer, because it was far from Sidon, and they had no ties with anyone. It was in the valley that belongs to Beth Rehob. So they rebuilt the city and dwelt there.* (NKJV)

aimlessly
Proverbs 18:9

The people of Laish had no idea when they woke up one fine morning that they were looking at their last sunrise. By evening they would be attacked, and their adversaries would burn their homes and put entire households to the sword.

> ## what others say
>
> ### Joni Eareckson Tada
>
> It's possible for *any* of us to drift spiritually or morally . . . Think of the powerful currents in your own life that can take hold and carry you along unless you make an effort to control the direction . . . I must continue to pull on the oars with all the strength God gives me.[13]

The problem with floating <u>aimlessly</u> is that you are exposed to every current, breeze, and undertow. Unless you don't mind being lost at sea, you must exert every effort to set your sail in the direction the Lord has prescribed.

God's Competition

JUDGES 18:29–31 *And they called the name of the city Dan, after the name of Dan their father, who was born to Israel. However, the name of the city formerly was Laish.*

Then the children of Dan set up for themselves the carved image; and Jonathan the son of Gershom, the son of Manasseh, and his sons were priests to the tribe of Dan until the day of the captivity of the land. So they set up for themselves Micah's carved image which he made, all the time that the house of God was in Shiloh. (NKJV)

Even though the people of Dan are removed by a great distance from their fellow Israelites, they want to remember who they are and

ark
1 Samuel 4:11

Israel
2 Kings 24:12–16

Jeroboam
1 Kings 12:26–30

to whom they are related. They rename the captured city after their forefather, Dan. This location now becomes the northernmost extremity of the Promised Land, and the expression "from Dan to Beersheba" is meant to encompass all of Israel.

With the pilfered priest and idols, the tribe of Dan sets up their own place of worship. Idolatry had been practiced privately for many years, but this is the first publicly acknowledged site of worship to be established as a rival to Shiloh within Israel. It remains a sanctuary for idol worship until the time of captivity. This "captivity" no doubt refers to the time when the ark of the covenant was taken from Shiloh, not the more publicized exile of Israel to Babylon in 586 BC. The probable writer of Judges would not have been alive at that time.

Later, Jeroboam, king of Israel, sets up a golden calf in the very place where Dan housed Micah's idols. Jeroboam did this as extra incentive to keep the northern tribes from traversing south to worship in Jerusalem after the split between Judah and the rest of the tribes of Israel occurred.[14]

This place is now known as Tel el-Qadi (Mound of the Judge). It rises 30 to 80 feet above the plain in a rectangular shape, 700 by 1,500 feet around the outer edge. Only surface excavations have been carried out so far, but what has been found is so promising that it is one of the most challenging sites in all of the biblical lands.[15]

Chapter Wrap-Up

- Micah sets up a shrine and installs a personal priest in the hills of Ephraim. (Judges 17:1–13)
- Five spies from Dan find a new place to settle and check out Micah's setup for worship. (Judges 18:1–13)
- When the warriors of Dan pass through Ephraim to their new home, they take Micah's gods and priest with them. (Judges 18:14–26)
- Warriors from Dan attack Laish, destroy it, and then rebuild the city for their own use. They set up a false system of worship. (Judges 18:27–31)

Study Questions

1. What mistaken opinions did Micah and his mother hold when it came to pleasing God?

2. Why were the people of Laish in such a vulnerable position?

3. How can we follow the example of the five spies in their exhortations to the tribe as a whole?

4. How did Micah reap what he sowed?

Judges 19–21
Gibeah's Punishment

Chapter Highlights:
• An Abomination in Benjamin
• A Massacre in Benjamin
• A Reconciliation in Benjamin

Let's Get Started

Later in history, the prophet Hosea looks back at what happened in Israel during this period of time, with much dismay. Shaking his head in disbelief, Hosea recalls Gibeah's <u>plunge</u> into corruption. (Gibeah is a small town in the tribe of Benjamin.) He remembers the drastic measures God had to take to expose the wickedness of these people. But the thought that truly breaks Hosea's heart is the realization that Israel, after this display of **flagrant** defiance, never again recovered its past glory. Because *all* of the people participated in their own forms of rebellion, they were *all* found responsible for the events at Gibeah, and had to <u>continue</u> to live with the consequences.

What happened? Why did all of Israel have to share responsibility for the wickedness of one of its districts? Why was Israel's relationship with God so debased that it could never be restored? The answers are found here in the last three chapters of Judges.

plunge
Hosea 9:9

continue
Hosea 10:9

flagrant
obviously contrary to any standards

An Abomination in Benjamin

JUDGES 19:1–3 *And it came to pass in those days, when there was no king in Israel, that there was a certain Levite staying in the remote mountains of Ephraim. He took for himself a concubine from Bethlehem in Judah. But his concubine played the harlot against him, and went away from him to her father's house at Bethlehem in Judah, and was there four whole months. Then her husband arose and went after her, to speak kindly to her and bring her back, having his servant and a couple of donkeys with him. So she brought him into her father's house; and when the father of the young woman saw him, he was glad to meet him.* (NKJV)

In theory God was the king, but in practice, each individual put himself in a position of authority. Immediately following the statement about Israel's instability and pursuit of personal pleasure is a depressing illustration of the disorder that resulted from this lack of restraint.

go to

danger
Proverbs 13:20;
Exodus 23:2

The passage does not state *how* the concubine was unfaithful—whether she had an affair and then returned to the refuge of her father's home, or simply disliked her husband and deserted him. But her father appears anxious for a reconciliation, probably because a breakup would bring him social disgrace.

Dillydallying

the big picture

Judges 19:4–10

The girl's father prevails on the Levite to stay and visit with him, so for three days he partakes of his father-in-law's hospitality. On the fourth day, the Levite prepares to get an early start, but the girl's father talks him into eating and drinking a little more, and every time he makes an effort to leave he is persuaded to stay a little longer. The fifth day begins the same way, but by afternoon, the Levite is determined to depart even though the father-in-law continues to press him to stay. So the man, his concubine, and two saddled donkeys finally take off toward Jerusalem.

The eating and drinking would be done by the two men, as women ate their meals separately at this time.[1] Entrapped by the hospitality of his host, the Levite lingered for several days.

On the fifth day, the Levite was thwarted once again by the insistence of the girl's father and his own indecision, but finally separated himself at what the father-in-law calls (in the original) "the pitching time of day," meaning when travelers ordinarily pitched their tents and prepared for nightfall.[2]

The calamity related in the next few pages might have been averted if the unfortunate Levite had just acted with more resolve and left when he originally intended.

apply it

There is a <u>danger</u> and a weakness in allowing ourselves to be talked into something against our better judgment.

On the Road Again

the big picture

Judges 19:11–15

They did not turn in at Jerusalem, although the day was almost gone, because the Levite preferred to spend the night in an Israelite town. So they kept on going until they reached Gibeah,

go to

opened
Job 31:31–32

hospitality
Titus 1:6–9

barbarians
from an uncivilized
culture

> just at sunset. They sat in the city square, but no one offered to put them up for the night.

It was a fatal misjudgment to assume that Gibeah would be safer because it was an Israelite town. The Levite and his concubine could scarcely have fared worse than they did. People who belong to God in name only can inflict just as much cruelty and fall just as deeply into vile behavior as the worst **barbarians**. Gibeah was four miles northwest of Jerusalem.[3] At this time, there were no inns or public accommodations available. Strangers had to rely on private hospitality. Most people in this part of the world were generous and willingly opened their doors to travelers, offering to share whatever they had. So it was very unusual that this couple did not receive even one invitation to spend the night. However, when we read of the contemptible character of the citizens of this town, it is no wonder the simple graces have been abandoned.

One indication of our spiritual maturity is our eagerness to offer hospitality.

Company for Dinner

> **the big picture**
>
> **Judges 19:16–21**
>
> Finally, an old man came in from the fields who was originally from Ephraim. Upon his inquiry, the Levite shared that he was also from Ephraim, and had just come from Bethlehem, and was going to the house of the Lord. He explained that he needed a place to stay for the night, but could supply his own food. The old man welcomed him into his own house, and warned that upon no condition should they remain in the square for the night. So they went with the man, fed their donkeys, washed up, and ate and drank.

Either the old man feels that it is a disgrace to the reputation of the town that a stranger should go uninvited for the night, or he is aware (because of the reputation of the townspeople) of the danger in remaining unprotected in the public square. At any rate, he urges them to come to his home.

The Levite has already declared that they had enough provisions for the journey so they will not have to impose upon their host for

go to

Lot
Genesis 19:1–11

heinous
shockingly evil and
wicked

anything but lodging. They were carrying their own rations, and for the donkeys he would have been well-supplied with chopped straw and balls of bran and barley meal.[4]

what others say

Corrie ten Boom

Mother loved guests. Her lovely blue eyes would brighten, and she would put her dark hair into place when she knew we would be squeezing another visitor around the table—already bursting with four children, three aunts, herself, and Papa. With a flourish she would place a little box on the table, and spreading her arms wide, she would say to our visitor, "You are welcome in our house, and because we are grateful for your coming, we will add a penny to the blessing box for our missionaries."[5]

Sodom Revisited

what others say

Judges 19:22–26

While they were enjoying themselves, wicked men of the city surrounded the house, pounding on the door and demanding that the visitor come out so that they could have sex with him. The old man tried to talk them out of their disgraceful behavior, even offering them his own daughter and the man's concubine to fulfill their desires. But they would not listen to his pleas, so the Levite handed out his concubine to them anyway. They raped and abused her all night, letting her go at dawn. She fell down at the door of the man's house.

The literal interpretation calls the wicked men who surround the house "sons of Satan."[6] They have abandoned all sense of right, honor, and decency. But even more shocking than the **heinous** actions of the townspeople is the inexplicable conduct of the old man and the Levite, whom we expect to maintain a higher standard. Although not stooping to the level of their depraved neighbors, their proposals to compromise the virginity of their own daughter and concubine reflect a wholly different level of degeneracy.

The old man from Ephraim found himself in a situation much like Lot. Both were good men in the middle of vile and corrupt communities. Both invited vulnerable visitors to spend the night. Both

their homes were surrounded by depraved citizens yearning to violate innocent guests. Both offered their own daughters to **assuage** the crowd so that their visitors could remain unmolested.

Homosexuality is not simply a personal choice to follow one's own natural inclination. God has made it clear that this behavior is a violation of his laws, set up to ensure that we experience the best he has to offer. Homosexuality is an <u>immoral</u> act that often has dangerous, unhealthful ramifications. It is treated in Scripture with great severity, yet it is also like every other perversion that starts with something good that God has created.

go to

immoral
Genesis 13:13;
18:20–21;
Isaiah 3:9

bottom
Psalm 51:1–8

assuage
provide relief from
pressure

Body Parts Shop

> JUDGES 19:27–30 *When her master arose in the morning, and opened the doors of the house and went out to go his way, there was his concubine, fallen at the door of the house with her hands on the threshold. And he said to her, "Get up and let us be going." But there was no answer. So the man lifted her onto the donkey; and the man got up and went to his place.*
>
> *When he entered his house he took a knife, laid hold of his concubine, and divided her into twelve pieces, limb by limb, and sent her throughout all the territory of Israel. And so it was that all who saw it said, "No such deed has been done or seen from the day that the children of Israel came up from the land of Egypt until this day. Consider it, confer, and speak up!" (NKJV)*

After sending his concubine through an experience that brought about her death, the Levite reacts indifferently to her form, collapsed in agony at the door. However, he is stirred enough to undertake the gruesome task of dismembering her body and sending a piece to each tribe, ensuring that the cruelty taken out on her will not go unpunished.

It is uncertain whether the people who receive her limbs were horrified at the sight of the mutilated body or were reacting to the story of the rape and murder when they said that "no such deed has been done or seen" (Judges 19:30 NKJV), but the whole nation speaks out in readiness to do whatever is necessary to rectify the problem.

Sometimes the very best thing that can happen to us is to suddenly be made aware of the scandalous straits into which we have fallen. This may not occur until we reach rock <u>bottom</u> and see what we have become, shocking as it may be. When the enormity of our sin

suffering
Matthew 10:29–31

seems to be unparalleled, God can use our disgusting behavior (if we allow him to) as the impetus to get us back on track.

God is not oblivious to the <u>suffering</u> of any individual, even though we may sometimes wonder where he is and why he has allowed it.

---

what others say

Amy Carmichael

I cannot recall a single explanation of a trial—we are trusted with the unexplained.[7]

A Massacre in Benjamin

JUDGES 20:1–3 *So all the children of Israel came out, from Dan to Beersheba, as well as from the land of Gilead, and the congregation gathered together as one man before the LORD at Mizpah. And the leaders of all the people, all the tribes of Israel, presented themselves in the assembly of the people of God, four hundred thousand foot soldiers who drew the sword. (Now the children of Benjamin heard that the children of Israel had gone up to Mizpah.) Then the children of Israel said, "Tell us, how did this wicked deed happen?"* (NKJV)

All the people, from border to border, moved as a single unit in rallying against the evil that had been perpetrated. The fact that the tribes are still acting in unison is one indication of the early date of these events. Later in Judges the tribes functioned quite independently. The girl had been cut into twelve parts—one for each tribe—so the Benjamites did not remain immobile because they lacked an invitation.

Repulsed as they are over the nature of this particular atrocity, Israel remains unconscious of its *own* acts of rebellion. God may use Israel to bring judgment upon the iniquity in Benjamin, but he will not allow them to go scot-free.

But first they are anxious to know the details.

Caught up to Speed

---

the big picture

Judges 20:4–11

The Levite gives his account of what happened that dreadful night and asks for a verdict. The people rise as one man,

---

The Levite recites the bare facts, for embellishment is not needed; the essentials are graphic enough. For the second and third times the men of Israel react to the Levite's appeal by acting "as one man" (Judges 20:8 NKJV), swearing to make up for the **debauchery** committed against this young woman, as if it were possible to undo the suffering and shame brought on by the **decadence** that affects them all.

One-tenth were selected to forage for food and provisions so the rest of the army could focus on bringing vengeance against the criminals in Gibeah.

Left-Handed Slingers

the big picture

Judges 20:12–16

The men of Israel sent emissaries to Benjamin asking for the surrender of the men who committed the violent acts, but Benjamin would not listen and instantly mobilized 26,700 swordsmen to fight against the Israelites. Among them were seven hundred left-handed men who could sling a stone at a hair and not miss.

Israel requests the Benjamites to **"purge"** the evil from Israel by relinquishing the wicked men, in the same way an orthodox Jewish family meticulously turns the house upside down at Passover to rid it of any residual flecks of leaven.[8] By refusing to comply with this demand, Benjamin aligns herself with the original evil and must take on its guilt. And now what began as a simple punitive operation escalates into a full-scale civil war.

The people of Benjamin should have corrected the problem long before it ever involved innocent parties, but their leniency and **cavalier** attitude will bring about their ultimate demise.

It is ironic that the father of this tribe—Benjamin—means "son of my right hand," for he has so many left-handed descendants.

quartermasters
army officers responsible for food and equipment

debauchery
unrestrained, selfish behavior

decadence
moral decline in society

purge
get rid of something undesirable

cavalier
jaunty arrogance

Although they boast of many skilled warriors, the odds are against Benjamin, considering the number of men Israel can place on the field of battle. In round numbers it was 26,000 to <u>400,000</u>.

The <u>acceptance</u> of evil often becomes a greater sin than the original commission.

Surprise Endings

the big picture

Judges 20:17-23

Israel went up to the house of God and asked him which tribe should lead in the warfare against the Benjamites. God replied that Judah should go first. The next morning they took up battle positions, but Benjamin wiped out twenty-two thousand of their men. Israel did not back down, but in the evening, they wept before the Lord and asked if they should continue the fight against their brothers. The Lord told them to go ahead.

Bethel means "house of God," so it is unclear whether Israel went to speak to God at the actual location called "Bethel" or at Shiloh.

The thought that they might experience anything short of absolute victory has never occurred to Israel, but they do ask direction from God as to the fighting order. Judah takes precedence as the established leader among the tribes.

The type of slaughter they suffer usually follows a blatant sin that God wants to draw to their attention, but the only thing they can figure out is that God is angry because they've taken up arms against their brothers. They have forgotten their own areas of weakness and that they have actually been wallowing in the same pit as Benjamin. All they see is the gross violation of one city, while the whole country is overrun with the **virulent** disease of sin.

go to

400,000
Judges 20:17

acceptance
Psalm 97:10;
1 Corinthians 5:1-2, 13

virulent
extremely poisonous and infectious

what others say

Beverly LaHaye

From our perspective, we are only winners when everything goes our way and we come out on top. We want to see the opposition lying at our feet . . . God's perspective is so much broader. He alone sees the whole picture. How, then, can we really judge the wins or losses? The answer is simple: we can't by using man's limited wisdom. We are victorious, however, because God has a different vantage point.[9]

God is more concerned about furthering our <u>maturity</u> than increasing our comfort.

Three's a Charm

go to

maturity
1 Peter 1:6–7

listen
Proverbs 3:11–12

contrite
deeply sorrowful

> **the big picture**
>
> ### Judges 20:24-28
>
> On the second day of battle, Benjamin cut down another eighteen thousand Israelites. All of the Israelites went to the house of God and wept, fasted, and presented burnt and fellowship offerings to the Lord. The ark was there, with Phinehas (son of Eleazar, son of Aaron).
>
> They asked God again if they should fight against their brothers in Benjamin, and this time God told them that the next day he would give Benjamin into their hands.

On the second day, the Israelites fight with the same spirit and from the same place, hoping to avenge their first defeat. But they have consulted the Lord to validate a previous opinion, not to find out if they needed to change anything in themselves. So, they again rush forward with unhumbled hearts, not understanding that God would use Benjamin to execute justice against them for idolatry and disobedience, at the same time they were punishing Benjamin for defending Gibeah's immorality.

Now the total casualties number a staggering forty thousand—10 percent of the entire force. Confounded by this, they finally search their own hearts, and for the first time they weep over their own unworthiness. The result is **contrite** fasting and sacrifices of repentance and renewal, performed at the tabernacle by the high priest.

And this time, when they come to God, he assures them of victory.

> **what others say**
>
> ### Joni Eareckson Tada
>
> God's pruning shears seem merciless. Nothing escapes the cutting edge of His will. Not the blossom of youth, not the bloom of good health, not the fruit of prosperity, not the sturdy, growing family . . . [But] new life is on its way.[10]

We should not give up when we experience failure. Rather, we should <u>listen</u> carefully to what God might be trying to say.

Ai
Joshua 8:17–22

metaphor
a comparison

Charlie Hedges

Most of us have a hard time with the idea of falling back to where we started . . . My hope is that all of us would learn to give ourselves permission to fail more . . . If we fail or proceed more slowly than we might have wished, so what? We learn and get better.[11]

Nothing Left That Breathes

Judges 20:29–48

Israel prepared an ambush for Gibeah. This time when they drew up before the city in battle formation, they were able to entice the Benjamites out of the city by allowing them to believe they were winning as they had done before. Once they got them out onto the roads, and let them inflict about thirty casualties, the ambush rushed into the city from the west and put it to the sword.

At a prearranged signal they started to burn Gibeah. At the same time, ten thousand of Israel's finest warriors made a frontal attack. The men of Benjamin were terrified at the squeeze and fled toward the desert but could not escape. All told, 18,000 Benjamites fell in the heat of battle, 5,000 were cut down on the roads, 2,000 more near Gidom, bringing the grand total to 25,000. However, 600 escaped to the rock of Rimmon where they stayed four months. The men of Israel left nothing else alive, putting even the animals to the sword, and burning all the towns and villages of Benjamin.

The Bible rendition of this encounter begins by relating all the events in general terms, then concludes with the details and particulars.

Even though Israel had the assurance of God behind them this time, they did not rush into warfare presumptuously. They took every prudent precaution, even allowing thirty men to perish before they sprang their ambush.

The psychological impact Benjamin must have felt when they found themselves caught must have been tremendous. It was actually the same game plan that Joshua had used in similar circumstances against Ai some years before.

The **metaphor** in the original language that expresses the cutting down of the Benjamites reads as follows: Israel "gleaned them in the highways," meaning they mowed them down as cleanly as a field of grain at harvest.[12]

The rock of Rimmon is about four miles east of Bethel. As the refuge of six hundred Benjamites for four months, it appears to be a secure natural fortress capable of withstanding a siege. A limestone hill, it is conical in shape and full of caves for protection from the elements and hiding from pursuers.[13]

In 1922–23, Albright found in the ruins of Gibeah, a layer of ashes, the date proving concurrent to the sacking of Benjamin by Israel.[14]

A Reconciliation in Benjamin

> JUDGES 21:1–3 *Now the men of Israel had sworn an oath at Mizpah, saying, "None of us shall give his daughter to Benjamin as a wife." Then the people came to the house of God, and remained there before God till evening. They lifted up their voices and wept bitterly, and said, "O LORD God of Israel, why has this come to pass in Israel, that today there should be one tribe missing in Israel?" (NKJV)*

We do not have any previous record of this oath, taken in haste when Israel was hot with indignation over Benjamin's defense of Gibeah. They did not take it with the intent of exterminating one of their tribes. Their objective was to treat Benjamin with the same disdain as the Canaanites, if Benjamin insisted on acting like them. Now they realize they've gone too far.

Israel's cries mingle self-reproach and entreaty—wondering how they could have got to this point, about to eradicate an entire tribe made up of their own brothers.

Counting Tallies

the big picture

Judges 21:4–9

Early the next day, the Israelites offer burnt and fellowship offerings to the Lord, and then try to figure out who did not join with them in making things right with God and fighting against Benjamin. They discover that no one from Jabesh Gilead had participated. Meanwhile, they had previously taken another oath to the effect that any group of Israelites who failed to join their gathering would be put to death.

If anything, we would hope that Israel might begin to recognize the danger of swearing oaths in passion and haste. But now they are about to make things worse by committing another evil to repair the first.

Their mission is to provide wives for the six hundred Benjamites still in hiding, but to pull that off they must engage in more violence and bloodshed. The focus of their fury now switches to the citizens of a city in the half tribe of Manasseh, who live on the east side of the Jordan not far from the Sea of Galilee.[15]

Everything in Israel, from the border specifications of the land itself to the stones in the high priest's breastplate, was laid out on the assumption that twelve tribes would make up the whole. It was unthinkable that one of the tribes should be omitted, especially that of Benjamin, who was so favored by their forefather Jacob, and whom the other brothers swore to protect.

400 Brides for 400 Brothers

the big picture

Judges 21:10-12

Twelve thousand fighting men were sent to kill everyone in Jabesh Gilead except for the young virgins. This accomplished, they brought back to the camp at Shiloh four hundred young women who had never slept with a man.

The virgins would have been easily distinguished by their mode of dress. The soldiers carrying out the objective were looking for unmarried but marriageable women.

How the young girls would feel toward their prospective husbands one can only imagine, seeing how the accomplishment of this union brought about the barbaric death of all they loved and the destruction of all they knew. We have absolutely no indication that God in any way supported the bloodbath at Jabesh Gilead.

what others say

Richard S. Taylor

Being estranged from God, man is also estranged from his fellows, hence his shocking "inhumanity to man," his abnormalities and perversions, his monstrous selfishness.[16]

Matchmaker, Make Me a Match

go to

Samuel's
1 Samuel 1:3

> ## the big picture
>
> ### Judges 21:13-24
>
> Israel sends an offer of peace to the Benjamites left in the rock of Rimmon. So the Benjamites return and are given the women from Jabesh Gilead. But there are not enough for everyone. The Israelites puzzle over this dilemma, realizing they cannot offer their own daughters because of the oath they have taken.
>
> Suddenly, they remember an annual festival that is about to take place—north of Bethel, east of the road from Bethel to Shechem, and south of Lebonah. They instruct the remaining two hundred Benjamites to hide in the vineyards nearby, and when the girls of Shiloh start to dance, each man should grab a girl and carry her off to be his wife. This they did, and the rest of Israel stood behind them, explaining the situation to the girls' fathers and brothers, clarifying that because they were ignorant of the scheme they were not guilty of breaking the oath, and asking for their cooperation.

emnity
ill-will or hatred

Feast of Tabernacles
seven-day holiday (festival), ordained by God (Leviticus 24), wherein the Israelites live in booths (huts) to commemorate crossing the wilderness after gaining their freedom from Egypt

Once assured that **enmity** no longer exists between themselves and the rest of Israel, Benjamin can safely leave the stronghold. Israel commiserates with the men who remain partnerless, until an entirely new idea strikes their fancy.

The party they plot to crash is most likely the **"Feast of Tabernacles,"** as it appears to be an outdoor celebration at a time when the vines are in full leaf (to conceal the men hiding in the vineyard).[17] This may have been the same event that later drew Samuel's parents to the area of Shiloh once a year. Men and women traditionally celebrate these festivals separately, the two sexes not participating in each other's entertainments.[18] So the seizing of the women could be done with comparative ease, since no men were present to defend their daughters and sisters.

Curtain Call

JUDGES 21:24–25 *So the children of Israel departed from there at that time, every man to his tribe and family; they went out from there, every man to his inheritance. In those days there was no king in Israel; everyone did what was right in his own eyes.* (NKJV)

wrong
Proverbs 16:25

promptings
Ezekial 36:27;
Psalm 32:8

directions
2 Timothy 3:16

Just like the occasion at the end of the book of Joshua when the people met with the Lord at Shechem and then returned to their own inheritances, in Judges they once again conclude their business at Shiloh and head back to the inheritance the Lord has granted each one. However, the outlook at the conclusion of *this* book is grim in contrast to the optimism at the end of Joshua.

Instead of renewing their commitment to total obedience, Israel has only partially grasped what God demands. Instead of affirming their desire to serve the Lord, they are more intent on serving themselves. Instead of seeking God's will, they are trying to solve their problems all by themselves.

The whole situation is summarized in the concluding statement. In the absence of any continuing leadership in Judges, every individual did whatever he wanted to do.

The natural bent of our hearts is always <u>wrong</u>. All the faculties at our disposal (apart from the Holy Spirit, who will live within us at our invitation) work in a warped and deceptive manner. Our only recourse is to depend entirely on God's <u>promptings</u> and <u>directions</u>.

Chapter Wrap-Up

- An innocent girl is raped and murdered by the licentious citizens of Gibeah, a town in Benjamin. (Judges 19:1–30)

- Israel unites to punish Gibeah, and Benjamin takes the other side. By the time the strife is over, 40,000 Israelites are dead and the entire tribe of Benjamin is wiped out, except for 600 men. (Judges 20:1–48)

- Israel seeks to restore wives to the remnant in Benjamin, and in doing so slaughters all the citizens of Jabesh Gilead (except 400 virgins), and kidnaps 200 other young ladies from a festival near Shiloh. (Judges 21:1–25)

Study Questions

1. How did the old man in Gibeah resemble Lot? How did his actions reveal his own depravity?

2. How can we explain the suffering of the innocent concubine?

3. Why did God seem to give Israel permission to fight Benjamin, when he knew all along they would lose a lot of men?

4. What did Israel forget when trying to provide each Benjamite with a wife?

Section Three
Ruth

Introduction to the Book of Ruth

What Is the Book of Ruth About?

The book of Ruth **chronicles** the most significant events in the life of a young Moabite woman named Ruth. In stark contrast to the previous book, whose pages were filled with continuing discord, vulgarity, and bloodshed, this is a very positive, even heartwarming story about ordinary people, living and loving and enjoying the blessings of God.

It begins with the death of Ruth's Israelite husband, then living in Moab, at which point Ruth decides to travel with her previously widowed mother-in-law, Naomi, back to the Jewish town of Bethlehem from which Naomi came originally. It relates how these two women make their way against tremendous odds by loving and supporting each other. Eventually Naomi encourages Ruth to remarry, and Ruth presents Naomi with the joy and affection of a family that Naomi never thought she would experience again.

When Did Ruth Live?

The first verse of the book of Ruth helps to position this beautiful story right in the middle of the rule of the judges. So we know that the events in Ruth's life happened *after* Joshua heroically led the Israelites into their new land, but *before* Saul became the first king in Israel.

As was suggested in the introduction to the book of Judges, the approximate dates for the leadership of the judges range from 1380 BC to 1043 BC. We have no clues as to what might have given Naomi's family cause to travel to Moab other than the indication of a famine that might have occurred during the <u>Midianite</u> invasion. If this was the case, Naomi would have made her return with Ruth after Gideon's deliverance, for she waited until she had received word that the Lord was once again supplying his people with food.

Midianite
Judges 6:2–6

chronicles
present an account in order

go to

mentioned
Ruth 4:17

died
1 Samuel 25:1

advice
2 Samuel 17:15–16

support
2 Samuel 15:19–21
15:32–37

own
2 Samuel 8:18

parents
1 Samuel 22:3

Josephus
ancient Jewish historian

canon
set of writings forming a compete body

vernacular
distinctive vocabulary spoken by a particular group

Who Wrote the Book of Ruth?

In ancient Hebrew Bibles, Judges and Ruth were closely aligned, giving one reason to believe that Ruth was written by the same author as Judges. **Josephus**, for example, is said to have lumped the two books together when reciting the Old Testament **canon**.[1]

If Samuel *was* the author, this book would have to have been written *after* David was annointed (for David is mentioned in the last chapter of Ruth), but *before* David was crowned (Samuel died before David was placed on the throne). Thus we can tentatively pinpoint the date of composition at around 1015 BC.[2]

The **vernacular** used in Ruth is similar to that of Judges.[3] And the classical style of Hebrew that Ruth was written in uses certain archaic forms that would be somewhat rare in later Hebrew writings, another reason to think of Samuel as a possible author.[4]

Something else to consider is the level to which interracial interaction was accepted at the time of its writing. The author obviously had no compunctions about Ruth, a Moabitess, being included in Jewish circles or listed in the genealogy of a king. This comfort with outsiders could have been common during the life of David. He had a tender heart toward the foreigner, going to them for advice and military support, even entrusting his own life and the lives of his parents into their care. Never again in the history of Israel would this level of cross-cultural contact be tolerated.[5]

This fact seems to point once again to Samuel, or one of his contemporaries, as the author. However, there is no hard evidence to support any particular individual, and Christian scholars remain divided between ascribing this book to Samuel and declaring that the author is unknown.[6]

What Is the Theme of Ruth?

Several concepts are furthered in this book. The value of legitimate friendship is one prominent theme, exemplified by the relationship between Ruth and Naomi. Another theme is the meeting of family obligations—daughter-in-law to mother-in-law, wife to deceased husband, and close relative to family members in distress.

The most likely reason for the existence of this book is to give a biographical sketch of one of David's ancestors, for David was destined in history to become Israel's greatest king. Ruth was actually David's grandmother. Thus the book of Ruth also counters **exclusivism**. If a Moabite woman could be "grafted in" to Israel, to both marriage and personal choice, and thus become the object of God's special care (even being included in the royal bloodline of Israel), then *any* nation or culture could experience God's attention and compassion.

His revelation must be kept free from the contamination of other systems of belief, and it must not be diluted by careless, halfhearted adherence to its principles, but God will never deny access to anyone who longs to know him, and his message will always be available to every seeking individual.

The book of Ruth also demonstrates God's active participation in human affairs. Every event, from the famine that sent Naomi's family to seek relief in Moab, to the concurrent death of her husband and her sons that forced her back to Israel, to Ruth's arbitrary choice of where to glean and Boaz's attraction to her even when he was not aware of their relationship, all show the divine hand of God moving in people's lives.

Last of all, this story is meant to give a perfect picture of the nature of a **kinsman redeemer**. Boaz is the only person who is in a position to save Ruth and Naomi from a life of poverty and disgrace. Out of the goodness of his heart, he takes the actions necessary, within the ancient Hebraic code, to make them a part of his own family and elevate them to a position of respect and honor.

Boaz makes a perfect <u>foreshadow</u> of the character of the Lord Jesus Christ as displayed in the New Testament. We (and the entire human race) are helpless in our personal struggle against sin. In kindness and compassion, Jesus did what was necessary to make us a part of his own <u>family</u>, even though it meant he had to suffer and <u>die</u> to bring it about. Because of his efforts in our behalf, we can be lifted out of our shame and be given all the benefits that belong to <u>royalty</u>. These blessings can be ours by acknowledging and personally accepting his offer of rescue and relief.

go to

foreshadow
Galatians 3:13–14
family
1 John 3:1
die
Romans 5:8
royalty
Romans 8:15–16

exclusivism
limited to a certain group of people
kinsman
male relative
redeemer
one who liberates by payment

Chapter Highlights:
• Naomi's Sorrows
• Looking for Love
• Ruth's Devotion
• God's Guidance
• Boaz's Kindness

Let's Get Started

In the Bible, the meaning of a person's name often gives an interesting glimpse into their character. For example, each member of the family we meet in the book of Ruth has a name that is significant to the account. Starting with the father, Elimelech, whose name means "God is King"—it appears that even though he moved his family into a foreign land, he never lost sight of who it was that he worshipped, raising his family with that consciousness as well.[1]

Naomi, his wife, has a name that means "my pleasantness," or "my sweetness." It is no wonder that, later in the story, when she experiences distress and heartache, she asks her friends to call her Mara (bitterness) instead.[2]

Elimelech and Naomi had two sons. One was named Mahlon (sickly) and the other Chilion (pining).[3] Perhaps they were physically weak their whole lives, but the only other information we have on them is that they marry two women from Moab, seem unable to father children, and before very long both die. The first wife is named Orpah, meaning "stiff-necked," and she is the one who goes back to her own Moabite family when given the opportunity.[4] Ruth was the other wife, and her name means "comrade, friend, or neighbor," which fits perfectly with the kind of relationship she freely offers to her mother-in-law.[5]

The only other person of significance in the book is the hero-type relative who rescues Ruth from her plight as a starving foreigner and widow. His name is Boaz—most appropriately meaning "in him is strength."[6]

Naomi's Sorrows

the big picture

Ruth 1:1-5

During the time of the judges, there was a famine in Israel, and Elimelech, a man from Bethlehem, his wife, Naomi, and their sons, Mahlon and Chilion, traveled to Moab to live. While there, Elimelech died and Naomi's two sons married Moabite women

income
1 Kings 17:8–16

creditors
2 Kings 4:1–7

defend
Psalms 68:5; 146:9

take
James 1:27

named Orpah and Ruth. Then, after ten years, the sons also died.

The famine mentioned here could very well have been the period of intense impoverishment brought on by the Midianite invasion of Israel. Like a cloud of grasshoppers, they swarmed over all available crops, feeding their cattle and voraciously grabbing up any edible produce before the Israelites could even touch the fruit of their labor. This would explain why Moab did not suffer any loss of harvest and why Elimelech would see this move as advantageous for his family.

Apart from this, natural factors could also have been in play. Bethlehem is on the eastern side of the central ridge in Israel, and would be quick to feel any drought as the moisture off the Mediterranean would naturally drop on the western side of the hills. In contrast, western Moab is known to be particularly fertile, receiving around sixteen inches of rainfall annually.[7]

Naomi eventually suffers not only the loss of her husband, but that of her two sons as well. Now she is in a strange land with no one left to take care of her.

> **what others say**
>
> **Robert W. Bailey**
> In this life God does not seek to shield us from pain, suffering, and death. He does seek to enable us to become genuine disciples of Christ. If we are open to the possibility, we can learn obedience to Christ in the midst of our suffering.[8]

A widow's misfortune in this time and culture was serious indeed. She would have no means of securing an <u>income</u> and little access to food. Without anyone to take her in, she would be at the mercy of her <u>creditors</u>. In the face of such dire and severe circumstances, God himself offers to <u>defend</u> the widows and later asks the church to <u>take</u> on the responsibility of looking after them.

<u>Country Road, Take Me Home</u>

RUTH 1:6–7 *Then she arose with her daughters-in-law that she might return from the country of Moab, for she had heard in the country of Moab that the LORD had visited His people by giving them bread. Therefore she went out from the place where she was,* *and her two daughters-in-law with her; and they went on the way to return to the land of Judah. (NKJV)*

God, as a principal character in this story, makes his first appearance in verse 6, "visiting" the people he loves in blessing and mercy. At other times he has had to make an appearance to <u>discipline</u> them for their outrageous behavior, but this narrative emphasizes his compassion.

In response to the rumor of better times, Naomi prepares to leave Moab and travel back to her homeland. Fact is, the original intention of her husband had never been to permanently migrate, but to "live for <u>a while</u>" in Moab until the worst of the famine was over. Instead, they had remained at least ten years.

discipline
Deuteronomy 31:16–18

a while
Ruth 1:1

monologue
a long speech delivered by one person

Looking for Love

the big picture

Ruth 1:8-15

Naomi encourages her daughters-in-law to return to the homes of their mothers, blessing them for the kindness they have shown to her and her sons and hoping they will find new husbands. They cry and express a wish to go with her.

Naomi reasons with them that she has no more sons to offer, is too old to marry again, and even if she got a husband and conceived that night, it would be ridiculous to wait for the sons to grow. She bemoans that God's hand is against her, and Orpah finally leaves with a kiss.

Ruth, however, clings to her, even though Naomi continues to push by encouraging Ruth to follow Orpah's example in returning to her people and her gods.

Naomi endorses the idea that the girls ought to go back to the homes in which they grew up. Her primary concern is that they will find good marital matches, and she believes their mothers would be the best ones to make arrangements for remarriage. It is a tribute to her character that both girls consider leaving everything that is familiar, kissing any second chance for romance good-bye, just to be able to stay with her. She is also their only remaining link with the true God.

Naomi's allusions to God, in her extended **monologue**, first call upon him to show her daughters-in-law kindness for past service, and blessings for future happiness. But in relation to herself she laments the difficult things he has brought her way. She feels that the struggles of her own life have been unreasonably harsh.

Ruth 1–2 Ruth's Character Tested ───── 309

go to

through
Romans 14:19; 15:2;
Ephesians 4:11–13

protégée
a young woman
receiving guidance
from someone older

Although Orpah is finally convinced to return home, Ruth clings to Naomi. The word for "cling" in the original means to stick or adhere. The noun form is the word for "glue."[9] But Naomi continues her pitch, trying to influence Ruth to return to her people and her false gods. This encouragement hardly seems like the message a godly woman ought to be promoting to a young, easily influenced **protégée**, But Naomi, in her own grief, is not thinking straight at this point.

what others say

Marilyn Meburg

I love the fact that God is a God who encourages relationships not just with himself but with each other. Jesus modeled that for us in the richness of His relationships with the twelve disciples. We are indeed rich when we have many friends and I'm thoroughly convinced that God loves us, encourages us, nurtures us and supports us <u>through</u> other human beings.[10]

Ruth's Devotion

RUTH 1:16–18 *But Ruth said:*
"Entreat me not to leave you,
Or to turn back from following after you;
For wherever you go, I will go;
And wherever you lodge, I will lodge;
Your people shall be my people,
And your God, my God.
Where you die, I will die,
And there will I be buried.
The LORD do so to me, and more also,
If anything but death parts you and me."
When she saw that she was determined to go with her, she stopped speaking to her. (NKJV)

The amazing thing about Ruth's bold declaration is that, by embracing Naomi and her lifestyle, Ruth was renouncing everything she would be expected to hold dear. Hers was a sixfold statement related to where she would go and stay, who would be her family and God, and where she would die and be buried. This set of deliberate decisions was related to both social and religious issues that would affect her whole life.

To confirm her oath she invokes the Hebrew name of the Lord

(Yahweh), not the Gentile form commonly used when taking a pledge (Elohim).[11] This signifies that Ruth has already come to faith and wants to identify herself with the people of God.

The Bible speaks of Ruth's determination to go with Naomi, using a word that comes from a root word meaning "stout, bold and alert." It is in the **reflexive** case, emphasizing that she strengthened *herself* in her resolve.[12] There was no changing of her mind, and Naomi refrains from any further urging after this.

The <u>phrase</u> that Ruth used to solemnize her oath—"The LORD do so to me, and more also, if . . ." (1:17 NKJV)—is found eleven times in the books of Samuel and Kings. It is thought that these words may have been accompanied with a symbolic gesture across the neck with the forefinger.[13]

go to

phrase
1 Samuel 20:13;
25:22;
1 Kings 20:10;
2 Kings 6:31

reflexive
referring back to the subject

ossuary
urn or vault to hold bones

what others say

Dee Brestin

As daughters-in-law, we need to become as vulnerable as Ruth. She told her mother-in-law everything![14]

Gordon McMinn

Many of us hesitate to give out of fear that someone will take advantage of us or walk all over us. Giving, in fact, runs counter to the "look out for yourself" philosophy which saturates the music and thinking of our culture.[15]

Burial practices in ancient Israel substantiate the fact that families were not separated even in death. Early family tombs can be found all over the land. It was common for them to have benches upon which to lay the most recent relatives taken in death. After decomposition, the bones would be gathered and placed in a common repository with the rest of the deceased (either an **ossuary** or a place hollowed out of the rock for that purpose).[16]

something to ponder

Half Empty or Half Full?

RUTH 1:19–21 *Now the two of them went until they came to Bethlehem. And it happened, when they had come to Bethlehem, that all the city was excited because of them; and the women said, "Is this Naomi?" But she said to them, "Do not call me Naomi;*

go to

later
Ruth 4:15

love
1 John 3:1

*call me Mara, for the Almighty has dealt very bitterly with me.
I went out full, and the LORD has brought me home again
empty. Why do you call me Naomi, since the LORD has testified
against me, and the Almighty has afflicted me?" (NKJV)*

The journey from Moab to Bethlehem had to be extremely arduous for the two women. First, they would have traveled north to
skirt the Dead Sea. Then, to cross over the Jordan, they would have
had to descend from a relatively high elevation to 1,290 feet *below*
sea level where the Jordan River enters the Dead Sea. After making
their way across the river, they would begin their ascent through
rugged terrain (about twenty-five miles as the crow flies), to reach
Bethlehem, 2,300 feet *above* sea level in the hill country of Judah.[17]
Not an easy trek.

There was great excitement and chatter over Naomi's return. She
must have been vastly altered in either appearance or demeanor for
her former neighbors to ask, "Is this really Naomi?" Naomi herself
feels like an entirely different person from the woman she was when
she left, so much so that she suggests a name-change might be
appropriate. Although it is true that she came back without her husband and sons, she still retained something of immense value that
she obviously overlooked. She had a rich relationship with her
daughter-in-law. It was not until later that she realized Ruth could
bring her more happiness than many robust sons.

Naomi traces the source of her sorrow back to God, the
"Almighty." In each of the Bible passages where this name for God
is used, the main idea being expressed is that God has the power to
do what he sees fit. Naomi could see that the events in her life were
not merely the product of chance, but they were brought on by a
God who carries out his purposes without resistance.

What we often fail to observe (and Naomi is a case in point) is that
this all-powerful God is motivated by grace and mercy. With the
same relentless drive that impels him to carry out his will regardless
of the obstacles, he will be driven by his love and compassion to do
what is best for us. The fullest meaning of the name "Almighty"
encompasses not just his might but his care as well.[18]

what others say

Max Lucado

It reminds me of the often-told story of two maestros who attended a concert to hear a promising young soprano. One commented on the purity of her voice. The other responded, "Yes, but she'll sing better once her heart is broken." There are certain passions only learned by pain. And there are times when God, knowing that, allows us to endure the <u>pain</u> for the sake of the song.[19]

God's Guidance

RUTH 1:22–2:1 *So Naomi returned, and Ruth the Moabitess her daughter-in-law with her, who returned from the country of Moab. Now they came to Bethlehem at the beginning of barley harvest.*

There was a relative of Naomi's husband, a man of great wealth, of the family of Elimelech. His name was Boaz. (NKJV)

These two verses are transitional but important for a full understanding of the rest of the story. Naomi and Ruth have arrived in Bethlehem in late April or May, just in time for the barley harvest, and one month before the wheat will be ready.[20]

We are also introduced to Boaz, a relative of Naomi's husband. How close a relative, the Bible does not reveal until later. He is a man of some influence in the community—the Hebrew word for influence meaning that he is important and powerful in some field.[21] Often this term is spoken of in relation to military rank, but in this case Boaz appears to be a rich landowner.

Backbreaking Labor

RUTH 2:2–3 *So Ruth the Moabitess said to Naomi, "Please let me go to the field, and glean heads of grain after him in whose sight I may find favor." And she said to her, "Go, my daughter." Then she left, and went and gleaned in the field after the reapers. And she happened to come to the part of the field belonging to Boaz, who was of the family of Elimelech.* (NKJV)

Ruth is not afraid of hard work and is more than willing to pull her share of the load. From a human perspective, Ruth's arbitrary choice of a field to glean in was purely accidental, but not from God's. He directed both the inclination of her heart and the direction of her steps toward the field that Boaz owned.

Gleaning was one of God's provisions for the poor. Landowners were instructed by law *not* to reap to the <u>edges</u> of their property and *not* to go a second time over their fields to pick up what was accidentally <u>overlooked</u> in the first pass. In spite of God's expressed wishes, however, the farmers were not always cooperative, wanting to squeeze the most profit out of every inch of land. That is why Ruth articulated a desire to find a landowner that was favorable toward herself.

Checking Her Out

> RUTH 2:4–7 *Now behold, Boaz came from Bethlehem, and said to the reapers, "The LORD be with you!" And they answered him, "The LORD bless you!" Then Boaz said to his servant who was in charge of the reapers, "Whose young woman is this?" So the servant who was in charge of the reapers answered and said, "It is the young Moabite woman who came back with Naomi from the country of Moab. And she said, 'Please let me glean and gather after the reapers among the sheaves.' So she came and has continued from morning until now, though she rested a little in the house." (NKJV)*

Ruth's first glimpse of Boaz occurs as he salutes the fieldworkers in the name of the Lord. From this she would be able to see his devotion to God, as well as the people's affection toward him as they returned his greeting.

Boaz immediately asks his foreman for information about the new girl, which reveals her willingness to work. The only break she took all day was a short respite in the tentlike shelter erected in the field for the workers' benefit.

go to

edges
Leviticus 19:9

overlooked
Deuteronomy 24:19

self-emptying
Philippians 2:3–8

gleaning
gathering usable parts of a crop after harvesting is done

what others say

Andrew Murray

<u>Self-emptying</u> and self-sacrifice, obedience to God's will, even unto the death of the cross—such was the character of Christ for which God so highly exalted Him. Such is the character of Christ that we are to imitate.[22]

Boaz's Kindness

RUTH 2:8–9 *Then Boaz said to Ruth, "You will listen, my daughter, will you not? Do not go to glean in another field, nor go from here, but stay close by my young women. Let your eyes be on the field which they reap, and go after them. Have I not commanded the young men not to touch you? And when you are thirsty, go to the vessels and drink from what the young men have drawn." (NKJV)*

Boaz is completely aware of the harassment a lovely young woman might face in the company of hired field labor and takes steps to ensure her safety. He seems to be quite smitten with the foreigner from Moab, for his watch-care is very touching and he grants special privileges that display a thoughtful tenderness. Boaz's reference to Ruth as "my daughter" may be an indication that he is older than she.

Your Reputation Has Preceded You

RUTH 2:10–13 *So she fell on her face, bowed down to the ground, and said to him, "Why have I found favor in your eyes, that you should take notice of me, since I am a foreigner?" And Boaz answered and said to her, "It has been fully reported to me, all that you have done for your mother-in-law since the death of your husband, and how you have left your father and your mother and the land of your birth, and have come to a people whom you did not know before. The LORD repay your work, and a full reward be given you by the LORD God of Israel, under whose wings you have come for refuge." Then she said, "Let me find favor in your sight, my lord; for you have comforted me, and have spoken kindly to your maidservant, though I am not like one of your maidservants." (NKJV)*

Ruth is overwhelmed by the kindness of Boaz. She must have felt awkward and out of place when comparing herself to Israelite women, for she makes mention of this distinction in her reply to Boaz. Perhaps the shade of her skin, an accent in her speech, or her manner of dress made her feel different and self-conscious.

But Boaz's generous reply ought to put her at ease. He speaks as if he'd already elevated her to a place of fine standing. Then he

go to

resources
Ephesians 2:6–7

humility
Colossians 1:12–18

places
Psalms 36:7; 91:4

benediction
an expression of
God's blessing

imagery
figurative language

bestows a bountiful **benediction** on Ruth, anticipating her faithfulness to be rewarded. It is ironic that Boaz, the one who conferred such a blessing, will be the one in the end to answer his own prayer.

Ruth counters his praise with humility and a wish that she will continue to bring credit to his confidence in her character.

---

what others say

Beth Mainhood

One Old Testament verse from the book of Ruth has been a key motivational force for me as I have tried to pay the costs. "May the LORD repay you for what you have done. May you be richly rewarded by the LORD, the God of Israel, under whose wings you have come to take refuge" (Ruth 2:12). I don't pay the cost in order to receive a reward, but I do know that my depleted <u>resources</u> will be graciously restocked by the God of all riches.[23]

David Seamands

Someone once asked Corrie Ten Boom how she could possibly handle all the compliments and praise that were constantly heaped upon her, without becoming proud. She said she looked at each compliment as a beautiful long-stemmed flower given to her. She smelled it for a moment and then put it into a vase with the others. Each night, just before retiring, she took the beautiful bouquet and handed it over to Jesus saying, "Thank you, Lord, for letting me smell the flowers; they all belong to you." She had discovered the secret of genuine <u>humility</u>.[24]

The **imagery** that Boaz chose to illustrate God's watch-care over Ruth relegates to God the characteristics of a bird. God does not actually possess a pair of wings that he uses to fly about the universe or under which he can place those he desires to shelter or protect. But the example brings to mind a beautiful picture of a nurturing parent bird wanting to offer security and comfort to its frightened fledgling that is not quite ready to make it on its own. This same level of care is spoken of in other <u>places</u> in Scripture as being available to *us* as well.

Teacher's Pet

mirror
Colossians 3:10

RUTH 2:14–16 *Now Boaz said to her at mealtime, "Come here, and eat of the bread, and dip your piece of bread in the vinegar." So she sat beside the reapers, and he passed parched grain to her; and she ate and was satisfied, and kept some back. And when she rose up to glean, Boaz commanded his young men, saying, "Let her glean even among the sheaves, and do not reproach her. Also let grain from the bundles fall purposely for her; leave it that she may glean, and do not rebuke her." (NKJV)*

Boaz clearly wants to share the best he has with Ruth. He offers her bread dipped in wine vinegar, which was sometimes diluted, combined with olive oil, and used with bread as a special refreshment. The roasted grain was made by plucking some of the fullest stalks, tying them together in a small parcel, and roasting them in a blazing fire until the chaff burned off. Then the grain could be eaten right off the stem.[25]

It was abnormal for the gleaners to follow too closely on the heels of the harvesters. Unwritten etiquette required that they stay at an appropriate distance until it was obvious that the workers were completely done. Boaz wants Ruth to get first pickings, and then he bends the rules even further. He asks his laborers to deliberately leave extra stalks for Ruth to find. Boaz allowed himself to be used of God to be a blessing to Ruth, but secretly, so as not to bring her embarrassment.

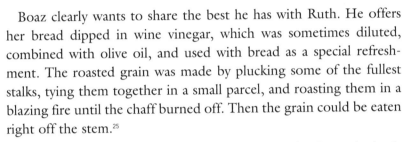

what others say

Corrie ten Boom

He makes us a <u>mirror</u> of his love. A mirror does not do much in itself: It hangs or stands in the right direction, and then it works. You and I do not do much; we only have to look at the Lord Jesus and he will make us a mirror.[26]

More Than Generous

RUTH 2:17–19 *So she gleaned in the field until evening, and beat out what she had gleaned, and it was about an ephah of barley. Then she took it up and went into the city, and her mother-in-law saw what she had gleaned. So she brought out*

Gideon
Judges 6:11

and gave to her what she had kept back after she had been sat-
isfied. And her mother-in-law said to her, "Where have you
gleaned today? And where did you work? Blessed be the one who
took notice of you." So she told her mother-in-law with whom she
had worked, and said, "The man's name with whom I worked
today is Boaz." (NKJV)

Normally, threshing was done with an oxen-pulled sledge, but an
individual might thresh a small amount of grain with a stick (like
<u>Gideon</u>). Ruth would rather carry a basketful of grain back to her
mother-in-law than a bundle of unwieldy stalks, so she separates the
grain right in the field before she makes her way back home. She
ends up with one-half to two-thirds of a bushel (between twenty-
nine and fifty pounds). This amount was abnormally large and would
be enough to feed the two women for several weeks.[27]

Naomi is so astonished that her questions tumble out in rapid-fire
succession. When she finally pauses for breath, Ruth identifies the
benefactor as Boaz. Boaz had shown compassion and kindness to
these two destitute and defenseless widow-women with no prospect
of reimbursement.

Naomi offered a heartfelt blessing on the individual who had rendered them such kindness. Generally, under a broad heading, the
"blessings of God" that she wished upon the man who took notice
of Ruth would encompass the following three areas:

1. numerous offspring (Genesis 1:28; 9:1)

2. riches (Genesis 24:35)

3. victory over enemies (Genesis 27:29; 49:8–12;
Deuteronomy 28:7)

Just Like Family

RUTH 2:20–23 *Then Naomi said to her daughter-in-law,*
"Blessed be he of the LORD, who has not forsaken His kindness to
the living and the dead!" And Naomi said to her, "This man is
a relation of ours, one of our close relatives." Ruth the Moabitess
said, "He also said to me, 'You shall stay close by my young men
until they have finished all my harvest.'" And Naomi said to
Ruth her daughter-in-law, "It is good, my daughter, that you go

out with his young women, and that people do not meet you in any other field." So she stayed close by the young women of Boaz, to glean until the end of barley harvest and wheat harvest; and she dwelt with her mother-in-law. (NKJV)

Feast
Leviticus 23:15–21;
Deuteronomy
16:9–12

For the first time since returning home, Naomi realizes that God's hand is upon her, not necessarily in judgment but in blessing, and she holds on to the hope that Boaz will function as their kinsman redeemer. Naomi encourages Ruth to continue in her labors, not just to provide for their needs but to further develop a relationship with the only man on earth (to her knowledge) who can offer a lasting resolution to their problems.

She has also been concerned about the safety of a single woman in the company of coarse and ill-mannered field hands, so knowing that Boaz is looking out for her daughter-in-law relieves her immensely.

The harvesting season lasts about seven weeks, culminating in the "Feast of Weeks," a festival celebrating the rich yield of the year's crops. Ruth remained with her mother-in-law all during that time, faithfully toiling to save up a store of provisions for them to live on.

The concept of the "kinsman redeemer" is primarily one in which a relative chooses to rescue a family member in trouble. For example:

1. If an Israelite became so poor that he had to sell his land to make ends meet, a kinsman redeemer might buy back the property and restore it to its rightful owner. (Leviticus 25:25)

2. If an Israelite got so far in debt that he had to sell himself as a slave, a kinsman redeemer might pay his purchase price and offer him his freedom. (Leviticus 25:47–55)

3. If an Israelite was murdered in cold blood, a kinsman redeemer might avenge his death by killing the one who had conspired against him. (Numbers 35:12–27; Deuteronomy 19:6)

4. If an Israelite died without producing any heirs, a kinsman redeemer might preserve the deceased man's name by marrying his widow. (Deuteronomy 25:5–10)

The last provision is the one that Naomi has clung to as a way for Ruth and herself to find happiness. If Boaz should take the notion,

action
John 15:12–14;
1 John 3:16–18

Christ
Matthew 1:5–16

he might decide to marry Ruth, and then they would be well-provided for the rest of their lives.

An individual cannot show Christ's love to another person without that emotion taking the form of an <u>action</u>.

If you travel a mile east of Bethlehem, you will find a place called the "Field of Boaz," where tradition claims Ruth gleaned so many years ago. Adjoining it is another plot of land called the "Shepherd's Field." Tradition declares that the birth of Jesus was announced at this place before the shepherds hurried over to Bethlehem to see the child that was born. It is interesting that Ruth's budding romance with Boaz, which eventually made possible the birth of the <u>Christ</u> child eleven hundred years later, occurred in approximately the same spot.

Chapter Wrap-Up

- Naomi's husband and sons die in Moab where they have been living, leaving her and her daughters-in-law without any means of support. (Ruth 1:1–15)

- Orpah returns to her former home, but Ruth will not leave Naomi, so they travel to Bethlehem where Naomi formerly lived. (Ruth 1:16–21)

- God leads Ruth to glean in the field of a compassionate man who watches out for her well-being. (Ruth 1:22–2:7)

- Naomi discovers that Ruth has attracted the attention of Boaz, who might decide to act as their kinsman redeemer. (Ruth 2:8–23)

Study Questions

1. What are the six statements Ruth makes in regard to her commitment to Naomi, and how do her words confirm that she has come to faith?

2. What did Naomi fail to realize when she considered how the "Almighty" had dealt with her?

3. For what did Boaz commend Ruth and offer his blessing?

4. What are the possible functions of a kinsman redeemer?

Ruth 3-4
Ruth's Character Proved

Chapter Highlights:
- At the Threshing Floor
- Party Time
- At the City Gate
- At Boaz's Own Home
- Cutest Little Grandkid

Let's Get Started

The book of Ruth is set up in a "problem-solution" type format. The first two chapters set up the complexity of the *problem*—Naomi and Ruth are both without husbands and children, and must face the reality of starvation unless they can personally figure how to make a living or how to avail themselves of the protection and security offered by somebody else.

The last two chapters reveal a possible *solution* to their seemingly insurmountable struggles. The path to attain relief will not be easy and is packed with its own temptations and trials, but the characters we've already met and learned to love continue to act honorably and nobly.

Every situation in which Naomi, Ruth, or Boaz could take advantage of the other or seek their own best interests will provide a fresh opportunity to demonstrate strength of character and personal integrity. It would be as refreshing to observe their exemplary conduct in our own day as it must have been during the time of the judges.

Boaz at the Threshing Floor

RUTH 3:1–3 *Then Naomi her mother-in-law said to her, "My daughter, shall I not seek security for you, that it may be well with you? Now Boaz, whose young women you were with, is he not our relative? In fact, he is winnowing barley tonight at the threshing floor. Therefore wash yourself and anoint yourself, put on your best garment and go down to the threshing floor; but do not make yourself known to the man until he has finished eating and drinking. (NKJV)*

Naomi had attempted to send her two daughters-in-law back to their mothers so they could arrange second marriages for them. But since Ruth opted to stay with Naomi, Naomi now feels the responsibility to follow up on any available prospects for her daughter-in-law.

Naomi realizes that if Boaz could be prevailed upon to become their kinsman redeemer, he would provide them with everything they could ever desire. Boaz had the power to restore the family property and perpetuate Elimelech's name by providing an heir. But although Boaz had treated Ruth very kindly the last two months, he had made no attempt to permanently fill the role of husband or savior.

Naomi is aware of Israelite custom and thinks long and hard about the best way to approach Boaz. Finally she figures out a way for Ruth and Boaz to meet alone, where Ruth can express her desires and they can talk undisturbed. She gives Ruth five suggestions:

1. Wash (or bathe).

2. Wear perfume (often **myrrh** mixed with oil and spices).

3. Put on your best clothes.

4. Go down to the threshing floor.

5. Don't let Boaz know you are there right away.

Ruth has placed herself under the authority of Naomi to receive wisdom and guidance. This **mentor-apprentice** sort of relationship is honored in the Bible as one of the best ways to receive spiritual input and to mature in the faith.

The **threshing** floor would usually be located on an exposed or elevated site so the westerly breeze that often blew in the late afternoon could aid in the winnowing process. After the animal-drawn sledge was pulled across the harvested grass, workers would throw the grain into the air with a fork. The breeze would then blow the chaff away while the part used for food would drop back down to the threshing floor.[1]

Mother May I

RUTH 3:4–6 *Then it shall be, when he lies down, that you shall notice the place where he lies; and you shall go in, uncover his feet, and lie down; and he will tell you what you should do."* *And she said to her, "All that you say to me I will do." So she went down to the threshing floor and did according to all that her mother-in-law instructed her. (NKJV)*

Naomi is full of advice, and Ruth accepts it freely. Four more instructions are given in addition to the five already doled out:

6. Note where Boaz lies down.

7. Go to where he is.

8. Uncover his feet.

9. Lie down.

After it became dark and the work was completed, Naomi knew that the grain would have to be guarded. After Boaz participated in the harvest festivities, he would lie down at the site so he could keep an eye on his harvested crop throughout the night. Following her mother-in-law's advice to the letter, Ruth went down to the threshing floor and did as she had been told.

Party Time

RUTH 3:7–8 *And after Boaz had eaten and drunk, and his heart was cheerful, he went to lie down at the end of the heap of grain; and she came softly, uncovered his feet, and lay down. Now it happened at midnight that the man was startled, and turned himself; and there, a woman was lying at his feet.* (NKJV)

Proverbs
Proverbs 31:10

troth
solemn promise to
remain faithful

Spreading a man's garment over a woman is symbolic of the protection offered in marriage. It has commonly been used as an actual part of the wedding ceremony among Arab people.³ So Ruth's action would have been an obvious request for marriage.

When Boaz stirs around midnight, he is stunned to find a woman lying at his feet. In all his years as a bachelor, nothing like this has ever happened before.

Rendezvous in the Moonlight

RUTH 3:9–11 And he said, "Who are you?" So she answered, "I am Ruth, your maidservant. Take your maidservant under your wing, for you are a close relative." Then he said, "Blessed are you of the LORD, my daughter! For you have shown more kindness at the end than at the beginning, in that you did not go after young men, whether poor or rich. And now, my daughter, do not fear. I will do for you all that you request, for all the people of my town know that you are a virtuous woman. (NKJV)

Boaz has to ask for verbal identification since it is too dark to see for himself. Ruth calls herself a servant, emphasizing the fact that her request is offered out of a humble heart.

Boaz commends Ruth for her kindness, first to Naomi, by staying and providing for her, and then to himself by not pursuing a younger and more handsome lover. Ruth may have actually received and rejected another marriage proposal, for the definite article preceding Boaz's mention of "younger men" suggests that he may have had a certain individual in mind.⁴

Boaz says that Ruth has a reputation as a woman of noble character. This speaks of personal virtue and moral worth. The same word is used to describe the ideal wife in the book of Proverbs.

Pledging His Troth

RUTH 3:12–13 Now it is true that I am a close relative; however, there is a relative closer than I. Stay this night, and in the morning it shall be that if he will perform the duty of a close relative for you—good; let him do it. But if he does not want to perform the duty for you, then I will perform the duty for you, as the LORD lives! Lie down until morning." (NKJV)

Boaz is quite willing to be Ruth's champion and personal prince, but a possible obstacle is suddenly introduced into the story line. There is another man who is more closely related to Ruth and Naomi and even more eligible than Boaz. Regardless, Boaz makes a firm commitment, establishing it with an oath, to marry Ruth if the law will allow.

Boaz swears that "as the LORD lives" he will take action to see that Ruth is redeemed. This expression in the taking of pledges is used some thirty times in Judges, Samuel, and Kings.[5] It means that as surely as Jehovah is the living God (and that is one fact that is unalterably irreversible), the individual making the promise can be counted on to fulfill his word.

Full and Running Over

RUTH 3:14–15 *So she lay at his feet until morning, and she arose before one could recognize another. Then he said, "Do not let it be known that the woman came to the threshing floor." Also he said, "Bring the shawl that is on you and hold it." And when she held it, he measured six ephahs of barley, and laid it on her. Then she went into the city.* (NKJV)

Although nothing immoral has occurred, Boaz is very sensitive about preserving Ruth's impeccable reputation. Rumors could quickly misconstrue an innocent event into a public scandal if it became known that a woman was observed in Boaz's vicinity on the threshing floor.

But before Ruth leaves, Boaz sends a gift. He loads Ruth up with six "measures" of barley. This could hardly mean six "ephahs," as that would amount to several hundred pounds. It would more likely be a "seah" (one-third of an ephah)—six seahs weighing approximately ninety pounds. Or it could mean an omer (one-tenth of an ephah)—six measures amounting to about twelve quarts.[6] Whatever the final amount, Boaz evidently had to lift and place it on her head, the traditional method of carrying a heavy burden.[7]

go to

waiting
Psalm 62:5

intrinsically
basically and
essentially

perseverance
steady persistance
for a long time and
in spite of difficulties

> ### what others say
>
> #### C. S. Lewis
>
> William Morris wrote a poem called "Love Is Enough" and someone is said to have reviewed it briefly in the words "It isn't . . ." The natural loves are not self-sufficient. Something else, at first vaguely described as "decency and common sense," but later revealed as goodness . . . must come to the help of the mere feeling if the feeling is to be kept sweet.[8]

Sit Tight

RUTH 3:16–18 *When she came to her mother-in-law, she said, "Is that you, my daughter?" Then she told her all that the man had done for her. And she said, "These six ephahs of barley he gave me; for he said to me, 'Do not go empty-handed to your mother-in-law.'" Then she said, "Sit still, my daughter, until you know how the matter will turn out; for the man will not rest until he has concluded the matter this day." (NKJV)*

Naomi is bristling with curiosity, for this whole affair was begun at her instigation and upon her recommendation (not to speak of the fact that her own fate is **intrinsically** linked to its outcome as well). Once Ruth tells her everything that happened and every word that was spoken, Naomi pronounces the verdict based on what she knows of the man. The only thing left to do is wait.

> ### what others say
>
> #### Tim Hansel
>
> **Perseverance** is not an easy quality, yet it's not a quality for a select few. Most of the time, it involves an amount of courage that we would never believe we could have. It's a unique combination of patience plus endurance. It's what makes life worthwhile in spite of adversity. And quite often, it involves a quality of letting go and letting God keep us at it, funneling his power through us to keep us from quitting . . . Sometimes perseverance is expressed in our <u>waiting</u> on God. I call this "wait training . . ."[9]

Boaz at the City Gate

> RUTH 4:1–2 *Now Boaz went up to the gate and sat down there; and behold, the close relative of whom Boaz had spoken came by. So Boaz said, "Come aside, friend, sit down here." So he came aside and sat down. And he took ten men of the elders of the city, and said, "Sit down here." So they sat down.* (NKJV)

People constantly passed through the gates of a city to work in their fields, to graze their animals, or to draw water, so the most likely place to connect with someone was at the gate. Traditionally, there was a large open space near the entrance to the city where business and legal matters would be transacted, where caravans would stop to offer their wares, and where townspeople would pause to gossip and share information.[10]

Boaz calls together ten elders of the town. Ten men were the required quorum to start a synagogue, and ten men were necessary to offer the benediction in a wedding, so this was undoubtedly the minimum number required by law.[11]

Many significant events took place at the city gate in other biblical passages. Here are a few:

1. Abraham purchased a burial plot for Sarah (Genesis 23:10).

2. Absalom sought to influence the people against his father (2 Samuel 15:2).

3. Kings would hold court (1 Kings 22:10; Jeremiah 38:7).

4. Trials would be enacted (Joshua 20:4; Deuteronomy 21:18–21).

Death of a Vision

> RUTH 4:3–4 *Then he said to the close relative, "Naomi, who has come back from the country of Moab, sold the piece of land which belonged to our brother Elimelech. And I thought to inform you, saying, 'Buy it back in the presence of the inhabitants and the elders of my people. If you will redeem it, redeem it; but if you will not redeem it, then tell me, that I may know; for there is no one but you to redeem it, and I am next after you.'" And he said, "I will redeem it."* (NKJV)

custom
Jeremiah 32:6–12

brothers
Deuteronomy
25:5–10

Naomi had been trying to sell her land in an effort to generate some income to live on (at least temporarily). As long as she had no capital to invest in making the land produce, she could not profit from its revenues. As her land was the only thing of value she had left, and she couldn't derive any benefit out of it anyway, she had placed it on the market.

Now Boaz offers the land to the next of kin, who has a responsibility to redeem it (according to the <u>custom</u>) for the sake of the family. Assuming the property belongs solely to Naomi and his obligation will be discharged with the purchase of it, the close relative agrees to buy the land.

what others say

Watchman Nee

If we give ourselves unreservedly to God, many adjustments may have to be made: in family, or business, or church relationships, or in the matter of our personal views. God will not let anything of ourselves remain. His finger will touch, point by point, everything that is not of Him, and will say: "This must go." Are you willing? It is foolish to resist God, and always wise to submit to Him.[12]

Read the Fine Print

RUTH 4:5–6 *Then Boaz said, "On the day you buy the field from the hand of Naomi, you must also buy it from Ruth the Moabitess, the wife of the dead, to perpetuate the name of the dead through his inheritance." And the close relative said, "I cannot redeem it for myself, lest I ruin my own inheritance. You redeem my right of redemption for yourself, for I cannot redeem it."* (NKJV)

After the nearest relation decides to fulfill the obligation of a kinsman redeemer, Boaz informs him that the job also entails taking Ruth as a wife to preserve the name of her deceased husband. (Originally, this principle of remarriage applied only to blood <u>brothers</u>, but by this time in Israel the obligation had extended to involve any near clansman.) Boaz's pronouncement throws the whole situation into an entirely new light. Now the man who was ready to plunk down his money so fast for Naomi's land comes to understand that the property would merely be held as a trust for whatever son might be born out of the union of Ruth and himself. This son would acquire the family name of Ruth's original husband, and the land that he would inherit would belong to the family of Mahlon.

The prospective kinsman redeemer starts to wonder. Would his own situation be in danger if he spent money to buy land that he could never own? He may have already been married and had sons of his own whose inheritance he did not wish to jeopardize. He wouldn't have wanted to take away from them to provide for a child as yet unknown.

Off with His Shoe

RUTH 4:7–8 *Now this was the custom in former times in Israel concerning redeeming and exchanging, to confirm anything: one man took off his sandal and gave it to the other, and this was a confirmation in Israel. Therefore the close relative said to Boaz, "Buy it for yourself." So he took off his sandal.* (NKJV)

It appears the author is explaining an earlier symbolic ritual, as if it is no longer in vogue at the time of writing. At any rate, the next of kin renounces his right to the land by removing his sandal, in the presence of witnesses, and presents it to the individual who has taken up the charge.

Archaeological discoveries at the Babylonian city of Nuzu have unearthed a large number of records substantiating the background information of many Old Testament stories.[13] These clay tablets have provided an excellent record of the social and cultural traditions of the period. The majority of the information consists of private documents about personal affairs. Included is solid substantiation of the shoe-removing ritual.[14]

Fame and Fortune

RUTH 4:9–12 *And Boaz said to the elders and all the people, "You are witnesses this day that I have bought all that was Elimelech's, and all that was Chilion's and Mahlon's, from the hand of Naomi. Moreover, Ruth the Moabitess, the widow of Mahlon, I have acquired as my wife, to perpetuate the name of the dead through his inheritance, that the name of the dead may not be cut off from among his brethren and from his position at the gate. You are witnesses this day." And all the people who were at the gate, and the elders, said, "We are witnesses. The LORD*

go to

hero
Hebrews 11:32–38

light
Matthew 5:16

Tamar
Genesis 38

Rachel
the favored wife of
Jacob (alias Israel)

Leah
the first wife of
Jacob, birthing ten
of his twelve sons

*make the woman who is coming to your house like Rachel and
Leah, the two who built the house of Israel; and may you prosper
in Ephrathah and be famous in Bethlehem. May your house be
like the house of Perez, whom Tamar bore to Judah, because of
the offspring which the LORD will give you from this young
woman." (NKJV)*

A spontaneous response from the bystanders in the form of a blessing shows how moved the townspeople were concerning this event.
They hold up **Rachel** and **Leah** as models for Ruth, for these two
women together produced the original twelve sons from whom all
of Israel was descended. The people trust that this union will
increase the good reputation that each has already individually established, and that many offspring will perpetuate their fine name in the
years to come. It is obvious that the people think highly of both
Boaz and Ruth and want them to experience the best.

what others say

Bruce Larson

To be someone's hero is a humbling experience. Every athletic
star, every top-flight business executive, every minister, youth
worker, and schoolteacher knows that it is both thrilling and
disquieting to be a "knight in shining armor" to one or two or
a dozen or a multitude of people. Yet I think there is a sense
in which every Christian should be a hero, at least to a few
people. The Bible speaks of Christians being the light of the
world and if we walk in the light we can't avoid being seen.[21]

It is interesting that the townspeople mention Tamar at this time.
Tamar and her son Perez are ancient ancestors of Boaz. But what
appears especially significant is that Tamar found herself in the same
position as Ruth—a childless widow waiting for someone to redeem
her and carry on the name of her deceased husband. When her family ignored the problem, she concocted an elaborate deception in
order to force someone to take on the responsibility. Her plan
brought years of sin and grief to her family. Unlike Ruth, Tamar
never learned to wait on the Lord for *his* solution.

Boaz at His Own Home

RUTH 4:13–14 *So Boaz took Ruth and she became his wife; and when he went in to her, the LORD gave her conception, and she bore a son. Then the women said to Naomi, "Blessed be the LORD, who has not left you this day without a close relative; and may his name be famous in Israel! (NKJV)*

center
Genesis 2:18–24;
Proverbs 18:22;
Mark 10:9;
Ephesians 5:25

prayer
1 Chronicles 16:11;
Ephesians 6:18;
James 5:13–16

The wedding festivities over, Ruth settles down to a life with Boaz, centered around the Lord, who brought them together. Every event that transpires is reason to bring praise and thanksgiving to God, who has made it all possible.

The women of the area now call the child that has been born to Ruth Naomi's "kinsman redeemer," instead of Boaz. The child fulfills the role in the following ways;

1. He took away the reproach of childlessness in the family.

2. He brought Naomi the joy of life in the aftermath of death.

3. He can be expected to provide for the family when she is old.

God's rightful position in any marriage is right in the <u>center</u>.

> ## what others say
>
> ### Dr. James C. Dobson
>
> It is impossible for me to overstate the need for <u>prayer</u> in the fabric of family life. Not simply as a shield against danger, of course. A personal relationship with Jesus Christ is the cornerstone of marriage, giving meaning and purpose to every dimension of living . . . In this day of disintegrating families on every side, we dare not try to make it on our own.[16]

The Cutest Little Grandkid

RUTH 4:15–17 *And may he be to you a restorer of life and a nourisher of your old age; for your daughter-in-law, who loves you, who is better to you than seven sons, has borne him." Then Naomi took the child and laid him on her bosom, and became a nurse to him. Also the neighbor women gave him a name, saying, "There is a son born to Naomi." And they called his name Obed. He is the father of Jesse, the father of David. (NKJV)*

go to

God's
Acts 13:22

fruit
Hebrews 12:11

her
Matthew 1:5–16

save
Matthew 1:21

chastening
disciplining

The contrast between the dejected Naomi who first dragged herself into Bethlehem, and the joyful and fulfilled Naomi who now proudly dandles a baby grandson on her knee, is sharp indeed. All of the struggles that she had to face were worth the delight and contentment she now experiences.

It is unusual that the neighborhood women take it upon themselves to name Naomi's grandson, but as the whole community seems to have taken an interest in this happy family, they include themselves even in this. Obed means "servant," and this perhaps suggests the role he will take in caring for Naomi later in life.[17]

At last we find out where this whole story has been leading. The man who is to become the greatest king that Israel will ever know (a man after <u>God's</u> own heart) is actually descended from the union of Boaz and Ruth.

> **what others say**
>
> **John Hunter**
>
> Although **chastening** is not pleasant, "afterward it yieldeth the peaceable <u>fruit</u> of righteousness unto them which are exercised thereby . . ." The fruit of chastisement is a righteous life which enjoys the peace of God. I have peace in my soul because my life is right with God, because I have put first things first, because I have humbled my heart before a Holy God.[18]

Family Trees

RUTH 4:18–22 *Now this is the genealogy of Perez: Perez begot Hezron; Hezron begot Ram, and Ram begot Amminadab; Amminadab begot Nahshon, and Nahshon begot Salmon; Salmon begot Boaz, and Boaz begot Obed; Obed begot Jesse, and Jesse begot David.* (NKJV)

Since the genealogy from Perez to David covers about eight hundred years, it is obvious that only significant family members are named.[19] The purpose of this directory is first to draw attention to David and his lineage, but second to point the reader to the coming Savior. For in spite of the conditions prevailing in Ruth's time, we are reminded as we read her story to look ahead to a day when the ultimate Redeemer would come from among <u>her</u> descendants to <u>save</u> not just her own posterity, but all of humanity.

consummation
a final, satisfying
conclusion

what others say

Charles Colson

Thus in the midst of the dark and habitual chaos of earth, a light penetrates the darkness. It cannot be extinguished; it is the light of the Kingdom of God. His Kingdom *has* come, in His people today, and it is yet to come as well, in the great **consummation** of human history.[20]

Chapter Wrap-Up

- Naomi encourages Ruth to approach Boaz on the subject of marriage. (Ruth 3:1–6)
- Ruth meets Boaz on the threshing floor in the middle of the night and he promises to marry her if the law allows. (Ruth 3:7–18)
- Boaz makes arrangements with the city officials to become the kinsman redeemer. (Ruth 4:1–12)
- Boaz and Ruth marry and start a family, which eventually results in the birth of a king of Israel. (Ruth 4:13–22)

Study Questions

1. What series of instructions did Naomi give to Ruth? What did Ruth do with all the advice that Naomi gave to her?

2. What immediate act of kindness did Boaz show after he made his commitment to Ruth?

3. What unforeseen obstacle arose that could have prevented Boaz from becoming the kinsman redeemer?

4. What did the townspeople wish for Boaz and Ruth? Why did they get so emotionally involved in the fate of this family?

Appendix A - The Answers

Joshua 1–2 PRELIMINARY PREPARATIONS

1. God offered Joshua the promise of victory in battle, a detailed plan for personal success, and his own presence to stay beside him at all times. (Joshua 1:3–9)

2. God encouraged Joshua to make his Word a part of every thought, action, and speech. (Joshua 1:7–8)

3. God wanted to demonstrate that his message of love can reach out to anyone—no matter who they are or where they've come from. (Joshua 2:1–21)

4. Rahab put her life on the line for a cause she believed in. Further, she kept her part of the bargain—bringing her family into her house, tying a cord in the window, and keeping the plans a secret. (Joshua 2:3–21)

Joshua 3–4 CROSSING THE JORDAN

1. The people of Israel had to wash their clothes, bathe, and abstain from sexual activity. (Exodus 19:14–15)

2. (1) Sanctify themselves from encumbering sin (Joshua 3:5); (2) Follow God's guidance (Joshua 3:3–4); (3) Step out in faith, trusting God to provide (Joshua 3:15–16).

3. Lists of personal struggles will differ, but the key to overcoming is focusing on the Lord instead of the problem. Joshua drew Israel's attention to the ark of the covenant and the Lord of all the earth. (Joshua 3:11)

4. The pile of stones was to serve as a reminder to future generations of what God had done, to give proof of God's power, and to instill a reverence for who he is. (Joshua 4:21–24)

Joshua 5–6 CONQUEST OF JERICHO

1. Circumcision represented a loving and submissive heart toward God. We should put aside our sinful nature just as circumcision puts aside unnecessary

flesh. (Deuteronomy 30:6)

2. Joshua needed to remember who was in charge and what the conflict was really about. (Joshua 5:14)

3. God knows the steps that need to be followed to ensure blessing. He is the ultimate source of truth; therefore, his instructions should be obeyed without deviation. (Deuteronomy 5:29; Joshua 1:7)

4. The first of anything received was given back to God. (Deuteronomy 26:1–10)

Joshua 7–8 TRAGEDY AND TRIUMPH AT AI

1. No one sins in isolation. The bad choices a person makes bring down his family, corrupt the character of his friends, and ruin the reputation of God. (Exodus 20:5)

2. God made the "Valley of Trouble" into a "Door of Hope." He also brought the whole nation together to experience victory from his hand. (Joshua 8:1)

3. Joshua was wise, perceptive, cautious, thorough, industrious, helpful, courageous, and unflinching. (Joshua 8)

4. The people offered sacrifices in thanksgiving and reaffirmed their covenant with God. (Joshua 8:30–32)

Joshua 9–10 THE SOUTHERN INVASION

1. The leaders of Israel relied on their own resources for wisdom in dealing with a questionable situation, instead of asking God for direction. (Joshua 9:14)

2. Once a promise has been made, God expects it to be kept. (Numbers 30:2; Deuteronomy 23:21)

3. God caused the sun to "rest" or "cease" for one whole day. (Joshua 10:13–14)

4. We can learn the following:
   a. We need to maintain our personal integrity. (Joshua 10:6–7)

b. Our qualifications and preparation are not good enough. We need God's help. (Joshua 10:8)

c. We ought to do what needs to be done, when God prompts. (Joshua 10:10)

d. Pray for God's intervention. (Joshua 10:12)

e. Have confidence that God will bring the victory. (Joshua 10:25; 2 Timothy 4:18)

Joshua 11–12 CONQUEST OF THE NORTH

1. They would no longer be looking to God and seeking his help. (Isaiah 31:1; Psalm 20:7)

2. Joshua followed every instruction of the Lord's and left nothing undone. (Joshua 11:15)

3. God hardened their hearts and they became deceived. (Joshua 11:20)

4. This was the only course of action because:

   a. The Canaanites' wickedness reached an intolerable level. (Genesis 15:16)

   b. Their wickedness would drag Israel right down with them. (2 Kings 16:3; 23:7)

   c. There are greater evils in the world than death. (Deuteronomy 28:67)

   d. This judgment was from God for a specific time and a specific place. (Joshua 11:15)

   e. The Canaanites could have repented at any time before the Israelites came into the land and God hardened their hearts. (Jeremiah 18:7–8)

   f. This was only one step in God's overall plan to rid the world of the poison called sin. (John 3:17)

Joshua 13–22 DIVISION OF THE LAND

1. Caleb asked for and was granted the portion of land where a race of giant people dwelt. He successfully drove them out of his territory, even though he was in his eighties, because he followed God with his whole heart. (Joshua 14:10–12; 15:14–15; 14:14)

2. The descendants of Joseph did not think they could conquer their enemies because the people of the plains were in possession of iron chariots. (Joshua 17:16)

3. God gave Israel everything he'd sworn to their forefathers, and every word that he had spoken was fulfilled. (Joshua 21:43–45)

4. Before assuming the guilt of the other party, the Israelites sent representatives to discuss the problem. The misunderstanding was resolved, and they did not have to fight each other. In the same way, we need to go to the erring party with a spirit of restoration and share what we see, listening for ways to understand and help. (Joshua 22:10–34; 1 Thessalonians 5:14; James 5:19–20)

Joshua 23–24 JOSHUA'S FAREWELL

1. The New Testament picture is of the vine and the branches. (Joshua 23:8; John 15:1–6)

2. Three results of apostasy:

   a. No more victory—only defeat.

   b. What we desire traps us.

   c. We become the object of disgrace and destruction.

   Three safeguards against apostasy:

   a. Obey God's Word.

   b. Separate from that which drags us down.

   c. Devotion to God (Joshua 23:6–16)

3. Remembering how God had brought them from obscurity, through dangers on all sides, confirmed that every achievement was dependent on God alone. (Psalm 44:1–3)

4. The children of Israel needed to throw away the idols they had collected because retaining them was the first step toward betrayal of a godly lifestyle. (Joshua 24:23)

Judges 1:1–2:15 LEADERLESS WITHOUT JOSHUA

1. Ephraim and Manasseh spent time gathering information about their enemies before they engaged in a confrontation. (Judges 1:22–26)

2. The message went as follows:

   a. God has worked in Israel's behalf.

   b. God is willing to keep his part of the covenant, if only Israel will be faithful to keep hers.

   c. Israel needs to avoid political and spiritual participation with neighboring nations.

   d. If Israel does not keep faith, God will withdraw his support. (Judges 2:1–3)

3. The parents did not take the time or energy to pass on a living faith, so the children grew up without knowledge of God and his work. (Judges 2:10–13)

4. Israel was subject to decline for the following reasons:

   a. Envy of the wicked

   b. Lack of spiritual accountability

   c. The pull of decadence and immorality

   d. Compromise of personal behavior (Judges 2:10–13)

Judges 2:16–3:31 EARLY JUDGES IN ISRAEL

1. The repeated cycle goes as follows:

   a. Israel cries out to God.

   b. God raises up a judge to deliver them.

   c. They go their own way in disobedience.

   d. God gives them over to their enemies.
   (Judges 3:7–12)

2. God wants to keep us ever aware that *he* is the overcomer. (Judges 3:1–3)

3. In the Old Testament, the Spirit came upon a particular individual in order to give him (or her) strength and courage to do a particular task. After Christ left the earth, he sent his Spirit to indwell all believers on a permanent basis.

4. God used left-handed Ehud to lead in Moab's defeat and helped Shamgar to overcome six hundred men with an animal prod. (Judges 3:15–16, 31)

Judges 4–5 DEBORAH, A LADY LEADER

1. Barak placed more confidence in a person than in God. He forgot that God equips those he calls. Thus two people had to do the work of one, and someone else got the credit for it. (Judges 4:8–10)

2. Jael did not hesitate to act on her convictions; she simply did what she could. (Judges 5:24–27)

3. Deborah spoke first to herself, which is where any call to action must start. (Judges 5:12)

4. Reuben's "resolvings" of heart turned to "revolvings" of heart, and conviction changed to deliberation. While others eagerly displayed courage and cooperation, Reuben's inactivity brought shame and correction. (Judges 5:15–16)

Judges 6:1–7:15a CONVINCING GIDEON

1. Gideon asks, "If God is with us, why has all this happened to us?" The answer is that their own personal choices have caused them to feel alienated from the very one who longs to deliver them. (Judges 6:13)

2. They uniformly exhibited a spirit of reticent humility. (Judges 6:15)

3. Gideon was instructed to tear down his father's altar to Baal, to cut down the Asherah pole, and to build an altar to the true God. Baal's failure to retaliate proved that he was not a true god. (Judges 6:25–32)

4. God may choose to honor any such request, but it's better to make certain that our lives are in line with his will so he can direct our decisions. (Judges 6:36–40)

Judges 7:15b–8:35 CONDITIONING GIDEON

1. Gideon gave a sympathetic and self-effacing reply. (Judges 8:1–3)

2. It was an act of disloyal treason to refuse aid to those who were risking their lives in defense of the nation. The townspeople weakened the soldiers both physically and emotionally. (Judges 8:4–9)

3. God was to serve as the supreme head to avoid having an earthly king usurping his control and furthering his own agenda. (Judges 8:22–23)

4. Gideon took his battle proceeds and fashioned a religious momento that became an object of worship. (Judges 8:24–27)

Judges 9:1–10:5 ABIMELECH, A KINGDOM-LESS KING

1. Abimelech murdered his brothers, destroyed an entire town, and was in the process of wiping out another when he met his end. (Judges 9:5, 45, 52)

2. Gaal didn't realize he would be held accountable for his idle words. He also didn't know how tightly Abimelech held the reins and the influence he still had in other places. (Judges 9:28–29, 38–41)

3. Gaal and his relatives suffered defeat and were driven out of town, the city of Shechem was totally destroyed, and Abimelech was killed by a woman with a millstone. (Judges 9:45, 53)

4. (a) Tola: (1) son of Puah, (2) grandson of Dodo, (3) delivered Israel from an oppressor, (4) lived in Shamir in the hills of Ephraim, (5) led Israel for twenty-three years, (6) buried where he lived. (b) Jair: (1) from Gilead, (2) led Israel twenty-two years, (3) had thirty-three sons with thirty-three donkeys, (4) controlled thirty-three towns named after an ancestor, (5) buried in Kamon.

Judges 10:6–12:15 JEPHTHAH, PLUS THREE

1. Israel needed to see that the restrictions of God are far less confining than the bonds of any other master. (Judges 10:15–16)

2. Because of Jephthah's ill-treatment, he developed the skills of a warrior and distinguished himself as a leader of men. (Judges 11:1–5)

3. A vow to the Lord is a promise in which an individual may demonstrate his or her love for God through the offering of gifts and services beyond what is normally required. (Judges 11:30–31, 34–35)

4. Ibzan, Elon, and Abdon were not recognized for any special deeds or abilities. (Judges 12:8–15)

Judges 13–14 SAMSON'S STRENGTH

1. Samson's mother needed to establish a habit of following the Nazirite restrictions so that when her son was born it would already be an established part of their household. (Judges 13:4–5)

2. Manoah was not ready for the full import of God's name, should the Lord have blurted it out. (Judges 13:17–18)

3. Samson violated God's command that Israelites should not marry outside the faith. (Judges 14:3; 17:6; 21:25)

4. The Spirit of God empowered Samson to do extraordinary works of strength. (Judges 14:6, 19)

Judges 15–16 SAMSON SUBDUED

1. Both Samson and Jesus voluntarily allowed themselves to be bound by the very ones they'd come to save in order to bring about their deliverance. (Judges 15:12–13)

2. Samson appears to have no particular purpose for being in Gaza, so his idle mind is soon occupied with sin. (Judges 16:1)

3. Samson made no attempt to separate himself from a dangerous situation. He started by making little compromises and when the consequences were not immediately noticeable, he believed himself to be invincible. (Judges 16:15–17)

4. Samson recognized God's role in his life for the first time; when he finally realized how helpless he was without God, he began to rely on him for enablement. (Judges 16:28)

Judges 17–18 MICAH'S MISTAKE

1. Micah thought he needed to add human inventions to God's plan. (Judges 17:3–4)

2. Laish did not retain any close ties with its mother country; its people were self-sufficient and unaware of danger. (Judges 18:7)

3. The spies encouraged the group by inspiring them with persuasive words to take action. (Judges 18:8–10)

4. Micah stole and then was stolen from. Micah placed too much significance on his objects of worship, so that when they were taken away, he was devastated. (Judges 17:2)

Judges 19–21 GIBEAH'S PUNISHMENT

1. Both Lot and the old man lived in corrupt communities. Both invited visitors for the night. Both were surrounded by neighbors who demanded to have their passions fulfilled. The old man showed his own depravity by offering the women in the house to absorb any violence toward himself and his guest. (Judges 19:16–24; Genesis 19:1–11)

2. We *cannot* explain away suffering. But, we do know that God is aware of every evil thing that happens, and he continues to care.

3. God used Benjamin to execute justice against Israel for idolatry and disobedience, even while they were punishing Benjamin for defending Gibeah's immorality. (Judges 20:18–28)

4. The Israelites never consulted God about their problems; they continued to try to solve things on their own. (Judges 21:7–23)

Ruth 1–2 RUTH'S CHARACTER TESTED

1. Ruth wanted to go and stay with Naomi, make Naoim's family and God her own, and die and be buried in the same place as Naomi. Ruth uses the Hebrew name of God to identify with him and his people (Ruth 1:16–17)

2. Naomi correctly attributed the events of her life to God's power and hiis ability to do whatever he purposes without resistance. However, she did not realize that his strength and power are motivated by grace and mercy. (Ruth 1:20–21)

3. Boaz commended Ruth for all that she did for Naomi after her own husband died. (Ruth 2:10–13)

4. A kinsman redeemer might buy back the land or freedom of a relative. Also, he might avenge his death or marry his widow. (Ruth 2:20)

Ruth 3–4 RUTH'S CHARACTER PROVED

1. Naomi told Ruth to: (1) wash, (2) perfume, (3) put on her best clothes, (4) go down to the threshing floor, (5) not let Boaz know, (6) note where he lies down, (7) go to him, (8) uncover his feet, and (9) lie down. Ruth did everything that Naomi told her to do. (Ruth 3:3–5)

2. Boaz sent a generous gift of grain home to the two widows. (Ruth 3:15)

3. A man more closely related to Elimelech than Boaz decided to become the kinsman redeemer. (Ruth 4:3–4)

4. The townspeople wished that this union would yield many children and increase the standing and fame of all involved. The plight of the two widows, the fate of Elimelech's lost line, and Boaz and Ruth's budding romance piqued their curiosity. In addition, they admired the upstanding reputation of both Boaz and Ruth. (Ruth 2:4, 6–7, 11–12; 3:11; 4:11–12, 14–17)

Appendix B - The Experts

Aldrich, Dr. Joe—pastor of Mariner's Church in Southern California, former president of Multnomah Bible College and leader of Northwest Renewal ministries

Aldrich, Dr. Willard M.—former president of Multnomah Bible College in Portland, Oregon

Allender, Dr. Dan B.—president and professor of counseling at Mars Hill Graduate School near Seattle, Washington.

Arthur, Kay—well-known Bible teacher and best-selling author, cofounder of Precept Ministries

Austin, Bill—pastor of the First Baptist Church of Ponca City, Oklahoma, and author of several books

Bailey, Robert W.—pastor of the First Baptist Church of Concord, North Carolina, and author of several books on pastoral care

Baker, Don—pastor for thirty-eight years in the Pacific Northwest and author of best-selling books

Barclay, William—professor of divinity and biblical criticism at Glasgow University, best-selling author, broadcaster on radio and television, and a regular contributor to widely circulated newspapers

Beers, V. Gilbert—prolific writer of Bible background and children's books, curriculum developer, and editor

Bertolini, Dewey—associate professor of Bible and youth ministry at Western Baptist College, Salem, Oregon, campus chaplain, and author of several books

Boreham, Frank W.—well-known speaker in the early 1900s, educated under Spurgeon, and a pastor in Tasmania, author of forty-six books

Brengle, Dr. Samuel—revered leader of the Salvation Army

Brestin, Dee—author of Bible study guides and books on women's issues

Bridges, Jerry—treasurer for the Navigators and Navigator Field Ministries before becoming vice president for corporate affairs for the Navigators, also the author of several books

Bright, Bill—founder and president of Campus Crusade for Christ, author of numerous books, columns, and articles

Briscoe, Stuart—pastor of Elmbrook Church in Waukesha, Wisconsin, director of "Telling the Truth" tape ministry, and author of many books

Burke, Tim—former major-league baseball player, now author and speaker

Burkett, Larry—founder and president of Christian Financial Concepts, Incorporated, well-known author and host of a nationally syndicated radio talk show

Bush, Dr. George—originally a missionary to Indiana in the early 1800s, most well-known as an author and a professor of Hebrew and Oriental Literature at New York University

Campolo, Toni—pastor, author, professor of sociology, founder of the Evangelical Association for the Promotion of Education, furthers inner- city schools for kids with learning disabilities

Carmichael, Amy—missionary to India until her death in 1951, originator of the Dohnavur Fellowship, and author of many books

Chafer, Lewis Sperry—founder and first president of Dallas Theological Seminary, his books on systematic theology are considered classics

Chambers, Oswald—Itinerant evangelist and Bible college teacher. Most of his works were compiled posthumously by his wife in 1917.

Clairmont, Patsy—author of best-selling books and speaker at Women of Faith Seminars

Cloud, Dr. Henry—clinical psychologist, co-director of the Minirth-Meier Clinic West, author, popular speaker, and host of a daily radio broadcast

Collins, Dr. Gary R.—professor of psychology at Trinity Evangelical Divinity School, licensed clinical psychologist and author of almost thirty books

Colson, Charles—former presidential adviser who went to prison during the Watergate era, currently founder of Prison Fellowship, a worldwide ministry

Crabb, Dr. Lawrence J., Jr.—psychologist, professor at Colorado Christian University, popular conference speaker, and author

DeHaan, Richard W.—teacher of the *Radio Bible Class,* contributor to the devotional series *Our Daily Bread*, and author

Dobson, Dr. James C.—psychologist, best-selling author, and founder of Focus on the Family

Edwards, Jonathan—a Puritan minister, preacher during the "Great Awakening," and president of Princeton University

Eims, LeRoy—director of Public Ministry Worldwide for the Navigators, speaker, seminar leader, and author

Elliot, Elisabeth—wife of martyred missionary, well-known speaker, and author

Elliot, Jim—one of five missionaries martyred for his faith among the Auca Indians in Quito, Ecuador

Ellison, Stanley E.—distinguished doctor of theology and professor at Western Conservative Baptist Seminary in Portland, Oregon

Engstrom, Ted—president emeritus of World Vision, and best-selling author

Evans, Colleen Townsend—serves on the board of governors at the College of Wooster in Ohio and Union Seminary in Virginia, is active in the Urban Task Force at the Presbyterian church in Washington, D.C., where her husband pastors, and is an author

Ford, Leighton—associate evangelist with the Billy Graham team, chairman of Lausanne Committee for World Evangelism, author, and frequent radio speaker on *The Hour of Decision*

Friesen, Garry—chairman of the Bible department at Multnomah Bible College, and best-selling author

Getz, Dr. Gene—professor of practical theology at Dallas Theological Seminary, and founder/pastor of Fellowship Bible Church in Dallas, Texas

Gothard, Bill—seminar speaker, and founder of the "Institute of Basic Youth Conflicts"

Graham, Billy—world-famous evangelist and best-selling author of several books

Hansel, Tim—founder of Summit Expedition, a wilderness ministry with life-changing impact, highly regarded conference speaker, and author

Havner, Vance—beloved evangelist, country preacher, and author

Hayford, Jack—pastor of Church on the Way in Southern California, composer of more than four hundred gospel songs and author of more than twenty books

Heald, Cynthia—Navigator staff member who gives seminars on "Women of Excellence," popular speaker, and Bible study leader

Heavilin, Marilyn Willet—popular speaker and best-selling author

Hedges, Charlie—former pastor of the ten thousand member South Coast Community Church in Irvine, California, now the principal of Hedges and Associates, a management development firm

Hendricks, Howard—professor and chairman of the Department of Christian Education at Dallas Theological Seminary

Hill, E. V.—pastor of Mount Zion Missionary Baptist Church for more than thirty years, preacher and teacher at conventions and revival meetings around the world

Hodges, Zane C.—professor of New Testament at Dallas Theological Seminary

Hughes, R. Kent—writer of numerous books, and pastor of College Church in Wheaton, Illinois

Hunter, John—associated with Capernwray and Major W. Ian Thomas, full-time worker with the Torchbearers organization

Hybels, Bill—pastor of Willow Creek Community Church in South Barrington, Illinois, and an author of Gold Medallion award-winning books

Johnson, Barbara—founder of Spatula Ministries, popular speaker and author of numerous best selling books

Johnson, Greg—literary agent for Alive Communications, founding editor of *Breakaway* magazine, served ten years in Youth for Christ/Campus Life and is an author of numerous books

Kahn, Robert I.—rabbi of Congregation Emanu El in Houston, one of the largest Jewish congregations in the south, frequent speaker at conventions and on radio and TV

Kessler, Jay—former president of Youth For Christ International, pulpit pastor at the First Baptist Church in Geneva, Illinois, and an author

LaHaye, Dr. Beverly—founder and chairman of Concerned Women for America, a nationally recognized advocate, author, and spokesperson for traditional family values

LaHaye, Dr. Tim—best-selling author of the Left Behind series, founder and president of Family Life Seminars

Larson, Bruce—director of Faith at Work, Presbyterian minister, and best-selling author

Lawrence, John—professor of Bible and theology at Multnomah Bible college

Lee, Dr. Richard—senior pastor of Rehoboth Baptist Church in Atlanta, and speaker on the nationally syndicated *There's Hope* radio and television broadcasts

Lewis, C. S.—teacher of English literature and language, and professor of medieval and renaissance English literature at Cambridge, and best-selling author

Linamen, Karen Scalf—freelance writer, editor, and author of several books

Lincoln, Abraham—sixteenth president of the United States, credited with holding the nation together in the Civil War

Little, Paul—assistant professor of evangelism at Trinity Evangelical Divinity School in Deerfield, Illinois, director of evangelism for InterVarsity Christian Fellowship, and popular speaker

Longfellow, Henry Wadsworth—most popular American poet, foremost of the Fireside Poets, wrote on subjects of general appeal to a family audience

Longman, Dr. Tremper, III—professor of Old Testament at Westminster Theological Seminary, author of several books, and many professional articles

Lucado, Max—minister at the Oak Hills Church in San Antonio, writer, speaker, and the voice of *Upwards*, a daily radio program

Luther, Martin—instigator of the Protestant Reformation in the early 1500s who promoted the concept that salvation was by faith alone; he nailed his thesis of ninety-five statements on the door of the Wittenberg church

Lutzer, Dr. Erwin—senior pastor at Moody Church in Chicago, former professor at Moody Bible Institute, and author of numerous books

MacArthur, General Douglas—supreme allied commander in the Pacific during World War II

MacArthur, Dr. John F., Jr.—pastor of Grace Community Church in Sun Valley, California, president of the Master's College, best selling author and radio preacher

Macauley, Susan Schaeffer—daughter of Francis and Edith Schaeffer, leader of L'Abri in Switzerland, and an award-winning author

MacDonald, Gordon—author, conference speaker, and consultant for churches and business groups

Mains, Karen Burton—frequent speaker and cohost of *Chapel of the Air*, and author of a best-selling book

Mann, Gerald—senior pastor of University Baptist Church in Austin, Texas, columnist for "Questions Youth Ask" in the *Baptist Standard*, and producer of a top-rated daily television show in Austin

Marshall, Catherine—wife of Peter Marshall (chaplain of the U.S. Senate in the late 1940s) and best-selling author of fiction and non-fiction works

Mayhall, Jack—former pastor, United States director of the Navigators, conference speaker, and author

McDowell, Josh—author of more than five best-selling books, traveling staff member for Campus Crusade for Christ, speaker at more than 580 universities in 57 countries

McGee, J. Vernon—Bible teacher of the *Thru the Bible* radio broadcast, pastor, and college lecturer

McMillen, S. I., M.D.—medical practitioner and author

McMinn, Gordon N.—professional counselor at Beaverton Family Counseling Center in Beaverton, Oregon, author of several books and numerous articles

Meburg, Marilyn—popular speaker at conferences and Women of Faith Seminars and an author

Meier, Dr. Paul D.—psychiatrist and executive vice president of Minirth-Meier Clinic, featured on a daily radio show

Miller, Keith—widely popular teacher, speaker, and best-selling author

Milton, John—ardent Puritan, called the greatest writer of the seventeenth century, wrote the great biblical epic *Paradise Lost*

Minirth, Dr. Frank B.—psychiatrist and president of Minirth-Meier Clinic and the Minirth-Meier Foundation

Mitchell, Curtis C.—professor of biblical studies at Bola University, well-known speaker at churches and conferences

Moody, D. L.—premier evangelist and soul-winner of the late 1800s in Great Britain and the U.S., founder of Moody Bible Institute

Morely, Patrick—founder and chairman of Morely Properties writes and speaks to men and women across the country

Mueller, George—founder and maintainer of orphanages in England in the late 1800's, caring for more than ten thousand orphans and raising millions of dollars through prayer alone

Murray, Andrew—devotional writer and well-known preacher in South Africa during the mid-1800s

Narramore, Dr. S. Bruce—professor of psychology at Rosemead Graduate School, author, and a licensed psychologist specializing in psychopathology

Nee, Watchman—a Chinese evangelist in the mid-1900s whose gifted preaching brought far-reaching results even to a persecuted church

Needham, David—teacher of Bible and theology at Multnomah Bible College, and author of several books

Ogilvie, Lloyd John—chaplain of the U.S. Senate, former pastor, author of numerous books and articles, speaker on radio and television

Ortland, Anne—listed in *Who's Who of American Women*, author of more than a dozen books, accomplished musician, and founder (along with her husband) of Renewal Ministries

Packer, J. I.—teacher of systematic and historical theology at Regent College in Vancouver, B.C., author of numerous books

Palau, Luis—international evangelist to more than three million people in thirty-seven nations (170 million more through radio and television broadcasts)

Pentecost, J. Dwight—professor of Bible exposition at Dallas Theological Seminary, pastor, and author of more than a dozen books

Phillips, Bob—director of Hume Lake Christian Camps, licensed marriage, family, and child counselor, and author of more than a dozen books

Phillips, J. B.—Anglican minister, best known for translating the New Testament into modern English

Pink, Arthur W.—a British scholar who served in pastorates in Australia and the U.S. during the early 1900s, originator of *Studies in Scripture*, a magazine on biblical exposition

Plummer, Reverend A.—master of University College, Durham, England

Prater, Arnold—pastor of First Methodist Church of Lebanon, Missouri, author of many articles and books

Price, Eugenia—successful scriptwriter for major television networks before becoming a popular writer in the Christian marketplace

Radmacher, Dr. Earl D.—professor at Western Baptist Seminary, Portland, Oregon, author and speaker

Redpath, Alan—senior minister at Moody Memorial Church in Chicago, more recently pastoring in Edinburgh, Scotland

Reeve, Pamela—dean of women at Multnomah Bible College in Portland, Oregon, and author of several books

Ridenour, Fritz—former youth editor for Gospel Light publications, and best-selling author

Rogers, Dale Evans—movie star in Hollywood Westerns, regular speaker at Billy Graham Crusades in the early 1950s, and author of *Angel Unaware*

Ryrie, Charles Caldwell—professor of Systematic Theology at Dallas Theological Seminary and the author of numerous books on the bible and Christian living

Sanders, J. Oswald—former director of Overseas Missionary Fellowship (OMF), principal of New Zealand Bible Training Institute, and author of many books

Schaeffer, Francis A.—founder of L'Abri Fellowship, philosopher and theologian, author of books selling in the millions

Schaeffer, Franky—author, filmmaker, and president of Schaeffer V Productions

Schwanz, Floyd—founder and director of TEAMwork Ministries, and pastor of Small Group Ministries at Wenatchee Free Methodist Church in Washington

Seamands, David A.—professor emeritus at Asbury Theological Seminary, former missionary and pastor, and best-selling author in the area of Christian psychology

Secker, William—seventeenth-century British clergyman and author

Sittser, Gerald L.—professor of religion and philosophy at Whitworth College in Spokane, Washington, and author of several books

Slessor, Mary—single woman missionary from Scotland to the cannibals in Calabar (now Nigeria) from 1876 through 1915

Smalley, Gary—nationally known speaker and writer on family relations, formerly a pastor of family life

Solzhenitsyn, Aleksandri—recipient of the Nobel prize in literature, called the greatest living master of the Russian language, imprisoned for his stand on human rights

Spurgeon, Charles Haddon—called the "prince of preachers," his sermons held throngs spellbound at the Metropolitan Tabernacle in London in the nineteenth century and now in written form

Stanley, Dr. Charles—senior pastor of the twelve-thousand member First Baptist Church of Atlanta and popular speaker for *In Touch*, a national television and radio program

Stedman, Ray C.—nationally recognized expositor, author of several well-known books, and a pastor

Stott, John R. W.—famous lecturer, author of numerous devotional books, and the rector of All Souls Church in London

Sweeting, George—former president of Moody Bible Institute, prolific author and Bible teacher

Swindoll, Charles R.—president of Dallas

Theological Seminary, host of the nationally syndicated radio program *Insight for Living*, and author of many books

Swindoll, Luci—vice president of public relations at Insight for Living, popular speaker, and author

Tada, Joni Eareckson—artist, speaker, and author of more than twenty books, president of Joni and Friends Ministries, which advances Christ's kingdom among the disabled

Taylor, Dr. Richard S.—professor emeritus of theology and missions at the Nazarene Theological Seminary in Kansas City

Tchividjian, Gigi Graham—eldest daughter of Billy Graham, columnist for *Christian Parenting* magazine, speaker, and author of several books

Ten Boom, Corrie—survivor of a WW II concentration camp, writer and speaker all over the world, and the inspiration behind the feature-length movie *The Hiding Place*

Tippit, Sammy—founder and president of God's Love in Action, evangelist in the United States and Europe (particularly in the former Eastern bloc countries)

Townsend, Dr. John—clinical psychologist, codirector of the Minirth-Meier Clinic West, author, popular speaker, and host of a daily radio broadcast

Tozer, A. W.—pastor, longtime editor of what is now called *Alliance Life*, the official magazine of the Christian and Missionary Alliance Church, and author of many books

Trent, Dr. John—associate director of Today's Family, conference speaker and former family life pastor

VanGorder, Dr. Paul R.—associate teacher of the *Radio Bible Class*, speaker on the TV series *Day of Discovery*, contributing writer for *Our Daily Bread*, and an author

Vester, Bertha Spafford—daughter of Horatio Spafford (who wrote the famous hymn, "It Is Well with My Soul," after his daughters drowned at sea), leading figure in the Christian Colony in Jerusalem in the early 1900s

Waalvord, Dr. John F.—chancellor of Dallas Theological Seminary, former president of that institution for thirty-four years, author, and co-editor of *The Bible Knowledge Commentary*

Wesley, John—circuit preacher who traveled over 250,000 miles on horseback, preached over 40,000 sermons, wrote over 6,500 hymns, and started the Methodist Church

White, John—associate professor of psychiatry at the University of Manitoba, prolific author of both fiction and nonfiction books, and helps to pastor a congregation in Winnipeg

Wiersbe, Warren—one of the evangelical world's most respected Bible teachers, author of more than one hundred books, and former director of *Back to the Bible*, a radio ministry

Wilcox, Michael—formerly director of pastoral studies at Trinity College, Bristol; is currently vicar of St. Nicholas Church in Durham

Woudstra, Martin H.—former professor of Old Testament studies at Calvin Theological Seminary, president of the Evangelical Theological Society, and writer of scholarly books and articles

Yancy, Philip—executive editor of *Campus Life Magazine*, editor of Campus Life Books, and an author

Endnotes

Introduction to Joshua, Judges, and Ruth

1. Alan Redpath, *Victorious Christian Living* (Grand Rapids: Revell, 1993), 52.

Introduction to the Book of Joshua

1. J. Vernon McGee, *Joshua-Judges* (La Verne, CA: El Camino Press, 1976), 7.

2. Charles F. Pfieffer, Old Testament, ed., *The Wycliffe Bible Commentary* (Chicago: Moody Press, 1980), 213.

3. Leon Wood, *A Survey of Israel's History* (Grand Rapids: Zondervan, 1973), 168.

4. Bruce Wilkenson, *Talk Thru the Bible* (Nashville: Thomas Nelson, 1983), 52; Kenneth L. Barker and John Kohlenberger III, consulting eds., *Zondervan NIV Bible Commentary* (Grand Rapids: Zondervan, 1994), 289; McGee, *Joshua-Judges*.

5. Gleason L. Archer, Jr., *A Survey of Old Testament Introduction* (Chicago: Moody, 1975), 264.

6. H. D. M. Spence and Joseph S. Exell, eds., *The Pulpit Commentary*, vol. 3, *Joshua to Nehemiah* (Grand Rapids: Eerdmans, 1980), i.

7. Marten H. Woudstra, *The New International Commentary on the Old Testament, The Book of Joshua* (Grand Rapids: Eerdmans, 1981),14; Pfieffer, *The Wycliffe Bible Commentary*, 205.

Joshua 1–2: Preliminary Preparations

1. McGee, *Joshua-Judges*, 11.

2. Warren Wiersbe, *Be Strong*, quoted in Max Lucado, *The Inspirational Bible* (Nashville: Word, 1991), 224–25.

3. A. W. Tozer, *The Pursuit of Man* (Camp Hill: Christian Publications, 1978), 3–4.

4. McGee, *Joshua-Judges*, 12.

5. Joni Eareckson Tada, *Secret Strength* (Portland, OR: Multnomah, 1988), 82.

6. Charles R. Swindoll, *The Quest for Character* (Portland, OR: Multnomah, 1987), 164.

7. Tada, *Secret Strength*, 34.

8. Eugenia Price, *Just as I Am* (Philadelphia: J. B. Lippincott, 1968), 168.

9. Pfieffer, *The Wycliffe Bible Commentary*, 208.

10. John Wesley, quoted in Robert J. Morgan, *Nelson's Complete Book of Stories, Illustrations and Quotes* (Nashville: Thomas Nelson, 2000), 151.

11. V. Gilbert Beers, *The Victor Handbook of Bible Knowledge* (Wheaton, IL: Victor, 1981),128–29; Earl D. Radmacher, gen. ed., *Nelson Study Bible* (Nashville: Thomas Nelson, 1997), 355–56.

12. Zane C. Hodges, *The Gospel Under Siege* (Dallas: Redencion Viva, 1984), 32.

13. Billy Graham, *Peace with God*, quoted in Lucado, *The Inspirational Bible*, 227.

14. Luci Swindoll et al., *Joy Breaks* (Grand Rapids: Zondervan, 1997), 51.

Joshua 3–4: Crossing the Jordan

1. Lloyd John Ogilve, *The Bush is Still Burning* (Waco, TX: Word, 1980), 42, 45.

2. Bertha Spafford Vester, *Our Jerusalem* (Jerusalem: Ariel, 1988), 232.

3. George Sweeting, *Talking It Over* (Chicago: Moody Bible Institute, 1979), 238.

4. Corrie ten Boom, *Not I, but Christ* (Nashville: Thomas Nelson, 1983), 94.

5. Anne Ortland, *My Sacrifice His Fire* (Dallas: Word, 1993), 191.

6. Luci Swindoll et al., *Joy Breaks*, 87.

7. Amy Carmichael, *Whispers of His Power* (Minneapolis: Grason, 1982), 216.

8. C. S. Lewis, *Miracles* (New York: Macmillan, 1947), 98-99.

9. Ray C. Stedman, *Birth of the Body* (Santa Ana, CA: Vision House, 1974), 104–6.

10. Joni Eareckson Tada, "More Precious Than Silver," *Power for Living*, June 25, 2000 (Colorado Springs: SP Publications), 7.

Joshua 5–6: Conquest of Jericho

1. Dale Evans Rogers, *My Spiritual Diary* (Westwood, NJ: Revell, 1955), 23.

2. Radmacher, *The Nelson Study Bible*, 360.

3. Redpath, *Victorious Christian Living*, 91–92.

4. John White, *The Fight*, quoted in Lucado, *The Inspirational Bible*, 231.

5. Jim Elliot, quoted in Elizabeth Elliot, *Journals of Jim Elliot* (Old Tappan, NJ: Revell, 1978), 68.

6. C. H. Spurgeon, *The Metropolitan Tabernacle Pulpit*, vol. 14 (Pasadena, TX: Pilgrim, 1970), 88.

7. A. W. Tozer, *The Pursuit of Man* (Camp Hill, PA: Christian Publications, 1978), 10.

8. Radmacher, *The Nelson Study Bible*, 362.

9. Charles R. Swindoll, *Growing Strong in the Seasons of Life* (Portland, OR: Multnomah, 1983), 251.

10. Woudstra, *The Book of Joshua*, 111.

11. R. Kent Hughes, *Living on the Cutting Edge* (Westchester, IL: Crossway, 1987), 77.

12. Ted Engstrom, quoted in Bill Bright, *The Greatest Lesson I Ever Learned* (San Bernardino: Here's Life, 1991), 60.

13. Beers, *The Victor Handbook of Bible Knowledge*, 132.

14. Herbert Lockyer, *All the Miracles of the Bible* (Grand Rapids: Zondervan, 1961), 83.

15. John J. Davis, *Conquest and Crisis* (Winona Lake, IN: BMH Books, 1974), 48.

16. Barbara Johnson et al., *Joy Breaks*, 170–71.

17. Charles Colson, *Kingdoms in Conflict* (Grand Rapids: William Morrow/Zondervan, 1987), 371.

Joshua 7–8: Tragedy and Triumph at Ai

1. Eugene Merrill, *An Historical Survey of the Old Testament* (Nutley, NJ: Craig Press, 1971), 158.

2. John MacArthur, *The Vanishing Conscience* (Dallas: Word, 1994), 116.

3. Hughes, *Living on the Cutting Edge*, 88.

4. Redpath, *Victorious Christian Living*, 116.

5. G. Ernest Wright, editor and adviser, *Great People of the Bible and How They Lived* (Pleasantville, NY: Reader's Digest Association, 1974), 106.

6. James M. Freeman, *Manners and Customs of the Bible* (Plainfield, NJ: Logos International, 1972), 145.

7. Swindoll, *Growing Strong in the Seasons of Life*, 133.

8. Beers, *The Victor Handbook of Bible Knowledge*, 203.

9. Hughes, *Living on the Cutting Edge*, 84.

10. Beers, *The Victor Handbook of Bible Knowledge*, 135.

11. Josh McDowell, *Answers to Tough Questions* (San Bernardino: Here's Life, 1983), 70.

12. Corrie ten Boom, *Each New Day* (Old Tappan, NJ; Revell, 1977), 175.

13. Pfeiffer, *The Wycliffe Bible Commentary*, 215.

14. Ibid., 215.

15. Radmacher, *The Nelson Study Bible*, 368.

16. Luis Palau, *Heart After God* (Portland, OR: Multnomah, 1978), 77.

17. Pfeiffer, *The Wycliffe Bible Commentary*, 215.

18. Radmacher, *The Nelson Study Bible*, 368.

19. Francis A. Schaeffer, *The God Who Is There* (Downers Grove, IL: InterVarsity, 1969), 50.

20. Redpath, *Victorious Christian Living*, 126.

Joshua 9–10: The Southern Invasion

1. Radmacher, *The Nelson Study Bible*, 369.

2. J. Oswald Sanders, *Bible Men of Faith* (Chicago: Moody Press, 1965), 79.

3. Oswald Chambers, *My Utmost for His Highest*, quoted in Lucado, *The Inspirational Bible*, 230.

4. Pfeiffer, *The Wycliffe Bible Commentary*, 216.

5. Ibid., 217.

6. J. I. Packer, *Knowing God*, quoted in Lucado, *The Inspirational Bible*, 232.

7. Woudstra, *The Book of Joshua*, 306.

8. Radmacher, *The Nelson Study Bible*, 371.

9. Gigi Graham Tchividjian, *Currents of the Heart* (Sisters, OR: Multnomah, 1996), 49–51.

10. Charles H. Spurgeon, *Faith's Checkbook* (Chicago: Moody , n.d.), 85.

11. Pfeiffer, *The Wycliffe Bible Commentary*, 218.

12. Radmacher, *The Nelson Study Bible*, 371.

13. Davis, *Conquest and Crisis*, 66–68.

14. David Needham, *Close to His Majesty* (Portland, OR: Multnomah, 1987), 23.

15. McDowell, *Answers to Tough Questions*, 105.

16. Joni Eareckson Tada, *Diamonds in the Dust* (Grand Rapids: Zondervan, 1993), November 17.

17. Max Lucado, *He Still Moves Stones*, quoted in Lucado, *The Inspirational Bible*, 243.

18. Radmacher, *The Nelson Study Bible*, 374.

19. Luci Swindoll et al., *Joy Breaks*, 158.

Joshua 11–12: Conquest of the North

1. Pfieffer, *The Wycliffe Bible Commentary*, 220.

2. Barker, *Zondervan NIV Bible Commentary*, 308.

3. Charles Stanley, *A Touch of His Freedom* (Grand Rapids: Zondervan, 1991), 43–44.

4. Radmacher, *The Nelson Study Bible*, 376.

5. Pfieffer, *The Wycliffe Bible Commentary*, 220.

6. Arthur W. Pink, *Gleanings in Joshua* (Chicago: Moody Press, 1969), 312.

7. Pfieffer, *The Wycliffe Bible Commentary*, 220.

8. Merrill C. Tenney, gen. ed., *The Zondervan Pictorial Encyclopedia of the Bible*, vol. 1 (Grand Rapids: Zondervan, 1977), 318.

9. Henry H. Halley, *Halley's Bible Handbook* (Grand Rapids: Zondervan, 1965), 164.

10. Schultz, *The Old Testament Speaks*, 100.

11. Halley, *Halley's Bible Handbook*, 164.

12. Bill Gothard, *Men's Manual*, vol. 1 (Oak Brook, IL: Institute in Basic Youth Conflicts, n.d.), 40.

13. Jerry Bridges, *The Practice of Godliness* (Colorado Springs: NavPress, 1983), 153.

14. Joe Aldrich, *Secrets to Inner Beauty* (Santa Ana: Vision House, 1977), 31–32.

15. Tada, *Diamonds in the Dust*, June 12.

16. Ten Boom, *Each New Day*, 93.

17. Eugenia Price, *The Burden Is Light* (Old Tappan, NJ: Spire Books, 1975), 167.

18. D. L. Moody, *The Way to God* (Chicago: Revell, 1912), 115.

19. Davis, *Conquest and Crisis*, 75.

20. H. H. Rowley, *The Rediscovery of the Old Testament* (Philadelphia: Westminster, 1946), 32ff.; James Muilenburg, *The History of the Religion of Israel*, as quoted in George A. Butterick, ed., *The Interpreter's Bible* (New York: Abingdon, 1952); 310.

21. Hughes, *Living on the Cutting Edge*, 95.

22. Pfieffer, *The Wycliffe Bible Commentary*, 206.

23. James Orr, ed., *The International Standard Bible Encyclopedia*, vol. 1 (Grand Rapids: Eerdmans,

1939), 550–51.

24. Paul E. Little, *Know Why You Believe* (Downers Grove, IL: InterVarsity, 1973), 88.

Joshua 13–22: Division of the Land

1. Pfieffer, *The Wycliffe Bible Commentary*, 222.

2. Radmacher, *The Nelson Study Bible*, 378.

3. Cynthia Heald, *Becoming a Woman of Excellence* (Colorado Springs: NavPress, 1986), 65.

4. Elliot, quoted in Elliot, *Journals of Jim Elliot*, 70.

5. Pfieffer, *The Wycliffe Bible Commentary*, 223.

6. Redpath, *Victorious Christian Living*, 201.

7. John MacArthur, *The MacArthur Study Bible* (Nashville: Word, 1997), 322.

8. Swindoll, *Come Before Winter*, 99.

9. Pfieffer, *The Wycliffe Bible Commentary*, 225

10. Ibid.

11. Dr. James C. Dobson, *Love for a Lifetime* (Portland, OR: Multnomah, 1987), 119–20.

12. J. I. Packer, *Knowing God* (Downers Grove, IL: InterVarsity, 1976), 210.

13. Radmacher, *The Nelson Study Bible*, 387.

14. Ibid.

15. Ibid.

16. S. I. McMillen, *None of These Diseases* (Westwood, NJ: Revell, 1963), 89.

17. Radmacher, *The Nelson Study Bible*, 388.

18. Arthur W. Pink, *The Attributes of God* (Grand Rapids: Baker, 1975), 39.

19. John F. Walvoord, quoted in Bright, *The Greatest Lesson I've Ever Learned*, 220.

20. Woudstra, *The Book of Joshua*, 326–27.

21. Pfieffer, *The Wycliffe Bible Commentary*, 228.

Joshua 23–24: Joshua's Farewell

1. MacArthur, *The MacArthur Study Bible*, 331.

2. McGee, *Joshua-Judges*, 13.

3. Tim LaHaye, *How to Study the Bible for Yourself* (Irvine, CA: Harvest House, 1976), 15.

4. Kay Arthur, *Lord, Only You Can Change Me* (Sisters, OR: Multnomah, 1995), 19.

5. A. W. Tozer, *The Knowledge of the Holy* (New York: Harper & Row, 1961), 9.

6. Dewey Bertolini, *Escaping the Subtle Sellout* (Wheaton, IL: Victor, 1992), 29.

7. MacArthur, *The MacArthur Study Bible*, 331.

8. Dan B. Allender and Tremper Longman III,

Bold Love (Colorado Springs: NavPress, 1992), 117–18.

9. Radmacher, *The Nelson Study Bible*, 393.

10. J. Dwight Pentecost, *The Glory of God* (Portland, OR: Multnomah, 1978), 99–100.

11. Stanley E. Ellison, quoted in William Kerr, *God What Is He Like?* (Wheaton, IL: Tyndale House, 1977), 91.

12. Hughes, *Living on the Cutting Edge*, 162.

13. Ten Boom, *Each New Day*, 15.

14. J. B. Phillips, *Your God Is Too Small* (New York: MacMillan, 1972), 58.

15. Stuart Briscoe, *Everyday Discipleship for Ordinary People* (Wheaton, IL: Victor, 1988), 168.

16. George Mueller, *Answers to Prayer* (Chicago: Moody Press, n.d.), 33.

Introduction to the Book of Judges

1. Pfieffer, *The Wycliffe Bible Commentary*, 233.

2. Davis, *Conquest and Crisis*, 94.

3. Bernard Grun, *The Timetables of History* (New York: Simon & Schuster, 1963), 4–5.

4. Ronald A. Beers, gen. ed., *Life Application Bible* (Wheaton, IL: Tyndale House, 1988), 343.

5. Davis, *Conquest and Crisis*, 93.

Judges 1:1–2:15: Leaderless Without Joshua

1. LeRoy Eims, *The Basic Ingredients for Spiritual Growth* (Wheaton: Victor, 1992), 74.

2. Pfieffer, *The Wycliffe Bible Commentary*, 235.

3. Ibid.

4. Ibid.

5. Tada, *Diamonds in the Dust*, November 5.

6. Barker, *Zondervan NIV Bible Commentary*, 331.

7. George Bush, *Notes, Critical and Practical, on the Book of Judges* (Minneapolis: Klock and Klock, 1981), 19.

8. Howard Hendricks, *Say It with Love* (Wheaton, IL: Victor, 1973), 73–74.

9. Willard W. Winter, *Studies in Joshua, Judges, Ruth* (Joplin, MO: College Press, 1969), 335.

10. Pfieffer, *The Wycliffe Bible Commentary*, 237.

11. Charles R. Swindoll, *Dropping Your Guard*, quoted by Max Lucado, *The Inspirational Bible*, 252.

12. Bush, *Notes, Critical and Practical, on the Book of Judges*, 22.

13. Gerald L. Sittser, *The Will of God as a Way of Life* (Grand Rapids: Zondervan, 2000), 52.

14. Arthur, *Lord, Only You can Change Me*, 56.

15. Pfieffer, *The Wycliffe Bible Commentary*, 238.

Judges 2:16–3:31: Early Judges in Israel

1. Fritz Ridenour, *How to Be a Christian Without Being Religious* (Glendale, CA: Regal, 1972), 61–62.

2. Bertolini, *Escaping the Subtle Sellout*, 47–48.

3. General Douglas MacArthur, quoted by McGee, *Joshua and Judges*, 113.

4. Jonathan Edwards, quoted by Francis Hodgins and Kenneth Silverman, *Adventures in American Literature* (Orlando: Harcourt Brace Jovanovich, 1980), 41.

5. Marilyn Willet Heavilin, *When Your Dreams Die* (San Bernardino: Here's Life, 1990), 81–82.

6. Winter, *Studies in Joshua Judges Ruth*, 355.

7. Arthur E. Cundall and Leon Morris, *Judges and Ruth* (Downers Grove, IL: InterVarsity, 1968), 72.

8. Karen Scalf Linamen, *The Parent Warrior* (Wheaton, IL: Victor, 1993), 146.

9. Davis, *Conquest and Crisis*, 106.

10. Billy Graham, *The Holy Spirit* (Waco, TX: Word, 1978), 220.

11. Davis, *Conquest and Crisis*, 107.

12. Winter, *Studies in Joshua Judges Ruth*, 361–62.

13. Cundall, *Judges and Ruth*, 77.

14. Bush, *Notes, Critical and Practical, on the Book of Judges*, 35.

15. William Secker, *The Nonsuch Professor in His Meridian Splendor* (Chicago: Revell, 1899), 69.

16. Bush, *Notes, Critical and Practical, on the Book of Judges*, 36–37.

17. Richard W. DeHaan, *The World on Trial* (Grand Rapids: Zondervan, 1970), 16.

18. Winter, *Studies in Joshua, Judges & Ruth*, 361.

19. Bush, *Notes, Critical and Practical, on the Book of Judges*, 40.

20. Pfieffer, *The Wycliffe Bible Commentary*, 241.

21. Ibid., 241

22. Davis, *Conquest and Crisis*, 109.

Judges 4–5: Deborah, a Lady Leader

1. *Bush, Notes, Critical and Practical, on the Book of Judges*, 42.

2. Radmacher, *The Nelson Study Bible*, 405.

3. Ibid.

4. Bush, *Notes, Critical and Practical, on the Book of Judge*, 43; Pfieffer, *The Wycliffe Bible Commentary*, 247.

5. Howard Hendricks, *Values and Virtues* (Sisters, OR: Multnomah, 1997), 204.

6. Bush, *Notes, Critical and Practical, on the Book of Judges*, 45.

7. Ibid., 46.

8. Barker, *Zondervan NIV Bible Commentary*, 336.

9. Bush, *Notes, Critical and Practical, on the Book of Judges*, 47.

10. Pamela Reeve, *Faith Is* . . . (Portland, OR: Multnomah, 1972), 4.

11. Don Baker, *Lord, I've Got a Problem* (Eugene, OR: Harvest House, 1988), 37.

12. Barker, *Zondervan NIV Bible Commentary*, 336.

13. Bush, *Notes, Critical and Practical, on the Book of Judges*, 53.

14. Pfieffer, *The Wycliffe Bible Commentary*, 14.

15. Patsy Clairmont et al., *Joy Breaks*, 47–48.

16. Radmacher, *The Nelson Study Bible*, 406.

17. Bright, *Believing God for the Impossible*, 12.

18. Radmacher, *The Nelson Study Bible*, 406.

19. Earl D. Radmacher, quoted in William Kerr, *God What Is He Like?* (Wheaton, IL: Tyndale, 1977), 26.

20. A. W. Tozer, *Whatever Happened to Worship* (Camp Hill, PA: Christian Publications, 1985), 30–31.

21. Tada, *Secret Strength*, 21.

22. Ten Boom, *Not I, but Christ*, 63.

23. Bush, *Notes, Critical and Practical, on the Book of Judges*, 66.

24. Leighton Ford, *Good News Is for Sharing* (Elgin, IL: David C. Cook, 1977), 186.

25. Bush, *Notes, Critical and Practical, on the Book of Judges*, 68.

26. Ibid., 69.

27. Lawrence J. Crabb Jr., *The Marriage Builder* (Grand Rapids: Zondervan, 1982), 112.

28. Barker, *Zondervan NIV Bible Commentary*, 336.

29. Ten Boom, *Not I, But Christ*, 135.

30. Pfieffer, *The Wycliffe Bible Commentary*, 244.

31. Swindoll, *Growing Strong in the Seasons of Life*, 380.

32. Jack Mayhall, *Discipleship: The Price and the Prize* (Wheaton, IL: Victor, 1984), 91.

Judges 6:1–7:15a: Convincing Gideon

1. Pfieffer, *The Wycliffe Bible Commentary*, 245.

2. Ibid.

3. Winter, *Studies in Joshua, Judges & Ruth*, 392.

4. Ibid. 395–96.

5. Vance Havner, *Consider Jesus* (Grand Rapids: Baker, 1987), 80.

6. Bush, *Notes, Critical and Practical, on the Book of Judges*, 85.

7. Sammy Tippet, *Fire in Your Heart* (Chicago: Moody Press, 1987), 74–75.

8. Bush, *Notes, Critical and Practical, on the Book of Judges*, 87–88.

9. Frank Boreham, quoted in Peter F. Gunther, compiler, *Frank Boreham Treasury* (Chicago: Moody Press, 1984), 33, 36–37.

10. Frank B. Minirth and Paul D. Meier, *Ask the Doctors* (Carmel, NY: Guideposts, 1991), 29.

11. Pfieffer, *The Wycliffe Bible Commentary*, 247.

12. Bush, *Notes, Critical and Practical, on the Book of Judges*, 93.

13. Winter, *Studies in Joshua, Judges & Ruth*, 400.

14. Pfieffer, *The Wycliffe Bible Commentary*, 246.

15. Winter, *Studies in Joshua, Judges, Ruth*, 400.

16. Gary R. Collins, *You Can Make a Difference* (Grand Rapids: Zondervan, 1992), 25.

17. John MacArthur Jr., *Found: God's Will* (Colorado Springs: Chariot Victor, 1998), 60.

18. Garry Friesen, *Decision Making and the Will of God* (Portland, OR: Multnomah, 1980), 223.

19. Bush, *Notes, Critical and Practical, on the Book of Judges*, 96.

20. Patrick Morely, *Walking with Christ in the Details of Life*, quoted in Max Lucado, *The Inspirational Bible*, 248.

21. Tim and Christine Burke, *Major League Dad*, quoted in Max Lucado, *The Inspirational Bible*, 235.

Judges 7:15b–8:35: Conditioning Gideon

1. Bush, *Notes, Critical and Practical, on the Book of Judges*, 103.

2. Pfieffer, *The Wycliffe Bible Commentary*, 248.

3. Andrew Murray, *Daily Secrets of Christian Living* (Minneapolis: Bethany, 1978), March 31.

4. Bush, *Notes, Critical and Practical, on the Book of Judges*, 105.

5. Abraham Lincoln, quoted in Morgan, *Nelson's Complete Book of Stories, Illustrations and Quotes*, 164.

6. Gordon N. McMinn, *Choosing to Be Close* (Portland, OR: Multnomah, 1984), 108.

7. Bush, *Notes, Critical and Practical, on the Book of Judges*, 109.

8. Philip Yancy and Tim Stafford, *Unhappy Secrets of the Christian Life* (Grand Rapids: Zondervan, 1979), 75.

9. Greg Johnson, *Life Is Like Driver's Ed . . .* (Ann Arbor, MI: Servant, 1996), 162.

10. Cundall, *Judges and Ruth*, 117.

11. Ibid.

12. Ibid., 118.

13. Susan Schaeffer Macaulay, *For the Children's Sake* (Wheaton, IL: Crossway, 1984), 10.

14. Cundall, *Judges and Ruth*, 120.

Judges 9:1–10:5: Abimelech, a Kingdomless King

1. Pfieffer, *The Wycliffe Bible Commentary*, 250.

2. Lloyd John Ogilve, quoted in Morgan, *Nelson's Complete Book of Stories, Illustrations and Quotes*, 270.

3. Pfieffer, *The Wycliffe Bible Commentary*, 250.

4. Bill Hybels, *Descending into Greatness* (Grand Rapids: Zondervan, 1993), 25–26.

5. Radmacher, *The Nelson Study Bible*, 346.

6. Keith Miller, *The Taste of New Wine* (Waco, TX: Word, 1967), 26–27.

7. Radmacher, *The Nelson Study Bible*, 346.

8. Pfieffer, *The Wycliffe Bible Commentary*, 250.

9. Bush, *Notes, Critical and Practical, on the Book of Judges*, 124.

10. Pfieffer, *The Wycliffe Bible Commentary*, 250.

11. Ibid.

12. Beers, *The Victor Handbook of Bible Knowledge*, 446.

13. Ibid., 484–85.

14. Beers, *The Victor Handbook of Bible Knowledge*, 245.

15. Bush, *Notes, Critical and Practical, on the Book of Judges*, 135.

16. Ibid.

17. Pfieffer, *The Wycliffe Bible Commentary*, 251.

18. Erwin W. Lutzer, *Hitler's Cross* (Chicago: Moody Press, 1995), 92–94.

19. Bush, *Notes, Critical and Practical, on the Book of Judges*, 128.

20. Barker, *Zondervan NIV Bible Commentary*, 347.

21. Pfieffer, *The Wycliffe Bible Commentary*, 251.

22. Bush, *Notes, Critical and Practical, on the Book of Judges*, 131.

23. John W. Lawrence, *Down to Earth* (Portland, OR: Multnomah, 1975), 24–25.

24. Tenney, *The Zondervan Pictorial Encyclopedia of the Bible*, vol. 5, 385.

25. Pfieffer, *The Wycliffe Bible Commentary*, 252.

26. Ibid.

27. Radmacher, *The Nelson Study Bible*, 418.

28. Aleksandr Solzhenitsyn, quoted in James and Phyllis Asdurf, *Battered into Submission* (Downers Grove, IL: InterVarsity, 1989), 59.

29. Gordon MacDonald, *Rebuilding Your Broken World* (Nashville: Thomas Nelson, 1988), 85.

30. Toni Compolo, *Who Switched the Price Tags*, quoted in Max Lucado, *The Inspirational Bible*, 283.

Judges 10:6–12:15: Jephthah, Plus Three

1. Pfieffer, *The Wycliffe Bible Commentary*, 253.

2. Bush, *Notes, Critical and Practical, on the Book of Judges*, 139.

3. Bertolini, *Escaping the Subtle Sellout*, 63.

4. John R. W. Stott, *Our Guilty Silence* (Grand Rapids: Eerdmans, 1969), 42–43.

5. Larry Burkett, "Are Allowances Scriptural?" *Moody* (Chicago: Moody Bible Institute, May 1982), 61.

6. Pfieffer, *The Wycliffe Bible Commentary*, 253.

7. Ibid., 254.

8. Swindoll, *Come Before Winter*, 233.

9. Pfieffer, *The Wycliffe Bible Commentary*, 254.

10. Bush, *Notes, Critical and Practical, on the Book of Judges*, 149.

11. Pfieffer, *The Wycliffe Bible Commentary*, 254.

12. Halley, *Halley's Bible Handbook*, 202.

13. Lewis Sperry Chafer, *He That Is Spiritual* (Grand Rapids: Zondervan, 1976), 24.

14. Radmacher, *The Nelson Study Bible*, 423; Bush, *Notes, Critical and Practical, on the Book of Judges*, 162–65.

15. Vance Havner, *Consider Him* (New York: Revell, 1938), 67.

16. Pfieffer, *The Wycliffe Bible Commentary*, 255.

17. Floyd Schwanz, *Growing Small Groups* (Kansas City: Beacon Hill Press, 1995), 115.

18. Pfieffer, *The Wycliffe Bible Commentary*, 256.

Judges 13–14: Samson's Strength

1. Beers, *The Victor Handbook of Bible Knowledge*, 52.

2. Barker, *Zondervan NIV Bible Commentary*, 353.

3. Beers, *The Victor Handbook of Bible Knowledge*, 158.

4. Oswald Chambers, quoted in Edythe Draper, *Draper's Book of Quotations for the Christian World* (Wheaton, IL: Tyndale House, 1992), 446.

5. Bush, *Notes, Critical and Practical, on the Book of Judges*, 175.

6. Charles Caldwell Ryrie, *You Mean the Bible Teaches That . . .* (Chicago: Moody Press, 1974), 89.

7. Beers, *The Victor Handbook of Bible Knowledge*, 157.

8. Linamen, *The Parent Warrior*, 22–38.

9. Bush, *Notes, Critical and Practical, on the Book of Judges*, 177.

10. Tada, *Diamonds in the Dust*, November 3.

11. Bill Austin, *The Back of God* (Wheaton, IL: Tyndale House, 1980), 67-68.

12. Pfieffer, *The Wycliffe Bible Commentary*, 256.

13. Pentecost, *The Glory of God*, 5.

14. Bush, *Notes, Critical and Practical, on the Book of Judges*, 182.

15. Ibid., 183.

16. John F. Walvoord, *The Holy Spirit at Work Today* (Chicago: Moody Press, 1973), 24.

17. Bush, *Notes, Critical and Practical, on the Book of Judges*, 183.

18. Barker, *Zondervan NIV Bible Commentary*, 355.

19. Radmacher, *The Nelson Study Bible*, 426.

20. Charles Haddon Spurgeon, quoted in Richard Ellsworth Day, *The Shadow of the Broad Brim* (Valley Forge, PA: Judson, 1934), 182.

21. Bush, *Notes, Critical and Practical, on the Book of Judges*, 189.

22. Ibid., 190.

23. Bush, *Notes, Critical and Practical, on the Book of Judges*, 191; Pfieffer, *The Wycliffe Bible Commentary*, 256.

24. Bush, *Notes, Critical and Practical, on the Book of Judges*, 192.

25. Ibid.

26. Bob Phillips, *Good Clean Jokes for Kids* (Eugene, OR: Harvest House, 1991), 51.

27. Pfieffer, *The Wycliffe Bible Commentary*, 258.

28. Barker, *Zondervan NIV Bible Commentary*, 356.

Judges 15–16: Samson Subdued

1. Barker, *Zondervan NIV Bible Commentary*, 356.

2. Everett Sentmen, "Jackal," *Grolier's Interactive Encyclopedia* CD-ROM (Grolier Interactive, 1998); Bush, *Notes, Critical and Practical, on the Book of Judges*, 197.

3. Pfieffer, *The Wycliffe Bible Commentary*, 258.

4. Ibid.

5. J. J. M. Roberts, "Gilgamesh," *Grolier's Interactive Encyclopedia* CD-ROM.

6. Greg Johnson, *Man in the Making* (Nashville: Broadman & Holman, 1997), 93.

7. Bush, *Notes, Critical and Practical, on the Book of Judges*, 201.

8. Ibid.

9. Samuel Brengle, quoted in Oswald Sanders, *Spiritual Leadership* (Chicago: Moody Press, 1967), 58.

10. Pfieffer, *The Wycliffe Bible Commentary*, 259.

11. Ten Boom, *Each New Day*, 154.

12. Bush, *Notes, Critical and Practical, on the Book of Judges*, 203.

13. Martin Luther, *The Table Talk of Martin Luther* (Grand Rapids: Baker, 1952), 290–91.

14. Barker, *Zondervan NIV Bible Commentary*, 358.

15. Pfieffer, *The Wycliffe Bible Commentary*, 259.

16. Tim LaHaye, *Transformed Temperaments* (Wheaton, IL: Tyndale House, 1971), 134.

17. Bush, *Notes, Critical and Practical, on the Book of Judges*, 207.

18. John Milton, quoted in Bush, *Notes, Critical and Practical, on the Book of Judges*, 212.

19. Wright, *Great People of the Bible and How They Lived*, 113, 125; Beers, *The Victor Handbook of Bible Knowledge*, 161, 170; Pfieffer, *The Wycliffe Bible Commentary*, 260.

Judges 17–18: Micah's Mistake

1. Bush, *Notes, Critical and Practical, on the Book of Judges*, 218.

2. Ibid., 219.

3. Gerald Mann, *The Seven Deadly Virtues* (Waco, TX: Word, 1979), 99.

4. S. Bruce Narramore, *You're Someone Special* (Grand Rapids: Zondervan, 1978), 158.

5. Richard Lee, *The Unfailing Promise* (Waco, TX: Word, 1988), 162–63.

6. Bush, *Notes, Critical and Practical, on the Book*

of *Judges*, 224.

7. Curtis C. Mitchell, *Let's Live!* (Old Tappan, NJ: Revell, 1975), 49.

8. Barker, *Zondervan NIV Bible Commentary*, 361.

9. Bush, *Notes, Critical and Practical, on the Book of Judges*, 227.

10. Arnold Prater, *Parables from Life* (Grand Rapids: Zondervan, 1963), 49–50.

11. Elisabeth Elliot, *Trusting God in a Twisted World* (Old Tappan, NJ: Revell, 1989), 124–25.

12. Dr. Henry Cloud and Dr. John Townsend, *Boundaries* (Grand Rapids: Zondervan, 1992), 84.

13. Tada, *Secret Strength*, 84.

14. Bush, *Notes, Critical and Practical, on the Book of Judges*, 231.

15. Frank Charles Thompson, compiler and editor, *The Thompson Chain Reference Bible* (Indianapolis: B. B. Kirkbride, 1990), 1785.

Judges 19–21: Gibeah's Punishment

1. Barker, *Zondervan NIV Bible Commentary*, 362.

2. Bush, *Notes, Critical and Practical, on the Book of Judges*, 234.

3. Ibid.

4. Ibid., 236.

5. Corrie ten Boom, *In My Father's House* (Old Tappan, NJ: Revell, 1976), 40.

6. Bush, *Notes, Critical and Practical, on the Book of Judges*, 237.

7. Amy Carmichael, quoted by Ruth Bell Graham, *Legacy of a Pack Rat* (Nashville: Word, 1997), 10–11.

8. Pfeiffer, *The Wycliffe Bible Commentary*, 264.

9. Beverly LaHaye, *Prayer* (Nashville: Thomas Nelson, 1990), 179–80.

10. Tada, *Secret Strength*, 73–74.

11. Charlie Hedges, *Getting the Right Things Right* (Sisters, OR: Multnomah, 1996), 228.

12. Bush, *Notes, Critical and Practical, on the Book of Judges*, 250

13. Pfeiffer, *The Wycliffe Bible Commentary*, 264; Bush, *Notes, Critical and Practical, on the Book of Judges*, 250; Barker, *Zondervan NIV Bible Commentary*, 366.

14. Halley, *Halley's Bible Handbook*, 173.

15. Radmacher, *The Nelson Study Bible*, 439.

16. Richard S. Taylor, *The Disciplined Lifestyle* (Minneapolis: Bethany, 1981), 50.

17. Radmacher, *The Nelson Study Bible*, 439.

18. Bush, *Notes, Critical and Practical, on the Book of Judges*, 256.

Introduction to the Book of Ruth

1. Cundall, *Judges and Ruth*, 230.

2. Radmacher, *The Nelson Study Bible*, 449; Winter, *Studies in Joshua, Judges, Ruth*, 580.

3. Barker, *Zondervan NIV Bible Commentary*, 368.

4. Cundall, *Judges and Ruth*, 236.

5. Ibid., 237.

6. Winter, *Studies in Joshua, Judges & Ruth*, 579.

Ruth 1–2: Ruth's Character Tested

1. Paul P. Enns, *Ruth: Bible Study Commentary* (Grand Rapids: Zondervan, 1982), 19.

2. Ibid.

3. Ibid.

4. Ibid., 20.

5. Winter, *Studies in Joshua, Judges & Ruth*, 578.

6. Enns, *Ruth: Bible Study Commentary*, 34.

7. Ibid., 18.

8. Robert W. Bailey, *Ministering to the Grieving* (Grand Rapids: Zondervan, 1980), 11.

9. Enns, *Ruth: Bible Study Commentary*, 26.

10. Marilyn Meberg et al., *Joy Breaks*, 138.

11. Radmacher, *The Nelson Study Bible*, 443.

12. Enns, *Ruth: Bible Study Commentary*, 28.

13. Ibid., 27.

14. Dee Brestin, *The Friendships of Women* (Wheaton, IL: Victor, 1988), 152.

15. McMinn, *Choosing to Be Close*, 68.

16. Edward F. Campbell Jr., *Ruth* in *The Anchor Bible* (Garden City, NY: Doubleday, 1975), 74–75.

17. Yohanan Aharoni, *The Land of the Bible* (Philadelphia: Westminster, 1967), 31.

18. Cundall, *Judges and Ruth*, 266-267.

19. Max Lucado, *A Gentle Thunder* (Dallas: Word, 1995), 29.

20. Barker, *Zondervan NIV Bible Commentary*, 371.

21. Enns, *Ruth: Bible Study Commentary*, 34.

22. Murray, *Daily Secrets of Christian Living*, May 27.

23. Beth Mainhood, *Reaching Your World* (Colorado Springs: NavPress, 1986), 105.

24. David A. Seamands, *Healing Meditations for Life* (Wheaton, IL: Victor, 1996), 89–90.

25. Cundall, *Judges and Ruth*, 278.

26. Ten Boom, *Not I, but Christ*, 6.

27. Barker, *Zondervan NIV Bible Commentary*, 373.

Ruth 3–4: Ruth's Character Proved

1. Pfieffer, *The Wycliffe Bible Commentary*, 270; Enns, *Ruth: Bible Study Commentary*, 48.

2. Colleen Townsend Evans, *The Vine Life* (Lincoln, VA: Chosen Books, 1980), 33–34.

3. Pfieffer, *The Wycliffe Bible Commentary*, 271; Enns, *Ruth: Bible Study Commentary*, 52.

4. Enns, *Ruth: Bible Study Commentary*, 53.

5. Ibid., 55.

6. Ibid., 56.

7. Radmacher, *The Nelson Study Bible*, 446.

8. C. S. Lewis, *The Four Loves* (New York: Harcourt Brace Jovanovich, 1960), 163.

9. Tim Hansel, *Holy Sweat* (Dallas: Word, 1987), 128–29.

10. Barker, *Zondervan NIV Bible Commentary*, 375.

11. Louise Pettibone Smith, quoted in George Arthur Buttrick, ed., *The Interpreter's Bible*, vol. 2 (New York: Cokesbury, 1953), 847.

12. Watchman Nee, *The Normal Christian Life* (Fort Washington, PA: Christian Literature Crusade, 1971), 70–71.

13. R. K. Harrison, *Old Testament Times* (Grand Rapids: Eerdmans, 1970), 74.

14. Pfieffer, *The Wycliffe Bible Commentary*, 271.

15. Bruce Larson, *Living on the Cutting Edge* (Grand Rapids: Zondervan, 1968), 92.

16. Dobson, *Love for a Lifetime*, 52.

17. Enns, *Ruth: Bible Study Commentary*, 69.

18. John Hunter, *Knowing God's Secrets* (Grand Rapids: Zondervan, 1967), 109.

19. Enns, *Ruth: Bible Study Commentary*, 69.

20. Colson, *Kingdoms in Conflict*, 371.

Index

Israel had the legal title, 7
Israelis' main headquarters about 1/4 mile from Jericho, 57
Israelite army, 72, 86, 108, 189
Israelite entrepreneur, 42
Israelites would be the catalyst to bring all nations to God, 16
Israelite visitors, 15
Israel's evolutionary development, 86
Israel's history, 94, 123, 232, 248
Israel's neighbors to the south, 89
Israel's response to Joshua is warm and affirming, 11
Israel's victories at the hand of the Lord, 90
Issachar, 61, 96, 156, 168, 221
itinerant
    definition, 178
I will not drop you, 7

J

Jabesh Gilead, 295, 296, 297
Jabin, 77, 78, 153, 154, 156, 159, 160, 162
Jabin's harassment, 156
jackdaw, 196
Jacob, 21, 33, 61, 90, 106, 119, 126, 232
    definition, 21, 96
Jacob sets up an altar, 111
Jael, 159, 160, 161, 162, 165, 171
Japhia, 68
Jarmuth, 68, 72
Jasher, 70
jaunty arrogance, 291
javelins, 80
jealousy, 117
Jebusites, 2, 78, 93, 124, 129
    definition, 124
Jedidah, 156
Jehovah, 5, 65, 90, 103, 180, 203, 272, 327
Jephunneh, 91, 92
Jericho
    definition, 13
Jeroboam II
    definition, 95
Jerubbaal, 156, 186, 189, 205, 207, 209
Jerusalem, 17, 41, 68, 93, 94, 124, 126–30, 262, 263
Jesus, the Savior to come, 183
Jesus Christ, 84, 99, 150, 305, 333
Jewish historian, 150, 304
Jezreel Valley, 156, 187
Joash, 95, 181, 186, 205

Jogbehah, 200
Johnson, Barbara, 42
Johnson, Greg
    on control, 257
    on God's breaking point, 199
Joppa, 132
Jordan, 6, 10, 11, 21, 23, 26–30, 78, 82, 86, 88, 89, 103
    definition, 21
Jordanites, 103
Jordan Valley, 25, 78, 147
    definition, 78
Joseph, 61, 90, 95, 119, 130, 197
Josephus, 148, 150, 304
    definition, 150, 304
Joshua attacks Makkedah, 74
Joshua built an altar, 59
Joshua died, 142
Joshua's authority, 9
Joshua's constant companion, 9
Joshua's metaphors, 109
Joshua's reputation, 42
Joshua's trust in God was based on absolute certainty, 7
Joshua tears his clothes and tosses dust on his head, 49, 50
Joshua was a great general, 59
Jotham, 209, 210, 211, 212, 213, 220
journey into marriage, 9
Judean hills, 22
judge, 12, 93, 139, 140, 146, 155, 220, 222, 230, 272, 292
judgment, 14, 55, 58, 87, 179
judgment maker after hearing both sides, 167
jurisdictional
    definition, 63
justice, 52, 82, 87, 112, 123, 127, 139, 150, 161, 166, 200, 218, 228, 293
justified
    definition, 18

K

Kadesh Barnea
    definition, 74
Karkor, 199, 200
Kedesh, 98, 99, 156, 157, 158
keen insight, 9
keep covenant with God, 32
keeping a heart that is soft and receptive to God, 12
keep watching and praying, 90
Kenaz, 91, 93, 127, 145
Kenite, 128, 158, 159, 160, 171
Kenizzite, 91, 92

Kenyon, Kathleen, 41
Keturah, 178, 204
Kidon, 58
kill or allow someone to die who's old or sick, 196
King David, 16
king of Ai, 56, 57, 58, 117
king of Eglon, 68, 72
king of Hebron, 68, 72
king of Jarmuth, 68, 72
king of Jericho, 13
king of Lachish, 68
king of Mesopotamia, 145
king of Moab, 91, 113, 147, 148, 230
King Saul, 66, 146
kings of the Amorites, 15, 31, 68, 114
kings of the mountains, 77
kinsman redeemer, 319, 324, 331, 333
Kirjath Arba, 92, 99, 127
Kirjath Jearim, 67, 278
Kirjath Sepher, 93, 127, 128
Kishon
    definition, 170
Kishon River, 154
Kissinger
    definition, 209
know God's Word, 107
Kohathite
    definition, 100
Korah, 168
Kyle, Melvin G., 128

L

Lachish, 68, 72, 74
LaHaye, Beverly, 292
LaHaye, Tim
    on daily feeding of the Word, 107
    on sinful acts seem normal, 264
Laish, 132, 277, 281
land of blessing, 7
land of bondage, 34
land of Mizpah, 77
land of the Philistines, 89
land was offered as an unconditional promise, 7
Lapidoth, 155
last book of the Bible, 39
law
    definition, 51
lawless behavior, 214
Lawrence, John W., 218
laws given by God, 22
laypeople, 66
lazy body, 90
lazy thoughts, 83
leadership, 6, 10, 11, 12, 90, 124, 157, 223, 273
Lebanon, 6, 63, 78, 82, 89, 211
Lebanon Mountains, 7
legacy, 91, 94, 118, 179

Lehi, 258, 259, 260, 261
length of time a position is occupied, 237
Leshem, 96
lessons of war, 84
let Baal contend, 156
let sin go unpunished, 55
Levi, 27, 90, 99
Levites
    definition, 99
Levites who are priestly descendants of Aaron, 100
Levitical
    definition, 27
Lewis, C. S.
    on natural love, 328
    on rules behind the rules, 27
libation
    definition, 211
liberal scholars and theologians, 86
liberate with payment, 235
Libnah, 74
license to kill, 87
licentiousness
    definition, 86
life is literally filled with God-appointed storms, 50
lifestyle, 16, 110, 116, 117, 124, 137, 203, 204, 310
limestone cliffs, 17
Linamen, Karen Scalf
    on impact of prayer, 144, 244
Lincoln, Abraham, 197
Little, Paul E., 87
livestock, 10, 56, 58, 80, 81, 102, 177
living out God's Word, 136
living sacrifice
    definition, 40
Living Water, 139
loaf of barley bread, 191
long, narrow crack, 257
Longman, Tremper, III, 110
long-awaited deliverer, 16
"lord of Bezek," 126
Lord's presence, 7
loved by the Lord, 156
loved one's death, 98
love God, 108
loving-kindness, 113, 124
lowland, 63, 77, 82, 127, 129
Lucado, Max
    on God allowing pain, 313
    on God as a faithful father, 74
luggage or burden carriers, 149
lust, 117
Luther, Martin, 262
Lutzer, Erwin, 214
Luz, 130, 131

M

MacArthur, General Douglas, 141
MacArthur, John
  on sin, 46
  on the will of God, 188
Macaulay, Susan Schaeffer, 202
MacDonald, Gordon, 221
Machir, 168
Madon, 77
magistrate, 123, 139
Mahanaim, 135
maintain his reputation, 173
make a covenant with us, 64
make peace, 64, 94
make two conflicting things compatible, 87
making things right, 103, 295
Makkedah, 69, 71, 72, 74
Manasseh, 10, 85, 90, 93–95, 99, 101–05, 130–31, 168–69, 181, 187, 195, 197, 201, 226, 236, 281, 296
mankind, 55, 108, 150
Mann, Gerald, 273
manna, 10, 22, 33, 34
  definition, 10, 22, 34
Manoah, 36, 240, 243, 244, 245, 246, 247, 249, 269
man of valor, 180
manslaughter, 98
man's spiritual history, 108
March, 28, 251
married a daughter of Hur, 91
marvelous intervention of God, 166
master, 42, 118, 138, 150, 154, 229, 289, 291
Mayhall, Jack, 175
McDowell, Josh
  on science and Scripture, 71
  on sin, 55
McGee, J. Vernon, 8
McMillen, S. I., 99
McMinn, Gordon
  on building and destroying bridges in life, 197
  on giving, 311
Meburg, Marilyn, 310
Mediterranean Sea, 7, 79, 84, 123, 157, 239, 252, 262
Mediterranean tree, 95
Megiddo, 154, 170
  definition, 170
Meier, Paul, 186
men of Israel, 64, 65, 72, 203, 219, 291, 294, 295
men of Penuel, 199
men of valor, 10, 37, 68, 150

mental image of God, 108
mentor, 107, 118, 324
  definition, 324
mercenary
  definition, 263
mercy seat, 22
Merom, 77, 78
Meroz, 171
Mesopotamia, 145, 152, 154
Messiah, 16, 241
  definition, 16
metaphor, 109, 294
  definition, 294
Micah, 271–72
Michal, 174
Midian, 177, 178, 189, 195, 204
  definition, 204
mighty men of valor, 10, 37, 68, 180, 227
mighty military force, 113
migrant
  definition, 147
migrate, 96, 132, 169, 309
military exercise, 72
military post where troops are stationed, 48
military standpoint, 60
Miller, Keith, 210
mingle with godless people, 107
Minirth, Frank, 186
miraculous deliverance, 112
"miraculous deliverer," 142
Miriam, 155
Misrephoth Maim, 79, 89
mixed marriages, 109
mixing of religious practices, 107
Mizpah, 77, 79, 226, 227, 228, 232, 290, 295
Mizpah Valley, 78
Moab
  definition, 5
"Molech," 223, 230
monarch, 126, 163
monarchy, 124, 154, 203
  definition, 203
monuments, 26, 80
Moody, D. L., 85
moral decline, 135, 291
moral decline in society, 291
moral deterioration of political power, 141
moral leader, 135
moral life, 83
moral purity and uprightness, 16
morals, 60, 211
moral transformation, 146
Moreh, 187, 189
more powerful people, 65
Morley, Patrick, 190
Mosaic Law, 160
Moses brings them to the threshold of the Land of Promise, 12
Moses's death, 61
Moses's leadership, 12

most important god of the Canaanites, 136
"mother in Israel," 165, 167
motivate God, 49
Mound of the Judge, 282
mountain city, 132
mountaineers, 129
mountains of Ephraim, 98, 118, 119, 150, 221, 274, 275, 278, 285
Mount Baal Hermon, 143
Mount Ebal, 59, 61
Mount Gaash, 118, 135
Mount Gerizim, 61, 210, 211
Mount Gilboa, 187, 189
Mount Gilead, 189
Mount Halak, 82
Mount Hermon, 79, 82
Mount Sinai
  definition, 2
Mount Tabor, 156, 157, 158, 159, 187
mourned, 5, 134
moving to different regions in source of work, 147
Mueller, George, 119
murder, 81, 87, 96, 98, 99, 116, 160, 201, 211, 213, 214, 218, 233, 280, 289
Murray, Andrew
  on character of Christ, 312
  on faith like the mustard seed, 195
mutiny, 12, 214

N

Naharaim, 145
Nahshon, 334
name only, 154, 287
names of other gods, 107
names of the Lord, 103
Naomi, 178, 303–4, 306–7, 309–14, 318–19, 323–34
Naphtali, 60, 96, 98, 131, 132, 156, 168, 169, 187, 195
Napoleon, 276
Narramore, Bruce S., 275
nationalities, 32, 61
nationals, 64, 94
nation's wickedness reaches an insufferable level, 87
natural talent, 9
nature and character of God, 119
Nazirite vow, 163, 242, 243
Needham, David, 71
Negev, 7, 74, 93, 94, 128
  definition, 74
neglect, 93, 136, 142, 179, 229, 234
neglect or idleness, 142
Nethinim, 67
never be forsaken by God, 7
new bodies, 146

New Testament, 16, 55, 86, 107, 305
New Testament truth, 86
Nile
  definition, 112
nine and one-half tribes, 89
Noadiah, 155
Nobah, 200
noble families of high social status, 216
no decision is too small for God, 65
nomadic fashion, 177
nomadic life, 96
nomadic people, 187
nomads
  definition, 147
nominally
  definition, 154
non-Christians exclude any real notion of the Law, 60
nonentity, 135
non-Jews, 32
no other option for survival, 107
no possibility of retreat, 24
no religion, 108
northeastern Sinai, 74
northern mountains of Lebanon, 89
no survivors, 74
no sustenance for Israel, 177
northern realm, 77
not able to bear children, 240
not biblical, 107
nothing of God dies when a man of God dies, 7
not one person survived, 113
noxious
  definition, 208
numerous offspring, 318
Nun, 5, 6, 13, 18, 118, 135
nuptial
  definition, 250
nursing infant, 181

O

oasis of springs and palm trees, 128
oath, 17, 66, 100, 233, 295, 296, 297, 310, 311, 327
obedience, 3, 9, 24, 45, 112, 134, 245, 272, 298, 314
"obedience is paramount," 90
object providing protection, 263
objects of disgrace, 110
object with magical powers, 275
obliterated, 100, 113
obscure people, 64
obscure village, 181
occult, 87

Ras Shamra tablets, 86
rational-spiritual nature of man, 83
raven, 196
reaching out everyone, even those outside our comfort zones, 61
readiness to comply with God's will, 12
reasonable and consistent, 65
reassurance, 100
Rebekah, 111
rebellion, 54, 109, 113, 141, 142, 153, 170, 216, 219, 255, 285, 290
rebellion against authority, 153
rebuke, 99, 104, 184, 204, 245, 261, 317
recalling what God has done, 114
received God's law at Sinai, 7
reciting various phrases, 61
reconciling
   definition, 87
reconnaissance, 13, 47, 130
   definition, 130
reconnaissance mission, 13, 47
records tax payments, 95
recreating power of the Holy Spirit, 147
recruit, 168
recurring forms of evil, 82
redeemed, 22, 40, 235, 327
   definition, 40, 235
redemption
   definition, 146
Redpath, Alan
   on Christian living, 48
   on manna, 34
Red Sea, 7, 12, 15, 16, 28, 112, 113
Reeve, Pamela, 158
references to God, 114
refuge, 74, 96, 97, 98, 99, 100, 151, 156, 201, 210, 294, 314
refusal to change a reprobate lifestyle, 16
refuses to believe the truth, 83
regional variety in a language, 236
regress
   definition, 193
regular temple services, 153
related to climate, 170
relating to marriage, 250
released from the guilt of sin, 18
religion, 37, 108, 140, 268, 272
religious converts, 160
religiously offensive, 235
religious practices, 107, 136
reluctant attitude, 169
remained friendly, 128
remain faithful to Jesus, 85
renunciation, 32, 217, 226
   definition, 226

renunciation of God by word or deed, 32
repeatedly performing, 119
repentance, 83, 133, 213, 267
repentant, 124, 134, 226, 273
   definition, 124
repose
   definition, 119
reprehensible
   definition, 214
representative leadership, 90
reputation, 15, 42, 45, 46, 49, 50, 64, 156, 173, 255, 287, 315, 326, 327, 333
resinous
   definition, 256
respects, 218
responsibility, 69, 87, 93, 116, 161, 167, 168, 179, 232, 285, 308, 332
restitution
   definition, 103
restoration
   definition, 104
restraint from indulging in something, 241
retaliation
   definition, 258
retributive
   definition, 127
returning something to its former condition, 104
return of Jesus Christ, 99
return to a worse state, 193
Reuben, 169, 175
revelation
   definition, 38, 247
revival, 165, 168, 204
   definition, 168
revolutionary, 182
rhetorical
   definition, 115
rich and opulent country, 112
riches, 102, 174, 316, 318
Ridenour, Fritz, 140
righteous living, 136
righteousness
   definition, 16
rival kingdoms, 153
river defining the eastern entrance into the land, 21
River Kishon, 156, 157, 158, 170
roasted on a skewer, 182
robber of everything valuable, 138
rock monument, 117
Rogers, Dale Evans, 33
"roll," 135
rugged terrain, 78, 312
rulers of the congregation, 65
rulers of the opposition, 73
ruminations
   definition, 173

Ryrie, Charles Caldwell, 242

S

sacrifice
   definition, 54
sacrificed peace offerings, 59
sacrifices, 103, 132, 134, 211, 293
sacrilege
   definition, 186
sadistic
   definition, 49
salmon, 334
Salt Sea, 26
Samaritan Ostraca, 95
Samuel, 124, 155, 179, 297, 304
sanctified
   definition, 23
sanctified Christian, 149
sanctify yourselves, 23, 51
Sanders, J. Oswald, 65
saracens, 187
Satan, 87, 98, 138, 257, 288
Satan worship, 87
satiated
   definition, 90
Savior, 85, 139, 183, 241, 324, 334
scars of rebellion last a lifetime, 109
scattered, 55, 75, 100
Schaeffer, Francis, 60
Schwanz, Floyd, 237
scimitar, 58, 80
Scorpion Pass, 131
Scotland Yard, 8
scourge
   definition, 112, 240
scribes
   definition, 272
scriptural passage, 189
seal
   definition, 146
Sea of Galilee, 78, 157, 296
seashore, 77, 169
seasonal wanderers, 147
seat of love and hate, 83
Secker, William, 149
secret law of the soul, 108
secure borders, 11
sedition
   definition, 153
seducer of Dinah, 119
seir, 82, 111, 164
seirah
   definition, 150
seizing of the woman, 297
Sela, 131
self-governing, 86
selfishness, 117, 210, 296
self-reliance, 190
"selling them away," 138
sergeant's command, 169
servant of the Lord, 5, 10, 59, 61, 80, 85, 91, 101, 118, 134, 136
servants, 66, 68, 150, 185

servant's heart, 59
served the Baals, 136, 144
serviceable clothing, 64
serving God, 115, 186
set apart as holy, 146
settlement of Canaan, 100
seven
   definition, 74
seven churches, 38
seven-day holiday ordained by God, 297
seven days, 38, 41, 250, 251, 252
seven priests shall bear seven trumpets of rams' horns before the ark, 37
seven seals, 38
seven trumpets, 38
severe devastation, 178, 255
shadow of the sun went backward, 70
shale
   definition, 201
Shamgar, 151, 152, 165, 221, 239
sheath, 80
Shebarim, 48
Shechem
   definition, 119
Shechem Valley, 60
shedding blood to atone for sin, 54
Shephelah, 129
Sheshai, 127
Shibboleth, 236
Shiloh, 95, 102, 103, 133, 137, 196, 281, 282, 292, 296, 297, 298
   definition, 133
Shimron, 76
shockingly evil and wicked, 288
shopet
   definition, 123
short, popular song, 260
Sidonians, 89, 143, 225, 277
Sihon, 15, 85, 229
Simeon, 61, 96, 100, 125, 126, 128, 169
Simeon's offspring, 96
Simon, 156
sinful and troubled soul, 85
Sisera's flight, 171
Sittser, Gerald L., 134
slaughter and extermination of entire people groups, 86
slaughter of Sihon and Og, 15
sleeveless shoulder vestment, 204
slings, 80
slip into an increasing state of complacency and compromise, 105
slow to understand, 63
"small," 135
smallest inroad, 208
smallest sin, 46
"small wars," 140